THE POLITICS OF GIVING IN THE
VICEROYALTY OF RIO DE LA PLATA

THE POLITICS OF GIVING IN THE VICEROYALTY OF RIO DE LA PLATA

Donors, Lenders, Subjects, and Citizens

VIVIANA L. GRIECO

UNIVERSITY OF NEW MEXICO PRESS

Albuquerque

19 18 17 16 15 14   1 2 3 4 5 6

LIBRARY OF CONGRESS CATALOGING-IN-PUBLICATION DATA

Grieco, Viviana L., 1969–
The politics of giving in the Viceroyalty of Rio de la Plata :
donors, lenders, subjects, and citizens / Viviana L. Grieco.
pages cm.
Includes bibliographical references and index.

ISBN 978-0-8263-5446-4 (cloth : alk. paper) — ISBN 978-0-8263-5447-1 (electronic)

1. Loans, Argentine—Spain—History—18th century. 2. Loans, Argentine—Spain—
History—19th century 3. Loans—Political aspects—Rio de la Plata (Viceroyalty)
4. Loans—Social aspects—Rio de la Plata (Viceroyalty) 5. Moneylenders—
Rio de la Plata (Viceroyalty) 6. Finance, Public—Rio de la Plata (Viceroyalty)
7. Argentina—Politics and government—1776–1810. I. Title.

HJ8569.G74 2014
336.3'4098209033—dc23

2013038468

BOOK DESIGN BY Lila Sanchez
TEXT COMPOSITION Adobe Caslon 10.5/13
DISPLAY TYPE Adobe Caslon

CONTENTS

CONTENTS

TABLES

INTRODUCTION

During the War against the French Convention (1793–1795), the merchants of Buenos Aires offered the crown 100,000 pesos in *donativos*. Their "loyalty" was amply rewarded as the king subsequently granted them the right to establish a *consulado*, a corporate body that represented their interests. The merchants of Buenos Aires had been petitioning for the establishment of a consulado in the viceregal capital for more than a decade. Atlantic warfare and the collection of donativos gave them the opportunity to provide an outstanding financial service to the crown that finally established the institution that gave them not only a corporate identity but also the right to collect taxes on behalf of the monarch. Some of the taxes collected by the consulado of Buenos Aires were earmarked to pay interest on the *donativo* the merchants had advanced to the crown, evidencing that, in this case, donativos referred to a lending operation that brought political and financial gains for both king and merchants.[1]

Throughout the military conflicts that dominated the Atlantic in the late eighteenth and early nineteenth centuries, individuals and groups provided financial support to the crown in the form of donativos. While the merchants of Buenos Aires advanced their corporate and financial interests at court, other prominent subjects sought alternative benefits in exchange for their donativos. In the early 1790s, doña Francisca del Risco, the widow of a wealthy attorney and entrepreneur from Charcas, tried to obtain from the Cámara de Indias a *cédula de gracias al sacar* to remove the "stain" of her adulterous birth. By then, the legitimation of *adulterinos* had become a difficult legal business as the *cámara* had increased the requirements as well as the fees for granting *cédula* petitions. Doña Francisca's 15,000-peso donativo, advanced during the War against the French Convention, finally pushed her legal case through. In 1796 the crown granted her legitimation, a grant she passed on to her children as well. In contrast to those of the merchants of Buenos Aires, doña Francisca's donativo initiated an individual bargain that yielded social and legal benefits instead of corporate and financial rewards.[2]

Another interesting case is that of Francisco de Ortega y Barrón, who in the 1790s filed several petitions at court claiming that his possession of a *juro de heredad* (right to inheritance held over an office) as well as other services rendered (including donativos periodically advanced to the crown by his ancestors) gave him the ownership of a profitable judicial appointment within the district of the audiencia of Charcas. Through his petitions, Ortega y Barrón argued that the creation of the Viceroyalty of Rio de la Plata in 1776 had diminished the profits generated by that office, a loss he estimated to be in the 50,000-peso range. To obtain a fair compensation from the crown, he requested his appointment to a lucrative position such as the intendancy of Cochabamba.[3] Donativos provided by the Ortega y Barrón family were associated with the sale of offices, a practice that periodically resurfaced in tandem with international warfare and compensated donors financially as well as politically.

In addition to prominent imperial players, Spanish subjects of lesser means also contributed donativos. Some were explicit about their expectations. Others utilized the language of gift giving and various euphemisms commonly fashioned to legitimately initiate bargains but simultaneously downplay their self-interest. In 1794 Idelfonso Pinto, the Indian lord of Sipaquí, contributed a significantly smaller donativo of 20 pesos. Although no war was being fought nearby, he additionally offered the king one-half of his annual income and substantial amounts of wheat "to sustain the army." Pedro Casas, a Catalonian merchant residing in Potosí, contributed a donativo of 148 pesos annually on behalf of his eleven-year-old son who, despite his young age, "had already expressed an interest in serving the monarch."[4] Unlike the previous cases, these donors did not openly state but rather hinted to the crown what type of compensation they expected from their donativos. They voiced their expectations by utilizing expressions that within the Spanish political tradition were commonly associated with the sale of offices.

Residents from the Guarani missions and Paraguay, Indians as well as Spaniards, and laymen and ecclesiastics also provided for the crown donativos in kind. The records refer to these donors as "very poor but loyal people, willing to express their love for their king by contributing donativos within their means."[5] As opposed to the documents recording the transactions involving elites, the ones involving donors of lesser means remain silent about donors' expected rewards.

Wars fought against "regicide" Frenchmen and "impious" Englishmen motivated Rioplatense ecclesiastics to engage in spiritual donativos by

offering Masses, prayers, and mortifications that invoked God's intervention in favor of the Spanish army. Although recorded on the same rosters
listing donativos in coin and in kind, donors advancing spiritual contributions did not necessarily expect worldly compensations. Nevertheless,
Masses and prayers offered at times of war reminded churchgoers that
the king needed their material support. By means of their spiritual contributions, religious men and women sponsored the politics of giving and
promoted public support for the monarch's political agenda.

The examples I have presented indicate that donativos effectively
tapped the wealth of subjects and excited their loyalty at times of war.
Additionally, donativos opened channels for donors to petition for economic, political, and social rewards. In this book I argue that within the
framework of the Spanish political tradition, donativos functioned as
legitimate conduits through which subjects advanced multiple interests
vis-à-vis their king. Although opportunities for bargaining emerged at
critical times and originated in the fiscal sphere, donativo-based negotiations had impacts beyond the fiscal and financial realms as they bound
king and subjects not only during but also after the crises in which these
negotiations emerged. By requesting compensations in exchange for financial support, donors laid claim to rights and turned donativos into
political acts. Thus, my analysis of donativos is a study of the political
economy and political culture of the Viceroyalty of Rio de la Plata in the
late eighteenth and early nineteenth centuries.[6]

In the case of the merchants of Buenos Aires and the Ortega y Barrón
family, donativos were a type of lending operation managed through corporate delegation and the sale of offices. Both practices were common in
early modern Europe and allowed kings to secure loans at lower interest
rates during times of war. By means of these practices, merchants and
bureaucrats tied their corporate interests to the financial fate of the crown
and became its economic beneficiaries as well as the king's partners in preserving the political establishment. Doña Francisca del Risco advanced
her donativo as part of a broader legal strategy deployed to obtain legitimacy of birth for herself and her progeny. In her case, a financial investment yielded valuable individual and social returns as rectifications of the
birth status of the elites sustained a relatively fluid yet hierarchical social
order that was jeopardized when passing became common.[7] Both Pinto
and Casas sought political and financial rewards in exchange for their
comparatively smaller monetary donativos. However, unlike Francisco
Ortega y Barrón, who bargained for a high-end political appointment,

they understated their claims by employing indirect references and euphemisms. Although those who appeared on the documents as "very poor people" expressed their loyalty to the monarch and built their bargaining capital by providing whatever resources they had, the surviving records indicate that they did not immediately obtain any social, political, or economic rewards in exchange for their contributions. Thus, as political and fiscal mechanisms donativos redistributed power and wealth following the established social hierarchies and according to the constitutional makeup of the Spanish Crown. They additionally revealed that the king was capable of mobilizing the support of a broad spectrum of subjects, although judging by the size of their contributions, their commitment to and investment in the established order was far from uniform. Whether more or less deferential, donors presented themselves as worthy of compensation and invoked their reciprocity compact with the king. Thus, my analysis of donativos also reveals the rules and boundaries of a hierarchical but competitive political community in which service and loyalty served as the entry point to rights.

Since males and females; Indians, *castas*, and Spaniards; ecclesiastics and laymen; individuals and corporations all gave donativos, it appears that anyone was able to make donativo-based bargains. However, the records indicate that only a small fraction of the population engaged in these negotiations, and those who did participate in them did not bargain equally. In the following pages, I will demonstrate that bargaining opportunities opened by donativos were in principle inclusive, but in practice they revealed a more selective political game. Nevertheless, a study of donativos ultimately reveals that social advancement was possible but contingent upon talent, service, patronage, and economic success.

Due to their capacity to articulate financial, social, and political claims, donativos were a versatile social mechanism. However, they were also ambiguous in that the rewards that were given to different individual and corporate donors were never clearly defined. From the donors' points of view, this ambiguity added uncertainty to their negotiations as they were unable to know when and how they would be compensated or if they would be compensated at all. My discussion of several examples of donativos collected in the Rio de la Plata between 1793 and 1810 shows that these difficulties did not discourage donors. On the contrary, every donativo mobilized subjects' support and resulted in the collection of impressive sums—evidence that the donors' confidence in the Spanish imperial project outweighed any uncertainties they may have had.

From the king's point of view, ambiguity was an advantage that allowed him to distribute rewards at his discretion. However, the Spanish contractual political tradition (known as *pactismo*) set limits on the royal will by regarding as legitimate only those monarchs who not only preserved the common good but also safeguarded the reciprocal obligations that bonded the king with his kingdom. Spanish monarchs were expected to be just and also capable of channeling individual and group interests toward the achievement of common aims. Monarchs acted legitimately when they arbitrated competing claims not by being impartial, but by being fair, that is, redistributing to each individual and group what they deserved according to their status and their contributions to the common good.[8] My analysis of donativos demonstrates that Spanish redistributive notions of justice sustained and legitimated what I call the politics of giving. The politics of giving was socially and politically successful because the king, through bargaining, modified but always maintained a hierarchical social order his subjects perceived as fair. Bargaining additionally sustained monarchical power as, in the process, the monarch emerged as ultimate arbiter over multiple, diverse, and competing claims.[9] Through donativos, in other words, subjects voiced and advanced their interests, while the monarch used these channels to legitimately distribute rewards and promote those groups and individuals who best served his short- and long-term political aims.

While advancing donativos during times of war helped the monarch secure the political and financial support of his subjects, some of the funds and commodities made available to him had to find their way into the royal treasuries. In other words, the logistics that made possible the collection of donativos mattered. Within the boundaries of a large politically and fiscally fragmented empire, the transfer of donativos (in coin and in kind) from subjects' pockets and storerooms to the royal coffers encompassed financial transactions that utilized a variety of financial instruments and, frequently, a variety of coins as well. Financial instruments included bills of exchange, the renegotiation of existing credit transactions, and coin arbitrage. A close examination of these complex financial operations reveals that, as in the case of other sources of revenue, the crown relied on the expertise of merchant-bankers to integrate a politically, fiscally, and economically disjointed space. Merchants charged commissions for their services and additionally profited from selling at substantial markups and distant markets the commodities advanced as donativos in kind. Commissions and profits attracted merchant-bankers to the lucrative donativo business, and by gathering from throughout the viceregal territory donors' funds and commodities, the merchants simultaneously capitalized their own private enterprises and enriched themselves. Put simply, donativos made possible the transfer of income from the less powerful to the more influential and richer subjects of the Spanish king who, in turn, became invested in preserving the Spanish monarchical order as well as the laws that safeguarded their interests.

From the examples discussed in this introduction, it appears that donativos frequently encompassed fiscal contributions as well as lending operations. Therefore, we should question why they were not simply called taxes and loans. I argue that Spanish constitutional arrangements allowed imperial subjects to effectively deflect and avoid uniform taxation. From the subjects' point of view, the principles of distributed justice also regulated taxation, and from the mid-eighteenth century onward, they successfully resisted several attempts to increase royal exactions that were perceived as detrimental to their social status and constitutional rights. In the 1790s, the Spanish monarch opted to collect donativos, which, far from diminishing the status of his constitutionally empowered subjects, served as efficient channels for them to voice and advance their interests. As for loans, the endurance into the eighteenth century of moral and canonical sanctions against usury explains the employment of euphemisms to refer to the pursuit of profit. However, in the Spanish world, canonical regulations over usury did not aim to suppress profit but rather to make compatible the political aims of the king and the commercial and financial interests of his Roman Catholic subjects. Spanish eighteenth-century denunciations of usury primarily targeted the financial groups that benefited the most from lending to the monarch. Following the principles of distributive justice, moralists did not censure the profit per se but the unwillingness of powerful lenders to share their returns with smaller investors who, at a smaller scale, were also considered legitimate beneficiaries of the monarchical order. In the chapters that follow, I will demonstrate that during international wars it became politically and socially preferable to call lending to the king at a profit "donativos" instead of "loans" as, under Spanish constitutional rules and moral canons, those who provided outstanding services to the common good ought to be rewarded proportionally.

The collection of donativos was successful because it generated political, fiscal, social, and cultural consensus within Spanish constitutional arrangements. But what type of arrangements were they? Since at the territorial and imperial levels the Spanish king did not share his sovereignty with English-style representative assemblies, the Spanish political system has been frequently associated with absolutism.[10] However, my study of donativos reveals that the Spanish monarch, far from being absolutely sovereign, worked *with* instead of *against* his subjects and promoted negotiation with those individuals and groups willing and able to support him financially. My analysis of donativos demonstrates that legitimate channels of negotiation existed and were frequently utilized to advance the interests of diverse individuals and social groups. Similar to the social compacts concerning poverty, donativos show that Spanish rule rested on tacit consent, voluntary appeals, and ideological hegemony rather than coercion on the part of a powerful state.[11] Often, financially and commercially powerful individuals, who regularly provided financial services to the crown, institutionalized their channels for negotiating with the monarch by requesting the creation of corporations to advance their sectorial interests. Examples of these practices can be found in the creation of *consulados* and *tribunales de minería*. Additionally, through the sale of offices royal servants bargained with the king and transformed bureaucracies into another conduit for corporate representation. At the local level, however, the channels of negotiation and representation were different. A strong tradition of municipal power embodied in the Castilian and Spanish American cities and their cabildos set limits on the royal authority as leaders legitimately vetoed royal ordinances that contradicted the fundamental laws of the kingdom. Additionally, the power of municipalities rested on a wider social base as they represented *the people* instead of a limited number of influential groups and subjects.[12] In order to understand how representation worked within the Spanish empire, it is imperative to study power and authority at the local, viceregal, and imperial levels. As recently suggested by Regina Grafe, historians of the Spanish world should abandon models that oppose English constitutional and absolutist continental regimes and develop instead research agendas that inquire about the locus of power and the rules that made its exercise not only possible but also legitimate. I approach this task by analyzing loans and donativos collected in the Viceroyalty of Rio de la Plata between 1793 and 1810.[13]

As legitimate mechanisms to raise revenue, donativos functioned according to Spanish constitutional rules. When donativos were collected at the viceregal level, they primarily channeled income and power toward prominent groups, that is, those who had prime access to representation.

At the local level, however, where representation had a popular base, the politics of giving was more inclusive, and consequently socially and racially heterogeneous groups legitimately claimed and appropriated a share of the social, political, and economic rewards available to donors.

From the 1790s through the Napoleonic invasion of the Spanish peninsula, the Spanish Crown collected donativos in the Viceroyalty of Rio de la Plata on four occasions. The first opportunity emerged during the War against the French Convention (1793–1795). The Naval Wars against England (1799–1802) followed this conflict, and a second collection of donativos ensued. Competition between Spain and England continued into the early nineteenth century, and consequently from 1806 to 1807 English troops temporarily occupied the cities of Buenos Aires and Montevideo. The expulsion of the enemy caused an unprecedented popular military mobilization and generated a permanent burden on the municipal treasury. These episodes, known as the British Invasions of the Rio de la Plata, provided the opportunity for the crown to collect a third donativo.

During the British Invasions the viceroy behaved as an incompetent political and military leader, and so the cabildo and the people of Buenos Aires deposed him. The municipality provisionally assumed political leadership over the region. The constitutional principles that sustained Spanish rule made legitimate the transfer of power from viceregal to municipal authorities, which under popular pressure designated as interim viceroy a military leader who had emerged during the British Invasions. Under these circumstances, the cabildo of Buenos Aires (instead of the viceroy and royal treasurers) collected the third donativo, thereby transferring the politics of giving from the territorial or viceregal to the municipal or local jurisdiction. This change makes it possible to analyze and compare the redistributive power of the politics of giving at both the viceregal and municipal levels. Once managed by the cabildo, the benefits of the politics of giving now reached the plebeian and racially mixed groups that through their recent military participation in the British Invasions had preserved not only the well-being of the community but also Spanish sovereignty over the region. Their paybacks included pensions, salaries, and dowries for soldiers, military widows, and orphaned children as well as the monetary compensations given to masters who agreed to free the slaves who had fought against the English. The cabildo financed these benefits not only with the funds it collected in donativos but also by taking loans and applying a new excise tax on viceregal capital. In other words, at the municipal level not only donors but also consumers financed the welfare and social inclusion of the racially heterogeneous, creole-popular sectors.

Finally, the Napoleonic invasion of the Spanish peninsula in 1808 called for a fourth donativo, the last one collected in the Viceroyalty of Rio de la Plata under Spanish rule. This new donativo serves as an example of the "new" politics of giving, which, for the first time, included among the donors newcomers into the world of municipal politics. The 1808–1809 donativo roster included not only the recently created racially heterogeneous militias but also widows receiving pensions as well as *libertos*, that is, the ex-slaves who had recently obtained their freedom in exchange for their military service. In sum, donativos continued supporting Spanish rule. Through the mediation of the cabildo, however, the popular sectors were included as beneficiaries of the imperial project, and as such they began supporting the crown financially and politically.

The examples just presented demonstrate that the collection of donativos produced significant evidence for a study of the late eighteenth- and early nineteenth-century political culture of the Viceroyalty of Rio de la Plata. Moreover, as they became a recurrent feature of the era of the Atlantic revolutions, they also provide us with strong grounds for gauging continuity and change in Spanish imperial and postimperial policy and practices. However, despite their documentary richness donativos have failed to attract significant scholarly attention. The few publications on this topic are for the most part descriptive and partial, focusing primarily on the funds advanced by one social group during one particular war.[14] Those that offer broader analyses exclusively emphasize the fiscal impact of donativos, characterizing them as compulsory devices employed by absolutist monarchs. Disregarding contemporary writings and treatises that discussed donativos, this viewpoint characterizes them as concealed forms of taxation and effective means of obtaining silver from the Americas within the boundaries of an imperial system branded as "predatory" and "extractive."[15]

This volume tells a different story about collections of donativos in the Viceroyalty of Rio de la Plata. While exclusively focusing on one viceroyalty and on the donativos collected between 1793 and 1809, in this book I challenge at least four assumptions held as truth for the entire Spanish Atlantic.

The first assumption contends that the Spanish monarchy wielded enough political and bureaucratic power to deploy over the Atlantic an imperial system capable of siphoning off enormous amounts of silver from the Americas that otherwise would have been utilized for financing development in the region. While it is undeniable that a large portion of the American silver crossed the Atlantic, as well as the Pacific, a significant share never did. Only a fraction of the funds collected as donativos left the viceregal economic space. And, as in the case of other revenues transferred across the imperial treasuries (or *situados*), donativo funds that remained within the viceregal territory promoted economic integration and the expansion of local and regional businesses.[16] Additionally, the financial mechanisms employed for collecting and transferring donativos demonstrate that there was nothing compulsory about them. On the contrary, they serve as evidence of cooperation between private and royal interests.

Secondly, this book challenges the supposition that under Spanish rule middle classes were very small and lacking in entrepreneurial spirit. The available sources indicate that a wide range of social groups that (based on their income) did not belong either to the elites or to the more disadvantaged sectors of the colonial order channeled their savings into donativos.[17] Their social, political, and financial expectations helped capitalize merchant-bankers and forged a chain of interlinked financial obligations that made possible the commercial expansion of the Viceroyalty of Rio de la Plata in the late eighteenth and early nineteenth centuries. Their contributions to the donativos also demonstrate that the crown drew its support from a wide social base.

Thirdly, this volume departs from modern understandings of corruption that associate gifting with influence peddling, uneven access to information, and the unfair distribution of privileges through informal means. This point of view implies that insiders systematically and unfairly exclude outsiders, who remain politically disenfranchised and economically and socially disadvantaged. Ultimately, corruption subverts social cohesion and stalls economic growth.[18] Following contemporary definitions of gifts and gifting (referred to as *donatio*), I argue that donativos were widely accessible to individuals and groups of different social statuses. Because in old-regime societies gifts belonged to the realm of contracts, they carried the obligation to reciprocate, and therefore they fostered communication and corporation among the participants in the gift economy. In other words, donativos delineated horizontally and vertically the boundaries of social, political, and economic inclusion, but they did not necessarily close the channels available to access it. Additionally, the fiscal efficacy of donativos depended on their proper and lawful performance. Unlike corrupt practices, which expand informally and illegally, the contractual obligations and legal procedures associated with donativos created formal, institutionalized, and socially sanctioned channels for engaging in negotiations with and obtaining rewards from the Spanish monarch. Thus, my argument that donativos distributed power and income legally and legitimately while they simultaneously molded social advancement.

Finally, the fourth assumption that needs to be revised contends with politics and representation within the Spanish Atlantic world. As already discussed, the financial services provided by individual and corporate subjects opened channels for bargaining vis-à-vis the crown and the municipal authorities. At the viceregal level, the merchants' negotiations resulted in the establishment of an institutionalized channel that represented their interests—the consulado in Buenos Aires—while civil servants turned bureaucracies into another bargaining forum. However, at the municipal level donativos collected following the British Invasions represented a transformative political experience for the donors as their collection coincided with the *vecinos'* engagement in a more active type of *vecindad*. Active vecindad shared many characteristics with modern citizenship as those who fulfilled the duties of vecinos acquired rights and improved their juridical statuses. The prospect of social improvement stimulated political mobilization and participation in a community that, aiming at the preservation of the common good, periodically demanded from its members the performance of services beyond individual, family, and corporate interests.[19]

Services promoting the common good facilitated the transformation of the traditional corporate and hierarchical body politic into a community of free and equal individuals. Thus, I argue that donativos collected in the city of Buenos Aires stimulated donors to further engage in active vecindad. The military mobilization of mixed-raced popular sectors during the British Invasions of the Rio de la Plata improved the social and political worth of these groups, and consequently they demanded material compensations from the municipal treasury in the form of salaries, pensions, dowries, and grants of freedom. Once included, they became involved in the preservation of a system that provided for their well-being and became active participants in the politics of giving by contributing donativos. Thus, collections of donativos provided for these political novices opportunities for exercising their newly acquired rights as vecinos. By 1809 active vecindad (which included contributing donativos) had become an essential experience in the transition from what historians call old to new forms of political representation. This volume expands on the existing studies that argue that Spanish subjects conceptualized modern citizenship not in a vacuum but in reference to their status as vecinos.[20] For undertaking these transformations, Spanish imperial subjects did not need to borrow from or refer to the French Enlightenment or the English constitutional tradition. They simply brought forward the principles that sustained Spanish pactismo, which sanctioned both exclusive and inclusive channels of negotiation for those who provided essential services to the crown and the common good. Spanish political culture and its representative channels and institutions were capable of bridging new and old forms of political action. In such a system, English-style representation in the form of a parliament and colonial assemblies was simply redundant.

SPANISH LOANS AND DONATIVOS

Atlantic Perspectives

STATES, REPRESENTATION, AND ATLANTIC EMPIRES IN THE EIGHTEENTH CENTURY

Donativos and Loans in Their Historical Contexts

During the early modern period, at a time of almost constant international warfare, European states expanded their military and fiscal capacities. In order to meet their financial obligations, the major European powers not only diversified their taxation systems but also increased the size of their permanent public debt. Servicing public debt in a timely manner demanded a broader social base of taxation and a more efficient collection of, or increases in, existing taxes as interest payments to bondholders and financiers absorbed a greater proportion of total state revenues. Politically speaking, fiscal pressures provided opportunities for rulers to consolidate their power by means of bureaucratic centralization, although the discussion of taxation simultaneously enhanced the powers of representative institutions (i.e., estates, parliaments, and the Cortes—the assembly representing free municipalities in Castile) and corporate bodies instrumental in borrowing and taxing. Thus, depending on the case, the emergence of what scholars call European "tax states" facilitated either administrative and fiscal fragmentation or centralization. When possible, lenders and taxpayers advanced their interests and voiced their concerns through the institutions that made possible the collection of revenues.[1]

The study of "tax states" or "military fiscal states" has produced an extensive bibliography of works analyzing the experience of different European powers. The comparative review that follows demonstrates that Spain does not fit into the absolute/constitutional dichotomy that dominates the existing scholarship. Understanding the institutional development of eighteenth-century Spain demands breaking from this framework. Although the main financial features of the European tax regimes developed throughout the sixteenth to the eighteenth centuries, in this chapter I will summarize and compare the experiences of England, France, and Spain in the eighteenth century. This review serves to place collections of loans and donativos in a broader historical perspective.[2]

Economists and historians have argued that government deficit financing was successful in England due to the convergence of crucial financial and political features. Between 1688 and 1783, England developed an effective system of tax collection (based on customs duties, excises, and, to a lesser extent, land taxes) that provided a regular and secure income and made borrowing comparatively cheap and simple. Regular income endowed the British state with generous public funds to service its permanent debt in a timely manner. Reliable taxation and tax collection coupled with punctual payments to creditors strengthened the state's credit and expanded its capacity to secure large loans at lower interest rates. Additionally, the English state managed its borrowing following the system developed by the Dutch in the seventeenth century. State loans were handled through a public bank, and the debt was based on long-term redeemable annuities and bonds sold to a substantial number of investors through a market in securities.[3]

England had a national representative body that provided the monarch with the consensus necessary to enforce unpopular policies (in particular increases in taxation), making resistance to tax collection an extremely difficult proposition. Parliamentary scrutiny of public finances gave the state financial policy a degree of transparency unknown on the continent, while parliamentary consent legitimated the state's financial choices and expanded its credit. Additionally, the parliament kept the English monarch from overspending and from infringing upon the property rights of his subjects to bridge financial gaps.[4] The New Institutional Economics (NIE) sustains that these features set England apart from other European powers as they created a unique path to long-term economic growth and development.

The development of the British fiscal-military state also advanced the interests of those who could provide funds when most needed. Bankers, moneyed men, investors, and stockbrokers became the most conspicuous beneficiaries of the state's financial policies, and consequently they were frequently criticized for living parasitically off the state's need to borrow money. The landed classes resented the rise of "financial interests," claiming that the activities of this class reduced the value of real property and restricted the landowner's borrowing power. The landed elites were also reluctant to invest in debt as they considered it a risky enterprise based on a "superfluous" form of wealth. However, as British public debt grew and the opportunities for investing in state bonds increased (and became more reliable), landowners eventually took advantage of the new financial opportunities and diversified their sources of income by buying government bonds on a large scale. In John Brewer's words, "support for debt paralleled its gradual penetration of society at large."[5]

In England, the powerful groups that made possible the growth of the fiscal-military state had access to its financial and political benefits. Instead of negotiating directly and secretly with the monarch, however, these groups had to channel their interests through the parliament. In post-1688 England, the parties whose interests were represented in parliament became the "deal makers." As Hilton R. Root demonstrates, the process of gaining economic concessions was long, difficult, and corrupt. Nevertheless, parliamentary procedures turned the distributive role of government, as well as the lobbying activities of private groups, into a public and consensual process. Consequently, English-style distribution of power and income was regarded as legitimate, readily accepted, and easily enforced.[6] Ultimately, the more transparent and more efficient allocation of economic rights brought to England not only political stability but also economic growth. For new institutional economists, the English historical experience became a paradigmatic model to be followed by any nation eager to achieve economic development.

The constitutional arrangements that secured increases in taxation to service public debt in the metropolis did not necessarily work across the Atlantic. After the Seven Years' War (1756–1763), British naval superiority was unquestioned. But since the English overseas possessions shared frontiers with territories under Spanish, French, and Indian control, England needed to improve its imperial defense system. In the 1760s imperial finances were stretched. Thereafter, England searched for the best way to make her metropolitan and American subjects share the cost of sustaining the empire. Innovations in military policy were resisted by the American colonies on many fronts, and Americans refused to commit to militia service for lengthy periods of time. Understaffed militias had to be supplemented by professional units whose salaries demanded increases in local taxation, which unlike Spanish American cabildos, local assembles were reluctant to approve. Military efforts required cooperation and the sharing of resources, which was hard to achieve without an established tradition of mutual assistance or widespread cooperation among the colonies. The failure of the Albany Congress in 1754 made these shortcomings apparent. It also made England aware that imperial defense could not be left in the hands of her colonial subjects.[7]

The alternative to an expanded, better-integrated, and trained militia consisted of the permanent deployment in North America of an English standing army. The assumption was that colonists would absorb their share of the military expenses by accepting subsequent increases in taxation. However, this proposition was met with constitutional resistance. On the income side, the program suggested a better collection of existing custom duties, the implementation of new taxes, as well as the regulation of independent currencies. The colonial assemblies resisted these policies and found in the "Stamp Act Congress" an institution that helped them bridge their local divisions.

John Elliott describes the constitutional stalemate of the 1760s as a "crisis of the British composite monarchy in the form it had assumed in the middle of the eighteenth century," that is, a partially composite parliamentary state. Since 1688, the king in parliament had exercised sovereignty. In 1707 the Scots had been granted parliamentary representation in compensation for the loss of their own parliament in Edinburgh. However, Ireland and the American colonies had been left out of the parliamentary union, and consequently they retained their elected assemblies. Since sovereignty was conceived as indivisible, colonial assemblies were subordinates and followed the directives sent out from Westminster. In the quite original English case, it was the parliament and not the king that asserted its rule over the different parts of the composite state. By making reference to their English liberties and rights, American subjects paradoxically were entitled to reject taxes they had not consented to while simultaneously remaining loyal to the English king.[8] Under these constitutional rules, the discussion of taxation would become a conflict over competing constitutional rights staged within a political culture that had exposed colonials to debate, political competition, and accountability. Despite the existence of slavery and ample disparities in wealth, historians have argued that in the North American colonies religious pluralism and widespread property ownership fostered a political and social environment that promoted dissent, egalitarianism, and individualism and facilitated the emergence of new ideas and alternative forms of political organization. In other words, free Englishmen who had grown disappointed with English parliamentary rule were capable of conceiving independence and republican government. In sum, the English fiscal-military state was successful at coordinating the interests of the crown with those of its subjects in the metropolis but failed to accomplish the same across the Atlantic.

France's fiscal path was different. From the mid-seventeenth century onward, despite the many attempts to enforce a thorough fiscal reform, the French monarchy failed to develop a system of public finance and public credit as reliable as the English one. Although the taxation base widened and France actually became in the eighteenth century "a kingdom of taxpayers," the French monarchy continued to draw revenue mainly from one source, the land, even as manufacture and commerce expanded. Additionally, French kings never solved the long-term political and financial problems associated with tax collection, the venality of offices, and borrowing, and as a result their credit suffered and interest rates soared. Although fiscal crises plagued France throughout the old regime, in the 1780s financial problems became deeply entangled with politics to the extent that a simple request for a loan would spark a revolution.[9]

Richard Booney argues that from the mid-seventeenth century to the end of the ancien régime, the French financial system was beset with unresolved structural problems. Central control over financial matters emerged only gradually, and the distinction between public finance and royal domain remained unclear until the end of the old regime. Additionally, the standard of probity of the finance ministers was low, allowing them to make fortunes while in office, especially in periods when the crown was financially weak. The finance ministry was also an office characterized by the high turnover of ministers, with the average tenure in office between 1746 and 1774 being just three years. In such an unstable setting, it was hard to implement consistent policies or carry out a comprehensive reform. Tax collection, as well as the enforcement of new fiscal policies, was thus left in the hands of the provincial intendants who became targets of growing fiscal and political discontent. The major problem was, however, the limited authority of the finance ministry over the king's expenses. While in peacetime expenditures were kept low, each major war led to massive borrowing (and financial chaos) as the war minister was able to run up bills practically unchecked.[10]

Other problems that hindered the king's ability to collect revenue (and eventually balance his budget) stemmed from the fragmented structure of the French economy and polity and various fiscal and political privileges. Regional and personal exemptions were hard to overcome in France as the crown granted or confirmed them in the process of assembling the kingdom. Additionally, even as revenue grew, exemptions spread to a larger number of individuals, not only nobles and clergy but also magistrates, venal officeholders, and wealthy city dwellers. Sometimes entire regions escaped taxation by virtue of privileges confirmed by the king. In the *pays d'état*, the estates not only negotiated favorable levies with the king, but also determined the distribution of the tax burden, collected the taxes, and used a large share of them locally. Consequently, fiscal and regional immunities deprived the king of France of many of the revenues collected in his name.[11]

Despite these drawbacks, the fiscal power of the French monarchy grew in the seventeenth and eighteenth centuries as did the social base of taxation. The taille was among the chief direct taxes collected in France throughout the old regime. It was collected in two forms. The *taille personnelle* established eligibility or exemption according to the status of the individual while the *taille réelle* was collected following the status of the land. However, the taille output alone was insufficient to finance the ambitious foreign policy of the Sun King and his successors, especially after 1692, when warfare demanded major operations on both land and at sea. These growing military demands led to the imposition of the *capitation* in 1695, followed by the *dixième* in 1710, and, later on, the *vingtième*.[12] The new taxes were levied on all subjects (including nobles and other exempted groups) without their consent, and the relative importance of established tax privileges declined as the king put more emphasis on collecting the new direct taxes and other tariffs. The new impositions, although collected regularly in wartime, became the focus of political contestation when peace resumed. Provincial courts imposed limits on their duration, and so they did not provide secure long-term income for the crown.

Borrowing, not taxes, provided the funds needed for sustaining and expanding the French state. But lacking a system of public credit and simultaneously constrained by a nefarious credit rating due to a history of defaults and unilateral write-downs on government loans, the King of France mainly borrowed from private parties using instruments that carried high interest rates (*rentes perpetuelles*, or perpetual annuity loans, and *rentes viagères*, or life annuity loans and tontines).[13] Alternatively, the monarch could borrow at lower interest rates from creditworthy corporate bodies such as the clergy, the *parlements* (courts in charge of registering the monarch's edicts regarding financial policies), venal officeholders, and provincial estates. Although this choice was financially attractive, it was also politically costly as these groups demanded concessions in return for their financial support. For instance, venal officeholders borrowed from private parties using their offices as collateral and then advanced these funds to the king. If their income was compromised, they opposed royal policies. Parlements, municipalities, and provincial estates collected local and royal taxes and used them to back loans. In return for these services, they received pensions, access to royal patronage, and the power to spend tax revenues locally and without royal supervision. Paradoxically, in old regime France those who enjoyed fiscal immunities and were politically powerful (and potentially obstructive) aided the king in two essential functions: borrowing and tax collection. And distinct from the case of England where the parliament controlled the budget and increases in taxation, France had no need for such a national institution as those issues were negotiated at local and corporate levels.[14]

In summary, the French king had access to different (and quite generous) lines of credit despite lacking a bank. A credit system without one single organized, private financial interest group such as the English moneyed interest, although expensive, allowed the French monarch to exercise uncontested powers over his own finances and over investors and their private property. These powers became evident with every financial crisis as the French king was able to manipulate his creditors at will by employing devices such as the *visa* (a general write-down of government loans) and the *chambre de justice* (a special court established to investigate and eventually prosecute financiers reluctant to renegotiate loans). Lending to the French Crown was dangerous and risky. However, potential profits encouraged lenders to do business with an extremely unreliable client until the end of the old regime.[15]

Through the 1780s, unopposed absolutist policies let the king clean up the mess left after each financial crisis. Foreseeable defaults followed by predictable increases in taxation allowed the crown to successfully manage the budgetary imbalances caused by warfare.[16] Visa operations breached existing contracts and violated the right to private property. However, neither investors nor public opinion nor the parlements questioned the king's regalian rights to enforce such measures. When in 1788 magistrates, taxpayers, and political thinkers openly defied royal policies, the king had no choice but to summon the Estates General to find a political solution to his inability to tax and borrow. Some scholars would argue that this financial stalemate sparked the French Revolution.[17]

For Hilton L. Root, the absence of a representative institution similar to the English parliament turned the French absolute king into the principal political deal maker; that is, he enjoyed a monopoly over defining and allocating political and property rights. These rights were granted through private negotiations and in exchange for political loyalty and financial support. Through the dispensation of special rights, the French kings secured the loyalty of a large, powerful, and wealthy clientele. However, since the French-style distribution of power and income was only open to loyal clients or cronies and controlled by one single authority, there was no incentive for more efficient participants to make political bargains.[18] Additionally, the French monarch was institutionally free to penalize right holders and even breach contracts. As noted, the confiscation of property was a common practice in old regime France. Although in theory the French monarchs were independent and strong, in practice they were too dependent on their cronies, especially the financiers. Instead of promoting fiscal stability by enforcing uniform taxes, the French kings reinforced tax exemptions and inequality before the law. In other words, the French monarchs created a market for privileges rather than a market for rights. Those privileges could not easily be traded because the monarch ultimately determined their value. Consequently, the French system of redistribution was prone to market inefficiencies, coordination failures, information asymmetry, civil disobedience, and resistance to taxation, corporate regulations, and state-sponsored monopolies. Thus, the NIE characterizes French absolutism as politically, institutionally, and fiscally unstable and therefore not conducive to sustained economic growth and development.

Bourbon Spain offers an interesting case for comparison because although it lacked metropolitan and empire-wide representative institutions, it was capable of obtaining revenues from its possessions in the Americas, especially in the late eighteenth century. Many scholars have regarded the fiscal capability of the Spanish monarchy as evidence of its absolute power to spend and tax unchecked, especially in relation to its overseas possessions.[19] However, the following review of the literature demonstrates that the Spanish monarchy did not enjoy unlimited fiscal power as, for most of the eighteenth century, it managed to keep its public debt within controllable levels without changing its composite political and fiscal constitutions.

The accession of the Bourbons to the Spanish throne brought the opportunity to further assimilate the kingdom of Aragon (which supported

Archduke Charles in the War of Spanish Succession) to that of Castile. The Bourbon financial reform aimed at achieving tax equality and uniformity within the two kingdoms as well as improving the administration of taxation. For that purpose two ambitious projects concerning revenues were proposed. The first was the *catastro* (land survey) to be followed by the *única contribución* (a single-tax scheme of 6 to 7 percent on income regardless of the economic activity or the ownership of the wealth). However, these plans were never implemented due to the resistance of the clergy and nobility, who opposed any advances on their fiscal privileges.[20] Thus, the traditional Spanish revenue system based on ordinary (regalian) and extraordinary (mainly concessionary) revenues remained unchanged.[21]

Nevertheless, between 1722 and 1779 the Bourbons managed to achieve financial stability without broadening the tax base or borrowing on a large scale. The incorporation of the Aragonese territories to those of the crown of Castile and the Bourbon administrative reforms coupled with sustained population and economic growth during the first half of the eighteenth century and the shipment of revenues from the American possessions explain the general increase in income within the existing system. In the 1780s, when a new cycle of international warfare pushed expenses upward, however, the discussion of fiscal inequity among provinces and subjects was reopened along with the imposition of a direct tax on landed property. The privileged groups and the territories that made up the Spanish composite monarchy successfully thwarted this reform. In the end, Charles III (1759–1788) had to borrow to cover the wartime deficit, creating a large permanent debt that would eventually lead to dire financial straits.[22]

In 1780, in order to finance the war with England, the Spanish government issued bonds (*vales reales*) for 9 million pesos. Initially, the bonds were very attractive as they paid a commission of 10 percent and an annual interest rate of 4 percent on their face value. The crown saw this measure as temporary as it planned to retire all bonds after twenty years. The first vales reales were easily sold, and consequently the crown issued more bonds worth an additional 5 million pesos the following year. However, the second issue lacked the financial backing of the first, and as a result, all bonds were devalued by 14 percent in 1782. That devaluation of the bonds also disrupted the economy in general as they had circulated as paper money, supplementing the scarce specie. In that year the crown established the Banco de San Carlos (antecedent of the Bank of Spain) with the purpose of sustaining the value of the bonds and simultaneously withdrawing them from the market. The creation of the bank came along with a third issue of vales reales, this time for the sum of almost 15 million pesos.[23]

The Banco de San Carlos was a relatively successful financial institution, and by 1788 the bonds had recovered their face value. However, existing vales reales were worth 23 million pesos, and servicing them required setting aside from the budget almost 900,000 pesos per year. Under Charles IV (1788–1808), the bonds were never redeemed. Instead, the international wars of the 1790s, as well as the subsequent Napoleonic Wars, necessitated issuing even more vales reales. For example, in 1794 (during the War against the French Convention) the crown issued bonds worth a total of 34.2 million pesos with an additional 30 million added the following year.[24]

From the mid-1790s onward the Spanish Crown diverted larger shares of its revenues toward sustaining the value of the bonds and eventually retiring them from the market. In 1794 the crown established the Fondo de Amortización (Amortization Fund) and endowed it with 10 percent of its ordinary rents and the total income of the tax on the export of silver (*indulto de extracción de plata*). Despite this backing, in the summer of 1795 vales reales lost 22 percent of their face value. Peace with France and a large ecclesiastical subsidy destined to support the bonds temporarily boosted their value. However, these measures did not guarantee financial strength in the long run. Toward that end, the crown implemented in 1798 a series of measures intended to restructure (*consolidar*) its public debt. First, it assigned to the Fondo de Amortización all the revenues from the Cádiz customs office and those from the monopoly on stamped paper. Second, it created the Caja de Amortización de Vales Reales for dealing exclusively with all matters concerning public debt (in essence it functioned as a parallel treasury). Finally, through the decree known as the Consolidación de Vales Reales, the crown invited the ecclesiastical authorities to sell properties belonging to hospitals, houses of charity, confraternities, and foundling homes with the condition that this capital would be placed in the Fondo de Amortización. Two other decrees put the properties of the Colegios Mayores on the market and ordered the owners of all entailed properties to sell them wholly or in part and deposit the proceeds from these sales into the Caja de Amortización. Through the Consolidación de Vales Reales, the crown did not actually seize estates but rather forced their sale in order to raise funds for the

Fondo de Amortización. The liquid capital possessed by lay or religious institutions affected by the decree was also channeled toward the same fund. In both cases, the owners received 3 percent annual interest for the funds deposited in the amortization fund. Thus, through this measure the crown exchanged expensive obligations for comparatively cheap loans extended by large landowners, the nobility, and the clergy.[25]

The Spanish American possessions experienced both the Bourbons' financial restructuring as well as an increase in fiscal pressure. From the mid-1760s, colonial fiscal reforms resembled those implemented in Spain and, to some extent, those enforced over the British Atlantic. They included the expansion of dynamic sectors of the economy (mining, agriculture, and trade), end of tax farming, establishment of the intendant system, setting up of monopolies on strategic commodities (mercury, tobacco, alcoholic beverages, stamped paper, and playing cards), creation of new customs offices, and raising of the *alcabala* (sales tax) from 2 to 6 percent. In many cases, the reformers simply strove for a more efficient collection of already existing taxes. Additionally, starting in the 1780s the crown not only collected taxes from its colonial subjects, but it also supplemented its revenues by requesting loans and donativos. Some scholars see the increased revenues shipped to the metropolis in this period as evidence of the success of the reforms. Others, however, challenge the capability of the crown to comprehensively tax as well as increase the volume of remittances to metropolitan treasuries. But most agree that the new fiscal demands were met with resistance, riots, and rebellions.[26]

The Bourbon fiscal reforms have already received extensive scholarly attention.[27] However, we know little about the loans and donativos of this period or the intricate functioning of imperial finances as a whole. Steps toward clarifying these issues can be found in the works of Carlos Marichal about colonial Mexico in the eighteenth century. His detailed studies on the ordinary and extraordinary transfers of funds from the Mexican treasury to the metropolis and to other colonies in the Caribbean regard revenues extracted from New Spain as vital in the imperial financial strategy since they not only paid the military expenses of Central America but also enriched the Spanish coffers. Marichal argues that the reason why the metropolitan budget was kept balanced until the 1790s (and with a comparable low debt) had less to do with the implementation of sound fiscal policies in Spain than with the increasing shipment of silver from the Americas, in particular from New Spain. In other words, in the second half of the eighteenth century, the Viceroyalty of New Spain was so profitable that it paid for its own expenses and even produced a surplus that was vital to the functioning of the empire at large.[28]

In the last decade of the eighteenth century, warfare put additional pressure on the Spanish purse. New Spain's ordinary revenues (taxes and monopolies) became insufficient. Under those circumstances viceroys implemented extraordinary measures including the collection of loans, donativos, ecclesiastical subsidies, and, eventually, the enforcement of the unpopular Decreto de Consolidación de Vales Reales in 1804. These measures, according to Marichal, deceived earlier scholars as it was believed that the colonial administration ran into a budgetary deficit and consequently took on debt. Instead, he contends that through loans and donativos that were shipped directly to the metropolis, the crown tapped an enormous amount of extra resources from its possessions and ultimately transferred a large share of its own debt to its colonial subjects. Donativos were never repaid, while the loans were serviced with the regular revenues collected within the colony.[29] Marichal concludes that the transfer of these funds to Spain delayed the politically costly implementation of a thorough fiscal reform in the metropolis and kept the taxes paid annually by Mexican subjects on average higher than those imposed on their Spanish cousins. Coupled with the regular shipments of specie to the mother country through trade and taxation, loans and donativos drew off from the colonies significant amounts of capital (and credit), delaying investment and sustained economic growth.[30]

Marichal's arguments support a widespread view of the Spanish imperial system in which Spaniards are understood to have developed an absolutist and interventionist imperial state. In contrast to the British North American experience, the Spanish American possessions were incorporated into the kingdom of Castile when the Cortes were in decline, and, despite its geographical extension, it was possible for the Spanish crown to uniformly impose its administrative and juridical apparatus on its overseas possessions, issue imperial directives without consultation, and closely scrutinize their application. Instead of creating a religiously plural and loose "empire of goods," Spaniards concentrated their efforts on the evangelization of natives and the exploitation of Spanish American mineral resources, which required a strict control over land and labor as well as on the creation of a centralized bureaucracy and a system of uniform administration and taxation. The combination of endowments and structural and institutional factors made possible the regular shipment of silver from the Americas to Spain. Ultimately, these divergent colonial experiences explain both the economic and political success of North America and the lack of development in Latin America.[31]

However, historical research has questioned the definition of absolutism as a comprehensive political and fiscal system, especially the assumption that early modern states were capable of raising revenue by obliterating their subjects' rights and freedoms and by implementing bureaucratic rationalization and political centralization.[32] Discussing seventeenth-century Spain, for example, Ruth MacKay highlights that in order to pay for warfare, the Spanish Crown relied upon a variety of taxes, silver from the Americas, grants from the church, inflation, donativos, and loans. She argues that the Spanish was "a [political] system that relied upon improvisation," revealing the "dispersed rather than consolidated nature of royal authority . . . [and] cast[ing] doubt on any necessary linkage between large scale military ventures and the development of powerful, central state institutions, fiscal or otherwise."[33] Spanish improvisation was born not only out of necessity but also "as a result of the way in which the king's vassals understood royal authority and the location of political power."[34] In other words, when military and fiscal demands soared, the relation between king and subjects mattered not only in the English Atlantic but also everywhere else.

Regina Grafe further questions the presumed absolutist and predatory nature of the Spanish Crown. She argues that scholars who followed the paradigm of the New Institutional Economics overstated Spain's fiscal imperatives under the assumption that all monarchs unconstrained by parliamentary representation would routinely overspend. In fact, her review of the existing literature demonstrates that even when lacking legislative initiative, the Spanish Cortes effectively restrained the monarch's ability to spend as, over time, they increased the share of revenues they periodically granted to the king.[35] Moreover, despite the defaults that, as discussed previously, in early modern Europe primarily functioned as multilateral renegotiations, the Spanish Crown successfully lowered the nominal interest rate paid for the *juros* from 10 percent in the 1550s to 2.5 percent after 1728, and in spite of the new issues of bonds, it retired substantial amounts of them from the market by means of redemptions throughout the eighteenth century. Although yields for investors are difficult to estimate, the evidence available demonstrates that Spanish interest rates fell within the range of most contemporary European states, except for the Italian city-states, which developed more efficient financial markets.[36] Even though Spanish finances worsened after the 1780s and debt issues increased by a factor of five between 1782 and 1794, Grafe points out that the Spanish debt per capita was 5 percent of the English debt per capita. By the 1800s, the Spanish Crown was capable of borrowing in Amsterdam at 4.5 to 5 percent annually, the same rates offered to the English king. In the eighteenth century, judging by the share of the annual budget it spent in servicing debt, Spain enjoyed relative financial health as it reached 7 percent on average and 12 percent in the 1780s, while England and France diverted toward debt payments between one-third and one-half of their annual budgets and the Netherlands between 40 and 70 percent. In sum, when placed in the broader European context the Spanish fiscal outlook in the 1700s was less disquieting than is generally assumed. It follows that parliamentary representation was not a prerequisite to the exercise of financial prudence and to enjoying a good credit rating even when warfare was almost constant.[37]

Moreover, the articles jointly published by Regina Grafe and Maria Alejandra Irigoin have challenged the scholarship arguing that the Spanish Crown was capable of extracting enormous revenues from its overseas possessions, and they have also challenged arguments for the existence of divergent fiscal structures in the metropolis and the empire (the former regarded as preserving overlapping jurisdictions and fiscal fragmentation and the latter portrayed as modern, centralized, and absolutist). Instead, they argue for ubiquitous fragmentation and contend that in the Americas—despite the creation by the Bourbon Reforms of a fiscal bureaucracy, cleaner-cut fiscal districts, and a lower incidence of tax farming—the fiscal system hardly qualified as "modern."[38] The lack of a single authority governing the creation and collection of uniform and universally applied taxes (especially over the *repúblicas de indios* and *españoles*) as well as the Catholic Church's prerogative to collect revenues evidence, on the one hand, that fiscal centralization was a desire and a political aim rather than a fact and, on the other hand, that colonial subjects were "not equal before the hacienda [treasury]."[39] In addition to fiscal fragmentation, the authors argue that other forces subverted the presumed Spanish fiscal absolutism. Through a sophisticated quantitative study of the late eighteenth-century intracolonial revenue transfers (situados) and expenditure, Irigoin and Grafe demonstrate that Spanish imperialism rested on the redistribution of funds across imperial treasuries (*cajas*) and comparatively low levels of remittances to the metropolis (only 5 percent of the revenue generated by the Spanish American treasuries).[40] Their findings regarding times of peace (1785–1789) and war

(1796–1800) additionally challenge other key assumptions sustained by the absolutist, extractive, and predatory thesis. Revenue transfers did not flow to coastal settlements primarily to fund defense spending. Instead, they followed local, regional, and international trade patterns and stimulated commerce and consumption by pumping cash and credit into the economically dynamic areas of the empire. These transfers brought to powerful merchants opportunities for supplying the administration and for lending funds to the crown, which in many cases resulted in the partial or complete privatization of the fiscal system. Thus, fiscal decision making was locally based and subject to local initiative and, therefore, incompatible with maximizing revenue transfers toward the metropolis. Additionally, Irigoin and Grafe's analysis demonstrates that revenue collected in mining and agricultural districts did not always flow toward those areas where income primarily originated in non-extractive activities such as trade and consumption. And in times of war when fiscal pressure intensified, the extra fiscal burden fell on domestic trade and consumption instead of on extractive activities. In sum, intracolonial transfers functioned independently from transfers to Spain, as those districts shipping substantial funds to the metropolis were not necessarily the ones receiving the larger intracolonial transfers.

These arrangements resulted in a system of fiscal redistribution and cross-subsidization that made weaker fiscal districts dependent on stronger ones. Instead of the intercolonial competition that characterized the Anglo-American experience, the Spanish system overall demanded fiscal cooperation among different districts as well as among powerful commercial and mining elites who greatly profited from it. Although the monarch was the ultimate arbiter, the spoils of the system emboldened Spanish American elites, and consequently they "avert[ed] and avoid[ed] impositions on their economic activities" so that when fiscal demands increased, they managed to dump the burden onto "ill-represented groups" and "softer targets, such as trade and consumption, or agriculture around mining towns."[41] Within this system, the incidence of colonial taxation was comparatively low, and challenging Marichal's findings, Irigoin and Grafe contend that colonial subjects paid on average lower taxes than their metropolitan cousins and in both cases were less burdened than the British, who supposedly fared better under parliamentary rule. The image of the Spanish imperial state as an extractive machine has been replaced by that of a "stakeholder empire" that thrived on the cooperation between king and powerful as well as humble subjects who were instrumental in financing the empire and who expected rewards from their contribution to empire building. The fiscal sphere created spaces for negotiation and collaboration between king and subjects in which the latter found opportunities to engage with imperial authority in mutually advantageous ways.

Irigoin and Grafe's characterization of the imperial system not only challenges the extractive hypothesis but also casts doubt on the role played by loans and donativos, at least as interpreted by the handful of historians who have studied them. The scarce research available on loans and donativos has generally presented these devices as compulsory measures and/or concealed forms of taxation that facilitated the shipment of silver to Spain. In fact, the majority of the existing works have primarily analyzed one donativo, the one collected in 1781, in which the king had stipulated the precise amount he expected to collect from his subjects according to their status.[42] The 1781 donativo was exceptional, since in all the other collections of loans and donativos, donors and lenders freely and unilaterally decided the size of their contributions, if they contributed at all. The existing research does not go beyond the fiscal scope of loans and donativos and generally minimizes their voluntary quality by arguing that the loyalty owed by the subjects to the monarch turned requests of assistance into "natural obligations" that left almost no room for the former to deny their financial support to the king or request compensations afterward. Moreover, authors who have regarded these fiscal devices as compulsory measures have analyzed exclusively their fiscal performance and have ignored a variety of other practices associated with collections of loans and donativos, such as the monarch's right to accept or decline offers from worthy and unworthy donors as well as the bargaining preceding and following the contributions. Although recorded on the books that listed the monetary value of loans and donativos as well as on the private and official correspondence exchanged between donors, lenders, brokers, and the king, most historians have omitted the qualitative information included in these sources. When they have acknowledged any negotiations at all, they have dismissed them on the assumption that absolute monarchs would promise repayment but most certainly breech contracts after securing the financial support of their subjects.[43]

In the following chapters, I will demonstrate that when analyzed in their broader political, legal, and cultural contexts, loans and donativos functioned as legitimate bargaining devices. My analysis demonstrates that far from being extractive mechanisms that secured the transfer of income from disenfranchised subjects to absolute monarchs, loans and donativos opened for the former channels for advancing their social, political, and financial interests. As noted in the introduction, a broad spectrum of imperial subjects accessed these channels and expected a variety of rewards in exchange for supporting the crown financially. Thus, through collections of loans and donativos the monarch distributed power and income among donors and lenders. Depending on the locale—that is, viceregal-territorial or municipal-local—donativos and loans facilitated different types of negotiations that resulted in distinct distribution patterns. When lenders and donors bargained at the viceregal or territorial level, they entered an exclusive and elitist system that benefited those at the top of the social order. At the municipal level, however, the politics of giving was more inclusive and made possible not only the participation but also rewarding of popular sectors that were generally excluded from the viceregal-wide type of bargaining.

Before analyzing how Spanish monarchs dispensed economic, social, and political benefits in exchange for financial support, I will review discussions of these devices by contemporary writers and treatises as well as the constitutional principles that made legitimate the practice of requesting and expecting rewards in exchange for loans and donativos.

DEFINING SPANISH LOANS
AND DONATIVOS

In the previous chapter, I stated that loans and donativos functioned as bargaining channels through which donors and lenders legitimately accessed the Spanish distribution of income and power in the eighteenth century. In this chapter, I will sustain my claim by reviewing the works published by early modern Spanish intellectuals. In the eighteenth century, civil legislation, canonical debates over usury, and customary gift practices impacted Spanish lending and giving. Thus, my overview considers not only the point of view of political economists interested in discussing royal revenue but also the legal framework that regulated giving and lending. In the Viceroyalty of Rio de la Plata, donativos and loans became reasonable fiscal tools in the 1790s, and so this chapter also offers a discussion of that historical conjuncture. References to historical and anthropological interpretations of the meanings of gifts also enrich this review. Finally, in the last section of this chapter I review the Spanish constitutional principles that legitimized requests for rewards in exchange for providing financial assistance to the monarch.

EARLY MODERN VIEWPOINTS: LAW AND CUSTOM,
POLITICAL ECONOMISTS, AND CANONISTS

I will start my discussion of the then-contemporary meanings of loans and donativos with José Canga Argüelles's *Diccionario de hacienda*, published in the early 1800s while he served as minister of royal finance (*secretario de hacienda*). The *Diccionario* defines donativos as "the subject's free and voluntary cession of income [*haberes*] for relieving [*socorro*] the treasury, he being the only assessor of the amount." While, in principle, donativos could only be free and voluntary, Canga Argüelles admits that "the magnitude of public crises [*emergencias públicas*], the lack of good judgment [*filosofía*] but above all the perception of an excessively exalted sovereign power, have occasionally converted them into violent acts, although by their nature they can only stem from freedom, thereby introducing within the exchequer's chaos [*combinaciones fatales*] the distinction between *free and forced donativos*" (italics in the original).[1]

At critical times, neither "free" nor "forced" donativos were capable of balancing the royal accounts as, according to Canga Argüelles, warfare "devoured in one day the wealth produced in one year." However, he acknowledges that "free and spontaneous" donativos yielded significant funds, while forced ones were in comparison "barren" (*estériles*) as they "combine[d] the contradictory attributes of compulsion and freedom." Canga Argüelles additionally lists several examples of voluntary and therefore financially profitable donativos that had been advanced to the crown since the mid-seventeenth century. The minister includes on his list the one provided by the Cortes in 1653, the 1684 contribution from the merchants of Andalusia, the donativo offered by the archbishops and bishops of Spain in 1784, and the one supplied by "all the classes of the nation" for fighting the War against the French Convention (1794). Additionally, for 195 years (1556–1750) the merchants of Cadiz annually had provided the Spanish Crown with hefty donativos. Canga Argüelles notes that the monarchs regarded the merchants' contributions as "heroic efforts [on the part of subjects] to express their loyalty."[2]

In contrast, the author of the *Diccionario* argues that the "forced" donativos established in 1629, 1632, 1635, and 1690 were either low yielding or "fruitless" and, in most cases, resisted. Canga Argüelles even cites Minister Pedro de Campomanes, who, when asked to assess the possibility of the implementation of forced donativos in Spain, declared them "inconsistent, detrimental to the subjects' status, and capable of arising problems and hatred as patently demonstrated by previous attempts." Forced donativos collected from the royal officers' salaries were the only exception to the rule of failure, as these donativos could potentially become a reliable source of income. Nevertheless, Canga Argüelles argues that officers regarded them as an "abuse of power" and a "violation of the principles sustaining the right to receive a salary," for the officers' earnings paid them "for their services and [were assessed] proportionally to the capital they invested to make them capable of serving the patria." The author even calls the 1689 forced donativo on salaries "a tribute under the deceitful title of donativo."[3] It is noteworthy that Canga Argüelles regarded the officeholders' salaries as a payment for their investments, indicating that in spite of their professional competence, many bureaucrats still accessed their offices through purchase in the eighteenth century. Moreover, bureaucrats considered the king's violations of their property rights simply unacceptable.

In a separate entry, Canga Argüelles succinctly defines loans as "expedients available to rapidly access funds when there is public confidence [in the government]." He follows his definition with commonsense financial advice for managing loans and recommends "extreme caution" when borrowing, as loans could push governments to take more debt simply to satisfy the payment of accrued interest or partially redeem the principal of past obligations. Canga Argüelles strongly advocates for the punctual payment of financial obligations, as falling into arrears would destroy public confidence, which, according to the author, rested on "thriftiness, efficient public accounts and government ideology." If for any reason public confidence in the Spanish government was compromised, the minister pointed out that the monarch could effectively "invigorate" it by using the "good name and credit of cities and corporations," which were able to perform the role of "intermediaries" between the crown and lenders. Canga Argüelles continues his commentary by listing the advantages and disadvantages of taking loans. Among the former, he lists the crown's capacity to raise "colossal funds" without "damaging the national industries" and "without forcing lenders" who, seeking profit, voluntarily advanced their capital. Loans, however, entailed significant shortcomings as they gave the government "enormous power to carry out whatever it wanted without resistance . . . bypassing the duty [*obligación*] to convene, listen, and consult the subjects." Ultimately, loans were "violent" not to lenders, but to the (Spanish) subjects as their repayment "demand[ed] the imposition of new contributions."[4]

By the early nineteenth century, Canga Argüelles had accumulated enough experience on the administration of royal and imperial finances to be regarded as an authority in the matter.[5] His comments on donativos reveal that they differed from regular taxation in that they were extraordinary and voluntary contributions in which donors independently assessed the amounts they contributed. Additionally, collections of donativos had impacts beyond the royal finances. The subjects' freedom could be compromised by the monarchs' attempts to compulsively enforce a contribution defined by its voluntary nature. While the loyalty of subjects and the independent initiative of lay and religious institutions guaranteed the successful collection of voluntary contributions, forced donativos served as examples of the abuse of power and the violation of rights.

The historical literature reviewed in chapter 1 demonstrates that the Spanish monarchs did not have to rely on the constraints of an English-style parliament to maintain a balanced budget. Canga Argüelles's writings reveal that he not only advocated for budgetary thriftiness but also enriched his discussions of fiscal matters with remarks that transcended the financial realm. He linked public confidence (a prerequisite for access to loans) to government ideology and to the capacity of cities and corporations to act as financial brokers or intermediaries for the crown. Additionally, loans were capable of tilting the balance of power in favor of the monarch and against his subjects as they allowed the king to gain an enormous power and bypass the duty to convene, listen, and consult them on financial matters. Finally, loans could indirectly disfranchise the people who ultimately bore the violent imposition of new taxes required to repay interest and principal. In summary, Canga Argüelles's definitions linked collections of loans and donativos to political, constitutional, ideological, and cultural practices. At stake were both the prerogatives of the Spanish king over the imposition of fiscal obligations as well as his subjects' rights to assess whether to comply with or resist them. Thus, for Canga Argüelles, royal finances constituted an arena for mutual consultation and compromise between subjects and monarch, a system of reciprocal partnership based on loyalty and voluntary cooperation in which compulsion could only play a disruptive role. And his words had further implications. The monarch should exercise financial prudence precisely because Spaniards were anything but complacent taxpayers.

As with other well-established legal practices in the Spanish world, loans and donations had been defined and codified in the Siete Partidas. The Quinta Partida included them among other contracts such as sales, purchases, and exchanges. Title I covered loans and lenders, property that could be loaned, and terms and conditions for extending loans. It defined loans as "contracts of courtesy" through which individual adult men received "pleasure and assistance" from others.[6] Ecclesiastical institutions, kings, cities, and minors (those under twenty-five years of age) were also legally capable of receiving loans. However, they enjoyed a privileged status, as their lenders would not be able to reclaim the principal unless they proved that the loans had been advantageous to these borrowers. Except for this caveat, the Quinta Partida did not establish a restrictive legal framework for taking or giving loans.

35

The Quinta Partida additionally established legal standards for donations, which, like donativos, reciprocally bound donors and beneficiaries. Title IV, Law I of the Quinta Partida defines donations "as good acts born out of nobleness and kindness of heart, when made without any compulsion," and refers to the act of giving as "a way to show favor and affection."[7] Additionally, donations were regarded as "more perfect and better" than the other contracts discussed in the same *partida* (loans, sales, commodatum, and deposits), "for a person who lends his property or places it in safe keeping, does so with the intention of recovering it, but he who gives it relinquishes it altogether." While loans primarily aimed at giving assistance, donations were "made through the favor or kindness of those who bestow them, or on the account of the merits of those who receive them."[8] However, not all men were considered equally competent at donating. Free men over twenty-five years of age were the only ones absolutely capable of donating their property or a portion of it to whomever they deemed deserving. On the other hand, the insane, the foolish, and spendthrifts (who were legally banned from disposing of their property) as well as heretics, convicts, and those suspected of sedition were inhibited from giving donations.[9] Thus, legitimate donations required an accurate assessment of both the qualities of donors and the merits of recipients. Additionally, due to their contractual nature, donations bound both parties, therefore initiating a chain of mutual obligations. Bonds of kindness, nobleness, and affection reinforced reciprocal commitments beyond the legal realm. In other words, donations created mutual bonds between free, sensible, and law-abiding adults willing to express their persistent loyalty and affection to one another.

These qualifications also applied to donativos. Manuel Josef de Ayala's *Diccionario de gobierno y legislación de Indias* (1792) as well as Fabian de Fonseca and Carlos de Urrutia's *Historia general de real hacienda* (commissioned in the 1790s and published in the 1840s and 1850s) compiled and reproduced the royal ordinances issued by the Spanish monarchs for requesting donativos.[10] Fonseca and Urrutia introduced their compilation with a brief definition that regarded donativos as "soft" resources (*ramo mental*) because they exclusively owed "their existence to the crown's [military] conflicts and [financial] hardships." While collected intermittently, donativos belonged among other "continuously successful" branches (*ramos*) of the exchequer as they were "strongly backed by the inexhaustible fidelity fund [Spaniards established] for their kings," a quality that "set them apart from other nations." Through collections of donativos, Spanish and imperial subjects not only expressed their "love" to their rulers but also recognized the "agreeable" choice made by their "superbly benevolent princes" who "surrender[ed] their prerogative to request by other means what [other] vassals are compelled to give to one who keeps them in peace and [under his] justice."[11] Although they did not explicitly cite the Quinta Partida, it is apparent that Fonseca and Urrutia significantly drew from it. By contributing donativos, Spanish subjects expressed their infinite love and loyalty for their benign monarchs, regarded as such because under financial pressure they made acceptable fiscal choices instead of bluntly exercising the allegedly universal right of kings to enforce objectionable (and presumably compulsory) exactions. The special qualities of donors and recipients made these transactions possible. Under Spanish rule, kings requested financial assistance from their subjects through congenial means. By means of these contributions, subjects and kings interacted in the fiscal sphere in a quintessentially Spanish fashion.

While the contractual nature of loans appears obvious, it is less evident (at least to modern observers) why donations belonged in the realm of contracts. The Quinta Partida established rules and qualifications for donors and recipients. However, it did not stipulate when beneficiaries were expected to reciprocate, nor did it state what they would return to those willing to relinquish their property altogether. Donations as described by the Quinta Partida were both gratuitous and ambiguous. However, they were also capable of creating the obligation to reciprocate. Consequently, they were similar to gifting practices widespread in archaic societies.[12] More importantly, donations in eighteenth-century Spain and Spanish America shared many features that characterized medieval and early modern European gift systems. As Valentin Groebner suggests, gifts are transactions in which the giver "cannot demand an explicit quid pro quo" without jeopardizing its efficacy. Gifts in late medieval Europe were powerful because they were "as far removed as possible from calculation and self-interest."[13] The author additionally describes the gift economy as a transitional space lying "between 'hard,' clearly fixed and, explicit (political) rules and 'soft,' ambiguous practice."[14] Natalie Zemon Davis found for early modern France that modern contractual and market exchanges did not historically replace gifts (donatio). On the contrary, gift systems coexisted with contracts and mercantile transactions as well as with the taxes and salaries commonly associated with the development of a bureaucratic and centralized state apparatus. According to Davis, properly performed gifting not only eased social relations but also opened and sustained personal channels of communication and assistance among individuals and groups of equal and uneven social statuses. As gifts circulated broadly, they curbed the autonomy of participants and fostered social integration.[15] When exchanged among nobles of different ranks, gifts maintained the participants' statuses but simultaneously confirmed that they belonged to the honorable classes. Gifts exchanged between lords and peasants were suitable for their ranks, and therefore, while binding, they preserved the deferential distance that helped sustain a hierarchical order.[16] Gifts circulated among professionals helped create and sustain corporate identities as well as patron-client relations. In other words, gifts shaped the boundaries of social inclusion both horizontally and vertically. The absence of gifting, however, did not automatically imply a feud but established a distance, an area defined by the absence of favor and communication. Coercion, on the other hand, subverted gift relations, generating uncertainty and mistrust.

Davis additionally emphasizes that the language and gestures associated with gifting mattered. References to service and gratitude accompanying gifts relaxed mutual interest without completely obliterating it. Among nobles, that language resembled feudal homage, which carried with it the acknowledgment of their superior status.[17] Moreover, personal bonds established by gifts set them apart from the standardized and anonymous world of contracts and sales. While the latter bore precise stipulations about their value and timing, the value of gifts was relative to the situation and persons involved, and the time and manner for reciprocating was kept open.[18] In other words, ambiguity gave strength to gift relations as it created an unending chain of mutual obligations.

The ambiguity that characterized donations and donativos helped them bypass canonical regulations concerning usury. In Spain, as elsewhere in Catholic Europe, commentators condemned and criminalized usurious practices. Medieval canonists, preachers, and moralists contended that money was "infertile," that is, incapable of producing more money or transforming itself into something else. They regarded interest charged on loans (usury) as a crime (theft or pillage) and a sin (avarice or sloth). From the viewpoint of canonists and moralists, usurers sold the time that elapsed between the moment the money was loaned and the time of its repayment. However, time belonged exclusively to God, and since there was no evidence he wanted to give it up, usurers stole God's patrimony against his will (pillage). Additionally, the usurers' trades ran against nature as they forced money to "give birth" to more money without the intervention of any physical work, thereby turning the usurer into a scandalous idler (sloth). Moreover, as money reproduced itself day and night, usurers violated the cycle of labor and rest prescribed by God. Ultimately, usurers engaged in unfair practices as they received more than what they gave. Usury was punished by excommunication and the denial of proper Christian burial rites. Salvation for the usurer was only possible upon returning the ill-gotten gains. If he refused, his relatives were required to perform the restitution as otherwise they would be equally damned. Under such draconian rules, only groups who could afford to ignore canonical censure, such as the Jews and Muslims, engaged in moneylending.[19]

In practice, however, usury was not routinely censured or criminalized but rather regulated, primarily by the setting of limits on interest rates. In medieval Spain, depending on the *fuero* (*juzgo, municipal,* or *real*), the amount of the transaction, and the kind of coin employed, interest rates varied between 12.5 and 50 percent. While the Siete Partidas forbade interest-bearing loans among Christians, in the sixteenth century regulation ensued, and the official rate was set at 10 percent, though it was reduced to 5 and 6 percent in the middle of the following century.[20] In spite of regulations, transactions such as the exchange of coins (*cambium*), the sale of notes and bills at a discount, the payment of annuities (*census,* also associated with simony), and *montepíos* (pawnbroking at low interest rate) continued to raise controversy as, in all cases, postponed payments implied a lending operation rather than a sale.

Commentators who regarded financial instruments as usurious argued that given the sterile condition of money, it was morally questionable to assign different values to the money physically present at the time a transaction occurred and that to be collected in the future. As trade and the instruments that made it possible expanded, however, sixteenth- and seventeenth-century scholastic canonists and theologians (especially those from the University of Salamanca) softened their points of view. They argued that while time did not affect money, "extrinsic" factors such as emergent loss, privation of gain, risk, and delay might influence the repayment of a loan. Taking into account these considerations, lenders were entitled to obtain profits. Moreover, these scholars even equated interest with a salary, thereby transforming the activity of bankers and financiers into a service deserving of fair remuneration.[21] In other words, the School of Salamanca reconciled the various interests of a deeply Roman Catholic but commercially and financially savvy people.

Eighteenth-century French merchants adopted similar values and turned their merchant courts into "bastions of virtue" that prioritized charity and the long-term well-being of the community over short-term individual gain, which, as in Spain, continued to be canonically censured. According to Amalia Kessler, the adoption of these values fostered commercial success and profit as they lowered transaction costs in the relatively underdeveloped economy of the old regime.[22] In the eighteenth century, Spain embraced the principles sustained by the School of Salamanca, which were incorporated into the Novísima Recopilación (1805). Nevertheless, controversy over usury continued, evidencing that despite the influence of the French Enlightenment, certain contracts were not completely divorced from morals or free from ecclesiastical public criticism in the Spanish financial world. Supporters of lending at a profit argued that lenders should be entitled to the same benefits as borrowers. Following the physiocrats, they held that free will in the making of contracts guaranteed their fairness, and they advocated for the lifting of all moral sanctions that precluded the channeling of wealth into productive activities. Detractors, on the other hand, condemned commercial and lending practices that yielded profits for merchants at the expense of weaker social actors such as peasants, artisans, and urban consumers. Morally dubious practices included the manipulation of the prices of basic foodstuffs and the purchase on credit of manufactures and commodities at prices below market values. Detractors of usury advocated for the enforcement of controls over prices and interest rates, especially for loans extended to consumers. Other critics directed their censures toward powerful commercial and financial guilds such as the Cinco Gremios Mayores of Madrid, which enjoyed a sizeable share of the lucrative military victualing business and invested in tax farming and royal lending.[23] Critics of the Cinco Gremios did not directly object to their members' right to obtain profitable rents but rather criticized their reluctance to pay reasonable profits to incoming and smaller investors, thereby keeping for the founding partners the bulk of the overall returns.

Despite royal efforts at sidelining controversies over usury, these debates acquired public notoriety and influenced public opinion, especially during the Motín de Esquilache, when increases in the price of bread and other staples sparked widespread rioting in Spain. Indeed, usury controversies coupled with social unrest forced the king in 1764 to issue a royal ordinance declaring "mandatory and legitimate" all the present and future contracts signed with the Cinco Gremios and pressuring the Gremios to secure theological approval for their business transactions. Thereafter, the Cinco Gremios were encouraged to call the credit instruments associated with public lending anything but mutuum (contracts in which the object borrowed must be returned by provision of an equivalent value) to avoid suspicion of usury.[24]

The post-1770s social and intellectual environments created the conditions for downplaying self-interest and profit when businesspeople used the instruments that financed both commercial capitalism and warfare. Under those circumstances, donativos became versatile tools. The evidence I present in the following chapters demonstrates that collections and transfers of donativo funds yielded financial gains to merchant-bankers in the form of commissions, fees, and coin arbitrage. When donativo funds were associated with lending operations, they additionally generated interest on the principal. However, donativos were free from the taint of usury, due to their ambiguity, because recipients of such gifts could legitimately return property exceeding the value of that of the original transaction. Within the gift economy, the repayment of obligations with the intention of expressing gratitude, displaying kindness, and nurturing friendship and social cohesion was exempted from moral, canonical, and theological censures. Moreover, since donors essentially provided a service to the monarch at times of war, donativos aimed, above all, to preserve the common good. Under the rules of Spanish pactismo, actions that positively impacted the well-being of the community granted to subjects inalienable rights, and as such the distribution of rewards (in coin or otherwise) in exchange for donativos was mandatory and unquestionably fair. Unlike contracts of mutuum, which were regulated by commutative justice, services provided for the preservation of the common good conformed to the tenets of distributive justice. Consequently, compensations distributed following donativos ought to be proportional to the donors' worth and the size and value of their contributions. If, by any circumstance, the monarch was unable to reward donors for their services, the principles sustaining common good practices held the entire community responsible for their fair compensation. It followed that taxes collected and enforced to repay donativos, unlike those raised to pay for loans, were unquestionably legitimate.

LOANS AND DONATIVOS ON THE GROUND

In the prior sections, I introduced the cultural, legal, and constitutional principles legitimizing donativos and loans. What follows is a discussion of the historical circumstances in which Spanish monarchs prioritized donativos and loans over other sources of revenue. Legitimate practices followed established procedures. Loans and donativos were no exception, and as such they were collected following established rules.

Before the late eighteenth century, the Spanish Crown had occasionally collected donativos in order to finance unexpected expenses. Requests for donativos were either particular (affecting certain individuals, groups, or institutions) or universal (aiming at all sectors of society). Generally, collections of donativos were particular, sporadic, and extraordinary, and they were intended to provide funds for specific purposes.[25] However, on two occasions (after the 1640s fiscal crisis and throughout the fiscal emergencies of the 1790s) collections of donativos became not only universal but also frequent events. In both instances, royal finances were stretched. The funds collected through these fiscal devices supplemented ordinary revenues and were partially channeled toward servicing public debt. Through these mechanisms and despite the crises, the crown mobilized the idle wealth of the propertied classes, expanded its domestic sources of credit (individual and corporate), and became less dependent on international bankers.[26] However, the most important benefit of donativos was constitutional, as they provided extraordinary revenues expediently and without calling the Cortes, which in the eighteenth century had expanded their prerogatives over tax collection. In other words, through loans and donativos, the crown bypassed the requirement that the Cortes consent to new taxes.[27] Unlike passive taxpayers, however, donors and lenders found in these fiscal contributions legitimate conduits to advance their individual and corporate interests. In other words, in the Spanish world subjects had both a voice and channels for bargaining with the monarch. Although they did not take the shape nor follow the rules of the English parliamentary culture, these mechanisms were accepted, effective, and agreed upon.[28]

Despite these advantages, from a strictly fiscal point of view donativos produced ambiguous results. Donativos were an honorable (and therefore agreeable) device for extracting revenue from traditionally tax-exempt groups and from those who successfully resisted increases in taxation. Generally, donativos were collected rapidly, carried low administrative costs, and, because they were voluntary, were collected without detriment to status.[29] Thus, my argument that loans and donativos were generally enforced after subjects successfully opposed attempts to expand the base of taxation through increased or new contributions. However, donativos always revealed the fiscal weakness of early modern composite monarchies as each community and private individual negotiated their contributions and the means employed to raise them separately. Regardless of their frequency and their capacity to raise funds, donativos evidenced the fragmentation of the fiscal space as, through these mechanisms, revenue collection became even more decentralized, localized, and unequal.

In the Iberian Peninsula, municipal authorities collected donativos by personally visiting the vecinos, accompanied by a priest and a notary. In order to encourage the people's support, donativos were commonly collected on a festive day or on Sundays at the end of religious services. Local authorities compiled a roster of donors, which was periodically updated and published. If donativos were aimed at all social groups, the officer in charge was supposed to visit each house and request support from the paterfamilias and his wife. Then, he asked for funds from sons and daughters and other dependents including domestics. The crown generally allowed donativos in kind to supplement those in specie.[30] Effective and congenial, donativos brought about political developments that reveal the inner workings of a polity concerned with social cohesion, the preservation of the common good, and the fair granting of rewards in exchange for financial support. Examples from the Iberian Peninsula additionally reveal that groups and individuals of unequal statuses put forward a variety of claims through these channels. For instance, in the seventeenth century several Castilian towns requested to be promoted to the status of villa in exchange for their donativos. Additionally, in 1638 the commissioners in charge of collecting donativos issued pardons and remissions of criminal sentences (including homicide) to several contributors. In 1643 a donor demanded that the crown issue a written assurance that no other taxes would be imposed upon any donativo contributor, and in 1679 a past administrator of the ice monopoly offered to donate a substantial sum in order to end a pending trial with the crown and recover his right to manage the monopoly.[31] Thus, the voice and bargaining power subjects found through collections of donativos undermined the ideals of absolute rule and uniform taxation.

In sum, donativos were incompatible with the exercise of absolute, predatory powers. On the contrary, the collection of large donativo funds depended on the involvement of local authorities and their skillful manipulation of the mechanisms that sustained a hierarchical yet competitive social order. By publicizing the names of donors, local authorities recognized their services to the common good and indirectly incited other vecinos to imitate both their peers and their social betters. Publicity coupled with the expectation of rewards created the conditions for the type of social competition that brought into the system ambitious donors. Thus, donativos reveal that the political and financial survival of a composite monarchy required the participation of financial brokers capable of mobilizing the support of the subjects residing within their fiscal districts. My analysis reveals that local and regional authorities who not only contributed but also collected large donativos within their districts were recognized and handsomely rewarded.

In the Viceroyalty of Rio de la Plata in the 1790s, collections of donativos became frequent events. International warfare also resumed in that decade. However, I argue that the civil disorders experienced in Spanish America after the 1760s created an environment conducive to the adoption of these fiscal devices. Similarly to the British North Atlantic, the post–Seven Years' War era in Spanish America witnessed increased demands for military service and revenue. These demands were met with resistance and revolt in the 1760s and 1780s. While the Bourbons crushed the rebellions, they did not necessarily disfranchise their Spanish American subjects. On the contrary, the adoption of loans and donativos demonstrates that they were aware of their rights and expected compensations in exchange for their financial support. Donativos demonstrate that in the late eighteenth century, Spanish American subjects were as politically experienced as the British colonial subjects and even more successful at bargaining with their monarch. Unlike the English king, who through financial pressure lost the loyalty and support of his American subjects, the Spanish monarch by implementing donativos kept open the channels that gave his subjects a voice. Within the boundaries of the transatlantic Spanish composite monarchy, Spanish rulers found strength in sharing the spoils of the imperial project with powerful and supportive subjects rather than in preying on them. Although donativos were a poor substitute for an annual system of direct regular taxation from a strictly fiscal point of view, they did yield substantial funds precisely because they were politically, culturally, and constitutionally more palatable than taxes. By requesting instead of demanding the financial support of its subjects, the crown allowed them to assess whether they wanted to contribute or not and how much they wanted to pledge. Likewise, those who helped the crown requested and expected rewards. Consequently, universal collections of donativos opened political negotiations in a fragmented, widespread, and defused manner that made English-style parliamentary representation redundant and unnecessary.

A thorough discussion of the crown's attempts at increasing taxation in Spanish America from the 1760s onward exceeds the purpose of this chapter. Instead, I will mainly focus on the fiscal aspects of tax-related uprisings as well as the political and ideological responses fashioned by the participants. Between 1760 and 1810, localized and spontaneous fiscal riots became commonplace in Spanish America. However, only four major rebellions directly challenged colonial rule. The first one occurred in Quito in 1765; the second was the Great Andean Insurrection of 1780–1783; the third was the 1781 *comunero* uprising in New Granada (which coincided with that of Túpac Amaru in the Andes); and finally, the fourth was the popular upheaval lead by Father Hidalgo in Mexico in 1810.[32] It has been noted that in Mexico most of the pre-1810 revolts arose from local grievances, while protests against new taxes or abuses by tax collectors were less important.[33] Additionally, in New Spain the viceregal government could afford to disregard the uprisings and even grant concessions to the dissenters because the treasury depended less on taxes extracted from the indigenous population than on revenues collected from trade and mining. On the other hand, in regions that were comparatively poorer royal officials had to increase their pressure to extract revenues, and therefore they upset the interests of a variety of groups ranging across the social and ethnic hierarchies. For instance, the Quito rebellion was a reaction to the first wave of reforms implemented after the Treaty of Paris in 1763, and the comunero revolt was a response to the administrative and fiscal changes implemented by Visitor General Gutierrez de Piñeres. Likewise, in Peru most of the uprisings of the 1760s and 1770s, as well as the great insurrection of the 1780s, were sparked by diligent corregidors who, counting on the support of illegitimate or mestizo curacas, reassessed mita quotas, collected tribute more efficiently, enforced the new monopolies and customs duties, increased the *alcabalas*, and imposed the *repartimiento de mercancías*.[34]

In his synthesis of the rebellions of the late colonial period, Anthony McFarlane notes that elites as well as popular sectors rebelled not only because they opposed economic exploitation but also because the

Bourbons' assertion of authority dramatically modified their political and social expectations.[35] In Spanish America, creoles and Indian leaders did not have representative assemblies for venting their grievances. But according to McFarlane, under Habsburg rule they did participate in the government through the many channels opened to them by the Austrian paternalistic governing style ("government by bureaucratic negotiation") or, in Colin MacLachlan's words, a spiritual and flexible political matrix that rested on bonds of loyalty rather than on unquestioned obedience.[36] Politically speaking, the Habsburg experience functioned as a training ground for the colonial subjects who were rehearsing and appropriating political rights that eventually became customary after two centuries of colonial rule. Although in most cases those who rebelled did not elaborate political programs, we have enough evidence to assert that leaders and popular groups generally supported a representative system and defended their rights to negotiation within the colonial administration. The uprisings of the late colonial period could therefore be best described as "disputes over the constitutional order of the colonial regime," evidencing that Bourbon reformism did not eliminate politics.[37] For example, the *comuneros*, who drafted a political program, expressed their ideas by reviving the customary right of the community (body politic) to defend its "common good" (if necessary by force) vis-à-vis the demands of the government. In Quito, the rebels, although lacking an articulate political agenda, expressed similar ideas by summoning a *cabildo abierto*, an institution that embodied urban autonomy and government by negotiation. And the Andean leaders, by referring to "Inca nationalism," defended their right to broker between the state and the indigenous communities.

The comunero revolt was, however, the only one that presented the crown with written demands regarding taxation. The comuneros' capitulations did not deny the subjects' obligation to pay taxes, nor did they put forward an egalitarian collection of dues. On the contrary, living in a society of inherent inequalities legitimized by a redistributive system of justice, the comuneros believed that taxes should be collected following economic, social, and racial hierarchies. That fact, however, did not keep them from defending their right to judge whether the king had a genuine need for imposing new taxes (or increasing existing ones), suggesting that legitimate revenues were only those that the community consented to pay.[38] McFarlane finds the same language of contestation in the case of the Quito uprising of 1765 and highlights the political dimension of the city's anti-fiscalism. This interpretation can be expanded to the rebellions that took place in the Andes in the 1770s. For instance, in 1779 mestizos, cholos, and *zambiagos* violently opposed visitor Areche's decree aimed at collecting tributes from them not only because it represented a new monetary burden but also because it lowered their status to that of the *indios tributarios*. In the Andes, people reacted similarly when the king attempted to impose the alcabala on products and groups traditionally excused from it. In that case, the people defended their customary exemptions against fiscal innovation.[39] Moreover, during the rebellion led by Tomas Katari (1777–1780), which combined violence with persistent juridical claims, the indigenous communities of Macha consistently delivered their tributes to the royal treasury and fulfilled their mita quotas as they considered them an integral part of the compact that not only bound them to the monarch but also granted them voice.[40] Spanish American subjects internalized so deeply the concept of socially and racially allocated taxes as bases for bargaining with the monarch that even slaves in New Granada championed it. In the course of the 1781 uprising, they petitioned for their freedom in exchange for paying tributes "as if they were Indians."[41] In other words, Bourbon attempts at "fiscal absolutism" made subjects very sensitive to the threat of social homogenization, fiscal equality, and the eventual disfranchisement implicit in uniform, universal, and absolute systems of taxation. Their claims to rights in exchange for contributions were grounded in the philosophical principles and the political culture that legitimized Spanish rule.

THE PHILOSOPHICAL PILLARS SUSTAINING
SPANISH-STYLE BARGAINING

The Spanish contractual political tradition (pactismo) established that the power of the king was limited by law and revocable and that it was legitimate as long as the subjects agreed to concede their sovereignty (*potestas populi*). Spanish political philosophy regarded as legitimate those kings who preserved the common good and safeguarded the reciprocal obligations binding the monarch and his kingdom.[42] Spanish common good built upon the classical and Christian traditions that perceived the political community as the natural vehicle for achieving collective ethical perfection. Common good rested on the principles of peace, material well-being, and the promotion of virtue among the members of a political community regarded as naturally hierarchical. Common good was not achieved by simply adding together individual interests or by caring for the well-being of the majority. On the contrary, it was a superior aim that transcended the individual and blended into one the private and public spheres. In this framework, the state functioned as a juridical corporation with its own rights and duties that included directing individual interests toward the achievement of common aims. Under these principles, politics was not morally neutral but rather an ethical exercise oriented toward the betterment of the individual. Justice was not impartial but fair (distributive) as it assigned to each individual and group what they deserved according to their statuses.[43] A king was also perceived as fair when he rewarded subjects proportionally to their contributions to the common good. As an ethical exercise, the preservation of the common good limited both the king's political autonomy and his subjects' obedience. Spanish pactismo established that political authority was not exercised under the law but within lawful limits and that political obedience was not given to a person but to the laws of the kingdom. Under the rules of common good, the lawful exercise of authority did not diminish the monarch's majesty, nor did obedience limit the subjects' freedom. Within this framework, disobedience to authorities who violated the principles sustaining the common good was a lawful act, almost a duty rather than a right.[44]

The philosophical principles that sustained the Spanish monarchy were transferred to the Americas. In their defense of the Indians, the Augustinian friar Alonso de La Vera Cruz (1507–1584) and the Dominican Bartolomé de Las Casas (1484–1566) extended Spanish liberties and rights to the indigenous communities under Spanish rule, and as such they became a separate republic represented by their own cabildos. Radical proponents of potestas populi such as Juan de Mariana (1536–1644) even asserted that communities, territories, and municipalities preserved the right to impose tributes, change or eliminate laws deemed unsuitable, and intervene in dynastic succession. The king possessed the prerogative to declare war, provide laws in times of peace, and select justices and magistrates. Absolutists, on the other hand, did not deny the contractual nature of authority but regarded God as the exclusive source of the prince's power.[45] According to historian Monica Quijada, potestas populi provided Spanish imperial subjects with an *imaginaire*, a flexible and multithreaded system that transcended the world of readers and academics as it furnished both the cultured and commoners with conceptual tools for understanding their social existence, behavior, and political action. *Imaginaires* functioned as "collective reservoirs of ideas" that presented to subjects practical political options in moments of crisis.[46]

My analysis of donativos demonstrates that donors, employing the tools made available to them by their political and fiscal imaginaires, voluntarily gave financial support to the crown and simultaneously advanced the rights that corresponded to their social statuses. Donors' bargaining with the crown in exchange for donativo contributions evidences that the Bourbon administrative reforms did not depoliticize nor did they disenfranchise Spanish American subjects. On this point, I follow the scholars who have challenged the efficacy of Bourbon reformism by emphasizing that representative and electoral practices at work in the Spanish American cabildos and other corporations made the Spanish contractual political tradition a permanent feature of the imperial political culture.[47] Administrative professionalization did not marginalize the role of corporate bodies either. On the contrary, they grew stronger as bureaucratic centralization required a better coordination of their roles and their articulation with the center.[48] As for cabildos, which were one of the pillars sustaining the *estado mixto* between 1765 and 1830, they not only expanded their jurisdictional and representative functions but also became indispensable for meeting increasing military and fiscal demands.[49] Following Ferdinand VII's abdication in 1808, the jurisdictional and representative prerogatives of Spanish American cabildos became even more apparent as, in the absence of a legitimate monarch, subjects reclaimed their right to exercise sovereignty at the municipal and regional levels and, as a result, actively contributed to the territorial disintegration of the Spanish empire.[50] This process revealed that the Spanish monarch ruled over a political community made up of multiple estates instead of individual holders of inalienable rights.[51]

In the Rio de la Plata, the cabildo of Buenos Aires claimed its right to represent the people and the king during the First English Invasion, that is, two years before Ferdinand VII handed his power over to Napoleon Bonaparte.[52] The political and military blunders of Viceroy Sobremonte (1804–1806) during the first English assault (he fled to Córdoba and failed to organize a military force to confront the invaders) generated distrust and eventually led to his removal from office and imprisonment. By summoning *cabildos abiertos*, the cabildo of Buenos Aires legitimately compelled Viceroy Sobremonte to delegate his political authority to the audiencia and his military command to Captain Liniers, who had emerged as a popular and talented military leader during the invasions. Afterward, the audiencia would confer on Liniers the title of interim viceroy.[53]

During the imperial crisis that followed the Napoleonic occupation of the Iberian Peninsula, the power and legitimacy of the cabildo of Buenos Aires expanded. Since revolutionary authorities in Buenos Aires opted not to send representatives to the Cortes in Cádiz, nor did they immediately call for a congress to draft a constitution and declare independence, their legitimacy was threatened by the viceroy, local audiencia, and cabildo as well as the representatives sent to the capital from other regions in the viceroyalty. In June 1810, a month after its establishment, the Junta, representing the legitimate rights of Ferdinand VII, deposed and expelled the viceroy and *oidores*, staffed the audiencia with loyal judges, and fashioned itself as the supreme authority in the viceroyalty. However, the Junta did not claim to legitimately hold sovereignty, because the constitutional makeup of the Spanish monarchy reserved that attribute for cabildos, especially those residing in viceregal capitals. It would have been constitutionally (and, I would argue, financially) risky to get rid of the cabildo. Instead, in October 1810, the Junta purged it and staffed it with city councilmen supporting the revolutionary cause. Despite the purge, the cabildo developed its own revolutionary agenda, and since the Junta still functioned at the fringes of legality, the cabildo continued challenging the Junta's legitimacy.[54] Following these constitutional principles, I argue that collections of loans and donativos strengthened the representative power and fiscal capacity of corporate and municipal bodies, which, paraphrasing Richard Bonney, evidences that meeting the demands of war turned the Viceroyalty of Rio de la Plata into an even more fragmented and therefore less absolute polity.[55]

Rights and privileges as defined by Spanish pactismo additionally conferred on Spanish subjects the status of vecinos. Despite local, regional, and imperial differences, in the Spanish world vecindad was the measure of a civic life, and consequently those without a "known citizenship" were regarded as dangerous social outcasts. According to Tamar Herzog, citizenship in Castile was achieved not only by legal formal procedures but also by performance, and thus, outsiders who established ties with a community and performed the ordinary communal duties (i.e., residence, militia service, payment of taxes) enjoyed citizens' privileges.[56] In the early stages of the conquest and colonization of Spanish America, citizenship developed similarly to its Castilian counterpart and was legally claimed by Spaniards, Indians, and foreigners alike. By the early eighteenth century, however, formal legal procedures were abandoned, and consequently the status of citizen was granted primarily upon the grounds of performance and reputation. Vecindad became a social construction, a mechanism that granted rights to those who acted like vecinos or were known to be such, even when absent from their communities. These changes coincided with the implementation of new forms of exclusion that made it harder for foreigners, Indians, Africans, and castas to legally gain citizen rights within Spanish settlements. Consequently, the gap between Spanish vecinos and the foreign and ethnically different outsider widened, while local communities developed a stronger ("national") Spanish identity.[57]

In the sixteenth and seventeenth centuries, Buenos Aires was primarily a frontier settlement antagonistic to, but also collaborating with, the Portuguese and the Indians. According to Herzog, this situation gave the city an early and acute Spanish character, blurring the difference between local and Spanish identities. By extension, services to the crown were perceived as services to the community. Additionally, those wishing to become vecinos had to be natives of the kingdom of Spain and were required to have a horse and arms to allow substitutes to fulfill vecinos' military duty during their absence from the city. Only exceptional foreigners, regarded as very useful and highly immersed in the local society, could be granted the status of vecino. During the union of the crowns of Portugal and Castile (1580–1640), these rules were overlooked. However, they were reinstated afterward, and consequently foreign immigrants were again regarded with suspicion and their activities closely supervised. Simultaneously, it was becoming apparent throughout Spanish America that the integration of Indians and Spaniards into a single community would not be easily accomplished. This realization coincided with the erection of ethnic and racial barriers between groups based on the perception of religious, political, and cultural differences. Thus, Indians, Africans, and castas who might have been considered potential vecinos (and, by extension, Spaniards) were regarded as permanently foreign to the community.

In reference to changes to the status of vecino, I argue that contributions in the forms of loans and donativos functioned performatively as mechanisms for sanctioning and achieving vecindad, and as such they became conduits for confirming and gaining rights. In the 1790s, most of the individual contributions came from a variety of prominent and middle-class donors. But starting with the British Invasions of Buenos Aires and continuing through the wars of independence, the plebs of Buenos Aires began to contribute small amounts, though in increasing numbers, to collections of donativos. Their stronger presence among the donors coincided with their military and political mobilization.[58] In other words, contributions to donativos became an additional channel utilized by the urban plebs and castas to achieve their inclusion into a community that had become socially and racially more exclusive.

In addition to the more exclusive definition of vecindad, between 1793 and 1816 social, commercial, political, and military developments profoundly changed the lifestyle of the popular sectors in Buenos Aires. Throughout this period, urban labor organization in Buenos Aires was transformed by the importation of great numbers of African slaves and the simultaneous destruction of the guild system. These transformations not only exposed the plebs to a fragile and volatile labor market but also cut them loose from the institutions and practices that had facilitated their subordinate incorporation into the old regime.[59] As in other Spanish American cities, guilds had performed many essential social roles in Buenos Aires. Workshops gave Spanish and *casta* workers control over labor recruitment and training and production standards. Additionally, they functioned as sources of mutual aid and corporate identity. Urban authorities even found in guilds effective mechanisms for controlling vagrancy, laziness, and crime.[60] In Buenos Aires the decline of the guilds coincided with the need to create popular militias and military units first to repel the English and, afterward, to fight the wars of independence. In this context, free black, casta, and creole artisans and laborers found in military mobilization "fluid hierarchies and [their] strong institutional loyalties provided [them with] alternative rituals, hierarchies, training regimes, and, more importantly, income."[61] Drawing from Lyman Johnson, Tamar Herzog (vecindad by performance as a channel for confirming and gaining rights), and Natalie Davis (donations as mechanisms for social integration and communication among groups of different social status), I argue that in the early 1800s, the plebs of Buenos Aires were able to harness the performative power of donativos to turn themselves into vecinos. They financially supported a system that opened for them opportunities for political influence, social advancement, and group identity (especially under the leadership of Santiago de Liniers and Cornelio Saavedra). Moreover, their services provided permanent employment, wages, pensions for veterans and military widows, as well as dowries for orphaned daughters.[62]

In the early 1800s, local and transatlantic circumstances prompted in Buenos Aires the active participation of increasing numbers of socially and racially diverse vecinos. The military and political crises fostered political sociability and simultaneously opened channels for the exercise of practices that foreshadowed modern forms of political representation. Popular militias debated in assemblies and through elected leaders. The popularity of coffeehouses and political and literary clubs coupled with the publication of an increasing number of newspapers and pamphlets stimulated political debate and broadened the boundaries of participation to include not only learned and propertied men but also women and the plebs.[63] This process transformed both vecindad and the vecino. Vecindad (especially in its active form) shared many characteristics with modern citizenship, and as such it became an essential experience in the transition from old to new forms of political representation and for the transformation of the traditional corporate and hierarchical body politic into a community of free and equal individuals. In other words, monarchical subjects conceptualized modern citizenship not in a vacuum but in reference to their status as vecinos.[64]

Several characteristics of vecindad facilitated its transformation. Vecindad was socially inclusive and malleable, as those who fulfilled the duties of vecinos acquired rights as well as a new and improved juridical status. Additionally, the prospect of social improvement stimulated political mobilization and participation in the community. Framed in the Castilian tradition of common good, vecindad demanded the performance of services beyond individual, family, and corporate interests for the betterment of a community that transcended those groups. Participation in the local government gave vecinos political autonomy vis-à-vis outsiders and royal representatives. Moreover, local identities and loyalties associated the local community with the *patria*, turning each of its members into *patricios* or *patriotas*.[65] Finally, in the early nineteenth century the status of vecino was a prerequisite for participating in elections, and while in different areas it referred to diverse social realities, in all cases the term grounded "the abstract citizen in the particular territorial and social conditions of a concrete community."[66]

In Buenos Aires there was an early identification between vecino, citizen, and patriota. Generally, *patria* referred to one's place of origin, but it differed from similar terms in that it excited deep personal feelings such as love and loyalty as well as strong and active commitment to the communal well-being. For Gabriel di Meglio, it was almost a sacred term that was generally evoked in emotionally charged expressions such as "defending the religion, the king and the patria." Through the revolutionary years, the term not only expanded its emotional dimension but also became highly politicized. Thereafter, *patria* transcended the local community to include "the common cause," and *patriota* identified all the Americanos as opposed to the Europeans. The defense and freedom of the patria demanded from all patriotas material contributions as well personal sacrifices. And, *patriotismo* referred to both the willingness to prioritize the common well-being over personal interests as well as the virtuous participation in the collective revolutionary cause. Thus, patriotismo became the "moral axis" of the system as well as the experience that separated active citizens from passive subjects.[67] In reference to changes in political representation, collections of loans and donativos counted among the old regime practices that enabled the transformation of subjects and vecinos into patriotic citizens. Employing the tools made available to them by the Spanish political culture and their political imaginaires, Spanish American subjects achieved not only political representation but also social inclusion.

REDISTRIBUTION OF POWER AND
INCOME AT THE VICEREGAL LEVEL

In this section, I analyze donativos and loans collected in the Viceroyalty of Rio de la Plata at the territorial or viceregal level. The crown requested the financial support of the Rioplatense subjects first during the War against the French Convention (1793–1795) and for a second time during the Naval Wars against England (1799–1801). In the three chapters that follow, I argue that through these devices the monarch distributed wealth and power among different regions and social groups. At the viceregal level, income distribution benefited prominent imperial groups such as merchants, merchant-bankers, and bureaucrats, which through corporate representation obtained a variety of rewards from the crown in exchange for their financial support. Groups lacking corporate representation contributed donativos as well. Following the principles of distributive justice, however, they accessed fewer and lesser compensations or, in many cases, none at all. Finally, distribution patterns were not fixed but rather changed over time. My analysis of these two collections of donativos additionally addresses the monarch's changing political agenda, his regulatory power, and his capacity for taking political initiative. Since Spanish kings prioritized the interests of those subjects instrumental to achieving their own imperial aims, the rewards they granted did not always favor the same groups or individuals. By analyzing both successful and unsuccessful negotiations, I additionally weigh the relative bargaining power of different donors and lenders confronting a rapidly changing political environment.

Late eighteenth-century wars impacted the Spanish empire both geopolitically and fiscally. The end of the U.S. War of Independence in 1783 marked a period of peaceful relations between Spain and England. Spain's partnership with France (which had been renewed through the Third Family Compact of 1761) allowed the crown to focus on economic growth and financial recovery from the 1760s to the 1780s. But in the early 1790s, as a consequence of the French Revolution, hostilities resumed. Charles IV, suspicious of the political developments in revolutionary France, courted England without breaking with France, thereby sending confusing signals to both nations. The increased radicalism spread by the French Revolution in 1792, followed by the execution of Louis XVI in 1793, forced Spain into an alliance with England against France. The War against the French Convention began in March of 1793 and continued until mid-1795, when France and Spain signed the Peace of Basle. The peace was followed by a renewed partnership against England in 1796.[1] The change in alliances, although short-lived, was financially costly for Spain. In order to finance the War against the French Convention, the crown issued bonds for 74.2 million pesos and created the Fondo de Amortización to sustain their value. Additionally, it received a large ecclesiastical subsidy and collected universal donativos in both Spain and in the Americas.[2]

Through the Peace of Basle of 1796, the military forces of Spain and France united against England, but Spain was allowed to maintain its neutrality against other nations at war with the French. Since France and England were already at war at the time the treaty was signed, England immediately attacked Spain. The Naval Wars against England at the end of the eighteenth century (1797–1802) were militarily and financially devastating for Spain, which was still trying to recover from the War against the French Convention. During the French war, shipping was not interrupted, as the Anglo-Spanish forces were superior to the French. During the Naval Wars against England, however, the English dominance (made even more apparent during the blockade of Cádiz) interrupted trade and the flow of silver from the Americas when they were most needed. Consequently, in 1798 the crown restructured its debt by issuing the decree known as the Consolidación de Vales Reales, which affected real estate property and liquid assets owned by the nobility and clergy. In the Spanish possessions, the crown first solicited loans and collected donativos, and finally, in 1804, it enforced the Consolidación decrees.

A NOTE ON THE SOURCES AND THE MECHANISMS EMPLOYED TO COLLECT LOANS AND DONATIVOS

In order to assess how loans and donativos had not only financial but also social and political impacts, we need to understand the mechanisms that made possible their collection across a fragmented fiscal space as well as the multiple transactions required to bring their yields into the royal treasuries. In the Viceroyalty of Rio de la Plata, loans and donativos were first collected at the local treasuries and transferred to Buenos Aires. Treasury officials in the viceregal capital recorded the amounts in the *libros de tomas de razón* as well as in the *libro manual* for donativos, a royal accounting book that noted both the amounts of the transactions and the financial instruments employed in the transfers. Royal officers additionally prepared detailed lists of donors and lenders to be sent to Spain along with the funds and the related official correspondence. I have compiled a database from the information available in these sources, which has allowed me to comparatively analyze different collections of loans and donativos. Unless indicated otherwise, the information presented on the tables is drawn from this database.[3]

Collections of loans and donativos produced a variety of qualitative records as well. Royal *bandos* and *proclamas* not only informed the public of the crown's financial needs but also mobilized popular support. Additionally, donors and royal officers followed both bureaucratic and ritualized procedures to validate these transactions. Upon announcements, prospective donors and lenders submitted letters to local royal officers expressing their willingness to contribute. These letters were forwarded to the viceroy, who decided whether to accept or reject the offers. Then, the viceroy formally notified donors and lenders of his decision by issuing letters of acceptance that served as notes of gratitude as well as written proof of the transactions. The records reveal that far from being a compulsory and predatory process, collections of loans and donativos involved bargaining from the outset.

In addition to monetary donativos, donors made contributions in kind. Religious men and women, for example, made spiritual donations (Masses, prayers, and mortifications). Lay donors frequently set specific conditions for their donations, indicating that they had a voice throughout the process. Some of them stated that their monetary donations would continue "for as long as the war lasted," while others specifically requested that their contributions "[pay] for the salaries" of one or more soldiers. The language employed in these transactions provides important analytical hints about the types of rewards expected by donors. These rhetorical tools had cultural and political meanings that transcended their literal meaning.

After being accepted, all the offers were entered in the libros de tomas de razón. While formal, these procedures were as far removed as possible from the surveys of wealth commonly conducted prior to the enforcement of forced loans and taxation. Unlike taxes, bureaucratic procedures associated with loans and donativos additionally carried low administrative costs, as they only demanded the sending of documents back and forth among the parties involved. The paperwork filed and the administrative steps followed for collecting loans and donativos were similar to those associated with the recording of gifts and the selling of annuities, which in Spain were commonly known as juros. Finally, the language employed in these sources reveals that donors, lenders, and the king not only shared the responsibility for but also actively participated in the conservation of the imperial order.

The majority of loans and donativos were expressed in *pesos fuertes* (for analytical purposes, those that were not have been converted into that currency).[4] In some cases, donors gave one-time contributions (noted in the source as *de contado*) and/or committed themselves to annual payments throughout the war (recorded as *anuales*). In processing this information, I have kept one-time contributions (de contado) separate from those that were advanced annually as the latter were expected to reach the treasury more than once. Donors who contributed annually periodically assessed the feasibility of receiving their expected compensations. The evidence available shows that if for any reason the terms and conditions of their bargains changed, they were able to discontinue their contributions. In other words, donors not only accessed bargaining channels but also had the power to periodically revise their deals.

Immediately after the War against the French Convention had been announced in Buenos Aires, the viceregal capital, both types of books that recorded loans and donativos (libros de tomas de razón and the libro manual) started registering offers that had been accepted. The earliest entry in the libro manual appears on 26 June 1793. The last contributions were recorded in the libros de tomas de razón in December 1794 (the closing date for accepting offerings), although the peace was made known in Buenos Aires on 4 September 1795. The discrepancy in the ending dates for both books does not affect one-time contributions. However, it does show a difference in the annual ones. The information available in the libro manual can help resolve this discrepancy as it shows that donativos continued arriving in Buenos Aires after December 1794. Also, in the case of several annual contributions, the books indicate that earlier offers were prorated through 4 September 1795—the date the peace was announced. Following the information available in these records, I will present and analyze annual donations as recorded in the libros de tomas de razón (through December 1794 or eighteen months) and as prorated through September 1795 (twenty-six months).[5]

Unfortunately, the available records for analyzing the donativos collected during the Naval Wars against England (1799–1801) are not as thorough as the ones available for the War against the French Convention. Nevertheless, it is possible to gloss the totals contributed by different regions and compare these totals with the previous collection of donativos.

THE PROFITABLE BUSINESS OF TRANSFERRING REVENUE, SALARIES, AND SUPPLIES

Donativos as a Source of Commissions and Private Capitalization

In this chapter I first discuss how donativos collected during the War against the French Convention (1793–1795) created opportunities for profit for the merchant-bankers involved in the transfer of donativos across the viceregal treasuries. This section is followed by a discussion of the social backgrounds of the donors as well as the sizes of their contributions. My analysis of the size and number of donativos demonstrates that, unlike taxes, donativos were not uniformly collected either across the different regions of the viceroyalty or among the different groups that chose to contribute their funds.

Loans as well as one-time and annual donativos were first collected in the local treasuries and then transferred to regional ones that generally transferred them again to the viceregal capital. Merchant-bankers involved in transferring these funds profited in different ways. First, merchants benefited from coin arbitrage. Second, they collected commissions from the monarch in payment for their financial services. Finally, they utilized loans and donativo funds to capitalize their viceroyalty-wide trading operations. Moneys collected in loans and donativos were frequently employed to pay the salaries and pensions of military men and bureaucrats serving across the viceroyalty. They additionally appeared as backing credit instruments issued for supplying the military and the bureaucratic apparatus serving in the different regions across the viceroyalty. By providing the king with a variety of essential financial services, merchant-bankers not only found opportunities for profit but also acted as indispensable partners in the financing of the imperial defense and administration. Simultaneously, merchant-bankers used these transactions to capitalize their businesses and facilitate the political and fiscal integration of a disjointed space.

In order to show how merchants profited from loans and donativos, I will first establish how much revenue these fiscal devices yielded and what share of that total the merchants retained in commissions and fees. Secondly, I will discuss the financial mechanisms that made it possible for the merchants to take their shares. As discussed in chapter 2, eighteenth-century Spanish moralists and canonists criticized merchant-bankers who profited from commissions, exchange in coins, and the farming of royal revenues. However, the evidence available shows that during international wars, profits linked to the preservation of the common good bypassed moral and canonical sanctions. Within the Viceroyalty of Rio de la Plata, each region or province combined a variety of financial instruments to transfer funds across the treasuries. In the analysis that follows I discuss and compare the mechanisms and financial instruments utilized in the three different areas that made up the viceregal territory: the Alto Peruvian provinces, Misiones and Paraguay, and the Rio de la Plata provinces.

For accuracy, my analysis considers one-time and annual contributions separately. Additionally, it is crucial to follow the transfer of donativo funds from local to regional treasuries and then from those to the one located in the viceregal capital. We also need to contemplate the fact that, frequently, the place of residence of donors differed from the place of departure of their funds (that is, the place of origin of the transfer). And finally, since the different accounting books recording these transactions occasionally provide incomplete or contradictory information, my analysis takes into consideration the different totals as recorded in various sources.

Table 3.1 shows one-time and annual donativos broken down by the place of residence of donors as it appears on the rosters. Among the places listed in the original sources, all but Misiones and Jujuy had their own treasuries (cajas). After the expulsion of the Jesuits in 1767, the administrative jurisdiction over the Guarani missions changed several times. Nevertheless, this area did not develop an independent *caja*. Thus, Jujuy and Misiones appear on this table under the "No caja" rubric.[1] Column B corresponds to eighteen months of annual contributions as recorded in the libros de tomas de razón, and column C prorates them through the end of the war (twenty-six months, following the libro manual).[2] The following column (A + C) records the total that should have been collected until the war ended. Column D breaks down the totals (both one-time and annual) by the places of origin of the transfers as they appear in the libro manual. The last two columns reproduce the net transfers broken down by treasury for one year (1796) and for the 1796–1800 period from the data compiled and published by Irigoin and Grafe.[3]

According to the libro manual, donativos yielded a total of 260,360 pesos during this war. These were significant funds as they represented 65 percent of the average revenue collected in customs duties in Buenos Aires between 1791 and 1794 and 23.5 percent of the situados (subsidies) received by the Buenos Aires treasury in 1796. Additionally, per capita donativos collected in the Viceroyalty of Rio de la Plata were double those simultaneously raised in New Spain as, throughout the same war, subjects from these viceroyalties contributed in donativos 0.52 pesos and 0.25 pesos per capita, respectively. In the Viceroyalty of Rio de la Plata, the per capita tax burden for the 1796–1800 quinquennium was 4.29 pesos, while during the same period it reached 9.15 pesos in New Spain.[4] It appears that donativos raised more funds in areas where subjects were relatively less burdened by taxation.

If we assume that all the annual contributions were paid throughout the twenty-six months of war, the total donativo should have reached at least 268,298 pesos.[5] In fact, between 1793 and 1795 the total deposited into the Buenos Aires treasury (*cartas cuentas*) in the *ramo* of *donativos voluntarios* was 250,422 pesos.[6] The evidence available reveals that the totals recorded in the libros de tomas de razón exceeded those recorded in the cartas cuentas by 9,938 pesos (eighteen-month collection) and by 17,876 pesos when prorated through the twenty-six months of war. Based on the available sources, I will argue that commissions and fees paid to merchants account for the difference between these totals.

Several scholars have stressed the strong reliance on intertreasury transfers (situados) within the boundaries of the decentralized, jurisdictionally and fiscally fragmented Spanish empire and have identified the opportunities for profit that this system provided to the merchants in charge of it, primarily in the form of commissions and business capitalization. Through situados, the more profitable treasuries periodically sent out remittances of funds to the less profitable ones, although the transfers frequently changed direction upon need. In the Rio de la Plata, the most substantial *situado* was sent from Potosí to Buenos Aires for the purpose of paying for the administrative and military expenses in the viceregal capital. This situado was scheduled to depart from Potosí at least three times a year. However, merchant-bankers frequently delayed situados, thereby forcing troops and royal servants to receive goods on credit from local merchants instead of their salaries. In fact, the situado system allowed local merchants to provide supplies on credit for the entire administration. When the situados finally arrived, the royal treasurers settled their accounts with the local merchants. Credit instruments backed by remittances of situados tied the everyday functioning of the imperial administration to local merchants, the *situadistas* (revenue-transfer farmers), and the high-ranking military and bureaucratic officers who generally partnered with them in business operations. In the Rio de la Plata, situados additionally integrated the interregional and transatlantic trades. Commercial credit networks supplied distant markets with domestically produced and imported goods and, simultaneously, collected a variety of coins necessary for trading in the Atlantic basin. The alleged delays in the transfer of situado funds evidence that the merchants in charge of moving these funds engaged in profitable but time-consuming trading operations before the situado funds finally reached their destinations. [7]

The management of situados in general and donativos in particular provides excellent examples of the workings of the Spanish revenue system on the ground. These examples also provide insights into the crown's regulatory power over competing merchant factions and over practices regarded as usurious. In the Viceroyalty of Rio de la Plata, profits to be made from situados were coveted, and consequently merchant factions frequently competed for the posts of situadistas, especially those transferring funds along the route that connected Potosí with Buenos Aires.[8] Additionally, since the value and quality of gold and silver coins varied throughout the viceregal territory and changed in value at different times, merchants maximized their gains by trading in a variety of monies at different markets. In areas in which coins were scarce, transfers of funds across the treasuries could only be accomplished through the trading of credit obligations such as bills of exchange and ordinance bills. Donativo transfers followed situado-backed credit patterns, making it possible for the king to raise funds. However, the monarch would not have been able to tap these funds within a fragmented fiscal space without the help of the merchant-bankers. Consequently, the monarch paid them bonuses and commissions, thereby sharing with them the revenue generated by donativos.

When donativos paid in gold or silver coins of higher quality reached the capital, the treasurers recorded in the books the transaction as well as the percentage paid in bonuses. For instance, one transfer from Potosí and another one from Salta were paid in high-quality silver coin and generated 3 percent in bonuses. In a transfer of donativo funds from La Paz to Buenos Aires, merchant and postmaster general Manuel de Basavilbaso included gold disks (*tejos de oro*) that produced bonuses proportional to their karat. Manuel Ortiz Basualdo, a merchant from Buenos Aires, made a donativo contribution of eight ounces of gold. His donativo did not involve the transfer of funds across treasuries as it was deposited directly into the Buenos Aires caja. This fact did not keep Ortiz Basualdo from receiving an 8 percent bonus.[9] In other cases, the sources recorded the payment of bonuses and commissions as percentages of the total deposited into the treasuries, but they did not indicate whether these percentages were estimated before or after the coins were exchanged. Occasionally, treasurers simply stated that they paid bonuses by adding the expression *con premio* next to the item deposited in the Buenos Aires treasury. But they omitted the formulas they employed to calculate these bonuses. The information available on the books makes it impossible to accurately estimate the profits individual merchants made per transaction. However, I argue that all donativo transactions absorbed the difference between the totals recorded in various accounting books and the totals entered in the treasury summaries (cartas cuentas), which, as mentioned, ranged between 9,938 and 17,870 pesos and represented between 4 and 7 percent of the total donativo.

One could claim, as in the case of France discussed in chapter 1, that a handful of merchants held the imperial administration in a patrimonial fashion, hoarding hefty rewards only for their sectors' benefit. Or that a weak monarch granted a monopoly over the transfer of donativos to one powerful merchant faction.[10] That was hardly the case, however, as during the War against the French Convention the libro manual recorded the names of at least twenty-one different merchants transferring and/or depositing donativos funds across and into the viceregal treasuries, indicating that merchant-bankers who engaged in these operations did not have the power to close the scheme to competitors but rather shared their gains within a system opened to market forces. Moreover, the evidence available indicates that the monarch exercised regulatory power over this business. The Reglamento de Situadistas, drafted in 1795, set commissions at 0.25 to 1.5 percent, indicating that at times of war, when the king needed to raise revenues quickly, the bargaining power of the merchant-bankers increased, while at the end of hostilities, the monarch strengthened his political initiative and lowered the transaction costs below the 5 percent ceiling tolerated by canonists and moralists.[11] Thus, the lack of a representative assembly did not automatically close other conduits for negotiation and cooperation between the Spanish monarch and elite and lesser merchants, nor did it grant the former unlimited possibilities for preying upon the property rights of the latter.

Fifty-seven transfers to the treasury in Buenos Aires, ranging from 12 to 22,155 pesos and making up about one-half of the funds collected in donativos during the War against the French Convention, evidence that a wide range of merchants had a share in this lucrative business. Merchants trading between Paraguay, Misiones, and Buenos Aires made their profits out of multiple small transactions ranging between 12 and 338 pesos (twenty-nine transactions), while the situadistas and other merchants operating along the profitable corridor that connected the Alto Peruvian provinces with Buenos Aires transferred fewer but significantly larger sums (six transactions, all of them more than 11,000 pesos). The remaining twenty-two transactions spread from 400 to 5,771 pesos, indicating opportunities for profit for the mercantile middle ranks.[12]

Broken down by region, these operations further illustrate that the donativo business accommodated a diverse pool of traders. Eight merchants and two situadistas collected and transferred donativos across the Alto Peruvian treasuries and from Potosí to Buenos Aires. For example, the situadistas Simón Sáenz de Robredo and Joseph de Larramendi transferred to Buenos Aires donativos collected in Potosí. Larramendi also transferred, along with the Potosí situado, 12,238 pesos collected as donativos in La Paz. On his way to Buenos Aires, merchant Marcos Rocha transferred donativo funds not only from Potosí but also from Córdoba, and Joseph del Ricón collected and transferred donativos from Potosí, Salta, and Jujuy. Merchant Ramón de Ballisbián traded alongside the La Paz–Cordoba axis and transferred to the treasury of Buenos Aires donativos from those areas. These transactions were recorded in the libro manual as deposits made into the caja of Buenos Aires and utilizing a variety of coins instead of relying on credit instruments. Even though collections of donativos began in June 1793, most of the funds that were transferred through Potosí reached Buenos Aires between June 1794 and December 1795.[13] As in the case of other sources of royal revenue, the delay in transferring donativo funds indicates that on their way to the viceregal capital, they were multiplied through the merchant-bankers' investments in private commercial ventures. The timing of these transfers additionally reveals that merchants and situadistas trading along the Potosí–Buenos Aires axis accessed better credit lines and were capable of waiting for longer periods of time for their investments to yield profits, while those who dealt in smaller sums saw more immediate but presumably lesser returns out of multiple transactions.[14]

The involvement of the postmaster general (*administrador general de la renta de correos*) in the transfer of donativos across the viceregal treasuries provides a good example of the advantages merchants sought from their participation in the system. The Real Renta de Correos started operating in Buenos Aires in the 1740s and managed a system of postal offices integrated with the ones already existing in the Alto Peruvian provinces and Chile, which conveniently overlapped with the location of royal cajas.[15] Under the Habsburgs, the offices of the royal postal service had been sold to private bidders who built far-reaching family networks across the empire. The Bourbons decided to recover the postal offices, and from 1768 onward, they started to incorporate them back into the royal administration. However, in the Rio de la Plata the sale of postal offices continued after that date and granted the Basavilbaso family control over key appointments. For instance, Domingo de Basavilbaso, one of the most successful merchants in Buenos Aires, held the office of *administrador general* from 1769 until his death in 1794.[16] That year, his son Manuel inherited this office, which he also held for a lifetime. Additionally, since its establishment in 1767, Domingo and Manuel jointly staffed the office of *administrador del correo marítimo* (director of the maritime postal service), sailing between La Coruña and Montevideo.[17] Finally, the Basavilbasos also purchased and preserved throughout the entire viceregal period the office of *escribano mayor de gobierno y guerra* (main notary for civil and military administration).[18] While situadistas operated at a regional scale, the postal service gave the Basavilbasos the opportunity to consolidate their transatlantic mercantile and bureaucratic power. Postal ships crossed the Atlantic four times a year and were authorized to engage in trade to cover their service costs. In addition to delivering official and private correspondence (which gave postmasters priority access to crucial Atlantic and regional information), the postal service shipped both overseas and inland luggage, jewelry, as well as private and royal moneys (including revenue and salaries for royal officers and military men), and it generated its own revenue stream from the fees charged for these services. The viceregal post offices and relay stations functioned as resting and supplying centers for travelers and troops. Their furnishing was a viceroyalty-wide business controlled by the postmasters. Administrators, haulers, and postmen did not receive salaries from the crown. Instead, they charged fees for their services, and they frequently engaged in trading operations financed with the funds they managed on behalf of the postal office.[19] Overall, the royal postal service became such a successful operation that by the early 1800s it was capable of advancing loans to the crown. Despite their power, the Basavilbasos' stake in the donativo business was minimal as they transferred only a total of 3,775 pesos from the Alto Peruvian provinces to Buenos Aires by means of two transactions. Yet both of them were made in gold, indicating that while donativos added one more source of capital to the postmaster general's transatlantic business, the opportunity for trading in coins or even hoarding good metals was not lost in spite of the small number of pesos involved.

Donativo funds collected within the Rio de la Plata provinces followed a different pattern from the one at work in the Alto Peruvian provinces as merchant-bankers did not rely heavily on situados to transfer funds to Buenos Aires but rather on a variety of debit and credit instruments that cleared in the treasury located in the viceregal capital (table 3.2). These instruments included discounts on civil and military salaries paid in Buenos Aires, direct deposits made by local merchants, exchequer and ordnance bills, and the combination of several of these in a single transaction.

For example, Santiago de Allende, an infantry colonel from Córdoba, contributed a donativo of 400 pesos per year, which was discounted from his salary paid at the Buenos Aires treasury. The libro manual did not disclose his total salary, but it recorded deductions of 133 pesos and 2 1/2 reales every four months until 4 September 1795, the day the peace was published in Buenos Aires. In the course of twenty-six months of war, the treasurers discounted from his salary a total of 861 pesos 2 reales in donativos. His case additionally demonstrates that the treasuries continued receiving payments of annual donativos after the closing of initial offers.[20]

Ambrosio Funes, leader of one of the most powerful political clans in Córdoba, donated 60 pesos per year, which were deposited in Buenos Aires by his proxy (apoderado), merchant Saturnino Joseph de Alvarez. It was not uncommon for prominent porteño merchants to keep cash deposits from which their business partners and customers drew funds upon need, usually for participating in financial and commercial opportunities available in the capital.[21] In this case, through the brokerage of Alvarez, Funes entered a donativo-based bargain. Josefa de La Quintana, also a resident from Córdoba, was the widow of Colonel Marcos de Larrazábal and received a military pension paid by the Buenos Aires treasury. She contributed a one-time donativo of 100 pesos, which the sources recorded as "discounted" (*descontados*) from her pension but "paid in Buenos Aires" (*enterados*) by the postmaster general, Manuel de Basavilbaso.[22] While other details of this transaction were not recorded in the donativo books, it is apparent that Basavilbaso's brokerage was essential in fulfilling this transaction. Thus, pensions and salaries deposited in the royal treasuries functioned as credit accounts managed by merchant-bankers. Their interventions facilitated not only the daily functioning of the imperial administration but also regional integration and access to commercial credit for those on the crown's payroll.

Santa Fe, Paraguay, and Misiones were areas in which coin was scarce, and so donors from these regions relied on a variety of financial instruments handled by multiple merchants to meet their contributions to the donativo. For instance, Joaquin de Alós, governor of Paraguay, issued a 2,000-peso draft (*libranza*) against the Buenos Aires treasury to fulfill his own donativo. He additionally endorsed and sent to Buenos Aires a bill of exchange issued by the cabildo of Asunción against the Paraguay treasury, corresponding to the donativo collected among the vecinos of Asunción and its hinterland. According to Alós's instructions, which had been approved by the viceroy, that bill ought to be cancelled against the funds available in Buenos Aires for financing the Partida de Demarcación (royal corps of surveyors), which had been drawing the boundaries between the Spanish and Portuguese territories since the end of the Spanish-Portuguese War in 1777. This transaction reveals that the treasury in Asunción kept the coin it had collected as donativos from its vecinos and sent to Buenos Aires an ordnance bill detailing what it had supplied the surveyors.[23] Donativos, trade credit, and royal finances overlapped in one transaction.

Diego Casero, who between 1785 and 1794 held the appointment of general administrator, managed the donativos originating in the Guarani missions. His administrative functions also included purchasing and selling commodities and supplies for the mission towns and earned commissions set at 2 and 8 percent, respectively.[24] Additionally, Caseros administered in the Buenos Aires treasury the salaries that paid for mission administrators, schoolteachers, and priests. In other words, his office combined services similar to those provided by merchant-bankers trading between Buenos Aires and Potosí. However, since in Misiones hard currency was scarce, Caseros primarily dealt in credit instruments. For instance, Guarani lords and commoners issued bills of exchange against

Caseros in order to contribute their donativos, while the Spaniards serving in the missions, who received salaries from the Buenos Aires treasury, issued drafts against that caja. Other donativo transactions managed by Caseros required the sale of commodities (primarily yerba maté) to generate the cash for making the contribution.[25] Thus, Caseros profited not only from the commissions he collected on sales and purchases but also from those he charged for trading in bills of exchange. In the case of the Spaniards who issued drafts against the royal treasury, the Buenos Aires caja functioned similarly to a modern bank account in which their salaries counted as deposits and their donativos as withdrawals.

Other donativos from Misiones bypassed Caseros but were met by those utilizing similar credit instruments. During the War against the French Convention, Mission San Angel sent to Buenos Aires donativos in the form of two ordnance bills totaling 561 pesos, which detailed the supplies they had advanced also to the corps of surveyors. In this case, donativos made it possible for Mission San Angel to transfer to the treasury in Buenos Aires credit instruments it held against the surveyors instead of making a contribution in coin. Bartolomé González, a surgeon stationed at the missions, also donated a credit of 700 pesos in past-due salaries that he held in the Buenos Aires treasury. These examples show that a variety of financial operations overlapped and cleared in the Buenos Aires treasury and additionally demonstrate that the collection and transfer of donativos combined a variety of instruments, including credits held against the real hacienda.

Finally, donativo funds originating from donors who resided in Buenos Aires were fulfilled primarily in two ways. If they came from merchants, the funds were deposited directly into the local treasury either in one single payment or in installments. If they came from bureaucrats, they were frequently managed as voluntary salary discounts following the inflow into the treasury of funds earmarked for the bureaucrats' remunerations. Donors from Buenos Aires also donated past-due salaries and other credits held against the real hacienda. Such was the case of the royal notary, Gervasio Antonio de Posadas, who, like the surgeon from Misiones discussed previously, waived, through his donativo, a credit in past-due salaries of 223 pesos. Likewise, merchant Juan Esteban de Anchorena donated 500 pesos out of a 1,200-peso credit he held in Buenos Aires in overpaid alcabalas (sales tax). Thus, Anchorena turned a tax credit into a donativo contribution. The Santa Fe treasury utilized a credit on the *ramo de arbitrios* to transfer 671 pesos in donativos to

Buenos Aires. While the sources do not provide any details about the origins of this credit, it is apparent that the Santa Fe treasury withheld the coin it collected in donativos and sent to Buenos Aires an instrument to settle the debt. These examples demonstrate that the royal exchequer found in donativos an agreeable means to settle its accounts with a variety of creditors. These settlements generated profits and created mutual obligations and shared interests among donors and creditors residing in different areas of the viceroyalty. The records left by these transactions challenge any idea about the presumed capacity of donativos to extract coin from donors' regions of residence and from the viceregal economic space at large.

The information in table 3.1 additionally reveals that donativo contributions were unequally distributed among the donors residing in the different regions of the viceroyalty. Donors from Buenos Aires contributed 47 percent of the total. Donors from La Paz and Charcas followed those from Buenos Aires by contributing 16 and 9 percent, respectively. Donors from Potosí, Misiones, and Paraguay respectively contributed 5, 4, and 3 percent, while those residing in the remaining regions contributed between 1 and 2 percent. In total, donors from the Alto Peruvian provinces contributed 38 percent to the donativo, thereby adding to the treasury in Buenos Aires an additional subsidy of 102,910 pesos. This subsidy most probably allowed Buenos Aires to extend credit to the cajas and donors located and residing within the Rio de la Plata provinces.

Comparisons between the places of residence of donors and the places of origin of large transfers of funds reveal how merchants made their profits by transferring donativos across the treasuries (table 3.3). While donors from the Alto Peruvian provinces contributed 38 percent of the total donativo (102,910 pesos), the transfers originating in these provinces reached 42 percent (111,846 pesos). The 4 percent difference was paid into another local caja or region but pumped into the Alto Peruvian treasuries prior to its final transfer to Buenos Aires. Donativos collected within the Alto Peruvian provinces were also transferred within the Alto Peruvian treasuries before they finally departed for Buenos Aires. For instance, donors from Charcas contributed 24 percent of the provincial total, but their transfers to Buenos Aires only accounted for 15 percent of the funds. The other 9 percent was sent to another regional treasury before it reached Buenos Aires. Transfers from La Paz to Buenos Aires were 8 percent smaller than the total originating in the La Paz treasury, while almost the entire donativo from Cochabamba was sent to another caja (presumably

Potosí) before it reached the viceregal capital. The available data demonstrate that Potosí, as a mining and commercial center, not only attracted trade from neighboring and distant areas but also functioned as a transshipment hub for royal revenue as donativos from this area only represented 5 percent of the viceregal total (table 3.1) and 12 percent within the region (table 3.3). However, the transfers leaving from the Potosí treasury represented 22 percent of the viceregal total (table 3.1) and 51 percent within the Alto Peruvian region (table 3.3).[26] As in the case of situados, donativo funds traveled across different commercial centers, multiplying the opportunities for merchant-bankers and situadistas to engage in trade and credit operations and profit from them. Simultaneously, they held these regions together by bringing them into their networks of credit and trust.

Compared to the net transfers for 1796 compiled by Irigoin and Grafe (table 3.1), the majority of donativo funds originated in treasuries that did not subsidize other regions, although La Paz performed that role toward the end of the century. In other words, donors had more capital to contribute to donativos and were presumably more willing to do so if they resided in regions that received but did not give away subsidies to other treasuries, which allowed the former to thrive commercially. Potosí provides an example of this trend. Between 1796 and 1800, Potosí increasingly subsidized other treasuries (especially Buenos Aires), and consequently its residents contributed a relatively modest donativo. However, this treasury managed to keep a positive balance on its accounts and expand commercially not only due to its mining boom but because of receiving transfers from other treasuries. In sum, the money trail left by donativos indicates that before reaching Buenos Aires, they circulated following intertreasury transfers and pumped capital into existing financial and trading networks.

Qualitative information related to the donativos collected during the Naval Wars against England (1799–1801) provides further evidence for these trends. In 1801 the treasurers in Buenos Aires were unable to sort out donativo sums that arrived into the viceregal capital from Potosí as, in their own words, they were "wrapped up in the *masa del común*" (i.e., unglossed sources of revenue). The treasurers consulted intendant Francisco de Paula Sánz in Potosí, who responded that donativos from La Paz, Cochabamba, and Charcas were first brought into the Potosí treasury by regional *asentistas del trajín de caudales* (revenue-transfer farmers or situadistas) and that they were subsequently shipped to Buenos Aires along with the situado. Sánz not only sorted the donativo sums out but also provided the dates for the receipts. The dates indicate that it took about two years for these funds to finally reach Buenos Aires.[27] We may assume that donativo funds did not remain unproductive in the Potosí treasury but rather were used to finance regional trade until they made their way to Buenos Aires via the situado.

As for the transfers to Spain, the records show that only a small portion of donativo funds actually left the viceregal territory. In September 1794, Viceroy Arredondo notified Minister Gardoqui that he had shipped to the metropolis 67,062 pesos in donativos, and in March 1796 Viceroy Melo de Portugal shipped another 15,560 pesos.[28] These figures only add up to 82,622 pesos, a fraction of the total recorded on the accounting books. While it is possible that other shipments of donativos were dispatched unreported, it is also reasonable to assume that a share of them was never sent to Spain. As Irigoin and Grafe demonstrated, the total amount of silver sent to Spain increased in the eighteenth century, but over time these shipments represented a smaller share of the expenditures, reaching their lowest levels in the 1797–1800 period.[29] We can conclude that at times of war, donativos collected in the Viceroyalty of Rio de la Plata were fiscal mechanisms that effectively capitalized regional and local mercantile and financial networks, but they were less successful at draining specie from the region.

WHO AND HOW MUCH?
IDENTIFYING THE SOCIAL PROFILES OF DONORS

In this section, I will discuss the social, racial, and occupational backgrounds of donors as well as the sizes of their individual one-time and annual donativos. Donativos were distributed unevenly across regions and social groups. Thus, the analysis presented in this section shows that donativos were dissimilar to uniform taxes. After describing the social profiles of donors, I will discuss the mechanisms that made it possible to channel power and income into their hands. As we will see, not all donors fared equally.

Unfortunately, the surviving sources are not detailed enough to allow us to estimate the exact number and sizes of all the individual donations. For corporate bodies as well as groups of individuals (i.e., vecinos from a certain place), the rosters occasionally recorded lump sums. However, it is possible to take from the records representative samples for one-time and annual donativos. Despite the lump sums, the sources detail 610 individual contributions totaling 143,889 pesos or 70 percent of the total one-time donativo. That is, 0.1 percent of the total viceregal population contributed

70 percent of the one-time donativo. Table 3.4 presents the breakdown of those 610 individual donativos by size. In an effort to represent the distribution of donation size as accurately as possible, I listed contributions smaller than 51 pesos in 5-peso increments, while those between 51 and 300 pesos were tabulated in ranges of 25 pesos. Starting at 301 pesos, all but three donativos were recorded in round numbers. I rounded up those three to simplify the table. Following the sources, I listed donativos ranging between 301 and 1,000 pesos in 100-pesos intervals, and those over 1,000 were listed by thousands. No contributions fell between the 11,000 and 14,999-peso range.

As table 3.4 indicates, 85 percent of the individual one-time donativos fell within the 1–100 range. Within that wide category, 63.5 percent of the contributions were equal to or smaller than 25 pesos, 32 percent were equal to or smaller than 10 pesos, and 14 percent fell between 1 and 5 pesos. The most frequent one-time donativo (mode) was 25 pesos (eighty-six contributions). At the other end of the socioeconomic spectrum, only a handful of donors were able to contribute donativos larger than 100 pesos, and those donating more than 1,000 pesos were truly exceptional.

The sample for individual annual contributions contains 476 cases totaling 36,017 pesos or 85 percent of the total annual donativo collected throughout eighteen months (table 3.5). In this case, 0.09 percent of the viceregal population contributed 85 percent of the total annual donativo. The individual annual contributions smaller than 301 pesos were distributed following the same ranges utilized in the one-time sample (table 3.4). Contributions between 301 and 500 pesos were broken into 50-peso brackets. The few contributions above 500 pesos were recorded in round numbers. No individual annual contributions fell between 601 and 999 or between 1,001 and 2,999 pesos. As in the case of the one-time donativo sample, the majority of the contributions fell below 100 pesos (86 percent), while 55.5 percent of those were equal to or smaller than 25 pesos, and 27.0 percent were smaller than 10 pesos. Contributions below 5 pesos represented 14 percent of the total, and the most frequent individual annual contribution was 10 pesos (mode, forty-six contributions).

It is possible to weigh the size of individual donativos against the fragmentary data available on wages and annual per capita expenditure in Spanish America. Kendall Brown has estimated that in Arequipa, the annual per capita expenditure of a mestizo family was 32 pesos, while that of Spanish families amounted to 60 pesos. Lyman Johnson's estimates of annual wages range between 123 and 420 pesos for unskilled and skilled workers in prosperous late eighteenth-century Buenos Aires, depending on what their daily pay was as well as the number of days they were at work.[30] Even the smallest donativos (1 to 5 and 5 to 10 pesos) represented a large portion of the annual salaries of the working classes, which in Arequipa ranged between 130 and 200 pesos. However, beyond the world of work was a dynamic group of relatively prosperous and ambitious imperial players who invested and accumulated capital by participating in the late eighteenth-century urban retail economy and by joining the ranks of the educated royal servants. As Jay Kinsbruner has persuasively argued, modest retail and grocery store owners, small wholesalers, and artisans across the Spanish empire frequently started their businesses with low initial capital investments and relied on credit not only to enter a trade but also to maintain their operations. In eighteenth-century Puebla, Mexico City, or Buenos Aires, it was possible to buy a *pulpería* (retail store) on credit by making monthly payments ranging between 10 and 40 pesos.[31] Thus, we can assume that the majority of the individual one-time and annual donativo contributions did not originate among elites but rather among a variety of middling groups. Their experiences under Spanish imperial rule were diverse. However, they shared the ability to save small and medium-sized funds, and they channeled their savings into collections of donativos. Within the boundaries of a sophisticated and mature imperial commercial economy, donativos offered these dynamic urban residents an opportunity to fulfill their duties as loyal subjects, although, unlike the merchant-bankers and other prime beneficiaries of the imperial system, they did not necessarily profit from them. Yet the prospect of gaining social, economic, and political rewards by entering into donativo-based bargains was a powerful incentive to keep them loyal to the king and engaged in the preservation of the imperial project.

Except for a few cases, the sources made reference to a donor's status, gender, ethnicity, and social background as well as corporate affiliations. Table 3.6 lists donativo contributions broken down by the categories mentioned on the donativo rosters, indicating that a wide spectrum of individual and corporate subjects with diverse social and ethnic backgrounds contributed to this collection of donativos. Those groups that regularly accessed cash or periodically accumulated capital (i.e., merchants, ecclesiastics, cabildos, and Indian communities) favored one-time donations, while those that depended on seasonal cash flows (i.e., the bureaucrats and the military) contributed annually. The large one-time donation under "Women" is misleading as the bulk of it (15,000 pesos) came from

Francisca del Risco, who, as mentioned in the introduction, was an exceptionally wealthy and powerful woman and in the early 1790s was legally fighting for her legitimation. Overall, merchants; bureaucrats; ecclesiastics; members of the military, militias, and indigenous communities; and a variety of middle-class vecinos provided the largest donativos.

The regional distribution of socio-occupational/ethnic categories did not follow a uniform pattern either. As table 3.7 demonstrates, bureaucrats, ecclesiastics, military men, and vecinos from everywhere in the viceroyalty contributed to this donativo, while the merchants from Buenos Aires were the only ones among the commercial elites who contributed substantially. Donors from the Alto Peruvian provinces came from every single category identified on the rosters, while in the other provinces donativos came exclusively from a handful of groups. As mentioned before, donativos in Alto Peru originated in areas that profited from their proximity to the Potosí market, although their treasuries did not regularly send out subsidies to other cajas. Donativos indicate that in these areas substantial as well as modest funds not only passed through but also remained in the hands of a variety of imperial subjects. Except for these general trends, however, the distribution of donativo funds within each province, treasury, and socio-occupational/ethnic group was anything but homogeneous, evidencing that donativos, like many other contributions, were collected in a disjointed fashion. Hence, an analysis by group appears to be a promising means of understanding why donors contributed donativos and what they expected in return. In the following chapter, I will discuss how different individuals and groups bargained with the crown by becoming donors during the War against the French Convention.

Table 3.1. Donativos by treasury, 1793–1795

Region	Cajas	By place of residence of donor								
		A. One-time transfer (pesos)	B. Annual transfers over 18 months (pesos)	C. Annual transfers over 26 months (pesos)	A + C (pesos)	% of total	D. By origin of transfer[a] (pesos)	% of total	1796 Net transfer[b] (pesos)	1796–1800 Net transfer[b] (pesos)
Alto Peru	Arica	0	0	0	0	0	0	0	-49,396	-307,091
	Carangas	0	0	0	0	0	0	0	-6,855	-98,240
	Charcas	19,954	3,025	4,369	24,323	9	16,630	6	0	0
	Chucuito	0	0	0	0	0	0	0	0	-389,534
	Cochabamba	7,160	6,235	9,006	16,166	6	600	0	0	0
	La Paz	38,093	3,880	5,604	43,697	16	37,568	14	0	1,144,524
	Oruro	0	0	0	0	0	0	0	-110,753	-324,613
	Potosí	3,125	6,589	9,517	12,642	5	57,048	22	435,755	831,755
	Santa Cruz de la Sierra	3,321	1,911	2,761	6,082	2	0	0	0	0
Río de la Plata	Buenos Aires	111,687	9,580	13,838	125,525	47	137,572	53	1,111,678	7,162,330
	Catamarca	0	0	0	0	0	0	0	0	-5,000
	Córdoba	2,920	2,419	3,494	6,414	2	4,759	2	0	-12,000
	Corrientes	148	100	144	292	< 1	150	0	-372	-2,814
	La Rioja	0	0	0	0	0	0	0	0	-1,184
	Maldonado	0	0	0	0	0	0	0	45,358	225,249
	Montevideo	413	596	861	1,274	0	206	0	0	0
	Paraguay	5,760	990	1,430	7,190	3	50	0	56,135	136,495
	Salta	1,579	2,797	4,040	5,619	2	2,055	1	0	0
	San Juan	500	0	0	500	0	0	0	7	37
	Santa Fe	772	810	1,170	1,942	1	0	0	3,972	-6,722
	Santiago del Estero	0	0	0	0	0	0	0	0	0
	Tucumán	1,518	546	789	2,307	1	1,245	0	-3,639	-3,639
No caja	Jujuy	1,105	98	141	1,246	< 1	1,138	0	0	0
	Misiones	8,677	2,036	2,941	11,618	4	1,133	0	0	0
Chile	Chiloe	0	0	0	0	0	0	0	20,032	17,439
	Concepción	0	0	0	0	0	0	0	0	0
	Mendoza	6	1,007	1,455	1,461	1	0	0	0	-7,066
	Santiago de Chile	0	0	0	0	0	0	0	0	0
	Valdivia	0	0	0	0	0	0	0	96,141	343,603
	Anonymous donor	0	0	0	0	0	206	0	0	0
Total		206,738	42,619	61,560	268,298	99	260,360	98		

Total donativos from cartas cuentas: 250,422 pesos.[c]

a. AGNA, XIII, 42-1-2.
b. Irigoin and Grafe, "The Spanish Empire and Its Legacy."
c. Te Paske et al., *The Royal Treasuries of the Spanish Empire in America.*

Table 3.2. Donativos by place of residence of donors and by origin of transfer in the province of Rio de la Plata, 1793–1795

Cajas, province of Río de la Plata	Place of residence of donor (pesos)	%	Caja of origin of transfer (pesos)	%
Buenos Aires	125,525	77	137,572	93
Córdoba	6,414	4	4,759	3
Corrientes	292	< 1	150	< 1
Montevideo	1,274	1	206	< 1
Paraguay	7,190	4	50	< 1
Salta	5,619	3	2,055	1
Santa Fe	1,942	1	0	0
Tucumán	2,307	1	1,245	1
Jujuy (no caja)	1,246	1	1,138	1
Misiones (no caja)	11,618	7	1,133	1
Total	163,427	100	148,308	100

Table 3.3. Donativos by place of residence of donors and by origin of transfer in the province of Alto Peru, 1793–1795

Cajas, province of Alto Peru	Place of residence of donor (pesos)	%	Caja of origin of transfer (pesos)	%
Arica	0	0	0	0
Carangas	0	0	0	0
Charcas	24,323	24	16,630	15
Chucuito	0	0	0	0
Cochabamba	16,166	15	600	< 1
La Paz	43,697	42	37,568	34
Oruro	0	0	0	0
Potosí	12,642	12	57,048	51
Santa Cruz de la Sierra	6,082	7	0	0
Total	102,910	100	111,846	100

Table 3.4. One-time donativos by size, 1793–1795

Range (pesos)	Number of donors	%	Range (pesos)	Number of donors	%	Range (pesos)	Number of donors	%	Range (pesos)	Number of donors	%
1–5	85	14.0	101–25	5	< 1.0	301–400	11	2.0	1,001–2,000	6	1.0
6–10	109	18.0	126–50	3	< 1.0	401–500	6	1.0	2,001–3,000	6	1.0
11–15	60	10.0	151–75	3	< 1.0	501–600	16	3.0	3,001–4,000	1	< 1.0
16–20	39	6.0	176–200	19	3.0	601–700	1	< 1.0	4,001–5,000	1	< 1.0
21–25	95	15.5	201–25	1	< 1.0	701–800	1	< 1.0	5,001–6,000	0	0
26–30	3	< 1.0	226–50	2	< 1.0	801–900	1	< 1.0	6,001–7,000	5	< 1.0
31–35	2	< 1.0	251–75	0	0	901–1,000	0	< 1.0	7,001–8,000	0	0
36–40	2	< 1.0	276–300	0	0				8,001–9,000	1	< 1.0
41–45	0	0							9,001–10,000	0	0
46–50	68	11.0							10,001–15,000	4	< 1.0
51–75	5	< 1.0									
76–100	49	8.0									
Total	517	85		33	5		36	6		24	4

Table 3.5. Annual donativos by size, 1793–1795

Range (pesos)	Number of donors	%	Range (pesos)	Number of donors	%	Range (pesos)	Number of donors	%
1–5	68	14.0	101–25	12	2.5	301–50	1	< 1.0
6–10	64	13.0	126–50	6	1.0	351–400	2	< 1.0
11–15	34	7.0	151–75	0	0	401–50	3	< 1.0
16–20	17	3.5	176–200	13	3.0	451–500	13	3.0
21–25	87	18.0	201–25	5	< 1.0	501–600	4	< 1.0
26–30	6	1.0	226–50	0	0	601–1,000	1	< 1.0
31–35	1	< 1.0	251–75	1	< 1.0	1,001–3,000	1	< 1.0
36–40	8	1.5	276– 300	6	1.0			
41–45	1	< 1.0						
46–50	59	12.0						
51–75	17	3.5						
76–100	46	9.5						
Total	408	86		43	9		25	5

Table 3.6. Donors by socioracial and occupational backgrounds, 1793–1795

	One-time donations (pesos)	%	Annual donations over 26 months (pesos)	%
Artisans	53	< 1	0	0
Bureaucrats	12,174	6	29,997	49
Cabildos	6,290	3	3,064	5
Colleges	2,100	1	1,083	2
Común del pueblo	531	< 1	0	0
Ecclesiastics	18,761	9	4,697	8
Indian communities	8,812	4	33	< 1
Indians (as individuals)	238	< 1	26	< 1
Merchants	100,000	49	286	< 1
Military and militias	12,434	6	12,690	20
Slaves	1	< 1	0	0
Unknown group	672	< 1	416	1
Vecinos	27,222	13	7,813	13
Women	17,450	9	1,455	2
Total	206,738	100	61,560	100

Table 3.7. Donativos by social, racial, and occupational groups distributed by caja, 1793–1795 (pesos), *continued across page spread*

	Caja		Artisans	Bureaucrats	Cabildos	Colegios	Común del pueblo	Clergy
Alto Peru	Charcas	A	53	167	0	500	0	0
		B	0	1,517	0	722	0	72
	Cochabamba	A	0	2,124	2,450	0	0	437
		B	0	5,762	72	0	0	1,445
	La Paz	A	0	2,488	1,000	0	531	12,238
		B	0	544	1,445	0	0	0
	Potosí	A	0	1,900	0	0	0	100
		B	0	1,805	0	0	0	614
	Santa Cruz	A	0	50	175	0	0	1,582
		B	0	144	0	0	0	1,729
Río de la Plata	Buenos Aires	A	0	1,708	0	1,600	0	1,000
		B	104	11,777	0	0	0	144
	Córdoba	A	0	0	0	0	0	2,670
		B	0	1,624	0	361	0d	36
	Corrientes	A	0	0	0	0	0	0
		B	0	0	0	0	0	0
	Montevideo	A	100	0	0	0	0	0
		B	0	861	0	0	0	0
	Paraguay	A	0	1,940	0	0	0	0
		B	0	1,358	0	0	0	0
	Salta	A	0	25	175	0	0	400
		B	312	1,300	0	0	0	0
	San Juan	A	0	0	500	0	0	0
		B	0	0	0	0	0	0
	Santa Fe	A	0	0	0	0	0	100
		B	0	809	0	0	0	361
	Tucumán	A	0	504	60	0	0	0
		B	0	214	189	0	0	0
No Caja	Jujuy	A	0	298	155	0	0	0
		B	0	141		0	0	0
	Misiones	A	0	970	1,775	0	0	228
		B	0	686	1,358	0	0	296
Chile	Mendoza	A	0	0	0	0	0	6
		B	0	1,455	0	0	0	0
	Total							

Note: A = one-time donations; B = annual donations (twenty-six months).

Indian communities	Indians	Merchants	Military and Militias	Slaves	Unknown	Vecinos	Women	Total
0	8	0	1,300	0	0	2,926	15,000	19,954
0	0	0	1,192	0	0	144	722	4,369
562	0	0	0	0	0	1,587	0	7,160
33	0	0	0	0	0	1,694	0	9,006
3,925	30	0	550	1	0	15,100	2,230	38,093
0	26	0	0	0	0	2,860	729	5,604
0	0	0	1,125	0	0	0	0	3,125
0	0	214	6,600	0	0	284	0	9,517
0	0	0	271	0	0	1,233	10	3,321
0	0	0	320	0	0	565	3	2,761
0	0	100,000	5,074	0	0	2,305	0	111,687
0	0	0	1,141	0	0	672	0	13,838
0	0	0	0	0	0	150	100	2,920
0	0	72	1,011	0	0	390	0	3,494
0	0	0	0	0	0	148	0	148
0	0	0	0	0	0	144	0	144
0	0	0	213	0	0	100	0	413
0	0	0	0	0	0	0	0	861
0	0	0	2,927	0	0	893	0	5,760
0	0	0	0	0	0	72	0	1,430
0	0	0	674	0	0	305	0	1,579
0	0	0	2,428	0	0	0	0	4,040
0	0	0	0	0	0	0	0	500
0	0	0	0	0	0	0	0	0
0	0	0	0	0	672	0	0	772
0	0	0	0	0	0	0	0	1,170
0	0	0	200	0	0	544	210	1,518
0	0	0	0	0	0	386	0	789
0	0	0	0	0	0	652	0	1,105
0	0	0	0	0	0		0	141
4,325	200	0	100	0	0	1,079	0	8,677
0	0	0	0	0	0	601	0	2,941
0	0	0	0	0	0	0	0	6
0	0	0	0	0	0	0	0	1,455
								268,298

GIVERS AND TAKERS IN THE POLITICS OF GIVING

The 1793–1795 Redistribution Patterns

In addition to the merchant-bankers who collected and transferred donativos across the treasuries (discussed in chapter 3), other powerful individuals and groups found in them opportunities for obtaining political and financial rewards. Despite their contributions, however, donors of lesser means were only rarely compensated. In this chapter, I analyze donativos provided by different individuals and social and corporate groups and discuss the justifications for an unequal distribution of rewards.

THE MERCHANTS OF BUENOS AIRES: DONATIVOS AS A LENDING OPERATION SECURED BY CORPORATE DELEGATION

During the War against the French Convention, the merchants of Buenos Aires contributed a one-time 100,000-peso donativo. This donativo stands out because it represented almost one-half of the 1793–1795 one-time donativo total yield, 90 percent of the Buenos Aires treasury's donativo total, and 40 percent of the grand total collected in donativos in the entire viceroyalty during this war (table 3.7). The merchants of Buenos Aires were the main beneficiaries of the policy of free trade as their fortunes had grown exponentially since its implementation in 1778. But because their businesses were hurt by warfare they advocated for a rapid end to hostilities.[1] Additionally, from 1778 onward, the porteño merchants, in particular wholesalers, grew stronger not only individually but also as a group. The creation of a consulado, a commercial guild and court, had been part of their political agenda since 1782; however, years of negotiations were required before it could be established in February 1794. The correspondence exchanged between the porteño merchants and their deputy at court demonstrates that their promise to collect a substantial donativo was what finally turned the tide in their favor. Their original offer was set at 25,000 pesos, but through the negotiations that figure quadrupled.[2] Similar to the case of the situadistas discussed in chapter 3, these negotiations show that while the king was willing to extend the merchants of Buenos Aires a coveted grant he did not lose political initiative at a time of war. On the contrary, the price of his favor was increased through bargaining.

Once established, the consulado of Buenos Aires soon collected the 100,000-peso donativo. These funds were raised by means of a complex lending operation in which the merchant guild functioned as the financial and fiscal broker for the crown. As mentioned in the previous chapters, donativos frequently were related to profitable lending operations, and the agreement between the merchants of Buenos Aires and the crown serves as an example of such. It established that the consulado would raise loans from individuals and local corporations and simultaneously collect taxes earmarked to pay the interest and principal back to lenders. The interest rate was set at 6 percent annually. The duties established for that purpose included 0.5 percent on the gold and silver exported from Buenos Aires and Montevideo (*derecho de avería*) and another 0.5 percent to be charged on the import and export of goods traded through those seaports.[3] Other consulados in the Americas frequently engineered similar operations when the crown needed to collect considerable sums quickly to finance international warfare. Consulados had been successful fund-raisers because they enjoyed good credit ratings due to the royal grants that allowed them to collect certain taxes on behalf of the crown. In sum, this credit operation was characteristic of the old regime as, in the absence of a bank, the crown used the local merchant elite and their corporation to attract capital and raise revenue. In return for such services, consulado merchants were not only able to advocate strongly for their political interests but also found a profitable investment for their own capital, which was temporarily idle due to warfare.[4] Finally, through this donativo the consulado channeled tax money into the merchants' pockets. The mechanism was simple. Since the consulado collected these taxes, its treasurers managed the yields. The *junta de comercio*, which governed the consulado, periodically authorized the treasurers to pay the accrued interest to lenders utilizing tax funds. The receipts detailing these payments survive, and they demonstrate that every year the consulado punctually paid interest to these investors.[5]

The minutes of the Consulado of Buenos Aires recorded the transactions concerning the funds raised for this donativo. Between January and November 1794, the consulado collected a total of 100,000 pesos of which 78,000 came from donativos advanced by merchants and other wealthy individuals, while the remaining 28,000 pesos came from the tax on the export of precious metals (*avería*). The taxes collected by the consulado were therefore utilized not only to pay interest to lenders but also as investment capital for the merchants' corporation. The names of the lenders additionally reveal that this donativo constituted a profitable opportunity for well-established merchants and women belonging to prominent merchant families who had been able to save impressive sums (table 4.1). For instance, Gaspar de Santa Coloma, who was among the most successful porteño merchants, donated a total of 20,000 pesos, while Juan Esteban de Anchorena invested 12,000 pesos. Maria Josefa Lajarrota, the widow of Agustin Casimiro de Aguirre, another prominent merchant of Buenos Aires, contributed 10,000 pesos, and her unmarried cousin Maria Catalina de la Quintana contributed 2,000.

Through a donativo that brokered an interest-bearing loan, we see that the crown channeled toward its treasury the savings of its wealthiest subjects when they were needed the most. Likewise, those who provided the funds found a safe investment opportunity for their otherwise idle capital.[6] Interest payments from the taxes collected by the consulado created a revenue stream favoring a group of powerful investors who, like the merchant-bankers involved in donativo transfers, counted among the beneficiaries of the imperial redistribution of wealth.

This case additionally shows that as a result of warfare, the fiscal constitution of the Rio de la Plata became even more fragmented and decentralized as the crown created one more corporate body for the purpose of raising funds on its behalf and simultaneously granted it the prerogative to tax in order to back those loans. According to Stephan Epstein, in premodern states "public debt derived its success from the fact that the main lenders were also members of the political elite who were charged with raising the taxes that funded the debt."[7]

Constitutionally speaking, this type of corporate representation was consistent with the Bourbon policy of promoting the corporate interests of groups that fostered economic development (or *gobierno económico* to use the jargon of the Spanish Enlightenment) and facilitated an increase in royal revenue.[8] In the second half of the eighteenth century, merchants (consulados), miners (Tribunal de Minería), and bondholders

(Banco de San Carlos) obtained corporate grants as well as other privileges. Simultaneously, these groups increased their political power at the expense of the cabildos as they were granted the right to create regional delegations (*diputaciones*) representing their interests throughout the viceregal territory instead of being confined to local municipal boundaries.[9] Once established in the Rio de la Plata, the *diputaciones de comercio* not only gathered statistical information for the promotion of economic activities but also acted as the regional financial brokers for the crown in subsequent collections of donativos.[10] Donativos confirmed the monarch's willingness to consult, convene, and listen to his subjects and utilize congenial means to raise funds, to paraphrase ministers of finance Canga Argüelles, Fonseca, and Urrutia. These were legitimate practices within the boundaries of Spanish pactismo and at odds with "violent" forced loans and impositions of taxation.

In the Spanish empire, at the territorial or viceregal level, those with economic and financial power who provided financial services to the crown not only obtained a share of the spoils of empire but also had access to institutionalized representation. It could be argued that, similar to the French case, this type of partnership made the merchants partially dependent on royal favor and vulnerable to changes in policy. However, the Spanish merchants retained significant power vis-à-vis the king. First, they had full control over the sources of revenue that guaranteed their loans, in this case the avería and export taxes. Second, as we will see in the following chapter, in the late 1790s and early 1800s they used their power to change commercial policies that were detrimental to their businesses. While donativos allowed a small group of merchants to become part-time rentiers, in their struggle with the king over commercial policies the majority advocated for the continuation of their risky commercial businesses even when international warfare altered Atlantic commerce.[11] In other words, by becoming the monarch's creditors the merchants did not abandon their entrepreneurial outlook.

The mutual partnership between crown and merchants not only delivered political gains to the merchants but also financial benefits to both parties. Nevertheless, when Viceroy Arredondo formally accepted the merchants' donativo he emphasized their disposition to "contribute to the honor of the Religion, to the Glory of the Armies, and the well-being of the Patria" and reported to the king that he had promptly expressed his gratitude on his majesty's behalf.[12] Neither the viceroy nor the merchants referred to this operation as a loan but exclusively called it a donativo.

As multiple records indicate, they utilized the language associated with gift giving and the preservation of the common good. References to the gift economy detached interest-bearing financial transactions from greed and self-interest, fostered social cohesion, ratified the voluntary nature of the agreement, and reinforced the freedom and high status of the donors, as discussed in chapter 2. Moreover, donors eluded suspicions of usury because through gifts, unlike loans, recipients were able to legitimately return to donors property exceeding the value established in the original transaction. Donativos' impact on the common good (in this case the defeat of regicide Frenchmen) made the rewarding of the merchants an unquestionably fair matter. While they profited from this transaction, on the donativo documents they fashioned themselves as selfless servants seeking only the well-being of the community.[13] Finally, because donativos were governed by the principles of distributive justice, compensations should be proportional to the contributions, and thus, the size and purpose of their donativo placed the merchants of Buenos Aires on top of the list of beneficiaries. Their commitment to the common good was so exceptional that they even controlled the taxes earmarked for the payment of interest on their donativo.

DONATIVOS AND THE SALE OF OFFICES: PROFESSIONAL BUREAUCRATS AS FINANCIERS

Ambiguity was a defining feature of donativos and made it possible for subjects to promote their self-interest by engaging in interest-bearing lending operations. Coincidentally, legal ambiguity also characterized the transactions associated with the sale of offices in Castile. Sales of offices were generally carried out through legal instruments and involved euphemisms that did not necessarily make reference to a sale. Francisco Tomás y Valiente has pointed out that an officeholder's resignation in favor of another party (*resignatio in favorem inter vivos* or *ad mortem*) was in fact the purchase of an office involving private parties. Conversely, the term *donativo*, when it appeared on service records of officeholders, denoted the purchase of an appointment directly from the king. In these cases, the documents referred to donativos as "services" provided to the monarch at a time of need, and the office or "reward" was called a demonstration of the monarch's "gratitude."[14] Additionally, since donativos were generally collected at wartime, bidders for offices commonly portrayed themselves as providing a "service" to "pay for the salary" of one or more soldiers and/or sailors on the documents recording these transactions. The adoption of this type of language protected donors against charges of usury. Like the merchants, officeholders downplayed their self-promotion by presenting themselves as servants of the common good. The cases that follow demonstrate that donativos collected in the Viceroyalty of Rio de la Plata among current and future officeholders actually referred to the sale of offices, and as such they functioned as mechanisms that transferred power and income to this powerful group.

Historians have pointed out that the Spanish policy toward the sale of offices was inconsistent throughout the early modern period. Prior to the sixteenth century, the crown gave away offices gratis and in perpetuity primarily for the purpose of building a network of loyal families. Resignations in favor of other parties occurred, but the monarch did not collect any fees over these lucrative transactions. The Catholic Monarchs (1476–1516) opposed this policy, and at the Cortes celebrated in Toledo in 1480 they banned sales in perpetuity. Under financial pressure, Philip II (1556–1594) reinstated the auctioning of offices, and thereafter the practice became a source of royal income not only through the sale of old and new offices themselves but also through the fees charged on private transfers. Nevertheless, the sale of offices did not extend over all types of appointments. While municipal, notarial, treasury-related, and lower-ranking political appointments entered the market, judicial ones were excluded as their sale would have jeopardized the king's monopoly over the administration of justice. In most cases, sales were conducted privately, that is, auctions were avoided, and they were masked under other legal procedures due to the 1480 ban. From the late seventeenth century onward, however, the crown started to recover offices sold in perpetuity both in Spain and in the Americas by paying to officeholders the price set in the original transaction. Inflation helped the crown recover (consumir in the language of the time) these offices, which were incorporated into the royal domain. Nevertheless, the sale of offices continued, though under tighter royal control, for the crown replaced the sale of offices in perpetuity with the sale of both long- and short-term appointments. [15]

Latin American historians have commonly interpreted the incorporation of offices into the royal domain as part of the absolutist and centralist policies enforced by the Bourbon dynasty, a tool developed by a state presumed to be interventionist and bureaucratic. They additionally associated Bourbon bureaucratic centralization with an increase in the professional qualifications required to become an officeholder. Most of these studies emphasize the creation of a centralized chain of command

and an increase in the professional qualifications of the bureaucrats.[16] Simultaneously, scholarship outside the Spanish world has pointed out that in the eighteenth century bureaucratic aptitude did not only include honesty and professional competence but also status, power, honor, and wealth. Monarchs highly valued these qualifications as they expected officeholders to mobilize their individual and family wealth and influence to support the monarchs in financially critical times. By either sale or grace, monarchs favored the concentration of offices in powerful but loyal families. At the same time, monarchs increased the qualifications needed to hold office, and therefore, the market price for entering office increased as well.

In the Spanish world, the *fojas de servicios* (service records) provide evidence of the corporate spirit of early modern bureaucracies and of the influence of corporate and collective structures over individual talents as they listed not only the personal achievements of a particular officeholder but also the variety of services provided by his ancestors, including their donativos.[17] Eighteenth-century bureaucrats were not simply administrators but permanent members of the political establishment recruited to provide essential administrative, political, and financial services to the crown. As in the case of the merchants, such services gave the bureaucrats access to representation in the form of petitions regularly sent to the monarch for requesting promotions and new appointments as well as positions for their male relatives, especially their sons. The auctioning of offices was one among many features of the compact uniting the king and his subjects, and depending on changes in imperial and financial circumstances, it was more or less extensively used. In fact, scholars have suggested that in the case of France, an increase in the number of officeholders had less to do with the demands of a modern administration than with the king's need to meet extraordinary expenses.[18] The discussion that follows reveals similar patterns in the Viceroyalty of Rio de la Plata throughout the 1790s.

While the sale of offices has been studied for seventeenth-century Spanish America, its continuation in the eighteenth century has received significantly less attention. In his analysis of the sale of fiscal offices in seventeenth-century Peru, Kenneth Andrien found that this practice increased the number of unpaid servants in the royal administration and stimulated the sale of *futuras* (appointments unavailable at the time the sale was made but to be held in the future by purchasers). These practices additionally disrupted the patterns of promotion, making it impossible to advance exclusively on merit. Purchasers who held appointments for long periods of time developed strong ties with the local elites and simultaneously undermined viceregal patronage. Susan Socolow has already demonstrated that in Buenos Aires, the rapid growth in the number of bureaucrats that characterized the creation of the Viceroyalty of Rio de la Plata in 1776 was followed by their slow career advancement and the growth of interim and unsalaried appointments.[19] My analysis of donativos collected in the 1790s adds a new dimension to the existing research as it links the proliferation of temporary and unsalaried positions and slow promotions with the sale of offices not only within the boundaries of the viceregal capital but also across the entire viceroyalty.

In order to avoid lawsuits from officeholders as well as the immediate disbursement of large funds in eighteenth-century Rio de la Plata, the crown incorporated offices gradually. While the men and practices associated with the sale of offices continued for several years, the newly appointed viceroys managed to partially exercise their own patronage against entrenched local interests through the incorporation of offices.[20] However, donativos collected in the 1790s changed this process and often created opportunities for officeholders to bargain directly with the crown, bypassing the brokerage of viceroys and, consequently, diminishing their power. Additionally, since no homogeneous policy was enforced over all the divisions of the administration, officeholders serving in the different branches embraced donativos, expecting a variety of rewards. Thus, the analysis that follows breaks down donativos not only by treasury but also by administrative division (table 4.2).

In the Viceroyalty of Rio de la Plata, sales of offices brokered through donativos followed the same trends as those described for Castile by Tomás y Valiente. Sales were more common among officers holding positions in the revenue-collecting agencies than among those serving in the political and judicial branches of the administration (table 4.2).[21] During the War against the French Convention, only four high-ranking political officers (either governors or intendants) contributed donativos. The remaining officers holding political appointments were serving either as administrators in the mission towns or as *subdelegados* in the Alto Peruvian indigenous communities. *Subdelegaciones* (which replaced *corregimientos*) and *administraciones* had always been regarded as profitable positions, and it is not surprising that men holding these offices sought extensions in their tenures in exchange for their donativos. Many of them stated on the documents issued along with their donativos that their contributions would continue not only throughout the war but also for "as long as they remain[ed] in office." José Agustín de Arce, *subdelegado* in Chichas, contributed 200 pesos annually under such conditions.[22]

However, high-ranking officers negotiated more successfully than their junior partners, as their donativos secured them lifetime appointments at posts that were generally held on average for five years.[23] The case of Francisco de Viedma best illustrates this trend. In 1786 Viedma was appointed as governor-intendant of Cochabamba. During the War against the French Convention, he contributed 1,400 and 3,000 pesos in one-time and annual donativos, respectively. Instead of being transferred at the end of an average five-year tenure, he kept his office until his death in 1809. It is quite impressive that Viedma was capable of contributing such funds while receiving a salary of 6,000 pesos annually.[24] One can safely assume that due to his standing and political acumen, Viedma generated trust among his peers and subordinates, who in turn supported the king financially. Thus, the collection of this donativo provided Viedma with an opportunity to display his bureaucratic competence according to eighteenth-century standards. The funds he collected in his jurisdiction represented 6 percent of the total donativo (table 3.1). Joaquín de Alós y Bru, who served as governor-intendant of Paraguay between 1787 and 1796, eased his way into the governorship of Valparaiso in Chile through his 2,000-peso donativo contributed during the War against the French Convention and remained in this office until the end of the Spanish domination in 1811. Like many of the new officers appointed by the Bourbons, Viedma and Alós were Spanish by birth. However, they remained in Spanish America for most of their adult lives, holding long-lasting tenures in a few positions. While Spanish born and presumably loyal to their king, they perpetuated the practices that prior to the Bourbon Reforms had made it possible for creoles to create strong interest groups. In 1797 the crown reduced the intendants' wages to 4,000 pesos. This measure indicates that because these positions had been transformed into profitable sources of income for the officeholders, the crown reduced its administrative costs.[25] Indeed, some of them became so profitable that donativo contributors competed for them. For instance, the documents recording the donativo of the Count of San Miguel de Carma included his petition to be appointed to the intendancy of Cochabamba as well. But his 1,000-peso donativo paled in comparison with the impressive sums advanced by Viedma.[26] In other words, a market was already in place for these offices, and their price increased along with the competition. Viedma's case demonstrates that in order to secure a lengthy tenure at lucrative posts, bidders not only had to be Spanish and educated but also capable of contributing substantial donativos and performing as successful financial brokers for the crown within their districts. Increased competition resulted in lower administrative costs for the crown in the form of lower salaries and a boost in donativo revenue.

During the War against the French Convention, officers serving in the judicial branch of the administration had few incentives to contribute donativos as the king held a tight grip on these offices. Judge José Cabeza Enriquez contributed a single 1,000-peso donativo, which amounted to almost one-third of his salary of 3,500 pesos annually. However, his career expectations went unrecorded as he passed away in 1798 while still holding the same position (table 4.2).[27] The other contribution from the judicial branch of the administration came from six American-born attorneys serving at the audiencia of Buenos Aires. Each one of them donated 60 pesos to a common fund. Employing a common euphemism associated with the sale of offices, they stated that their contributions were intended "to pay for the salaries of six Spanish foot soldiers throughout the war."[28] Thus, the solicitation of donativos opened the game (at least on a smaller scale) even to creoles, although they were expected to be outsiders in Bourbon politics and administration.

Bourbon reformism did not affect the notary positions, which continued to be sold until the end of the Spanish rule. Judging by the small number of large donativos that came from the notaries, we can see that these were still very profitable positions, although it appears that by the 1790s there were not that many openings in this branch (table 4.2). The regional differences are noteworthy, as the notary appointed to the Royal Mint in Potosí could afford both one-time and annual contributions of 500 pesos each, while others holding less profitable posts donated one-third or one-half that sum.

Revenue-collection agencies were financially profitable, and consequently men serving in these branches contributed large donativos (table 4.2). In the Rio de la Plata, as mentioned in chapter 3, the sale of offices at the Royal Postal Service continued despite the early efforts at incorporating them into the royal domain. Securing positions in this branch provided officeholders with profitable commercial opportunities since the postal offices and relay stations also functioned as places to rest and resupply for travelers and troops. Unsurprisingly, postal officers counted among the donors contributing over 100 pesos, a sum that is quadruple the mode.[29] Likewise, the treasurers from almost every region in the viceroyalty contributed donativos, most of them also exceeding 100 pesos. However, in Potosí and Buenos Aires, the ends of the axis linking Alto Peruvian silver production with the Atlantic trade, their donativos were exceptionally large.[30] For instance, the senior accountant from the Royal Mint in Potosí contributed 1,000 pesos as a one-time donativo, while men like Pedro Medrano and Antonio Pinedo, both treasurers in Buenos Aires and members of powerful bureaucratic networks, each donated 500 pesos annually. As for customs, all the officers holding positions in Buenos Aires, including *meritorios* (unsalaried employees), made donativo contributions, evidencing that these payments were similar to those for the purchase of future appointments discussed earlier in this chapter. Likewise, the interim overseer (*alcaide*) in the Montevideo customs house contributed his entire annual salary, probably seeking a permanent appointment in retribution.[31]

The purchase of futuras (future appointments) and promotions through the contribution of donativos appealed to donors who already held or wanted to hold bureaucratic positions at the time they made their contributions. In many cases, these donors intended to secure posts not only for themselves but also for their sons. Such was the case of Juan Carrillo de Albornoz, member of the Cochabamba city council in perpetuity, who contributed 1,000 pesos for himself and the same amount "on behalf of his son Manuel." The donativo records do not mention which position Manuel was to be rewarded with, confirming that ambiguity characterized these open-ended bargains. Nevertheless, after securing an appointment in perpetuity for himself, Carrillo de Albornoz started building his son's "bargaining capital." Further evidence sustaining this point can be found in the records of the donativo of Pedro Casas, a Catalonian merchant residing in Potosí. His eleven-year-old son "had already expressed an interest in serving the monarch," leading Casas to donate 148 pesos annually on his behalf. Finally, Ambrosio Funes, who led a powerful family in Córdoba, donated 60 pesos for not one but three sons. As members of the local establishment, the Funeses were already secure in their prominent positions. However, they did not miss the chance to contribute to this donativo in order to enhance the political and clerical careers of their offspring.[32]

The market for futuras not only illustrates the mechanisms employed in the crafting of administrative family networks but also makes evident that donors laid claims to rights through their donativo contributions.

The Count of San Miguel de Carma was a resident in Charcas when he contributed 1,000 pesos in donativos during the War against the French Convention. In 1803 he submitted a petition to the crown requesting to be awarded with a political appointment, in particular the governorship of Cochabamba, in compensation for his donativos and "other merits he had both acquired and inherited."[33] As already mentioned, Francisco de Viedma, whose donativo was six times larger than the count's, outbid him and the other candidates also competing for the same lucrative spot. Similarly, Juan Andres de Arroyo, who served as the administrative assistant in the superintendency of Buenos Aires, requested a reward for his financial services in the form of donativo contributions. In the same letter that he submitted to express his willingness to support the monarch during the war against the French, he petitioned the viceroy to "employ him in the office of his choice."[34] Thus, donors of lower status and lesser means also entered the market of donativo-based bargains to give voice to their expectations, although in a subtler manner than the more powerful bidders. The uncertainty implicit in these negotiations did not keep them from taking risks. In fact, it appears that the risk involved in these transactions made middle-ranked donors more resourceful. For instance, Pedro José Ballesteros, interim accountant (*supernumerario*) serving at the Tribunal de Cuentas (Court of Audits) in Buenos Aires, contributed an annual donativo of 166 pesos during this war. The records indicate that those funds came from annuities (*censos*) he collected from the Cinco Gremios Mayores in Madrid and from the yields of a hacienda he owned in Spain. Accountants like Ballesteros seem to have been familiar with investing opportunities across the Spanish empire and also aware of the advantages of diversifying their investments. By successfully combining his political and financial capital, Ballesteros finally obtained a permanent appointment as treasurer in the Court of Audits of Buenos Aires.[35]

Finally, employees serving in the Royal Tobacco Monopoly contributed the largest number of individual donativos (table 4.2). The rapid growth and subsequent crowding of this new branch of the administration explains the intense competition for advancement within it. Under these circumstances, donativos became an important instrument utilized by the Royal Tobacco Monopoly employees to increase their chances in the highly competitive world of offices. Until the creation of the Viceroyalty of Rio de la Plata in 1776, the Royal Tobacco Monopoly operated under the jurisdiction of the Peruvian headquarters. Thereafter, it developed its own regional administrative structure and experienced rapid bureaucratic growth with positions being filled primarily by those exercising royal patronage (as we have no evidence indicating they had been sold). Donativos reversed this trend, however, as bureaucratic mobility within this branch decreased, even while it continued to hire a large number of meritorios (unsalaried workers) as well as second and third officials for the same positions. Although in the 1790s the tobacco monopoly employed in the city of Buenos Aires twenty-three officers, the donativo roster lists sixty-one contributors from this branch (table 4.2). Twenty-five held office, while the others were *estanquistas*, that is, the shopkeepers licensed to sell tobacco products. The estanquistas, however, did not receive salaries from the exchequer but needed to secure the royal favor in order to keep their licenses. It seems that, in this case, the salaried employees of the monopoly acted as brokers channeling the estanquistas' capital toward the royal treasury.

The records of the salaries paid to the employees serving at the tobacco monopoly have survived, and therefore, we can compare them with those of individual donativos. While donativos represented between 2 and 24 percent of the employees' annual salaries, the size of their contributions was not proportional to their earnings (table 4.3). Officers contributing large shares of their salaries were either holding interim positions (the *oficial mayor tesorero interino* contributed 21 percent of his salary, for example) or were at the end of the advancement queue, holding posts that a modern bureaucracy would consider redundant. The second officer in the treasury, the first to the second officer in the general administration, the second to the second officer, the third officer, the fourth officer, and the fifth officer contributed in donativos between 9 and 16 percent of their salaries (table 4.3). Francisco de Paula Saubidet, although holding a permanent position as an accountant, contributed 24 percent of his salary. However, he had been slowly advancing in this branch since 1777 when he started as a *meritorio*.

There are interesting lessons to be learned from the donativos collected among the employees in this branch. First, a market for advancement through the ranks and into permanent positions existed and expanded even within the branches of the administration that had become targets of Bourbon reformism. Second, from the royal administration viewpoint, the creation of unsalaried and interim positions was an unwise choice if royal servants were primarily appointed to provide professional administrative services. However, if officers were expected to financially support the crown by purchasing offices and pooling financial resources from family members, friends, and acquaintances, then the promotion of bureaucratic crowding and career immobility became sound royal policy.

In the Viceroyalty of Rio de la Plata, then, bureaucrats serving across the ranks and branches contributed donativos. The records strongly indicate that royal servants engaged in the donativo process voluntarily, as most of their contributions were given more than a year before the king suggested to Viceroy Melo de Portugal the implementation of 4 percent mandatory discounts on their salaries. As mentioned in chapter 2, these were the discounts monarchs generally enforced during international wars, and in spite of their satisfactory financial performance, Minister Canga Arguelles strongly discouraged them. When Viceroy Melo received the decree to establish such discounts, he considered its enforcement to be unnecessary and emphasized that many of the voluntary donativos contributed up to that point by royal officers "accounted for more than 20 percent of their salaries and most of them were larger than 10 percent."[36] In a clear example of the viceroys' prerogative to obey but not comply (*obedezco pero no cumplo*), Melo decided to adapt royal policy to the more favorable local circumstances. He put the royal decree on hold and instead kept on collecting larger voluntary donativos from officeholders eager to vie for promotions.

While the royal officers in high-end and life-long appointments were able to attain political, financial, and social goals, low- and middle-ranking bureaucrats worked in a more competitive environment where compensations became harder to obtain. That fact did not discourage them from contributing donativos. As already mentioned, officers of the quill and in the revenue-collection agencies obtained salaries and pensions and collected service fees, and in the case of the postal employees, holding office brought along opportunities in trade. Under these circumstances, the crown did not need to create new taxes to repay the bureaucrats for their financial services during the war. If this had been a modern bureaucracy, outstanding services would have been exclusively rewarded with increases in salaries and faster promotions. As we have seen, the crown took the opposite path, reducing salaries and promoting overcrowding, which ultimately stalled advancement. Nevertheless, greater competition meant that bureaucrats entering into these bargains had to be more highly qualified.

Paradoxically, salary reductions increased and advancement through the revenue collection department slowed following collections of donativos. Yet a larger share of revenue was spent locally.[37] Thus, officers had incentives to collect more despite the less advantageous working conditions. In the 1790s and early 1800s, the crown also sent to the Viceroyalty of Rio de la Plata several inspectors to "straighten out" the accounting books. Presented with this evidence, most scholars have been inclined to see "corruption" and "embezzlement."[38] Instead, based on the evidence available in donativo records, I propose an alternative reading of these trends that links these practices to the political culture of the Spanish world. Similar to consulados, the Spanish imperial bureaucracy functioned as a bargaining forum, a dynamic political arena in which the crown and officers not only compared their relative power but also defined their interests over time. By analyzing these practices, we can also grasp the rules of a complex political game. While the officers on the ground had direct access to revenues and fees and could have easily pocketed more than their fair share, the crown did not lose its regulatory power, nor did it give up its political initiative. It periodically sent out envoys not to make the accounts more transparent but to make the distribution of the spoils fairer to all sides. Retaining political initiative did not necessarily mean that the monarch had unconstrained power or could violate the property rights of the officers by breaching donativo-based contracts. In chapter 3 (table 3.6), I pointed out that officeholders heavily favored donativo contributions paid annually (49 percent of the total) instead of opting for the one-time donativos (6 percent). Their choice indicates that as active members of the political establishment, bureaucrats were aware of the risks involved in financing an imperial state at war, and consequently they took certain precautions to protect their political and financial investments. By spreading their contributions over time, bureaucrats retained their capacity to periodically evaluate the risks of, modify, and even exit their donativo-based bargains as they assessed whether their offices yielded enough funds (or other benefits) to be worth continuing with their contributions. Expressions indicating that donativo contributions were contingent on the officeholder's continuation in office evidence these employees' capacity to periodically gauge their commitments. For instance, José Agustín de Arce, subdelegado in Chichas, contributed 200 pesos annually "as long as he remained in office," while Geronimo Garmendia, interim accountant in Buenos Aires, stated that his donativos would be offered to pay the salary of one soldier for as long as he lingered in his current position.[39] Manuel Fernandez, who resigned from his office while this donativo was still being collected, immediately stopped his annual contributions.[40] Ultimately, this partnership between the crown and entrepreneurial bureaucrats was the most advantageous solution for all sides, as cooperation made possible the channeling of power and wealth to participants in collections of donativos.

Yet, as in the case of merchants and bankers, the principles of distributed justice dominated the allocation of rewards among bureaucrats. Larger donativos, such as those provided by Viedma and Alós, secured donors for life in powerful and profitable positions, while players of lesser means only advanced slowly, competing against a crowd of unprivileged peers. Increased competition and risk did not discourage middle- and lower-ranking players. On the contrary, some of them became emboldened by the prospect of rewards and recycled into the system increasing shares of their smaller earnings. As noted, lower-paid officers contributed proportionally larger donativos. In other words, pressure from peers and social betters within a hierarchical yet competitive social order was more effective to mobilize the financial resources of subjects than the presumed absolute power of the king.[41] Men like Ballesteros, who were endowed with bureaucratic and financial skills as well as patience, advanced to coveted permanent positions, such as treasurer in the Court of Audits of Buenos Aires, while the Count of San Miguel de Carma was unable to compete against Viedma, despite his individual and family record of good service and his hefty donativo. While the market for bids was open to competitors of diverse social backgrounds, the king utilized the principles of distributive justice to define and sustain a hierarchical order that rewarded certain groups at the expense of others. Donativos collected during the Naval Wars against Britain (1799–1802, see chapter 5) demonstrate that similar principles facilitated the advancement of Spaniards to the detriment of American-born royal servants.

DONATIVOS CONTRIBUTED BY THE MILITARY AND MILITIAS: CREOLES AND CASTAS AS DISADVANTAGED PLAYERS IN THE POLITICS OF GIVING

When combined, donativos from the military and militias totaled 12,434 pesos (6 percent, one-time total) and 8,786 pesos (20 percent, annual total over eighteen months). Their contributions to this donativo were comparatively substantial (table 3.6). Paradoxically, at times of war the Spanish king not only requested but also accepted financial contributions from the military and militias instead of increasing their salaries and power. In this section, I will analyze this seemingly inconsistent policy.

Before considering the donativo contributions from these groups, I need to outline the characteristics of the military institution in Spanish America. Throughout the eighteenth century, and in response to threats from other European nations (especially after the English occupation of Cuba in 1762), the Bourbon kings undertook enormous efforts intended to professionalize and make more attractive and honorable the military career on both sides of the Atlantic. An efficient defense of the overseas possessions required the creation of a professional military as well as the setting up of regular units stationed in major cities and vulnerable seaports. The extension of the Spanish possessions and the costs of keeping garrisons staffed and properly supplied left the Spanish Crown with no other choice but to rely largely on powerful American-born men and their capital for financing and manning the military.

Three branches made up the military organization in the Indies. The first one was the Ejército de Dotación or Fijo (garrison troops), composed of infantry regiments charged with defending the larger Latin American cities. As implied by its name, the units that made up this branch were intended to remain stationed within the region in which they served. The officers that joined this division were all professionally trained and came from wealthy or noble families. This was also the branch of the army in which the creole presence was the most noticeable.[42] The Ejército de Refuerzo (supplementary army) was an itinerant army frequently sent from Spain to the Indies with the purpose of reinforcing the units of the Ejército de Dotación either when the latter were undermanned (which was often the case) or when a foreign invasion was feared. Members of the Spanish lesser nobility predominantly made up the officer corps of this branch, although a few of them were Europeans recruited outside the Iberian Peninsula. Between 1739 and 1800, the crown sent the Ejército de Refuerzo to the Indies at least thirty-six times, and depending on the scale of the mission, the number of soldiers dispatched fell between 200 and 1,400 men.[43] Finally, the Spanish king promoted the creation of militias (both rural and urban) as a supplement to the existing professional military establishment.

Castilian law, which was also enforced in the Americas, established that vecinos between the ages of fifteen and forty-five must provide military assistance to the king. In the eighteenth century, although the ranks and recruitment of the militias remained unchanged, the crown attempted to professionalize these units. A series of ordinances issued from the 1770s onward (Reglamentos e Instrucciones) provided the militias with a similar organization to that of the regular troops and allowed the crown to keep a closer check on their recruitment, training, and discipline. Although the military and militias followed homologous methods, the nature of the service in these branches remained distinct. Militia officers and soldiers did not usually receive a regular salary, nor were they professionally schooled or housed in barracks. Militias only responded to the chain of command when mobilized and wore uniforms mostly for ceremonial occasions. However, as they constituted the largest number of men bearing arms, they became the crown's only reliable source of military reserves.[44]

Men who organized, led, and financed the militias were generally landowners and merchants who frequently profited from supplying the militia forces under their command. In the frontiers, especially in areas lacking cabildos, merchants and landowners additionally found in the militia leadership opportunities to practice social and political control locally.[45] Additionally, militia service made it possible for free men of color to achieve social recognition within a socioethnic order that, in spite of their freedom, frequently relegated them to a lower social status. In sum, in the eighteenth century the Army of the Americas (Ejército de las Americas) became an institution where creoles and castas found not only opportunities for commercial entrepreneurship but also social advancement, legal protection (*fuero militar*), tribute exemptions (especially for the free people of color), and outward displays of social standing (by wearing uniforms and bearing arms).[46] Thus, militias tied local, generally powerful and predominantly creole interest groups to the imperial project. While the crown benefitted from the militias' service and their leaders' financial assistance (which often compensated for the decline in revenue caused by tribute exemptions granted to colored militias), the expectation of socioeconomic rewards and a chance at local political leadership explains the willingness of creole and castas to join these forces.

The Viceroyalty of Rio de la Plata followed the imperial military blueprint, and consequently both regular troops and militias served in the region. The Ejército de Refuerzo was dispatched to this area only four times during the eighteenth century. However, the troops that remained in the area after the campaign of the mid-1770s against Portugal constituted the bulk of the viceregal Ejército Regular. It is noteworthy that with the exception of the Atlantic coastline and the Chaco frontier, the crown stationed regular troops in no other regions. Thus, the territorial defense and internal security of this viceroyalty were largely left in the hands of militias.[47]

The geographical distribution of donativos contributed by military and militia personnel during the War against the French Convention mirrored the regional distribution of regular troops and militias. They additionally show that the crown relied more heavily on the financial support of the creole militias than on Spanish military men (table 4.4). In Buenos Aires, Salta (Chaco frontier), and the Banda Oriental (regions that hosted regular troops), contributions originated with a small number of military men, while in the other areas all contributions came from militias. Donors identified as members of the regular army in areas that did not host regular troops were either temporarily stationed in that region or simply passing through.[48]

The figures on table 4.4 additionally indicate that individual donativos contributed by military men were equal to or larger than 100 pesos. Officers exclusively made these large individual contributions, as soldiers generally contributed to a common fund collected by the sergeant in charge of each unit. While the salaries of officers contributing donativos are unknown, the smallest individual contribution (100 pesos) is four times the most common amount collected across the viceroyalty (25 pesos) during this war. As mentioned in chapter 3, it was common for military commanders to partner with merchant-bankers in the lucrative business of transferring situados and supplying the army. Judging by the size of their donativos, high-ranking military men also served the king as financial brokers by pooling together capital from their subordinates, friends, and families. Thus, their role was similar to that of the Spanish officeholders, as their professional qualifications not only included schooling and training but also their capacity to assist the crown financially. They additionally exercised their social pressure over their subordinates and civilians alike, presumably in a more assertive fashion than the royal servants, in order to ease the transfer of financial resources from the more vulnerable to the more powerful members of the imperial order.[49] Nevertheless, the evidence available indicates that the example of and pressure exercised by the higher-ranking officers coupled with the expectations of rewards rather than the king's capacity to implement homogeneous exactions worked together to secure donativo contributions from the members of the military establishment.

As already mentioned, militia members did not regularly receive monetary compensation for their services to the king and the well-being of their communities (common good). Nevertheless, they contributed significant donativos, which indicates that they valued the tax exemptions, judicial privileges, and outward displays of social standing their militia services conferred on them. Compared to those of the military, the militia members not only individually contributed in larger numbers but also collected a larger total donativo. Except for Santa Cruz, individual donativos contributed by militia commanders and captains were on average considerable (table 4.4). Additionally, in Potosí and Buenos Aires, where militias contributed the largest one-time and annual donativos, not only officers but also militia soldiers were listed as donors. While these men were regularly employed in a variety of trades, the listing on the donativo rosters of their militia identity indicates that by means of their contributions, militia members sought to reaffirm their acquired status in different ways. First, colored militias', especially *pardos*', contributions to the donativo confirmed that they were relatively wealthy men, free and exempted from tribute.[50] Unlike taxes and tributes, as I have already mentioned, donativos did not compromise the social status of donors but rather enhanced it. Additionally, in Potosí militia soldiers contributed on average 25 pesos in donativos, which represented a large share of the salaries paid for skilled and unskilled labor in the region.[51] Second, creoles' adoption of the militia identity while they were performing the role of donors made it apparent that at critical times they were capable of providing essential services for the crown, even when the growing presence of Spanish battalions constituted a threat to their honor and standing and, to a certain extent, called into question their competence as military leaders.[52] In summary, the politics of giving reveals that by the late eighteenth century, it had become harder for creoles and castas to gain access to and preserve positions of leadership and social prestige because, due to the growing presence of Spanish competitors, they had to proportionally invest more capital and provide more services in order to access a shrinking share of the spoils of empire.

An analysis of the donativo contributed by the Cuerpo de Caballería de Blandengues of Buenos Aires further demonstrates that in the eighteenth century creoles had more difficulty successfully engaging in the politics of giving. In 1752, in an effort to contain the frequent Indian attacks on the Buenos Aires frontier, the cabildo of Buenos Aires decided to create this militia. Simultaneously, the cabildo paid for its expenses by temporarily establishing an excise tax on wine and liquor shipped to the viceregal capital from the Cuyo provinces (*ramo de guerra*). As in the case of most militias, the Blandengues started as a unit funded by local authorities. Unlike other units, however, they received regular salaries paid for by taxes collected locally. These measures reveal that fiscal frag-mentation endowed city councilmen and cabildos with strong political initiative. In 1761, while serving as governor of Buenos Aires (1757–1766), Pedro de Cevallos transferred the authority over the Blandengues as well as the funds earmarked for their salaries from the cabildo to the royal treasury. Since the royal treasurers prioritized other expenses, salary payments for the Blandengues fell behind, and consequently they expe-rienced a sharp decline in their numbers throughout the 1760s. However, Viceroy Vértiz (1778–1784) implemented several measures intended to professionalize this militia, including rules and regulations concerning the use of uniforms and weapons. As a result, under his administration the number of recruits increased again, and their performance improved. In 1784 the Blandengues were granted the status of *tropa veterana*; that is, they were incorporated into the regular army.[53]

By the time the crown collected donativos to support the War against the French Convention, the Blandengues enjoyed a mixed status; de-spite being a locally recruited and creole militia, their salaries were paid for by the royal treasury. Records detailing their remuneration survive, and thus we can compare what percentage of their salaries they con-tributed as donativos (table 4.5). Unlike the Spanish bureaucrats, who at the lower ranks contributed proportionally more in order to bargain for advancement (table 4.3), the Blandengues militia members' donations strictly followed the hierarchy of ranks. Additionally, Blandengues of-ficers sharing the same military rank always donated identical sums.[54] The commanders donated 100 percent of their monthly salaries, while those ranking below them settled for a proportionally smaller contri-bution. It is noteworthy that all of these donativos represented over 60 percent of the Blandengues' monthly earnings, even in the case of soldiers who received a modest income. As in the case of all other do-nors, the Blandengues freely assessed how much they wanted to con-tribute. However, they were the only group who decided to contribute donativos proportionally to their income. In other words, their dona-tivo was similar to a self-imposed and quite burdensome income tax. While their services to the crown and the common good were valued, other groups such as Spanish military men and bureaucrats competed more successfully for benefits, advancement, and social recognition. In the 1790s, Atlantic warfare coupled with the presence of other compet-itive groups and the principles of distributive justice broke the quasi-monopoly over military recognition that creoles and castas had held in the past. Facing a competitive and market, they found themselves investing more to obtain returns that had become both more uncertain and harder to access.

DONATIVOS AS JUROS AND CENSOS?

In the seventeenth century, when other attempts at increasing revenue failed, the Spanish Crown borrowed from its subjects by selling juros. *Juro* contracts established that individuals or corporations who advanced capital to the crown would receive interest annually (generally 5 percent) in the form of a pension backed by revenue. Thus, juros were part of a program of state-sponsored annuities in which investors found a safe a venture for their idle capital. Juros also became inalienable property that could be traded, sold, or inherited.[55] In Spanish America, Indian communities, widows, and minors as well as religious institutions, cabildos, and universities (*colegios*) had historically invested in royal debt primarily by purchasing juros. The crown preferred to sell juros to these groups instead of to merchants, landowners, and miners to avoid draining capital from the most productive and entrepreneurial sectors of the economy.[56] In other words, the sale of juros shows that the Spanish Crown was capable of enforcing financially sound policies while simultaneously wedding multiple interest groups to the imperial project.

As already discussed, in the 1780s the crown's attempts to increase taxation were met with resistance across the empire, which thereby created the conditions for the collection of donativos and eventually the sale of juros. Additionally, the donativo collected by the consulado of Buenos Aires was in fact a lending operation that resulted in the creation of long-term annuities backed by revenue. Hence, it is pertinent to ask whether the crown wanted to extend similar opportunities to traditional juro holders in the 1790s. In this section, I will examine the donativos contributed by widows, religious institutions, indigenous communities, cabildos, and universities—that is, traditional juro holders—in order to determine if the politics of giving offered them an investment opportunity recorded under the donativo rubric.

A look at donativos from women reveals a rather polarized picture (table 4.6), as only a few women from Buenos Aires and Charcas were capable of contributing significant sums, while those from the other regions contributed smaller funds. In fact, donativos from women from Córdoba, La Paz, Tucumán, and Santa Cruz followed the general trends described for the viceroyalty at large and ranged from 12 to 500 pesos out of which one-half were smaller than or equal to 25 pesos.

As already discussed, elite women who channeled their donativos through the consulado of Buenos Aires were actually engaged in a lending operation. While one of them was a widow and another one a single woman, they were both members of powerful Spanish merchant clans from the viceregal capital. Two women from Charcas also donated large funds. However, their donativos were not associated with lending operations but rather with other types of bargains. For instance, doña Francisca del Risco contributed 15,000 pesos—the largest individual donativo in the Viceroyalty of Rio de la Plata during this war. In her case, a financial investment yielded primarily social returns. Doña Francisca was the widow of Vicente Tardio de Guzmán, a wealthy and powerful attorney and entrepreneur who also served as the legal adviser of the president of Charcas. Tardio de Guzmán made his fortune by combining a variety of lucrative activities, including agricultural enterprises, silver mining (owning both mines and mills), and moneylending. Doña Francisca was the child of a prominent but adulterous couple from La Plata, and, like many other notables, she attempted to achieve legitimation by petitioning for a cédula de gracias al sacar. Her donativo must have influenced the decision of the Cámara de Indias, which granted her legitimation in 1796. This grant was exceptional as the legitimizing of adulterinos had become much harder and more selective than it was earlier in the century. Doña Francisca stated on her offer that her contribution was on behalf of herself and her children, revealing that she was fully aware of the rules governing both the politics of giving as well as legitimation.[57]

The Marchioness of the Valle de Toxo (or Tuxu), also from Charcas, contributed 500 pesos in donativos annually. She was a member of a powerful creole family as well as the heiress of an enormous entailed estate.[58] A few other relatively wealthy creole women could afford donativos equal to or larger than 100 pesos (eight in total). However, I have not found any evidence indicating that they were offered annuities in exchange for their contributions. In summary, donativos in the 1790s offered profitable ventures exclusively to elite women connected to merchant families, but the outstanding donativo from Francisca del Risco was tied to a social rather than a financial bargain. Other creole women, while wealthy, were not offered comparable benefits in exchange for their contributions. In other words, not all women benefited equally from the distribution of wealth and power at stake in the politics of giving.

The crown had traditionally secured long-term loans from the Indian communities by drafting *censo* agreements. Censos were similar to juros because in return for advancing their capital, the Indian communities received interest payments of 5 percent annually that were guaranteed by the treasury. Funds invested in censos came from the Indian communities' treasuries (*cajas de comunidad*). Indian lords as well as local and regional religious and lay authorities were called upon to verify these lending transactions. Scholars have regarded censos as one among many compulsory mechanisms that perpetuated the Indian communities' poverty and subordination to Spanish rule.[59] But if donativos were in fact censo agreements, the small number of indigenous communities listed on the rosters reveals that as compulsory measures, they were poorly enforced (table 3.7).

In the Alto Peruvian provinces, the Andean rebellions of the 1780s not only restrained the crown's ability to enforce new taxes but also set limits to the politics of giving. As a result, in the early 1790s only a few Indian communities from La Paz and Cochabamba contributed donativos (table 3.7).[60] Donativos collected among the Indian communities from La Paz were substantial. Pacajes and Chulumani contributed the largest sums (960 and 1,546 pesos, respectively), while the donativos from Omasuyos, Sicasica, and Larecaja were comparatively modest (525, 584, and 310 pesos, respectively). Even a handful of caciques from this region financially supported the king throughout this war. For instance, Idelfonso Pinto, cacique of Sipaqui (Larecaja), contributed 20 and 18 pesos in one-time and annual donativos, respectively. Pinto additionally offered as donativos one-half of the annual income of his *cacicazgo* and twelve cargas of wheat "to sustain the army."[61] That was an expression frequently utilized in donativo-based negotiations. Additionally, the sizes of Pinto's individual contributions, while below the mode (25 pesos), were larger than the smallest ones, evidencing that indigenous caciques figured among the middle groups that contributed the majority of the individual donativos. Indians from La Paz historically resisted and rebelled against Spanish authorities, although they did not always openly question monarchical legitimacy.[62] It is reasonable to assume that donativos counted among the strategies they employed to negotiate with the crown. However, the sources do not indicate that their donativos yielded safe financial returns. The treasury summaries from La Paz (cartas cuentas) did not list through the 1790s a ramo (accounting item) for collecting or repaying *censos de Indios*.[63] In other words, if theirs was a financial investment, it did not enjoy the type of backing that guaranteed the payment of interest for the most powerful juro investors. Unlike the bureaucrats, Indian communities did not have direct access to salaries and fees to lower the risk implied in these transactions. While donativos made it possible for the indigenous communities to engage in the politics of giving, their bargaining capital (political as well as financial) was too modest to secure safe returns.

Compared to those from La Paz, donativos from the indigenous communities of Cochabamba were almost trivial (table 3.7). It is actually quite surprising that these communities had any funds available at all as by 1793 all of them were under extreme economic pressure. While in bountiful years these peasants had successfully competed in the marketplace with larger landlords, in 1792 frost and drought ruined their crops, forcing the Indians of Cochabamba to purchase grain at high market prices.[64] Hence, donativos constituted an additional burden for the Indians of Cochabamba. Intendant Viedma must have prompted the collection in order to enhance his own bargaining power rather than to give the Indians a chance to negotiate with the crown.

The Guarani Indians also contributed substantial donativos. As described in the previous chapters, these donativos lubricated profitable trading and credit networks that integrated the mission towns with the Buenos Aires market and its treasury, the caja where their donativos finally cleared. Donativos from the Guarani were collected from their cabildos (recorded in the sources as "el corregidor, cabildo y administrador" from such and such a pueblo), their communities (noted as "la comunidad y naturales" from such and such a pueblo), as well as from individual Indians (table 3.7). Donativos from the Guarani are puzzling not only due to their magnitude but also because they were collected in the post-Jesuit era, a period most scholars associated with the weakening of the mission system and an overall worsening of the economic conditions in the area. However, recent scholarship emphasizes a slow process of decline over a thirty-year period characterized by adaptations and compromises that included the expansion of profitable commercial opportunities. These strategies, however, brought only short-term gains, and in the long run, they depleted productive resources (primarily high-quality yerba maté fields and cattle herds) and eroded the missions' communal structure.[65] Nevertheless, not all missions fared equally. For instance, Mission San Miguel set aside territory for the reproduction of wild cattle and became the supplier for other missions that needed livestock. San Juan, which depended on cattle supplies from San Miguel, profited from the exploitation of wild yerba maté bushes, which was a commodity that sold at premium prices in Buenos Aires and Potosí. These transformations partially explain the large donativos from the Guarani, which included contributions of 1,000 pesos each from the communities of San Juan and San Miguel, another 1,000 pesos from the cabildo of San Juan, and a few individual contributions as high as 200 pesos from the Indians of San Miguel. In the case of San Juan's cabildo, donativo funds most probably came from the sale or leasing of communal lands, a resource this mission could dispose of when its livestock withered and market conditions favored harvesting wild yerba maté.[66] To summarize, large donativos from the Guarani indicate that commercial opportunities in the 1790s slowed the missions' decadence. However, they created wider disparities of wealth among and within the Guarani communities. The sources did not record what the Guarani expected from their donativos, and we have no evidence indicating that they were associated with censo agreements either. Similar to the indigenous communities of La Paz in the early 1790s, the Guarani contributed donativos at their own risk, in hopes of building up their present and future bargaining capital.

During the War against the French Convention, a few Spanish cabildos contributed donativos, though only those in Cochabamba and La Paz donated substantial funds. Cabildos generally derived their income from the selling and leasing of lands (*propios*), fees charged on licenses, fines collected from the violation of city ordinances, rental of market stalls, and excise taxes. As regular municipal income was frequently insufficient to meet expenses, municipalities occasionally took loans mainly from small- and medium-sized lenders seeking short-term, safe investments.[67] Hence, it should not be surprising to find cabildos capable of providing donativos (either from their own funds or loans), especially in the areas where intratreasury transfers created conditions for profitable commercial and financial ventures.

I have already mentioned that the Bourbons erected or strengthened powerful offices and corporations whose influence transcended the municipal jurisdiction. Toward the end of the eighteenth century, however, the political and financial dynamism of Spanish American cabildos also increased. Municipal bodies were not politically marginalized by the Bourbon administrative reforms but rather grew stronger as the success of the reforms depended on the cabildos' cooperation, especially for meeting increased financial and military demands. Cooperation between municipal and royal authorities implied for the cabildos not only greater involvement in public administration and public works but also a more efficient collection and management of municipal revenues and finances, which made serving in municipal positions quite attractive. Thus, donativos from Spanish cabildos could have functioned as negotiations concerning not only the sale of juros but also municipal offices. In any case, the Spanish cabildos' capacity for generating income put municipal corporate donors in an advantageous position as, unlike the Indians, they had direct access to sources of political rewards (municipal offices) and financial compensation in the form of taxes and fees collected locally.

Corporate donors additionally included the regular and secular clergy as well as the institutions that provided higher education, such as the Colegio de San Carlos in Buenos Aires, the Colegio Nacional de Monserrat in Córdoba, and the University of Saint Francis Xavier in Charcas. The crown generally favored the financial support of these institutions because, according to the official viewpoint, they did not drive out capital from the productive sectors of the economy. While the church had traditionally extended loans to private parties and supported the crown financially, the sources recording the 1793–1795 donativo do not indicate that the crown sold juros through donativos.[68] But since donativo contributions came in different sizes and involved a variety of transactions, the ecclesiastics' participation was neither uniform nor compulsory.

Ecclesiastics contributed 18,761 pesos to the one-time donativo but only a fraction of that sum annually (4,697 pesos; see table 3.6). Compared to the merchants and bureaucrats, their financial support was weak. However, their spiritual support, which stimulated other groups to emulate leaders and peers, was very strong. In the early 1790s, the church was committed to backing the crown in the war. The execution of Louis XVI followed by the confiscation of ecclesiastical property and the secularization decrees provided compelling reasons for the church to fight against the French Convention. Consequently, unlike the bureaucrats who by means of their annual contributions periodically assessed whether they wanted to continue or not with their financial backing, the church as a corporation opted for one-time donativos supplemented with countless Masses and spiritual exercises intended to mobilize the people in support of the crown.[69]

Table 4.7 indicates that the bulk of the donativos provided by the church came from the members of the secular clergy (16,478 pesos in one-time donations and 2,283 pesos annually) and that the cathedral chapter of La Paz contributed the most funds (12,238 pesos). Donativos from the regular clergy were significantly smaller even in the cases of the wealthiest orders. For instance, the friars of La Merced of Buenos Aires and Salta and the Franciscans from Córdoba respectively contributed 1,000, 300, and 580 pesos in one-time donativos. The 580 pesos from the Franciscans originated in a loan extended to the order by a local merchant whose name the documents do not disclose. As discussed in chapter 3, it was a common practice to contribute donativos through credit instruments. Even in the case of religious institutions (with ready access to cash), donativos did not necessarily imply disbursements of coin but rather a settlement over an existing credit operation involving a variety of partners.[70]

However, regular and secular clergymen also had available to them alternatives to monetary donations. When funds were short, they supplemented their donativos denominated in coin with sizable gifts in kind. Such was the case of the bishop, the cathedral chapter, and the Dominican convent of Buenos Aires, which together donated 2,216 fanegas of wheat. This wheat was shipped to Spain, indicating that these clergymen coupled donativos in coin with the profitable Atlantic trade in commodities. Other members of the ecclesiastical order offered their particular knowledge and skills. For instance, the Bethlemites of Buenos Aires and the friars of the Convent of San Juan de Dios in La Paz volunteered to take care of the wounded on the battlefields and made available to the crown their "medicines and surgical instruments."[71]

Spiritual donations made their way to the donativo rosters and were recorded following monetary contributions, which fell under the heading of *ofertas temporales* (worldly offerings). The recording of both types of donativos on the same rosters further indicates they had a multiplicity of meanings. Most of the priests and friars listed as donors offered prayers and chanted Masses "for the success of the Spanish Army" and for the "Health and Glory of the King of Spain." The Capuchin nuns and the Franciscan brothers of Buenos Aires went a step further and expressed their allegiance to the Spanish king not only with their prayers but also by performing "spiritual sacrifices and mortifications."[72] Widespread public demonstrations of loyalty and allegiance sponsored by the church, though spiritual in nature, served the political aims of the Spanish kings. Masses and prayers offered on behalf of the Spanish army placed in the public sphere of the pulpits the current political agenda of the monarchy. Moreover, the War against the French Convention was extremely popular among Spanish and Spanish American subjects, as they feared the spread of the subversive ideology of the French and Haitian revolutions.[73] In this context, the purpose of religious services and spiritual exercises transcended the religious realm, and they became mechanisms for informing the public as well as mobilizing the people's financial support. The positive response on the part of the ecclesiastics provides evidence of good communication and the sharing of mutual interests between church and state. In March 1793 the crown, aware of the power and usefulness of the religious structures, requested through a royal ordinance the celebration of "public prayers to beseech the intervention of God in favor of the Catholic Armies." As in eighteenth-century England, when the crown needed the financial support of its subjects it mobilized public opinion. However, within the Spanish empire the Catholic Church instead of the press performed this task.[74]

THE ILL-REPRESENTED GROUPS: VECINOS AND THE "POOR BUT LOYAL PEOPLE"

Prominent local authorities collected donativos by personally visiting vecinos in the company of a priest and a notary. Collections of donativos appear to have been more successful if staged on festive days following religious services, and the publication of the sums donated by prominent vecinos also encouraged others to pledge. Additionally, when collections of donativos were aimed at all social groups the officer in charge visited each household and requested support from the paterfamilias, his wife, and his dependents, including domestics. In areas where coin was scarce, the royal officers accepted donativos in kind.[75]

The words and examples of patriarchs, social betters, and peers were therefore more effective at mobilizing the financial resources of local communities than the presumed absolute power of a distant monarch. Contributions from vecinos represented 13 percent of both one-time and annual donativos. While their individual donativos fell within a wide range (between 1 and 2,000 pesos), they most frequently contributed between 1 and 25 pesos. In Misiones and Paraguay, where specie was scarce, many vecinos opted for donativos in kind, which included yerba maté, cloth, tobacco, cattle, and horses. The sources referred to them as "very poor but loyal people, willing to express their love for their king by contributing within their means." The language of gifts glossed over these transactions not to reflect social closeness but rather to maintain the distance that separated the king from his humble subjects.[76] Artisans and the undefined urban *común del pueblo* were also described in the sources as humble but loyal subjects. The absence of the honorable title of "don" by their names, if they were recorded at all, additionally confirms their lower social status and distance from elites and kings.

Unlike groups enjoying corporate representation, most vecinos acting as individual donors did not find in the politics of giving opportunities for advancing their interests. At best, they could see their names listed on the published roster and obtain a notarized certificate of their support to be used in the future either by themselves or by their offspring, if they entered the upper echelons of the social order. Those who contributed in kind were even worse off since in giving up commodities such as yerba maté and textiles, which sold at immense markups in distant markets, they not only relinquished their property but also transferred the profits to the merchants who commercialized these products.[77] Profiting from lending to and trading with peasants counted among the practices censored by the detractors of usury. However, within the legal and cultural framework of donativos these practices were considered a service that virtuous merchants provided to the crown. Donativos did allow the members of the popular classes to play the role of vecinos at a time in which vecindad had become socially, ethnically, and racially more exclusive. However, while plebeians might have sought this type of recognition, the authorities recording donativos continued to draw boundaries between vecinos of full right and those in the making, as they frequently omitted the names of donors they regarded as members of the "común del pueblo." Instead of listing them as individuals, the authorities compiling the donativo rosters referred to them by their occupations: "dos cirujanos" among the donors from La Paz, for instance.[78] This type of recording implies that donors' chances for obtaining compensations by participating in the politics of giving were slim as it would have been impossible to individualize them.

Although only a few contributions came from artisans, and most of them were small (ranging between 1 and 12 pesos), a few wealthy tradesmen such as the silversmiths could afford donativos equal to or larger than 100 pesos. However, the sources indicate that artisans obtained, at best, social recognition for their substantial donativos, most frequently in the form of visible status symbols. After collecting a donativo of 216 pesos from a silversmith, the governor of Salta requested that the viceroy authorize the silversmith "to wear a uniform or another noticeable distinction in recognition for his generous soul and hard work."[79]

Manuel Iriondo, a black slave from La Paz, offers an interesting but contradictory case, as he contributed a 1-peso donativo to financially sustain the Spanish monarch, the ultimate guarantor of his enslavement. The sources do not mention his occupation, nor do they describe the circumstances of his action. Yet he was referred to by his full name. Perhaps he was compelled by his master to contribute this donativo, although one wonders why other masters did not behave like Manuel's. Manuel could have also been in the process of purchasing his freedom and decided to obtain a notarized record of his involvement in the community he was about to embrace as a *liberto*. If that was the case, his donativo evidences that he had internalized the correlation between taxes and status. If he was on the path to freedom, he qualified as a donor and vecino, not as a *tributario* or taxpayer.

CONCLUSION

During the War against the French Convention, the Spanish Crown collected in the Viceroyalty of Rio de la Plata more than 260,000 pesos in donativos. These were substantial funds by the fiscal standards of this viceroyalty. The transfer of donativos across the viceregal treasuries indicates that donativo funds met crucial imperial needs. First, donativos as well as the financial instruments associated with them were utilized to pay for military defense, especially the expenses of those units deployed on territories bordering those of the Portuguese. Second, merchant-bankers in charge of transferring revenues across the viceregal treasuries not only profited from transferring donativos but also found in them a source of capital that boosted their businesses. Third, donativos channeled toward the royal treasury the savings of upper- and middle-class subjects and to a lesser extent the resources of the popular sectors. Finally, despite fiscal fragmentation, the financial instruments employed to transfer donativos fostered the financial cooperation of subjects and the integration of geographically distant regions.

Since only a small portion of donativos funds left for Spain (about 30 percent), those that remained in the viceregal space paid for royal expenditures and simultaneously subsidized private entrepreneurship. Additionally, the low remittance of donativo funds demonstrates that local authorities not only had incentives to increase revenues but also wielded substantial power to make decisions about these monies.

Unlike the taxes the English king attempted to enforce over the

American colonies (which ultimately alienated the support of the British North American subjects), donativos aligned in the fiscal and political spheres the interests of the Spanish monarchy and those of its most prosperous subjects. The surviving sources do not disclose the exact number of individuals who contributed donativos. However, they reveal that less than 1 percent of the viceregal population contributed the bulk of donativo funds. Far from being a comprehensive expropriator, the Spanish king tapped the resources of relatively prosperous subjects but only rewarded those who were instrumental in supporting him politically as well as financially.

As for the donors, the examples discussed in this chapter demonstrate that powerful corporate groups such as merchants and bureaucrats found in donativos an effective channel to communicate and bargain with the king and obtain his favor. These channels were accessible and efficient. And while they did not run through an imperial representative body, they operated within an institutional framework shaped by laws and lawful procedure. As elsewhere in the eighteenth century, these conduits for negotiation were not equally open to all. Nor were the rewards equally distributed. For instance, the merchants of Buenos Aires, who provided an outstanding donativo, bargained through their proxy at court and obtained, along with the creation of their own consulado, corporate representation as well as a new cash flow generated by the avería. The bureaucrats, who advanced their interests through individual petitions, found in donativos the opportunity to extend their tenures in office and augment profits. Ecclesiastics and military men added donativos to the list of essential services they regularly provided to the crown in an effort to retain and eventually increase their own corporate bargaining capital.

Unlike the French, Spanish American subjects who benefitted the most from the redistribution of power and income at the viceregal or territorial level were relatively well protected against the presumed confiscating instincts of the Spanish monarch. They not only had direct control over the revenues that guaranteed their profits but also could periodically revise their bargains by spreading their contributions over time. Additionally, the monarch had few incentives to violate the property rights of those groups that were instrumental in holding together a transnational composite monarchy. Instead of chastising bureaucrats and merchants, the Spanish king shared with them the spoils of empire.

There is no point in judging the redistributive practices associated with donativos according to modern standards of probity. Bureaucrats and merchant-bankers provided essential services to the crown, and they rightfully demanded compensations for their services. In fact, bureaucratic standards of the time required successful royal servants to be capable of mobilizing financial resources on behalf of the monarch. Unlike contemporary British officers, Spanish American bureaucrats and merchants were not necessarily corrupt, as they did not engage in illegal practices to access the redistribution of benefits. It could be argued that their methods brought them closer to French cronyism since they were partially institutionalized. Unlike French cronyism, however, Spanish redistribution through donativos was subject to market forces, and therefore it stimulated donors to invest more to successfully compete for social, political, and economic rewards. Through competition, the most efficient bidders (that is, the ones who combined the largest number of skills, including their capacity to mobilize financial resources for the crown) gained bureaucratic appointments (which provided political, financial, and social benefits), a share of the situado business, or a cash flow that backed their investments. Moreover, these practices did not have a disruptive economic impact on the Viceroyalty of Rio de la Plata, and instead of draining capital from the area, they recycled funds within its boundaries and fostered commercial expansion.

Because their social, professional, and economic existence depended on the empire's survival, merchants, bureaucrats, military men, and ecclesiastics contributed the most funds to this donativo. As for individual donors, stronger bidders such as doña Francisca del Risco found in donativos channels for advancing particular interests, although the rewards doña Francisca obtained strengthened and preserved a fluid but hierarchical social order. While she and her offspring were the prime beneficiaries of a gracias al sacar, the fact that their births would be thereafter regarded as legitimate impacted the society at large. Players of lesser means, such as the cacique of Sipaqui, seem to have been equally aware of the advantages of engaging in the politics of giving, indicating that the system promoted the participation of those who were inferior in wealth and status as well. For individual donors who lacked corporate representation, however, the returns were remote or nonexistent. As we saw in the case of the militias and lower-ranking bureaucrats, their comparatively more substantial donativo contributions show that they entered the politics of giving to protect and, if possible, advance their interests in a system that had become increasingly competitive. Contributions from individual vecinos made apparent that a majority of them perceived donativos not only as an opportunity to exercise responsible vecindad but also to measure their status against their peers and community leaders. Their donativos also confirmed their status as tax-exempt subjects, an important marker in defining local identities. Eventually, they would build their own individual political capital, although before obtaining any rewards their participation in collections of donativos made possible the transfer of wealth toward already powerful and wealthy subjects. Thus, the prospect of social advancement to the higher echelons of the imperial order and to better positions for negotiating with the monarch coupled with social pressure worked as effective incentives to bring into the system individuals of lesser means. Their positive engagement with the politics of giving additionally indicates that small-sum donors perceived as legitimate the redistributive practices associated with donativos. In other words, unlike the Frenchmen and the British North American colonists, by the 1790s donors of lesser means did not feel compelled to subvert the system.

Finally, regardless of intent and outcomes, donativo transactions were recorded utilizing the language of gifts, service, aid, and fidelity for the purpose of downplaying profit, calculation, and self-interest, which occasionally sparked public censure and subverted social cohesion. This language, as well as the philosophical and moral principles it referred to, allowed a Roman Catholic transatlantic monarchy to develop a sharp commercial and financial edge that was supported by a hierarchical community that valued the common well-being.

Table 4.1. Donativos channeled through the consulado of Buenos Aires, 1793–1795

Loan date	Name of lender	Amount (pesos)	Due in (years)	Interest rate (%)
1 January 1794	Gaspar de Santa Coloma	10,000	6	6
	Maria Josefa Lajarrota	10,000	2	6
	Antonio Garcia López	6,000	2	6
	Esteban Villanueva	4,000	6	6
	Martin Boneo	2,000	2	6
6 September 1794	Manuel Rodriguez de la Vega	10,000	6	6
	Gaspar de Santa Coloma	8,000	5	6
	Juan Esteban de Anchorena	6,000	4	6
	Antonio Garcia López	6,000	4	6
17 November 1794	Juan Esteban de Anchorena	6,000	4	6
18 November 1794	Josef Xavier de Amenábar	6,000	2	6
	Gaspar de Santa Coloma	2,000	4	6
	Maria Catalina de la Quintana	2,000	3	6
Total		78,000		

Source: Archivo General de la Nación (Argentina), Consulado de Buenos Aires,1:503–14.

Table 4.2. Donativos from bureaucrats by treasury and administrative branch, 1793–1795

Region	Cajas	Political				Judicial				Notarial				Customs			
		A pesos	n.	B pesos	n.	A pesos	n.	B pesos	n.	A pesos	n.	B pesos	n.	A pesos	n.	B pesos	n.
Alto Peru	Charcas	117	2	300	2	0	0	0	0	0	0	0	0	0	0	0	0
	Cochabamba	1,474	2	3,319	3	0	0	0	0	0	0	0	0	0	0	0	0
	La Paz	1,551	7	352	2	0	0	0	0	0	0	0	0	0	0	0	0
	Potosí	0	0	200	1	0	0	0	0	500	1	500	1	0	0	0	0
	Santa Cruz	50	1	100	2	0	0	0	0	0	0	0	0	0	0	0	0
Río de la Plata	Buenos Aires	0	0	0	0	1,000	1	360	6	223	1	406	2	0	0	2,039	23
	Córdoba	0	0	500	1	0	0	0	0	0	0	150	2	0	0	0	0
	Montevideo	0	0	0	0	0	0	0	0	0	0	0	0	0	0	596	2
	Paraguay	1,940	1	0	0	0	0	0	0	0	0	0	0	0	0	0	0
	Salta	0	0	288	1	0	0	0	0	0	0	288	1	0	0	0	0
No Caja	Jujuy	200	1	0	0	0	0	0	0	0	0	0	0	0	0	0	0
	Misiones	970	8	475	7	0	0	0	0	0	0	0	0	0	0	0	0
	Total	6,302	22	5,534	19	1,000	1	360	6	723	2	1,344	6	0	0	2,635	25

Region	Cajas	Treasury				Tobacco Monopoly				Postal Service			
		A pesos	n.	B pesos	n.	A pesos	n.	B pesos	n.	A pesos	n.	B pesos	n.
Alto Peru	Charcas	50	1	750	8	0	0	0	0	0	0	0	0
	Cochabamba	650	2	470	3	0	0	0	0	0	0	100	1
	La Paz	700	3	0	0	237	*	25	1	0	0	0	0
	Potosí	1,400	5	550	2	0	0	0	0	0	0	0	0
Río de la Plata	Buenos Aires	485	1	2,464	20	0	0	1,884	25	0	0	1,000	8
	Catamarca	0	0	0	0	0	0	0	0	0	0	0	0
	Córdoba	0	0	251	3	0	0	174	3	0	0	50	1
	Paraguay	0	0	830	*	0	0	110	2	0	0	0	0
	Salta	25	1	216	1	0	0	108	1	0	0	0	0
	Santa Fe	0	0	0	0	0	0	560	19	0	0	0	0
	Tucumán	200	1	0	0	4	1	48	1	300	1	100	2
No Caja	Jujuy	40	2	40	2	8	1	8	1	50	1	50	1
Chile	Mendoza	0	0	675	3	0	0	332	13	0	0	0	0
	Total	3,550	16	6,246	43	249	2	3,249	66	350	2	1,300	13

Note: A = one-time contribution; B = annual (eighteen months).

* The sources recorded a lump sum without making reference to the number of donors.

Table 4.3. Donativos and salaries at the Royal Tobacco Monopoly, 1793–1795

Tobacco monopoly offices	Donativo (pesos)	Salary[a] (pesos)	Donativo as percentage of salary
Administrador de almacenes (warehouse administrator), Francisco Castellanos	72	1,700	4
Administrador general (general administrator), Rufino Cardenas	100	1,700	6
Contador general (general accountant), Manuel José de la Valle	200	2,500	8
Contador de libros de almacenes (warehouse bookkeeper), Vicente Falcón	60	800	8
Contador interventor de la adminstración general (accounts overseer), Francisco de Paula Saubidet	72	300	24
Dependiente destinado en la tercena del resguardo (clerk deployed to customs), Juan Gómez	25	250	10
Escribiente (scribe), José Manuel Cárdenas	20	250	8
Interventor de fábricas (warehouse overseer), Francisco Xáuregui	24	300	8
Oficial mayor (major officer), Antonio Paula Marín	96	1,400	7
Oficial primero de la adminstración gral. (first officer in the general administration), Joachin Urdaneta	25	300	8
Oficial segundo de la adminstración gral. (second officer in the general administration), Miguel Goñi	25	350	7
Oficial segundo de tesorería (second officer in the treasury), Bernardo Gonzalez	48	300	16
Oficial segundo primero (second to the first officer), Leon de Altolaguirre	100	800	13
Oficial segundo segundo (second officer), Vicente Capdevilla	72	800	9
Oficial tercero (third officer), Vicente Mariano Reyna	48	500	10
Oficial cuarto (fourth officer), Antonio Cordero	36	400	9
Oficial quinto (fifth officer), Miguel Márquez de la Plata	36	400	9
Oficial del director (officer assisting the general director), Silvestre de Ochagarria	60	600	10
Oficial escribiente del director de fábricas (scribe assisting the warehouse director), Joseph Cevallos	60	600	10
Oficial mayor tesorero interino (interim major treasury officer), José Elizalde	72	350	21
Sobrestante de fábricas (factory inspector), Manuel Frutos	36	400	9
Teniente primero del resguardo (first lieutenant deployed to customs), Ramón Palacios	24	500	5
Tercenista de la administración gral. (wholesaler in the general administration), Manuel de Figueroa	24	400	6
Visitador del resguardo de la capital (inspector deployed to oversee customs in the viceregal capital), Angel Vázquez del Viso	50	600	8
Visitador del resguardo de la ronda volante (itinerant inspector deployed to oversee customs), Joaquín de Vona	12	600	2

a. Socolow, *The Bureaucrats of Buenos Aires*, 166–68.

Table 4.4. Donativos from military and militia personnel, 1793–1795

Region		Military				Militia			
		One-time		Annual		One-time		Annual	
		pesos	n.	pesos	n.	pesos	n.	pesos	n.
Alto Peru	Charcas	0	0	0	0	1,300	2	825	3
	La Paz	0	0	0	0	550	2	0	0
	Potosí	0	0	456[a]	?[b]	1,125	3	4,113	60
	Santa Cruz	0	0	0	0	271	27	221	26
Río de la Plata	Buenos Aires	0	0	0	0	5,074	246	790	6
	Córdoba	0	0	0	0	0	0	700	2
	Montevideo	213	?	0	0	0	0	0	0
	Paraguay	2,927[c]	12	0	0	0	0	0	0
	Salta	674	5	1,033	3	0	0	648	4
	Tucumán	0	0	0	0	200	1	0	0
No Caja	Misiones	100[d]	1	0	0	0	0	0	0
	Total	3,914	?	1,489	?	8,520	281	7,297	102

a. 8th Company of the 3rd Battalion from the Ejército de Buenos Aires.
b. Unknown number of donors (lump sum).
c. 3rd and 4th Partidas de Demarcación (surveyors) deployed for establishing boundaries with Portuguese.
d. Soldier temporarily residing in the area.

Table 4.5. Salaries and donativos from the Cuerpo de Caballería de Blandengues de Buenos Aires, 1793–1795

Number of officers	Ranks	Salary per month (pesos)[a]	One-time donativo (pesos)	Donativo as percentage of salary[b]
1	Sargento mayor (commander)	115	115	100.0
1	Capitán (second commander)	80	80	100.0
6	Capitanes de compañías (captains)	80	50	62.5
6	Tenientes (lieutenants)	40	32	80.0
6	Alferezes (second lieutenants)	35	25	71.5
5	Capellanes (chaplains)	30	20	66.6
5	Cadetes (cadets)	0	10	—
—	Soldados (soldiers)	7	5	71.5

a. Beverina, *El virreinato del Río de la Plata*, chap. 6.
b. AGI, Buenos Aires 120, Duplicado 288; AGNA, IX, 8-7-12.

Table 4.6. Donativos from women, 1793–1795

	Buenos Aires		Charcas		Córdoba		La Paz		Tucumán		Santa Cruz	
	pesos	n.	pesos	n.	pesos	n.	pesos	n.	pesos	n.	pesos	n.
One-time	12,000[a]	2	15,000	1	100	1	2,230	23	210	2	10	1
Annual (18 months)	0	0	500	1	0	0	0	0	0	0	2	1

a. Managed by the consulado of Buenos Aires.

Table 4.7. Donativos from secular and regular clergy, 1793–1795

Region	Caja		Secular		Regular	
			pesos	n.	pesos	n.
Alto Peru	Charcas	A	0	0	0	0
		B	50	1	0	0
	Cochabamba	A	437	4	0	0
		B	1,000	11	0	0
	La Paz	A	12,238	?	0	0
		B	0	0	0	0
	Potosí	A	100	1	0	0
		B	425	4	0	0
	Santa Cruz	A	1,582	25	0	0
		B	1,197	27	0	0
Río de la Plata	Buenos Aires	A	0	0	1,000	1
		B	100	1	0	0
	Córdoba	A	1,990	1	680	3
		B	25	1	0	0
	Salta	A	0	0	400	0
		B	0	0	0	0
	Santa Fe	A	100	1	0	0
		B	250	2	0	0
No Caja	Misiones	A	25	1	203	5
		B	0	0	200	7
Chile	Mendoza	A	6	2	0	0
		B	0	0	0	0

Note: A = one-time contribution; B = annual.

CHAPTER 5

DONATIVOS AND LOANS COLLECTED DURING THE NAVAL WARS AGAINST ENGLAND (1797–1802)

The Naval Wars against England put Spain under increased financial pressure as the superior English navy interrupted trade and the flow of silver from the Americas. In 1798 the crown restructured its debt and issued the Consolidación decrees. In 1804 these measures were also enforced over the Spanish American possessions. It is noteworthy that even under financial pressure the crown did not increase existing taxes, nor did it implement new ones affecting the fiscal status and property rights of lay subjects. Instead, it opted for another donativo. Additionally, during this war the crown openly requested both interest-bearing and interest-free loans. Unlike the loans taken by the crown during the War against the French Convention, however, a large number of the lending operations brokered to finance the Naval Wars against England were negotiated separately from donativos.

This chapter analyzes donativos collected between 1799 and 1801. Through these years, changing political circumstances coupled with warfare prompted the crown to change existing commercial policies. The new commercial policies impacted both donativos and loans. The first section of this chapter discusses financial and commercial policies implemented in the 1790s. The analysis that follows demonstrates that instead of draining specie from the viceregal economy, donativos pumped capital into the areas that benefited from the new commercial arrangements. As in the past, donativos stimulated commercial expansion and regional integration and remained an ineffective tool for transferring funds to Spain. The collection of new donativos included not only transactions in coin but also the issuing and trading of a variety of financial instruments that cleared in the royal treasuries. Additionally, donativos continued to channel power and income toward influential interest groups. Under the new commercial, political, and financial conditions, however, the politics of giving changed and therefore facilitated the advancement of certain powerful groups to the detriment of others.

POLITICAL CIRCUMSTANCES AND COMMERCIAL AND FINANCIAL POLICIES AFFECTING THE COLLECTION OF DONATIVOS DURING THE NAVAL WARS AGAINST ENGLAND

Donativos collected from 1793 to 1795 as well as the new ones collected during the Naval Wars against England (1799–1801) aimed at providing financial support for the crown. The first ones were collected earlier in the cycle of costly Atlantic warfare. However, in 1799, when the second collection started, the Spanish Crown was still struggling to financially recover from the previous war. Consequently, the crown took a more aggressive approach toward mobilizing the monetary resources of its subjects and even offered solid guarantees for the repayment of loans.

In 1798 the king requested from Viceroy Olaguer Feliú "the shipment to Spain of all funds available in the royal exchequer . . . as well as those taken as loans from wealthy [*pudientes*] subjects and corporations [*comunidades*] interested in investing their idle [*parado*] capital."[1] The crown promised to pay 5 percent interest annually backed by royal revenues and rents. The terms of these agreements were similar to those regulating the issuing of juros discussed in chapter 4. Simultaneously, the crown opened the subscription for voluntary donativos and "patriotic" loans and discounted bureaucratic salaries by 4 percent; patriotic loans would be returned with no interest within ten years after the peace was signed. These ordinances additionally made clear that the call went beyond the rich and powerful, as they stated that the king was willing to accept "voluntary donations in coin and jewelry from subjects belonging to all classes and hierarchies [with the intention to extend] the honor of such dignifying service to everyone [but making sure contributors did not] relinquish the capital they need to continue with their businesses."[2] Significantly, the ordinances spoke of "dignifying service" instead of taxation, indicating that even when facing continuous financial challenges, it was not necessarily easy for the Spanish Crown to tax at will. And by requesting donativos and loans instead of imposing taxes, the crown allowed contributors to stipulate the size and value of their contributions. It is also apparent that the king did not want to jeopardize the financial well-being of the contributors and trusted their ability to assess their own capacity to extend financial support to the monarch. Finally, these ordinances indicated that the Spanish monarch was willing to mortgage present and future revenues to back the repayment of loans and donativos.

These royal orders combined the language of contracts and services. In their correspondence and on the decrees issued to publicize the royal will, however, the Rioplatense viceroys emphasized the latter. Interim Viceroy Olaguer Feliú (1797–1799) and his successor, the Marquis of Avilés (1799–1801), regarded this call for financial support as evidence of "the righteousness [*piedad*]" and "benevolence" of the king, who, despite the enormous expenses caused by warfare, "was unwilling to oppress his beloved subjects in Spain and the Americas with new taxes." To the viceroys, this policy additionally provided his majesty's subjects with an instance to "display the love and loyalty they professed for their monarch."[3] Although the crown was under heavier financial pressure, according to the viceroy, the king chose not to tax, although one might question if he actually could enforce new levies over noncomplacent taxpayers.

Moreover, the issuance of these ordinances by both king and viceroy further demonstrates that subjects and monarch negotiated their interests in the fiscal sphere. During the War against the French Convention, subjects took the initiative to bargain by sending to court petitions requesting favors in exchange for their past and current donativos and loans. Later on in the eighteenth century, the crown initiated through royal decrees the discussion over the choices available for donors and lenders willing to finance warfare. These channels of communication proved to be effective. Although (or perhaps because) they perpetuated regional, corporate, and individual tax inequality, they successfully mobilized the subjects' financial resources.

Political circumstances also changed at the turn of the century in part due to the sudden death in office of two viceroys and the inability of the crown to secure long-term appointments for the region. Viceroy Melo de Portugal, who took office in 1795, died in 1797. Field Marshal Antonio Olaguer Feliú, who held the office of subinspector general of the Royal Army, was then appointed as interim viceroy. In 1799 the Marquis of Avilés became the new viceroy, but he only served for two years as in 1801 the crown sent Joaquín del Pino to Buenos Aires to replace him. In early 1804, Viceroy Del Pino died in office and was replaced by another interim viceroy, Rafael de Sobremonte, who was finally confirmed in his position later that year. While the average time in office for the previous viceroys was about five years, at the turn of the century the average term was reduced to about two years, and consequently five different viceroys commanded the region between 1795 and 1804. Moreover, the wars against England also required increased military vigilance along the shores of the Rio de la Plata due to the threat of a naval invasion. Viceroys frequently left Buenos Aires to inspect and direct the troops stationed in Montevideo. While the political leadership and military capacity of viceroys was by then unquestioned, changing local and international circumstances made more challenging their dispensation of royal patronage. More than any other officer, the successful viceroy had to master not only military and political skills but also be capable of exercising financial brokerage. Collections of loans and donativos tested the viceroys' ability to perform that role.

By the 1800s, a decade of international warfare had also affected trade. Normal commercial patterns established by the free-trade decree of 1778 were modified as traditional seaports and sea routes were closed or became unsafe. The English blockade of Cádiz was immediately felt in the Spanish south Atlantic as exports from Buenos Aires fell from 5,479,675 pesos in 1796 to 334,408 in 1797. The prices of imports subsequently soared.[4] That year, the crown legalized the so-called trade with neutral nations, which provided alternative outlets for commodities produced in the region and allowed the importation of foreign goods. This policy attracted to the Rio de la Plata ships from the United States, Denmark, Brazil, and, through neutral intermediaries, even the British, who cut a share of this trade despite their status as a belligerent nation. The new policies additionally encouraged local merchants to explore commercial outlets in the overseas dominions controlled by neutral nations. During these years, Rioplatense merchants expanded their operations not only in Rio de Janeiro and Bahia but also in Hamburg, Senegal, Angola, Mozambique, and Mauritius in the Indian Ocean. Merchants from neutral nations additionally partnered with local tradesmen in purchasing ships, chartering vessels, transferring money, and engaging in contraband trade.[5] While neutral trade represented a threat to both Spanish and local manufactures as well as to the Spanish monopolistic policy, imperial administrators reasoned that, as in the past, when peace resumed Spanish trade would dramatically increase, and the preeminence of Spanish industries over the American markets would be again secured. Above all, neutral trade generated revenue for the crown through taxes and the sale of licenses, which was needed to back the bills the crown had issued against the Spanish American treasuries to pay for its regular expenses in the peninsula.[6]

These new commercial policies provided profitable opportunities for merchants who exported hides, flour, tallow, salted beef, and silver to the newly opened seaports and imported foreign goods and slaves, a trade that, aided by tax breaks, peaked in the region during the 1790s. Trade with neutral nations offered other advantages as well. Routes to neutral seaports were safer and covered shorter distances, making cargoes less likely to spoil. Additionally, this trade was carried out in smaller vessels that required significantly less start-up capital. Thus, merchants who engaged in neutral trade came upon faster, safer, and easier returns. In the Rio de la Plata, the scale of neutral trade demanded a larger stock of ships, and consequently it stimulated the purchase and transfer (*españolización*) of foreign vessels as well as the development of shipbuilding in Paraguay. Shipping gave new impetus to the logging and lumber industries already expanding in this region, which in turn increased the production of rope and cordage used to build and repair vessels.[7]

Simultaneously, merchants from Buenos Aires such as Tomás Antonio Romero, Francisco del Sar, Manuel de Sarratea, and Pedro Duval pioneered the African slave trade and established permanent connections with American and German trading houses. In 1796 merchant Casimiro Francisco de Necochea opened a shipyard in Paraguay, where labor was cheap and forest abundant.[8] In 1799 Necochea additionally promoted the surveying and opening of the small port of Ensenada de Barragán. This harbor soon took its share of the Rioplatense traffic to the detriment of Montevideo. Traders of lesser means profited by exporting local pastoral products to Brazil following the already well-established coastal commerce that linked Montevideo and Buenos Aires to Rio de Janeiro and Bahia, the seaports where they could purchase not only slaves but also sugar, rum, and foreign goods.[9] Trade with neutral nations impacted other regional economies as well by promoting the expansion of cattle ranching in Misiones, Paraguay, and Córdoba and the demand of regional products that served as temporary substitutes for Spanish imports. The price and demand for wine, liquor, dried fruits, and nuts from Mendoza and San Juan, cotton cloth and brandy from Catamarca, as well as hardware (knives, axes), sugar, dyes, and porcelain from Chile increased in the 1799–1801 period, although in the long run these commodities would be replaced by a new flood of *efectos de Castilla*. Between 1798 and 1802, measuring by their tithe outputs, many of these regions experienced unprecedented economic growth.[10]

However, trade with neutral nations did not deliver equally for all. Merchants who were tied to Spain as the main source of their European goods and credit suffered from these polices as it became harder for them to supply the Rioplatense market at competitive prices. Changes in international trade disrupted regional trading patterns, making transactions more unpredictable than in the past. Cycles of market saturation followed by scarcity became the norm, adding new stress to a system reliant on trade credit. Commodity prices rose in the 1790s across the viceregal territory, although in the city of Buenos Aires the effect of trade disruptions combined with a drought took the local prices to usually high levels. Additionally, Spanish credit lines, which had enriched the most prominent members of the Buenos Aires mercantile community since the establishment of free trade in 1778, shrunk or dried up due to payment delays and defaults caused by bankruptcies.[11]

CONTINUITIES AND CHANGES IN COLLECTIONS OF DONATIVOS

Unfortunately, the surviving archival sources for my analysis of the donativo collected between 1798 and 1801 are not as thorough as those for the War against the French Convention (1793–1795). The libro manual recording this donativo did not survive, and the information compiled in the libros de tomas de razón is less detailed than in the previous case. From 1799 to 1801, the treasurers recorded many lump sums without explaining whether they came from one-time or annual donativos, and in most cases they did not provide a detailed list of donors. Occasionally, they recorded the type of transaction employed to collect and transfer donativo funds.

The available data indicate that the changing Atlantic conditions did not hinder the collection of a new donativo (table 5.1). On the contrary, between 1799 and 1801 donativo funds reached 358,246 pesos, an increase of 38 percent over the total donativo collected during the previous war. Donativos per capita leaped from 0.52 pesos for the 1793–1795 period to 0.71 pesos at the end of the century. However, this estimate is probably low as for the latter period the sources did not sort out one-time from annual contributions. It is therefore not possible to prorate annual donativos throughout this war.[12] In any case, the evidence indicates that people still had powerful incentives for contributing donativos in the late 1700s. The less methodical record keeping could also be related to the fact that a large share of these moneys were expected to be spent locally, and thus, viceroys, governors, and treasurers spent less time glossing them. Despite the records' shortcomings, it is possible to partially discern a pattern of donativo transfers and financial instruments that made it possible for these funds to reach the royal treasuries. The records indicate that during this war, significant funds long remained in their treasuries of origin before their eventual transfer to Buenos Aires. In some cases, the funds never left their treasury of origin at all. Finally, a portion of donativo funds flowed into other local treasuries instead of being transferred to Buenos Aires. In sum, donativo funds added capital into regional treasuries and economies.

As in the past collection of wartime donativos, the 1799–1801 donativo funds collected in the Alto Peruvian cajas were trans-shipped to Potosí before they were sent on to Buenos Aires (table 5.1). A few merchant-bankers managed these transactions, including the proxy for the *situadista* Tomas Villota and a handful of Potosí merchants.[13] The treasury receipts indicate that beginning in 1799, donativos from Charcas, Cochabamba, and La Paz had been periodically transferred to Potosí. However, they arrived into Buenos Aires via situados only in 1801, suggesting that those who accessed these funds profited from this capital over a two-year period. As discussed in the previous chapters, this practice was common among merchants who regularly transferred other royal revenues across the different treasuries. In this case, however, the time span was unusually long, as situados were generally sent to Buenos Aires every three or four months. The new cycle of Atlantic warfare best explains this delay. Donativos circulated within the viceregal economic and fiscal space for a longer period of time due to the interruption of shipments of silver across the Atlantic. Thus, war represented an opportunity for profit for merchant-bankers.

Other situadistas transferred donativo funds from Potosí to Buenos Aires, and along this route they additionally collected donativo moneys that had been deposited into the other Rio de la Plata treasuries. For example, in 1799 the situadista Pedro González Rubín brought to Buenos Aires donativos from Salta, Jujuy, and Tucumán, while another situadista, Juan Felix de Ezcurra, did the same for Salta in 1801. Jujuy's and Tucumán's donativo funds had been previously transferred to Salta before being sent to Buenos Aires. Salta and its treasury functioned as a commercial center and financial hub that facilitated the integration of the outer cajas (or *cajas foráneas*), such as Jujuy and Tucumán, into the Potosí–Buenos Aires axis. Finally, a third situadista, Juan Francisco de Miranda, delivered to Buenos Aires 9,679 pesos in donativos from Córdoba. However, the sources do not make clear whether his operations integrated the Alto Peruvian and Rio de la Plata spaces or solely the last leg connecting Córdoba to the viceregal capital.[14]

A few donors from the Alto Peruvian provinces bypassed the situadistas. Instead, they drafted financial instruments against prominent Buenos Aires merchants. For instance, Pedro Vicente Cañete, the legal adviser for the intendant in Potosí, sent to the treasury of Buenos Aires a bill drawn against merchant Martín de Alzaga, while three other vecinos provided similar instruments drawn against Antonio de Las Cagigas, Anselmo Sáenz Valiente, and Ignacio de Rezábal. These examples indicate that by 1799, powerful merchants from the consulado of Buenos Aires not only brokered loans through this corporation but also more broadly by trading commercial paper that made it possible for donativo funds to reach the treasury located in the viceregal capital.[15]

As for the Rio de la Plata treasuries, donativo funds that were not transferred by the situadistas reached the viceregal capital in different ways. The postmaster general continued transferring donativos, although in 1799 he managed exclusively the funds provided by the postal employees from the entire viceregal territory. The treasurers from Catamarca transferred to Buenos Aires a large portion of the funds they collected in donativos (1,720 out of 5,091 pesos) by drafting against merchant Pedro Diaz de Vivar. Gaspar de Santa Coloma was financially responsible for paying into the treasury of Buenos Aires a 10,000-peso donativo contributed by the bishop of Santiago de Chile. Santa Coloma figured among the most prominent merchants of Buenos Aires whose businesses suffered due to the new commercial policies. Through these years, commissions and fees charged for providing financial services became an alternative means to profit, although in his correspondence Santa Coloma expressed a strong preference for trade over finance.[16]

As in the prior donativo collection, the merchants' credit and financial expertise continued binding distant regions and subjects across the viceregal space. Several examples illustrate this trend. For instance, in 1799 Francisco Tadeo Diez de Medina was a creole judge who served and resided in the audiencia of Chile. However, his landed estates and businesses were in La Paz, his family's hometown. Diez de Medina's 2,500-peso donativo was deposited into the La Paz treasury, presumably through the intervention of local merchant-bankers, and transferred to Buenos Aires by either one of the situadistas mentioned previously.[17] Francisco Ibañez, a priest from Santiago del Estero, was another donor whose transaction combined different instruments and connected distant regions within the viceroyalty. In 1799 he contributed a 441-peso donativo by transferring to the treasury an obligation owed by Francisco Garcia Petisco, a landowner from the Banda Oriental. Father Ibañez had extended to Garcia Petisco a loan of 125 pesos. However, it had accumulated interest for almost a decade, and therefore, by 1799 principal and unpaid interest totaled 441 pesos. Garcia Petisco acknowledged this debt although he was unable to meet this payment on call. The treasurers granted him an extension until this donativo contribution finally materialized in the Buenos Aires treasury via the hands of a local merchant, Manuel Ventura de Haedo. In this case, a donativo contribution connected three different regions (Santiago del Estero, the Banda Oriental, and Buenos Aires) and involved the transfer of a credit obligation from a private party to the royal treasury. The merchant who facilitated this transaction presumably collected commissions from all the parties involved.

Manuel Fernandez de Celis, a modest trader from Asunción in Paraguay, also recycled a credit obligation in order to make a contribution to this donativo. In 1799 he signed over to the crown a debt of 40 pesos he had been trying to collect from Bernabé Duarte, a resident from the county (*partido*) of Santiago, also in Paraguay. Fernandez de Celis additionally provided the royal treasurers in Asunción with an itemized copy of Duarte's debt. The receipt included eighteen small transactions of between 4 reales and 7 pesos each, making it apparent that Fernandez de Celis was a retailer (*tendero* or *pulpero*) who, like many others of his class, frequently advanced small loans as well as merchandise on credit. Copies of the original documents involving his donativo were sent to the subdelegado in Santiago, who finally managed to collect Duarte's debt. In other words, Father Ibañez as well as Fernandez de Celis found in donativos not only an opportunity to serve the crown but also the chance to get rid of bad (or slow-paying) debtors. Their cases indicate that donors, unlike taxpayers, not only decided the amounts they wanted to contribute but also the means by which they would make their contributions. These cases additionally serve as examples of the binding obligation contained in donativo-based contracts. As private parties, Ibañez and Fernandez de Celis struggled to collect their debts. By converting them into donativos, they were able to pressure their debtors to repay the loans into the royal treasury. While Ibañez and Fernandez de Celis did in fact relinquish their income, their status as donors presumably increased their present and future bargaining capital vis-à-vis the crown.

In sum, the instruments that made possible the collection and transfer of donativos during the Naval Wars against England were similar to those employed during the War against the French Convention. Over time, however, the amount of funds collected at each treasury changed (table 5.1). Except for those of Charcas, donativos collected in all the Alto Peruvian treasuries were comparatively smaller in 1799–1801. On the other hand, in Chile donativos from Mendoza tripled during the Naval Wars against England, while Santiago sent to Buenos Aires an unprecedented one-time donativo of 12,000 pesos as well as 1,000 pesos annually. Donativos from Córdoba also increased significantly. Those originating in Misiones were augmented almost by 50 percent, while donativos from Paraguay increased more than tenfold, from 7,190 in the 1793–1795 period to 107,587 pesos in 1799–1801. As mentioned previously, these were the regions that profited handsomely from trade with neutral nations, and so we should not be surprised to find in these areas financial instruments as well as capital ready to be channeled into the collection of donativos.

The sources are silent about transfers of donativo funds to Spain throughout these years. The viceregal correspondence does not make any specific reference to this matter. Unlike for the 1793–1795 donativo, the treasurers did not periodically draft summaries of donors to be sent to Spain. As already mentioned, the lack of interest on the part of the royal officers in keeping comprehensive rosters of donors to be sent to the crown suggests that they expected to manage these monies locally. Also, loans and donativos collected in the Alto Peruvian provinces during the Naval Wars against England were "wrapped up" in the masa del común (unglossed lump sums), evidencing that the treasurers in Potosí did not think it crucial to single them out from other sources of revenue they transferred to Buenos Aires.[18] During the 1799–1801 donativo collection, moreover, the viceroy authorized the governor of Paraguay to transfer, within the Asunción treasury, funds that were collected as donativos into the ramo (accounting item) that paid for local military expenses. Instead of leaving for Buenos Aires, these donativos were recycled into the regional economy.[19] Thus, the opportunities for recycling a larger share of revenue locally and regionally increased with warfare.

MISIONES AND PARAGUAY:
DONATIVOS, NEUTRAL TRADE, AND ENCOMIENDAS

Earlier in this chapter, I discussed how trade with neutral nations increased the demand for commodities and labor available in the Guarani missions and Paraguay. Commercial expansion and the collection of substantial donativos, which were pumped into Paraguay and the Guarani missions instead of being sent to Buenos Aires, stimulated agriculture and local industries. These and other circumstances prompted the governor of Paraguay to keep rosters of donors. I was able to locate a variety of archival sources related to the collection and management of donativos in these districts. The analysis that follows links trade with neutral nations with the collection of large donativos. I will also argue that donativos facilitated the ending of the Paraguayan encomiendas, which up to the late eighteenth century continued to provide labor services to both encomenderos and local landowners.

As in the past, donativos collected in the Guarani missions offered a variety of profitable options to the administrador general in Buenos Aires, a position that since 1795 had been in the hands of Manuel Cayetano Pacheco. However, by 1799, due to the jurisdictional changes imposed on the missions, the administrador's access to the mission's funds had significantly diminished.[20] Thirteen pueblos settled on the Parana River fell under the jurisdiction of the governor of Paraguay, and consequently they diverted their donativo contributions as well as their trade toward the treasury located in Asunción (table 5.2). These funds represented almost 73 percent of the total donativos contributed by the Guarani missions between 1799 and 1801. Although the donativo funds managed by Pacheco were comparatively smaller, the financial transactions that made them possible merit discussion as they illustrate the type of businessmen and practices that developed under trade with neutral nations.

Manuel Cayetano Pacheco was a Portuguese merchant who had arrived in the Rio de la Plata in the early 1780s on board a ship captained by Joaquín de Acosta Bastos. This vessel docked in Montevideo by means of a forced *arribada*, the request by a ship in distress to be able to make repairs in port. Once permitted in port, ships requesting *arribadas* engaged in trade as they had permission to auction off their cargoes to pay for repairs. In the Rio de la Plata, arribadas became an excuse commonly used by foreigners to engage in illicit trade.[21] Pacheco and Acosta Bastos's arguments for their arribada must have been at first unconvincing as both men were jailed on the grounds that they engaged in contraband trade. Although they were freed, about a decade of litigation not only in Buenos Aires but also in Spain was needed before they could clear their names and obtain monetary compensation for the merchandise that the port authorities had seized upon their arrival in the Rio de la Plata. In the meantime, Pacheco requested and obtained a *carta de naturaleza* (declaration of citizenship). This practice was common among the Portuguese residing in the Rio de la Plata as it granted them the privileges and rights of Spanish-born citizens. Spanish citizenship allowed Pacheco to enter the military, hold office, and engage in commerce. In 1789 he obtained from Spanish authorities a license to import African slaves, and in partnership with Acosta Bastos, he organized a lucrative trade in Brazilian woods, sugar, rum, and rice. Like other merchants profiting from neutral trade in the 1790s, Pacheco developed a small commercial fleet that included a brigantine, a frigate, and other smaller vessels that had adopted the Spanish flag (españolización) for legally sailing to Brazil, Africa, and Europe. Acosta Bastos also became involved in the administration of the Guarani missions by holding the position of *oficial primero*, which made him Pacheco's right hand. Simultaneously, Acosta Bastos filed his own petition for Spanish citizenship. However, his request encountered administrative obstacles, which he overcame by making a monetary contribution (presumably a donativo or a loan) to the royal treasury for the payment of interest and principal on vales reales.[22] By the early 1800s, Pacheco and Acosta Bastos were prepared to take advantage of profitable bureaucratic appointments, trade with neutral nations, and the collection of a new donativo. Their commercial networks integrated private credit and royal revenue as well as Atlantic trade and shipping in one of the most dynamic regions within the viceroyalty. Ambitious men like Pacheco and Acosta Bastos primarily managed multiple small- to medium-sized transactions. However, as they worked under exceptionally advantageous Atlantic conditions, they became quite prosperous.

In managing donativos, Pacheco employed financial instruments similar to the ones that had been utilized by Diego Caseros when he held the position of administrador general. These instruments included discounts on the salaries of the missions' administrators, priests, and members of the corps of surveyors; bills of payment issued directly against Pacheco; and the auctioning in the Buenos Aires market of donativos in kind (yerba maté, tobacco, and cloth) at premium prices. However, in the late 1790s, and by means of similar transactions, a few merchants from Buenos Aires also extended their financial services to this region and became involved in the transfer of donativos from the missions to Buenos Aires. For instance, Pedro Diaz de Vivar, the recipient of the donativo bill of payment from Catamarca discussed previously, received two smaller ones from Missions Yapeyú (50 pesos) and Salto (43 pesos). Isidro Balbastro and, after Balbastro's death, his son Joseph also received smaller bills from Missions Santo Tomé and La Candelaria. And Marcelino Durán, in partnership with Joseph Antonio Barroso, received cloth and yerba maté also from La Candelaria.[23] Like Pacheco, many of these men represented a rising mercantile class whose smaller-scale businesses thrived under neutral trade policies. Similar to the cases discussed in the prior chapter, donativos lubricated their relatively smaller mercantile operations. Thus, the management of royal revenue remained opened to entrepreneurs of modest means.

It is noteworthy that during the Naval Wars against England donativos collected in Paraguay showed the most impressive increase (table 5.1). However, only half of the funds were collected utilizing financial instruments that cleared in Buenos Aires (54,060 pesos). As for the other half, Viceroy Avilés authorized the governor of Paraguay to spend them locally. Thus, instead of draining capital from this area donativos supported the growth of the regional economy. Additionally, the Asunción caja received a hefty subsidy from donativos collected in the thirteen Guarani missions on the Parana River, which at this time were placed more firmly under the jurisdiction of the governorship of Paraguay (table 5.2). Moreover, almost the entire donativo that originated in Paraguay (100,100 pesos) came from the Paraguayan indigenous communities (table 5.3), evidencing that the benefits of the new commercial policies trickled down.

Unlike the authorities residing in other areas, those in Paraguay drafted comprehensive records of the donativos collected during the Naval Wars against England. In fact, it was Viceroy Avilés who requested from Governor Rivera the submission of copies of all the original receipts and other related documents as part of his inquiry about the funds donated by the indigenous communities from Paraguay and the Guarani missions. Prior to this investigation, Avilés and Rivera had been at odds over the extent of the jurisdiction the governor enjoyed over the ex–Guarani missions as well as the steps to be taken toward the abolition of the encomiendas in Paraguay, a policy Rivera successfully implemented, although without necessarily following Avilés's guidelines.[24] Viceroy

Avilés inquired about the origins of the donativo funds, the instruments employed to meet them, and whether they had encompassed the sale of assets or commodities owned by the indigenous communities. Although he was carrying out mundane administrative procedures, Viceroy Avilés stated on his missives that "the love they [indigenous communities] professed for the monarch as well as their patriotism should not be detrimental to their ultimate well-being [*felicidad*]."[25] The language employed in his missives echoes that of the royal ordinances issued by the monarch to encourage subjects to engage in the politics of giving.

Rivera's reports, as well as the treasurer's receipts from the Asunción caja, reveal that the *administradores* for the indigenous communities or their proxies, that is, the men who were best positioned to tap the communities' resources, managed these contributions.[26] As for sizes (table 5.3), donativos from the Paraguayan indigenous communities ranged from 200 (Ipané) to 18,000 pesos (Caazapá), while those from the Guarani missions on the Parana River (table 5.2) fell between 100 (San Ignacio Miní) and 3,200 pesos (Itapúa). In many cases, the sources made reference to the origins of the funds as well as the transactions involved. According to Rivera, Mission San Ignacio Guazú had sold landholdings for 11,725 pesos out of which it contributed 1,000 pesos in donativos. The receipts from Belem indicate that its 532-peso donativo came from the sale of yerba maté. Others combined a variety of financial instruments, many of which cleared in Buenos Aires. For instance, the community of San Joaquín contributed 15,000 pesos in donativos, the bulk of which (13,400 pesos) was met by a bill issued against the Buenos Aires merchant Alberto Calcena y Echeverria. In order to meet its 20,000-peso donativo, the community of Yutí issued two bills, one of 17,500 pesos against Pedro Martinez Fernandez and another against Pedro Alvarado for the remaining 2,500 pesos. Mission San Cosme engineered a complex financial operation to raise 4,000 pesos for donativos. It negotiated a loan of 3,000 pesos with merchant Pedro Benitez Robles, also from Buenos Aires, which would be repaid in shipments of yerba maté, cloth, and sugar. San Cosme paid for the remaining 1,000 pesos by transferring to the treasury in Buenos Aires the credit instruments it had issued for supplying the corps of surveyors.[27] Similar mechanisms had been employed during the prior wartime donativo, although by 1799 the involvement of third parties was a more frequent event. The more numerous and diverse interests that came together in each transaction demonstrate that fiscal fragmentation created both vertical and horizontal financial bonds.

They also demonstrate that the recycling of credit instruments coupled with the collection of royal revenue made possible the expansion of both domestic and international trade in this borderland region.

However, other missions were not as successful at recycling past-due obligations. Mission Trinidad attempted to transform into a donativo a debt of 114 pesos owed to them by merchant Pedro Nolasco Domeq for cattle and labor they had advanced to him on credit during a trip to Paraguay. Domeq rejected Mission Trinidad's effort to transfer his debt to the royal treasury on the grounds that he had paid for the supplies and services earlier by endorsing another bill originally issued against Mission San Cosme. Upon examining the documents, Viceroy Avilés declared Mission Trinidad's donativo offer null. In 1799 Mission Santa Rosa also attempted to transform into donativos a debt of 1,200 pesos in yerba maté shipments advanced to merchant Manuel del Cerro in 1795. Out of that total, Del Cerro accepted only 370 pesos in past-due payments and made Mission Santiago, the third party involved in this transaction, responsible for the rest. Viceroy Avilés did not admit this donativo either.[28] These cases indicate that not all creditors were successful at transforming past-due obligations into donativos. Nor were royal authorities always capable of enforcing the collection of debts transferred by private parties to the royal treasury. Thus, no uniform policy was enforced over this aspect of the collection of donativos.

As mentioned previously, donativo funds collected in Paraguay did not leave this caja. In June 1799, after discussing the risks and costs involved in shipping donativo moneys downriver to Buenos Aires, Viceroy Avilés authorized Governor Rivera to transfer them within the Asunción treasury from one ramo (donativos) to another (otras tesorerías or real hacienda). This ramo paid for administrative and military expenses, which had soared from the 1770s onward, when the Spanish Crown reclaimed control over this area from both the Portuguese and the Jesuits. While the movement of funds across branches was primarily aimed at simplifying and speeding up the payment of regional expenses, this transaction also demonstrates that, when needed, local officers disbursed royal revenues locally. Thus, local expenses and commercial expansion were prioritized over the financial needs of the monarch at war.[29]

As for the donativos provided by the indigenous communities, during the Naval Wars against England the Guarani missions administered by Manuel Cayetano Pacheco reduced their donativos, while the indigenous communities under the jurisdiction of Governor Rivera (whether in the mission system or not) dramatically increased theirs and even advanced substantial patriotic loans (tables 5.2 and 5.3). As discussed in chapter 4, in the post-Jesuit era a number of Guarani missions successfully profited from new commercial opportunities, while others did not, indicating that the decline of the mission system was a very uneven process. Missions contributing donativos during the War against the French Convention were those that adapted to commercial opportunities, although in the process they might have misused and even depleted their productive resources, including livestock and land. The 1799–1801 donativo contributions made apparent a similar process. Donativo receipts demonstrate that the mission towns obtained their funds from selling landholdings, yerba maté, cloth, and sugar as well as by extending goods on credit not only to the military outposts on the border with the Portuguese but also to other missions. However, the most successful missions were those that were commercially and financially integrated not only with Buenos Aires but also with Asunción.

Paraguayan indigenous communities that had not been under the Jesuit mission system provided labor services to landowners and encomenderos until the early nineteenth century. The decline of the encomiendas in Paraguay has already attracted significant scholarly attention. However, the available works do not evaluate how donativos might have impacted their decline. Based on the evidence related to the collection of donativos during the Naval Wars against England, I argue that these contributions were instrumental in wiping out the encomienda system. Likewise, they allowed Governor Rivera to tighten the royal grip over powerful yet uncooperative encomenderos. The discussion that follows links the end of the encomienda system to the donativo contributed by the Paraguayan Indians between 1799 and 1801.

Two encomienda systems survived in Paraguay into the eighteenth century. *Encomiendas originarias* required the Indians to permanently reside with encomenderos at their places of residence either in the cities or on their rural estates. Indians under this system were compelled to perform all kinds of labor services upon demand and without limitations based on age or sex. *Encomiendas mitarias* provided labor for planting, harvesting, herding, cutting timber, gathering yerba maté, and transportation without permanently changing the place of residence of the Indians in service. By law, only able-bodied young men owed labor services to their encomenderos for a period of sixty days a year, although in reality the demands exceeded the legal limits. The communities that provided labor to the *encomienda mitaria* included Atirá, Altos, Caazapá, Guarambaré, Ipané, Itá, Tobatí, Yaguarón, and Yutí. From the early 1770s onward, the governors of Paraguay had attempted to eliminate both types of encomiendas primarily by enforcing existing legal regulations on these drafts. Despite the tenacious opposition of the encomenderos, governors in Paraguay systematically inspected the indigenous communities bound to this service, forced encomenderos to treat their charges humanly, withheld labor privileges from those who violated the laws, and, more importantly, stopped awarding vacant encomiendas for the regular two-life terms, opting instead for temporary grants.[30]

As table 5.3 demonstrates, the number of Paraguayan encomiendas overall diminished in the last quarter of the eighteenth century. However, those indigenous communities that provided substantial loans and donativos during the Naval Wars against England gave this institution its last blow. For instance, in 1790 Caazapá provided Indian workers for eleven encomiendas. By 1802 it only supplied labor for one, a change I strongly believe was facilitated by the community's donativo of 18,100 pesos contributed in 1799. Throughout the same period, the communities of Yaguarón and Yutí also witnessed significant reductions in the labor services they owed to their encomenderos. Like Caazapá, both contributed donativos and patriotic loans, and in the case of Yutí, by 1802 its labor obligations were completely eliminated. On the other hand, Altos and Atirá, whose donativos were smaller, were less successful in reducing their labor obligations. By 1802 they were still providing labor drafts for six and four encomiendas, respectively.

I have not found any official correspondence or donativo-related documents directly linking these developments. However, Paraguay in the late 1800s was similar to the Andes in the sixteenth century in that the king and viceroys together struggled to put an end to the encomiendas that had been granted to the first conquistadores. In both cases, royal authorities encountered the resistance of powerful encomenderos. In both areas, these power struggles coincided with a period of commercial expansion in which indigenous communities found opportunities for profit. And in both instances, throughout their negotiations Andean and Paraguayan Indians raised their stakes in the bargaining process by offering their financial support to the king.[31] Labor policies enforced by Governor Rivera further support my hypothesis on the elimination of the encomiendas in Paraguay. As encomiendas declined, the number of indigenous free workers increased, which Rivera funneled into the developing industries of the region. Jerry Cooney has argued that throughout the 1790s, the rope and cordage industries as well as shipping and logging enterprises received contingents of Indian workers, especially from Yaguarón and Yutí, two communities that had successfully eliminated their labor drafts. Simultaneously, Rivera made it mandatory for their employers to pay wages and directly deposit their income into the communities' cajas. Employers even complained about the high salaries they were requested to pay for unskilled workers.[32] In my view, Indian salaries coupled with the profits generated by land sales and rentals as well as the income obtained through the expanding trade in yerba maté, hides, and sugar made it possible for these communities to contribute hefty donativos and advance the crown interest-free loans. In other words, by means of the politics of giving, royal authorities took Indian labor and income away from the encomenderos and diverted them toward merchants, industrialists, and the crown. The Paraguayan Indians eliminated their labor services, although at a high cost as in the process they transferred land, commercial profits, and income toward private entrepreneurs and the royal treasury. As in the prior collection of donativos, powerful interest groups, in this case commercial as well as industrial ones, benefitted over the ill-represented ones that paid higher costs for obtaining their rewards. As in the past, the crown arbitrated over competing interests and prioritized those that best served its needs. Moreover, in typical eighteenth-century Atlantic capitalist fashion, commercial opportunities associated with neutral trade contributed to the extinction of encomiendas in Paraguay while they simultaneously made possible the expansion of the slave trade and slavery in other areas of the Rio de la Plata. In Buenos Aires for instance, the increasing availability of slaves in the 1790s transformed labor relations among artisans and the urban plebs.[33] These changes also impacted subsequent collections of donativos.

WHO AND HOW MUCH?
IDENTIFYING THE OTHER 1799 DONORS

Except for Buenos Aires, Paraguay, and, in part, Misiones, Salta, and Jujuy, the surviving records do not provide information about the amount of the individual contributions or the donors' socio-occupational and ethnic backgrounds. However, sources are reliable for interpreting trends and drawing comparisons between this and the prior collection of donativos.

The merchants of Buenos Aires contributed in 1799 another 100,000-peso donativo by means of a lending operation similar to that of 1794. The consulado acted as the financial broker for the crown again and offered its revenue from the avería (the tax collected on the export of silver) as collateral for interest payments to lenders that channeled their capital through the merchants' corporation. The briefs of the consulado meeting held on 31 January 1799 state that "despite its current financial burdens [the consulado] agreed to donate another 100,000 pesos to profess its love for the king and its zeal for the well-being of the state."[34] The language of gift and service reemerged to present this lending operation as morally and canonically legitimate.

During both wars, the merchants of Buenos Aires contributed the same amounts in donativos by engineering similar lending agreements. However, that seemingly consistent attitude disguised a split within the merchant community throughout the 1790s. While the monopolists who dominated the merchant corporation during the first years of its creation constantly petitioned for the abolition of neutral trade, merchants who exported hides and imported slaves supported the continuation of this policy. Later in 1799, a royal ordinance abolishing trade with neutrals reached Buenos Aires, and the argument over this issue divided the consulado into two irreconcilable factions. In spite of the royal order ending neutral trade, merchants who benefited from it obtained from Viceroy Avilés individual extensions of their grants by arguing that their businesses were tied to deals that had been contracted within the legal framework allowing neutral trade. In the early 1800s, local authorities had room to follow their own criteria not only when they decided upon expending royal revenue locally but also when it came to implementing royal ordinances affecting trade.

Factional disputes over trading policies affected the politics of giving in 1799. Merchants who provided funds for the donativo collected during the Naval Wars against England included Manuel Rodriguez de La Vega (20,000 pesos), Anselmo Sáenz Valiente (17,000 pesos), and Manuel de Arana (13,000 pesos). José Martínez de Hoz and Esteban Villanueva also contributed 5,000 pesos each (table 5.4). Together, these merchants supplied 60 percent of the donativo managed by the consulado of Buenos Aires. All of them were members of the monopolist faction that vocally opposed both the slave trade and trade with neutral nations. Their efforts must have been coordinated with those merchants clustered in the consulado in Cádiz as this powerful institution was simultaneously lobbying to abolish trade with neutrals. However, in 1801, under extreme financial pressure, the crown temporarily reestablished trade with neutral nations in order to financially back new drafts it had issued in Spain against the American treasuries. But in 1802 trade with neutrals had to be banned again, evidencing that it continued to be an effective policy for the crown in spite of the objections put forward by merchants of the consulados.[35]

By means of their donativos, monopolists on both sides of the Atlantic had the opportunity to invest significant funds that would otherwise be idle due to the adverse effect the existing policies had on their businesses. However, one wonders if the new trading policies that the monopolists in Buenos Aires opposed so vocally were truly detrimental to their trades, as otherwise they would not have been able to raise such impressive sums. As already discussed in this and the prior chapters, the merchants of Buenos Aires charged commissions and fees when they extended their financial services to other regions within the Viceroyalty of Rio de la Plata. Yet without trade, they would not have been able to collect the avería tax that backed their donativo-based lending operations. Although their businesses combined commerce with lending, their politics revealed that they would rather continue diversifying operations instead of specializing in finance.

The merchants' factional struggles provide an excellent case for analyzing the bargaining strategies of competing interest groups as well as the monarch's arbitrating power both at the imperial and local levels. In the 1800s, under changing Atlantic conditions, the crown prioritized the interests of those entrepreneurs that better served its immediate needs. Through these years, neutral trade policies favored merchants who operated outside the Cádiz–Buenos Aires axis. Competition from the trade with neutral nations prompted the monopolist faction in Buenos Aires to provide a second 100,000-peso donativo. This contribution changed trade policies at court. As previously mentioned, the crown temporarily suspended trade with neutral nations. However, it fell short of affecting local decision making as the viceroy in Buenos Aires continued honoring grants of neutral trade, at least on an individual basis. The monopolists continued their campaigns against their competitors even though the payment of the interest on their prior and newly contributed donativos was bound to the collection of the avería. The surviving receipts indicate that donativo investors punctually received their dividends from the revenue generated by the avería throughout this period in spite of the interruption of monopolistic trading practices.[36] Although they bitterly argued against neutral trade, the financial investments of the monopolist faction depended on the commercial success of the neutral-trade bloc. Monopolists were reluctant to admit this fact. Nevertheless, the politics of giving reveals that the monarch managed to arbitrate over competing interest groups and make them work together to best serve his imperial needs.

In 1799 the list of investors who channeled their funds through the consulado also included one woman, Bernarda Lezica, who shared many characteristics with Josefa Lajarrota, listed among the donors in 1793 (table 5.4). Lezica and Lajarrota were both widows of prominent merchants (Francisco de Segurola and Agustin Casimiro de Aguirre, respectively), and both managed their late husbands' estates. Both also found in the collection of donativos an attractive venture, as they contributed 10,000 pesos each.[37] The remaining funds came from the dean of the cathedral chapter, Pedro Ignacio Picazarri (22,000 pesos), and the rector of the Colegio de San Carlos (8,000 pesos). It appears that after the enforcement of the Consolidación decrees, religious institutions opted for a safe investment brokered by the consulado and backed by the avería instead of advancing funds directly to the monarch.

In 1799, in addition to the merchants of Buenos Aires, thirty-two donors from Paraguay appeared listed on the roster as belonging to the mercantile classes under the general heading of *del comercio*. Together, their contributions totaled 918 pesos, made up of individual pledges that ranged between 2 and 100 pesos (table 5.3). Compared to the donativos provided by the merchants of Buenos Aires, those from Paraguay were negligible, although they indicate that the commercial expansion in this region allowed a group of vecinos to identify themselves primarily as belonging to a mercantile group.[38] Some acted as consignees for the merchants of Buenos Aires. Others were attracted to the logging business, which required relatively little start-up capital (about 1,000 pesos) but yielded up to a 30 percent return on investment.[39] Many of them traded in smaller local stores or peddled around the countryside. Only five among these men were able to contribute 100 pesos in donativos, while half of them could only afford contributions of less than 15 pesos. The most frequent amount was 25 pesos (seven contributions), which matched the mode for the 1793–1795 collection.

During the Naval Wars against England, Spanish vecinos from Paraguay who did not identify their trades contributed a total of 4,413 pesos in donativos. However, their numerous individual contributions were significantly smaller than those from the local merchants. As table 5.5

indicates, one-half of individual donativos from the Paraguayan vecinos fell within the range of 1–5 pesos with the most frequent contribution being 2 pesos (twenty-two contributions). For Paraguayan standards, however, these were substantial donativos as Paraguayan unskilled workers received at most a wage of 2 reales per day.[40] Vecinos of Jujuy collected 1,901 pesos in donativos. However, one individual made the remarkable contribution of 1,000 pesos, while half of the remaining funds fell within the range of 1–10 pesos. The most frequent contribution from this treasury was 6 pesos (eight contributions). Although most donativos from Salta were also small, the mode remained at 25 pesos, the most frequent contribution amount during the War against the French Convention.

While the evidence is incomplete, it indicates that each war presented the Spanish monarchs with the challenge of mobilizing capital not only in the hands of wealthy elites but in those of subjects of reduced means. These modest donors included indigenous communities, retailers, and a variety of middle-class Spaniards. And just as during the prior collection of wartime donativos, ill-represented groups did not generally obtain immediate rewards in exchange for their contributions. At best, they built up bargaining capital for future generations.

Although lacking corporate representation, individual donors who contributed comparatively larger donativos (that is, equal to or greater than 100 pesos) were relatively successful in their bargaining with the crown. In Salta and Jujuy, for example, city councilmen gave donativos that ranged between 100 and 250 pesos. Contrary to the prior collection, these contributions were not managed corporately by the municipalities but rather advanced individually, that is, met by vecinos who served in the cabildo when the crown requested their financial support. Indeed, the cabildo members of Jujuy appeared to be taking the opportunity to perpetuate their families' power as in addition to their individual pledges, two members contributed donativos on behalf of their own children as well. Such was the case of Manuel de La Quintana, *alcalde de segundo voto*, who added to his donativo of 100 pesos three more of 25 pesos each for his three young sons, the oldest of whom was seven. City councilman Alberto Puch, whose own donativo was also of 100 pesos, made a second contribution, equal in value, on behalf of Patricio, his twelve-year-old son. As discussed in the prior chapter, donativo contributions made on behalf of the young offspring of donors were associated with the purchase of futuras.[41] Angel de La Bacena, another cabildo member of Jujuy, contributed the single 1,000-peso donativo. Although he did not add any children to this pledge, his donativo was fulfilled by a bill of payment against his son-in-law, Ignacio Noble Carrillo, and cashed in the Buenos Aires treasury in January 1800. In addition to holding municipal office, these men were powerful landowners and merchants who frequently extended credit to local peasants and militiamen. It should not be surprising that they found in donativos an opportunity to increase their political power and simultaneously recycle capital into their own regional trading networks.[42]

Larger donativos from vecinos residing in Paraguay also initiated negotiations for a variety of royal grants. For example, on the statement sent along with his pledge of 100 pesos, Bernardo de Argana declared that he had been unemployed (*fuera de todo giro*) "ever since he auctioned off the office of Alferez Real." After selling an office, Argana appears to have initiated the bargaining process for the purchase of another one by contributing donativos. In 1799 Blas de Acosta Freyre, a military commander and vecino from Villa Real (located northwest of Asunción), made an exceptionally large donativo contribution of 2,000 pesos. For that purpose, he issued a bill of payment against Josefa Florentina Gomez, the widow of Miguel Gonzalez Noriega, another merchant from Buenos Aires. Along with this donativo, Acosta Freyre requested from the crown the cession of two properties that, according to the petitioner, were located "along the frontier with the infidels" but had been abandoned by their prior owners. Governor Rivera sent Acosta Freyre's request to Viceroy Avilés, who, after cashing the bill issued against Josefa Gomez, instructed the governor to grant hearings to all the parties and decide on the matter.[43] Although the final word on this case is unknown, this example along with the others demonstrate that donativos provided by wealthy individuals facilitated their access to land and offices. This transaction additionally reveals that while the viceroy ultimately accepted Acosta Freyre's donativo, he trusted Governor Rivera for the local administration of royal grants.

Acosta Freyre's donativo was comparatively large not only for Paraguayan but also for viceregal standards, and it was only surpassed by the individual contribution of 3,000 pesos made by the Marquis of San Joaquin y Pastor. The marquis was a nobleman from Valencia who was traveling through Buenos Aires at the turn of the eighteenth century. His donativo was the only one recorded on the 1799 roster drafted for Buenos Aires that did not originate among local merchants or bureaucrats. In Spain, the marquis's family had accumulated an enormous fortune from commerce and lending to the extent that his ancestors were able to purchase a title of nobility.[44] While the sources do not mention whether or not the marquis intended to obtain any grants in exchange for this contribution, it is pertinent to question why a Spanish member of the tax-exempted titled nobility would relinquish 3,000 pesos while traveling through Buenos Aires. Clearly, donativos, unlike uniform taxes, were voluntary engagements that did not impinge upon a donor's status but rather initiated new or cemented old bonds between donors and the monarch.

DONATIVOS AND THE PURCHASE OF OFFICES

In 1799 bureaucrats continued purchasing offices by contributing donativos. Additionally, the treasury summaries (cartas cuentas) indicate that the 4 percent salary discounts were as poorly implemented as during the War against the French Convention.[45] In fact, the uneven implementation of this measure suggests that instead of a uniform holdback, a group of bureaucrats agreed to relinquish a portion of their salaries, while others successfully averted this royal ordinance. Despite these similarities, bureaucrats showed different reactions to the 1799–1801 donativo. First, except for the officers serving in the postal service, the number of bureaucrats contributing donativos in 1799 dropped from the 1793–1795 levels across all government branches and even in the revenue-collection agencies (tables 4.2 and 5.6). Second, fewer officers holding political appointments made annual donativos in 1799. Instead, most of them preferred one-time contributions. Finally, there was an increase in the number of men holding high-ranking judicial appointments who contributed donativos during this war.

As discussed in chapter 4, the offices of the royal postal service were lucrative and continued to be sold by the crown through the 1790s. But during the War against the French Convention, only a small number of officeholders serving in this branch of the administration provided donativos, and the majority of them held high-ranking positions at the central administration in Buenos Aires. Through the 1790s, as domestic trade increased, so did postal traffic, especially in the areas that produced lucrative commodities such as hides, yerba maté, textiles, liquor, and wine. Thus, we may assume that positions in the postal service in places like Córdoba, Catamarca, Paraguay, Mendoza, and Misiones must have become even more lucrative than they were earlier and, consequently, worth preserving through the contribution of donativos (table 5.6).

The 6,000-peso donativo from Viceroy Avilés stands out not only among the political appointments but also because it represented 30 percent of his annual salary. During the War against the French Convention, Intendant Francisco de Viedma and Governor Joaquin de Alós extended their appointments by advancing large donativos. In fact, Viedma held his office for the remainder of his life, while Alós held his until the end of Spanish domination. The scarce paper trail left by Viceroy Avilés's donativo does not make any reference to his political aspirations. However, in 1801 he began his tenure as viceroy of Peru, one of the most prestigious imperial positions. It is noteworthy that officers like Viedma and Avilés, who held leading political appointments and successfully bargained for promotions by means of donativos, also collected substantial donativo funds from the subjects residing in the districts where they served. This fact confirms that ambitious eighteenth-century bureaucrats had to add to their lists of professional skills not only their individual financial resources but also their capacity to mobilize the financial support of others under their command. Viceroy Avilés excelled in this particular task as he collected from the Rio de la Plata almost 360,000 pesos in donativos.

The remaining donativos from political appointees were comparatively modest, although they were typically connected to lucrative positions, explicit requests for advancement, or unusually long tenures in office. For instance, donativos from bureaucrats appointed to Misiones came from Governor Zabala and from eight administradores serving in the now lucrative Guarani missions. In the case of Paraguay, Governor Lázaro de Rivera requested and obtained his position in 1796 after his predecessor's departure for Valparaiso.[46] Born in Malaga, Rivera had migrated to Peru at a young age and graduated from the University of Lima with a degree in geography and topography. In the early 1780s, he received his fist royal commission as a surveyor deployed to Chiloé to assess the island's strategic importance. In 1784, after finishing this mission, he traveled to Buenos Aires, where he was informed that he had been selected for two appointments, the governorship of Mojos as well as the commandership of the 3rd Corps of Surveyors deployed in the frontier between the Spanish and Portuguese territories. Despite the existing scholarly emphasis on the Bourbons' higher administrative standards, Rivera accepted and served in both positions simultaneously for about one year until he decided to keep the governorship exclusively. During Rivera's tenure as governor of Mojos, Ignacio Flores, the president at the audiencia of Charcas, accused him of embezzling royal revenue and ordered his detention. In order to obtain a fair hearing before the viceroy, Rivera escaped the royal prison and traveled undercover to Buenos Aires. Viceroy Loreto heard his case and forwarded it to Madrid. Enjoying the viceroy's patronage, Rivera was confirmed as governor of Mojos and remained in that position until 1792.[47] When his appointment at Mojos came to an end, he moved back to Buenos Aires from where he sent petitions to the court in Madrid requesting employment. In one of them, Rivera mentions that he has already spent 10,000 pesos and invested many years of hard work in serving the king. His service, he writes, made him "deserving of a governorship" such as the one vacant in Paraguay.[48] Once in Paraguay, he added to his service record the 500-peso donativo he contributed during the Naval Wars against England.

As discussed in chapter 4, bureaucrats who simultaneously contributed donativos and held unusually long tenures were utilizing their donativo contributions to purchase offices. This practice continued during the Naval Wars against England. For instance, Juan de La Luz became the governor-intendant in Salta in 1796. In 1799 he contributed 300 pesos in donativos. According to John Lynch, the average tenure in this office was 4.2 years. However, La Luz remained in the same position until he died in 1807, that is, for eleven years.[49] His legal adviser (*asesor letrado*), Tadeo Dávila, provided donativos for both the War against the French Convention and, later, the naval confrontation with England. His double donativo (one of 288 pesos and the other of 200 pesos) probably facilitated his promotion to the governorship of La Paz, a position he obtained in 1805. Finally, Pedro Vicente Cañete, the legal adviser of the intendant of Potosí, contributed 180 pesos in donativos annually. A native of Paraguay with a doctoral degree from the university in Santiago, Chile, Cañete had been successful in obtaining similar positions that required his expertise, both in Buenos Aires (judge advocate) and in La Paz (inspector of accounts). In spite of his legal and accounting competence, Spanish administrators repeatedly complained about Cañete's temper as well as his inclination to upset powerful officers and corporate bodies everywhere he served.[50] Since notary and legal advising positions in the political and judicial branches remained on the market, officers generally accessed them through purchases. However, by the early 1800s Cañete aimed higher by requesting a vacant judgeship in the audiencia of Buenos Aires.[51] Despite his competence, extensive service record, and donativo, Cañete did not obtain this appointment. Instead, he was transferred to Charcas to serve again as a legal adviser, this time for the audiencia.

The rejection of Cañete's petition could be interpreted as evidence of the new Bourbon policies toward judicial appointments. During the "age of authority" (1751–1808), the sale of audiencia positions in the Americas was supposed to be terminated. "Outsiders" (men who were born anywhere but where they served), especially married ones, displaced "native sons" in order to limit the influence of powerful local families over the judiciary. However, the cases I will discuss make clear that the increasing number of judges contributing donativos as well as their involvement in local politics signaled the continuation of practices that had characterized the so-called "age of impotence," which in the past had coincided with recurrent wars and increasing financial demands.[52] Moreover, salary cuts implemented to reduce audiencia expenses empire-wide made the political ground even more fertile for negotiations between the crown and the judges who were contributing donativos.[53] Thus, the challenges of Atlantic warfare turned the administration of justice into a fluid bargaining forum. Yet the professional qualifications for serving in the judiciary remained high.

In 1799, except for the prosecutor and one of the judges, all the ministers serving in the audiencia of Buenos Aires were suspected of advancing the interests of powerful local factions. These "outsiders" with strong local bonds had contributed donativos. After conducting a thorough investigation, Viceroy Del Pino (1801–1804) accused Regent Benito de La Mata Linares of interpreting the royal ordinance that suspended trade with neutral nations in such an original manner as to favor those profiting from this type of trade. Another investigation conducted by Del Pino revealed that *oidor* Sebastian de Velasco had invested directly in neutral trade in partnership with powerful local merchants, even after the renewed ban had been promulgated. Moreover, Judge Tomas de Ansótegui figured among a group of magistrates the viceroy regarded as indulgent toward contraband trade. Oidor Joaquin de Campuzano did not engage in illegal trade, nor did he issue sentences favoring trade with neutral nations. Instead, he had married into a powerful local family even after his request for a marriage license had been turned down.[54]

Judges serving in Buenos Aires were not punished but rather obtained transfers to similar positions and promotions or continued serving in Buenos Aires until the 1810 junta expelled them from the city. It could be argued these magistrates violated administrative standards of conduct and that their donativo evidenced the workings of a corrupt administration. The politics of giving, however, provides an alternative interpretation.

While mandatory donativo contributions representing 4 percent of bureaucrats' incomes were never thoroughly implemented in the Viceroyalty of Rio de la Plata, donativos from judges under investigation did equal 4 percent of their annual earnings. After the enforcement of empire-wide salary reductions, the regent of the audiencia of Buenos Aires received a remuneration of 5,250 pesos annually and made a donativo contribution of 210 pesos per year, while Judges Campuzano, Velasco, and Ansótegui also contributed the same proportion of their reduced salaries (that is, each contributed 140 out of 3,500 pesos annually). The judges who had been investigated by the viceroy contributed their donativos on an annual basis, while those who had not made a one-time contribution. As previously discussed, donors making annual contributions periodically assessed whether they wanted to continue with or terminate their commitments. This option was valuable for the magistrates as they made their donativo contributions at a time in which policies and local politics changed rapidly.

The judges' involvement in setting up the legal framework that facilitated trade with neutral nations provides another angle for understanding the complexities of imperial and local politics. As discussed earlier in this chapter, Viceroy Avilés approved individual grants that made possible the continuation of trade with neutral nations in spite of the royal ordinance suspending such trade. On the other hand, Viceroy del Pino, his successor, favored the monopolist faction and censored Regent La Mata Linares's interpretations of the ban. In order to be politically successful, mercantile interest groups had to be capable of influencing not only the decision-making process at court but also the local execution of the royal will, which required the consent of both viceroys and audiencia judges. This case thus demonstrates that far from being independent administrative chains of command prone to engage in corruption, imperial bureaucracies served as forums for articulating the interests of powerful competing groups. In the end, judges and viceroys who best interpreted and advanced the interests of the crown, both politically and financially, were rewarded. Viceroy Avilés collected an impressive donativo in his district and contributed an equally outstanding one on his own behalf. He was also a skilled politician who made possible the continuation of trade with neutral nations despite the opposition of the monopolist merchants and its prohibition by the crown. When his term in Buenos Aires ended, he was promoted to lead the viceroyalty in Peru. The magistrates who supported trade with neutral nations also continued advancing their careers either in Buenos Aires or in other districts. Judge Velasco retired in Buenos Aires in 1804, while Ansótegui continued serving in the viceregal capital until the junta established in 1810 invited him to leave the city. He returned to the Americas in 1811 to serve as regent in the Audiencia de Charcas and was subsequently promoted to Lima. In 1816 the revolutionary authorities in Peru expelled him from the Americas for a second time. Regent La Mata Linares's career culminated with a high-end appointment in Spain at the Cámara de Indias.[55]

Like the bureaucrats serving in the other branches of the administration, judges were expected to serve the monarch in different ways. Their legal training was an essential feature of their qualifications. But from the point of view of the politics of giving, they were also expected to create the legal environment for the legitimate reconciling of local interest with royal policies. And they were also expected to provide financial support to the crown by contributing donativos.

The statements the judges drafted to declare their intent to contribute donativos also serve as examples of their honed political skills. All of them expressed their commitment to the imperial project and their loyalty and gratitude to the monarch. However, they simultaneously complained about the high the cost of living in the viceregal capital, the recently implemented salary reductions and pension plan, and the fees associated with office holding. Some of them also reminded the king of other family members who had been, continued to be, or would be interested in serving in the royal administration. For instance, prosecutor Joseph Marquez de La Plata made reference to the challenge of "educating and finding a decent career path for his seven children, all of them minors" as well as taking care of his three sisters and nephews, who had also become orphans when their fathers died serving the monarchy during the War against the French Convention. Judge Sebastian de Velasco complained of his current financial situation and stated that with his reduced salary he found it difficult "to keep with decorum" his three sons, two of whom had been serving in the royal army in Spain, while the third one had been pursuing a law career. Additionally, he had been entrusted with the guardianship and material well-being of his two nieces, whose parents had died during the siege of La Paz by the forces of Túpac Katari in the 1780s. Regent Benito de La Mata Linares declared that his donativo aimed to facilitate the "glory and prosperity of the Spanish Army." As if he were justifying his support for neutral trade, he added that in Buenos Aires, subjects were "suffering from the scarcity of everything, which had caused an excessive increase in prices."[56] And Judges Campuzano and Garasa complained about the *media annata* and *montepío* fees as well as the debts they had incurred for traveling to and settling in Buenos Aires in order to serve the king.[57] In other words, while they added their financial support to the list of services they provided to the crown, judges also used the channel opened by the collection of donativos to vent their complaints about the policies they found detrimental to their corporate interests. Their language shows that they raised the stakes in their bargaining with the crown out of the confidence they had acquired from serving at challenging times. While bureaucracies generally created spaces for the political articulation of imperial interests, the judges found their strongest corporate voice during collections of donativos.

The donativo provided by Judge Francisco Tadeo Diez de Medina, who served in Chile, stands out: his 2,500-peso one-time contribution and his 1,000-peso annual donativo significantly exceeded the funds donated by judges serving in the Buenos Aires district. As mentioned earlier in this chapter, he was not a Spaniard but a criollo who belonged to a wealthy family from La Paz. At first glance, his appointment in Chile seems to have followed the rules of the "age of authority," as it was not his native district. However, his lavish donativo appears to have eased his access to this prestigious position. Cañete, the other creole who, during this period, unsuccessfully bargained for a judgeship, had also built an excellent service record. However, his 180-peso donativos did not take him very far. Like the militias that contributed to the donativo for the War against the French Convention, creole legal advisers and judges found that in the late eighteenth century, they had more difficulty successfully engaging in the politics of giving. The growing presence of Spaniards in the military as well as in the royal service forced them to provide the king with increasing services and amounts of capital in order to obtain proportionally smaller benefits.

Contrary to the prior collection of wartime donativos, the number of contributions from the officers holding positions in the customs, treasury, and tobacco monopoly departments significantly decreased (tables 4.2 and 5.6). Throughout the 1790s, bureaucratic advancement in these government agencies became more difficult due to overcrowding. Therefore, we should not be surprised to find only a few officers willing to contribute donativos.[58] The small number of donativo contributions from officers serving in the revenue-collection agencies indicates that by 1799, these profitable positions were already secured in the hands of the current holders, who had contributed donativos during the prior war.

In 1799 all of these trends converged in the customs office of Buenos

Aires. The creation of the Viceroyalty of Rio de la Plata in 1776 followed by the establishment of free trade in 1778 had increased the number of paid and unpaid positions in this agency, which subsequently hired accountants, clerks, tax collectors, and overseers. But despite its early growth, through the 1790s the careers of custom officers stalled.[59] In the 1793–1795 period all twenty-three officers appointed to customs contributed donativos, while in 1799 only three of them had an interest in providing the crown with this type of financial support. Moreover, the few custom officers listed on the 1799 donativo roster found bargaining much harder than in the past. Like the judges, customs officers utilized donativos as channels for communicating with the crown. And following the example of the magistrates, they included complaints in their 1799 donativo statements about the general increase in prices, the fees charged on their offices, and the challenges of maintaining on low-paying salaries the lifestyles that corresponded to their status. A treasurer of the Royal Tobacco Monopoly even bargained for a salary increase, and on his statement he mentioned that officers serving in similar positions in other viceregal capitals were paid better than he was.[60]

The case of Joseph Calderon de La Barca illustrates these developments very well. In 1799 he held the office of second customs inspector (*segundo vista*) in the *aduana* of Buenos Aires. In a crowded agency his slim possibilities for advancement heavily depended on his capacity to serve the king not only professionally but also financially.[61] His 1799 donativo represented 4 percent of his salary, which he voluntarily relinquished by written consent. However, he indicated on the same document that the increase in prices in the viceregal capital and the fees charged to officeholders kept him from contributing a larger donativo.[62] Finally, in order to boost the value of his contribution he added to his statement that during the War against the French Convention his donativo had equaled 8 percent of his annual wages. Despite his efforts, La Barca's financial contributions did not secure him a promotion. The first *vista* position remained, until 1810, in the hands of Juan Francisco Vilanova, who, counting on the support of one of the most powerful local bureaucratic clans, had secured it in 1778 and continued serving in it until the end of Spanish rule. In the early nineteenth century, the politics of giving became more competitive not only for creoles but also for lower-ranking Spanish bureaucrats.[63]

Francisco de Ortega y Barrón's frequent and substantial donativo contributions provide one of the best examples of the strategies employed by officers who had acquired extensive experience in imperial bargaining.

As in the case of other creoles bidding for office, however, only outstanding donativos guaranteed royal favor. As discussed in chapter 4, Ortega y Barrón, as well as the Count of San Miguel de Carma, had unsuccessfully petitioned to be appointed to the intendancy of Cochabamba, which instead remained in the hands of Francisco de Viedma until his death.[64] In spite of this early setback, Ortega y Barrón ultimately landed a prestigious office. In 1797 he became the director general of the Royal Tobacco Monopoly with jurisdiction over the entire Viceroyalty of Rio de la Plata. In this position, he headed an expanding government branch that additionally granted tax exemptions and judicial immunities and provided access to substantial profits.[65] During the Naval Wars against England, Ortega y Barrón voluntarily contributed a donativo equal to 4 percent of his salary of 3,000 pesos. However, the paperwork produced by his numerous petitions for political appointments demonstrates that donativos, coupled with other services, were instrumental to ambitious individuals and families in building their political capital.

Throughout the year of 1795, either Ortega y Barrón or his proxy systematically filed at court (almost on monthly basis) petitions for appointment to different political positions including the intendancies of Cochabamba, Huamanga, Arequipa, Córdoba, Santa Cruz de la Sierra, Puno, and La Paz. The reason behind his tenacious campaign was strong. Based on a juro de heredad (right to inheritance held over an office generally obtained by the payment of substantial donativos) as well as other services provided, including additional donativos advanced to the crown by Ortega y Barrón's ancestors, he owned the office of *contador entre las partes* within the district of the audiencia of Charcas.[66] However, the creation of the Viceroyalty of Rio de la Plata and the subsequent shrinking of the jurisdiction of Charcas diminished the profits generated by this position, which Ortega y Barrón estimated to be in the 50,000-peso range.[67] He probably had access to insider information as he was aware of the ending date for the tenure of each of the offices he requested and made a timely claim in each case. Ortega y Barrón's strategies additionally reveal his preference for long-term investments in royal service over instant monetary compensation, which, according to the records, had been accepted by other officeholders who also found their rights to office challenged by the redrawing of administrative boundaries. While he did not obtain any of the political appointments he requested, the honors and income associated with the directorship of the Royal Tobacco Monopoly must have made this position acceptable to Ortega y Barrón. In 1799 the new war gave Ortega y Barrón another chance to increase his bargaining capital. Following his ancestors' path, he contributed yet another donativo.

The Count of San Miguel de Carma was equally persistent. In 1794 he counted among the bidders for the intendancy of Cochabamba, which remained in the hands of Viedma. In 1803 he was still petitioning for this position, although this time he enjoyed the support of Viceroy Del Pino, who added his recommendation to the count's appeal to court. The written request drafted by the Count of San Miguel de Carma made reference to the merits "he had acquired and inherited" and added to his other qualification the monetary contributions he had advanced "during the past wars with England and France." The donativos he provided throughout a decade of war totaled 2,200 pesos. This amount was substantial, although at court it was not regarded as sufficient to grant a creole the governorship of Cochabamba.[68]

In 1800 the death in office of Angel Izquierdo, the administrador of the customs office of Buenos Aires, opened his position to bidders. Gabriel Güemes Montero, a royal treasurer serving in Salta, was among the petitioners who listed in his request the 108-peso donativo he gave annually to the monarch during the War against the French Convention. Juan de La Luz, the governor of Salta who, as mentioned, had secured his own position for life by contributing donativos, endorsed Güemes Montero's request. Additionally, he counted on the patronage of Viceroy Avilés, who enthusiastically forwarded his petition to court. Despite Avilés's backing, the request of this American-born officer was not granted either.[69]

In sum, donativos provided by officeholders demonstrate that regardless of the general increase in professional qualifications demanded by eighteenth-century bureaucracies, these and other corporate bodies continued to function as channels for bargaining with the monarch. In order to achieve his political and fiscal aims, the king utilized these conduits not only to mainstream political discussion but also to market rewards in exchange for political support. Through these outlets, individuals and interest groups voiced both their common and competing claims. The competition between individuals and groups made it possible for the king to arbitrate and ultimately favor those who best interpreted his policies and served his political and fiscal needs. Within the rules of the politics of giving, the qualifications and political skills of Spanish officeholders made it increasingly difficult and expensive for current and aspiring American-born bureaucrats to bargain successfully with the monarch.

By the late eighteenth century, the crown was collecting extraordinary funds in donativos through a competitive political system.

NO GIFT: THE ECCLESIASTICS' REACTION
TO THE CONSOLIDACIÓN DECREES

In 1799, as I have mentioned, corporate donativos advanced by the cathedral chapter of Buenos Aires were channeled as a loan through the local consulado. In addition to the donativo provided by Father Ibañez, the surviving rosters of donors record only a few individual contributions from religious men. Most of these donors served either in Buenos Aires or in the Guarani missions.

Four members of the cathedral chapter of Buenos Aires contributed individual donativos ranging between 200 and 600 pesos. It is noteworthy that these individual pledges were advanced separately from the funds the chapter invested through the consulado of Buenos Aires. As in the case of the magistrates, individual ecclesiastics utilized this channel of communication with the monarch not only to express their loyalty but also to promote their personal and family interests and voice their concerns. Pedro Ignacio Picazarri, who served as dean of the cathedral chapter in Buenos Aires, gave a one-time donativo of 600 pesos. On the document he submitted along with his pledge, he mentioned that the funds would be delivered through the hands of his nephew, Provost Jose Antonio Picazarri, a rising figure within this powerful clan of clergymen. As members of the local elite, the Picazarris used the means available to them to consolidate and expand their collective influence, which also included actively participating in the politics of giving.[70] Canon Francisco Tuban y Sala defined himself in his pledge documents as a man interested in "enlarging, preserving and making prosperous" the Spanish monarchy. However, due to his illness and medical expenses he split his donativo into two 150-peso installments. Price inflation did not keep Canon Francisco Xavier Divido y Zamudio from supporting the monarch at war either. However, he simultaneously vented important concerns. Moreover, his donativo statement was openly worded as a bargain: "In spite of the increase in prices of the commodities [*generos*] indispensable for keeping myself and my family and the ecclesiastical *media annata* payments [tax on ecclesiastical salaries] that I have to bear [*sufrir*] . . . I commit myself to help the monarch financially during this war [by donating] 200 pesos annually as long as [the monarch] does not impose additional discounts on my income [*rentas*]." Following the rules of the politics of giving, although in an unusually transparent tone, Zamudio made the continuation of his donativo contributions contingent on his obtaining specific grants from the crown. By contributing his donativo on annual basis, he also kept in his hands the capacity to exit this negotiation at any given time.[71]

Unlike in 1794, in 1799 ecclesiastics did not supplement their few monetary pledges with contributions in kind. Moreover, at the turn of the century religious men and women even became shy about their spiritual support. None of the hospital-based orders offered to care for the wounded, nor were chanted Masses, mortifications, or prayers performed for securing God's intervention in favor of the Catholic armies and the glory of the Spanish king. Although it did not automatically imply a feud, their lack of gifts did reveal distance and disfavor. The passing of the Consolidación decrees in 1798 probably explains this attitude on the part of the ecclesiastics as these decrees negatively affected the financial interests of the church in Spain. Although those measures were not extended to the Americas until 1804, this type of behavior on the part of the crown did in fact subvert its customary gift relations with the church, thereby generating uncertainty and mistrust.

DONATIVOS AND LOANS

In addition to donativos, in 1799 the crown opened the subscription to both interest-bearing and patriotic loans. As stated on the royal ordinances discussed at the beginning of this chapter, the former paid 5 percent annually in interest, while the crown would repay patriotic or interest-free loans in full within ten years after signing the peace treaties. As the figures on table 5.7 show, only the cajas of Paraguay and Charcas managed to collect significant amounts in the form of loans. Residents from Paraguay tied their loans to political bargains, and as such they extended them to the crown free of interest. In Charcas, on the other hand, the bulk of the loans extended during this war bore interest. Only 14,500 out of 80,900 pesos collected in loans in the Charcas treasury were lent free of interest, while the rest paid 5 percent annually.

Unfortunately, I was not able to locate a list of lenders. However, it is noteworthy that the loans collected in Charcas were in fact shipped to Buenos Aires along with the situado, while the surviving sources for Paraguay do not provide any details about the transfer of loans other than those that involved bills of payment issued against the merchants of Buenos Aires. Thus, it is not possible to establish whether these funds left this treasury or whether, as in the case of the donativos, they were transferred to another ramo (accounting item) within the same treasury.[72]

CONCLUSION

As Atlantic warfare increased the pressure on imperial finances, the Spanish monarch continued to request loans and donativos. The royal ordinances issued to mobilize the support of the subjects clearly stated that these devices were as far removed as possible from taxes. First, they were not imposed uniformly on the Rioplatense subjects. Second, the assessment of the amounts regarded as fair and legitimate contributions was left in the hands of the donors. Finally, the crown offered existing and future revenue as guarantees for repayment.

The issuance of royal ordinances regarding collections of loans and donativos additionally confirmed that in the Spanish Atlantic, the fiscal sphere constituted an arena of negotiation in which both king and subjects could take the initiative. This channel of representation effectively mobilized financial resources from a fragmented transatlantic monarchy in which subjects retained the power to accept or reject certain contributions. Within this fragmented system, the crown granted regional, corporate, and individual exemptions. This fiscal arrangement created a system in which financially and politically influential subjects wielded sufficient power to limit the king's ability to tax and shape policy independently. However, the king remained the ultimate arbiter for individuals and corporate groups capable of voicing their claims. In fact, this system empowered the monarch to promote the interests of certain individuals and groups at the expense of others. Thus, records of loans and donativos show that revenues increased even while the royal will prevailed, although the monarch was not an independent or autocratic judge but rather one who listened to and mediated among his subjects through a variety of channels. The collection of donativos and loans constituted one of them.

The cases discussed in this chapter illustrate the arbitrating capacity of the Spanish monarch. For instance, the monopolist faction's commercial losses were partially compensated for with financial privileges that came from the revenue generated by the avería, which continued to be earmarked to pay for the interest earned by their past and present donativos. The collection of the avería depended on the export of silver, which, due to the English naval superiority, was primarily carried out through the hands of merchants engaging in neutral trade. And since warfare increased the risks of regular transatlantic trade, the crown had little choice but to open alternative commercial routes to retain its share of the Atlantic commerce. Thus, it opened a legal and profitable trading outlet to the neutral-trade faction. Moreover, the collection of a new donativo coupled with the increased demand for commodities produced domestically gave prominent monopolists the opportunity to trade in commercial paper. This type of investment yielded low but safe returns, generally set at 1.5 percent.[73] As demonstrated by the transactions associated with collections of donativos throughout this period, prominent monopolists like Martín de Alzaga, Gaspar de Santa Coloma, Anselmo Sáenz Valiente, and Antonio de Las Cagigas expanded their financial brokerage beyond the boundaries of the consulado of Buenos Aires and utilized their financial expertise to make possible the transfer of donativos across the viceregal treasuries. Despite these benefits, they continued to advocate for the end of trade with neutral nations, showing their preference for riskier commercial businesses over safer financial investments.

Bureaucrats continued bidding for appointments, promotions, and extensions in their tenures through the bargaining channels opened by donativos. But since the prior collection of donativos had already allowed officers to hold their positions for longer periods of time, by 1799 it had become harder for new bidders to be granted the appointments and promotions they expected and even more difficult for them to obtain a positive response from the crown upon drafting a petition. Heightened competition for appointments increased the requirements for a successful negotiation. By the 1800s, the king promoted the interests of petitioners capable of combining professional qualifications with experience in royal service, the ability to access the highest levels of patronage, a willingness to give (and have given) generous donativos, and the capacity to mobilize the financial support of other subjects. The grants obtained by Viceroy Avilés, Francisco de Viedma, and Francisco Tadeo Diez de Medina as well as the continuous commitment displayed by the members of the Pinedo and Casamayor clans best illustrate these trends.

However, bidders with fewer qualifications were not discouraged by increased competition. On the contrary, they continued bargaining, lured by the prospects of social, political, and financial gains. In other words, by the early 1800s the Spanish monarchical system enjoyed robust and widespread consensus. The negative responses received by Pedro Vicente

Cañete, the Count of San Miguel de Carma, Joesph Calderon de La Barca, and Gabriel Güemes Montero showed not only the limits of an overcrowded system but also the uneven access to information within a competitive and hierarchical order. On the other hand, the donativos provided by the judges serving in the audiencia of Buenos Aires demonstrate that the crown valued their capacity to create the legal and political frameworks that made possible the implementation of imperial trading policies regarded as detrimental to a powerful local merchant group. In the eyes of Viceroy Del Pino, who favored the monopolist faction, magistrates supporting neutral trade failed to perform according to Bourbon bureaucratic standards. However, their advancement at the end of their tenures in Buenos Aires indicates that the monarch strongly disagreed with Del Pino's assessment. This fact did not stop the judges from voicing their dissatisfaction with a higher cost of living in the viceregal capital, the recently implemented salary reductions, and the pension plan. As skilled politicians, they vented these concerns through the documents they drafted to consent to contribute donativos.

The increased costs of warfare additionally opened donativo-based bargaining to donors of lesser means. As stated on the royal ordinances, the crown invited subjects of "all classes and hierarchies" to donate their coin and jewelry. The surviving sources for this donativo do not permit even an approximate head count of donors. However, the trends discussed in this chapter indicate that the redistributive power of donativos continued to attract donors of modest means. Unlike powerful bidders, financially weaker neophytes brought into the redistribution system the capital that was ultimately channeled into the pockets of the most powerful imperial players. Nevertheless, not all small donors gave up their capital. Men like Father Ibañez and the retailer from Paraguay, Fernandez de Celis, recycled into the royal financial system debt obligations that had become too hard to collect.

The politics of giving allowed the king not only to extend his support to and withdraw it from different corporations but also to promote the interests of underrepresented groups against those powerful ones. The Consolidación decrees violated the customary rights held by the Catholic Church, while changing commercial policies mainstreamed competing interests put forward by conflicting merchant factions. Donativos from the indigenous communities of Paraguay facilitated the extinction of the encomiendas while simultaneously strengthening the power of royal officers vis-à-vis the Paraguayan encomenderos. After being transferred to the ramo of real hacienda, the donativo funds from Paraguay paid for the Spanish military presence on the frontier shared with the Portuguese. As we have seen, these funds came from the lands and labor sold by Paraguayan indigenous communities. In other words, ending encomiendas by engaging in the politics of giving might have weakened their own economic survival in the long run.

In summary, the collection of larger donativos did not imply the implementation of rapacious policies or an increase in the amount of silver shipped to Spain.[74] It rather translated into more opportunities for bargaining and for both king and subjects.

Table 5.1. Donativos by treasury, 1793–1795 and 1799–1801

Region	Cajas	Donativos by origin of donor				Donativos by origin of transfer				From Irigoin and Grafe[a]	
		1793–1795		1799–1801		Libro manual		Libros de tomas de razón		1796	1796–1800
		One-time (pesos)	Annual 26 months (pesos)	One-time (pesos)	Annual (pesos)	1793–1795 (pesos)	%	1799–1801 (pesos)	%	Net transfers (pesos)	Net transfers (pesos)
Alto Peru	Arica	0	0	0	0	0	0	0	0	-49,396	-307,091
	Carangas	0	0	0	0	0	0	0	0	-6,855	-98,240
	Charcas	19,954	4,369	31,351	0	16,630	6	0	0	0	0
	Chucuito	0	0	0	0	0	0	0	0	0	-389,534
	Cochabamba	7,160	9,006	12,621	0	600	14	0	0	0	0
	La Paz	38,093	5,604	25,799	0	37,568	0	0	0	0	-1,144,524
	Oruro	0	0	0	0	0	0	0	0	-110,753	-324,613
	Potosí	3,125	9,517	700	180	57,048	22	71,863	20	435,755	831,755
	Santa Cruz de la Sierra	3,321	2,761	0	0	0	0	0	0	0	0
Rio de la Plata	Buenos Aires	111,687	13,838	110,990	2,214	137,572	53	192,802	54	1,111,678	7,162,330
	Catamarca	0	0	5,091	75	0	0	0	0	0	-5,000
	Córdoba	2,920	3,494	17,265	265	4,759	2	16,995	5	0	-12,000
	Corrientes	148	144	0	0	150	0	0	0	-372	-2,814
	La Rioja	0	0	0	0	0	0	0	0	0	-1,184
	Maldonado	0	0	81	0	0	0	0	0	45,358	225,249
	Montevideo	413	861	107,587	0	206	0	0	0	0	0
	Paraguay	5,760	1,430	3,090	0	50	0	66,188	19	56,135	136,495
	Salta	1,579	4,040	162	73	2,055	1	6,263	2	0	0
	San Juan	500	0	514	97	0	0	0	0	7	37
	Santa Fe	772	1,170	457	0	0	0	114	0	3,972	-6,722
	Santiago del Estero	0	0	0	0	0	0	0	0	0	0
	Tucumán	1,518	789	1,317	82	1,245	0	0	0	-3,639	-3,639
No Caja	Jujuy	1,105	141	1,956	25	1,138	0	0	0	0	0
	Misiones	8,677	2,941	17,412	0	1,133	0	0	0	0	0
Chile	Chiloé	0	0	0	0	0	0	0	0	0	17,439
	Concepción	0	0	0	0	0	0	0	0	0	0
	Mendoza	6	1,455	5,632	10	0	0	0	0	20,032	-7,066
	Santiago de Chile	0	0	12,200	1,000	0	0	0	0	0	0
	Valdivia	0	0	0	0	0	0	0	0	96,141	343,603
	Anonymous donor	0	0	0	0	206	0	0	0	0	0
Total		206,738	61,560	354,225	4,021	260,360		354,225	0		

1793–1795 Total: 268,292 pesos

1799–1801 Total: 358,246 pesos

a. Irigoin and Grafe, "The Spanish Empire and Its Legacy."

Table 5.2. Donativos from the mission towns, 1799–1800

Pueblos de Misión						
Under the jurisdiction of Administrador Pacheco			Under the jurisdiction of Governor Rivera			
Pueblos del Uruguay	Donativo (pesos)		Pueblos del Paraná	Donativo (pesos)		Patriotic loan (pesos)
	1793–1795	1799–1801		1793–1795	1799–1801	
Concepción	0	125	Candelaria	0	952	0
De la Cruz	0	293	Corpus	0	500	3,000
San Borja	0	500	Encarnación de Itapua	0	3,284	0
San Carlos	0	350	Jesus	0	160	0
San Francisco Xavier	0	170	Loreto	0	600	1,000
San Jose	0	10	San Cosme	141	4,000	0
San Juan Bautista	1,000	21	San Ignacio Guazú	97	1,000	500
San Lorenzo	300	17	San Ignacio Miní	0	100	100
San Luis	0	160	Santa Ana	0	200	600
San Miguel	1,000	322	Santa María de la Fe	97	1,000	500
San Nicolas	500	312	Santa Rosa	97	0	0
Santa María La Mayor	0	12	Santiago	194	1,200	1,900
Santo Angel	561	0	Trinidad	0	2,000	0
Santos Apóstoles	0	24				
Santos Mártires	0	12				
Santo Tomé	169	0				
Yapeyú	169	145				
Total	3,699	2,473	Total	626	14,996	7,600

Table 5.3. Donativos, loans, and encomiendas from Paraguay, 1799–1802

Pueblos de Indios from Paraguay under the jurisdiction of Governor Rivera										
Pueblos	Donativo 1799–1801 (pesos)	Patriotic loan (pesos)	Number of encomiendas[a]				Type of encomienda[b]	Number of mitarios[b]		
			1688	1778	1790	1802		1774	1802	Increase (%)
Altos	1,455	0	21	8	8	6	Mitaria	848	909	7.1
Atirá	1,970	500	18	6	7	4	Mitaria	903	978	8.3
Belem	532	0	0	0	0	0	NA	0	0	0
Caazapá	18,100	0	27	9	11	1	Mitaria	NA	NA	0
Guarambaré	1,164	0	14	2	2	0	Mitaria	236	486	105.9
Ipané	194	0	16	1	4	1	Mitaria	NA	NA	0
Itá	2,000	0	39	7	10	6	Mitaria	952	1,022	19.9
Itatí	17,500	0	0	0	0	0	NA	0	0	0
San Estanislao	19,700	0	0	0	0	0	NA	0	0	0
San Joaquin	15,000	0	0	0	0	0	NA	0	0	0
Tobatí	485	2,000	7	7	7	5	Mitaria	812	1,102	35.7
Yaguarón	2,000	4,000	13	8	8	2	Mitaria	1,398	1,745	24.8
Yutí	20,000	0	20	6	6	0	Mitaria	NA	NA	0
Total	100,100	6,500	175	54	63	25				

a. Maeder, "La población del Paraguay en 1799."
b. Seager, "Survival and Abolition."

Table 5.4. Contributors to the donativo collected by the consulado of Buenos Aires, 1799

Loan Date	Name of lender	Amount (pesos)	Interest rate (%)
14 February 1799	El Sr. Dean, don Pedro Ignacio Picazarri	22,000	5
	Manuel Rodriguez de la Vega	20,000	5
	Anselmo Sáenz Valiente	17,000	5
	Manuel de Arana	13,000	5
	Bernarda Lezica	10,000	5
	El Sr. Rector del Colegio de San Carlos	8,000	5
	José Martínez de Hoz	5,000	5
	Esteban Villanueva	5,000	5
Total		100,000	

Source: Archivo General de la Nación (Argentina), *Consulado de Buenos Aires*, 4:85–99.

Table 5.5. Donativos by size, 1799–1801

Caja	Paraguay				Salta		Jujuy		Buenos Aires	
Range	Merchants		Vecinos		Vecinos		Vecinos		Vecinos	
	n.	%	n.	%	n.	%	n.	%	n.	%
1–5	4	13	51	49	8	15	12	28	0	0
6–10	4	13	20	19	8	15	9	21	0	0
11–15	8	25	4	4	4	8	6	14	0	0
16–20	3	9	2	2	5	10	1	2	0	0
21–25	7	22	11	11	9	17	6	14	0	0
26–30	0	0	2	1	0	0	1	2	0	0
31–35	0	0	0	0	0	0	0	0	0	0
36–40	0	0	0	0	2	4	0	0	0	0
41–45	0	0	0	0	0	0	1	2	0	0
46–50	0	0	5	5	0	0	2	5	0	0
51–75	1	3	0	0	8	15	0	0	0	0
76–100	5	15	4	4	0	0	4	10	0	0
101–25	0	0	0	0	3	6	0	0	0	0
126–50	0	0	2	1	1	2	0	0	0	0
151–75	0	0	0	0	0	0	0	0	0	0
176–200	0	0	4	4	3	6	0	0	0	0
201–50	0	0	0	0	1	2	0	0	0	0
251–300	0	0	0	0	0	0	0	0	0	0
1,000	0	0	0	0	0	0	1	2	0	0
2,000	0	0	1	0	0	0	0	0	0	0
3,000	0	0	0	0	0	0	0	0	1	100
Total	32	100	106	100	52	100	43	100	1	100

Table 5.6. Donativos from bureaucrats, 1799–1801

Region	Cajas	Political				Judiciary				Notarial				Customs			
		A (pesos)	n.	B (pesos)	n.	A (pesos)	n.	B (pesos)	n.	A (pesos)	n.	B (pesos)	n.	A (pesos)	n.	B (pesos)	n.
Alto Peru	Potosí	0	0	180	1	0	0	0	0	0	0	0	0	0	0	0	0
Buenos Aires	Buenos Aires	6,000	1	0	0	400	1	890	6	0	0	0	0	0	0	284	3
	Paraguay	500	1	0	0	0	0	0	0	0	0	0	0	0	0	0	0
	Salta	500	2	0	0	0	0	0	0	100	1	0	0	0	0	0	0
No Caja	Misiones	770	9	0	0	0	0	0	0	0	0	0	0	0	0	0	0
Chile	Santiago de Chile	0	0	0	0	2,500	1	1,000	1	0	0	0	0	0	0	0	0
	Total	7,770	13	180	1	2,900	2	1,890	7	100	1	0	0	0	0	284	3

Region	Cajas	Treasury				Tobacco Monopoly				Postal Service			
		A (pesos)	n.	B (pesos)	n.	A (pesos)	n.	B (pesos)	n.	A (pesos)	n.	B (pesos)	n.
Buenos Aires	Buenos Aires	400	2	572	4	0	0	268	3	50	2	0	0
	Catamarca	0	0	0	0	0	0	0	0	91	12	75	8
	Córdoba	0	0	0	0	0	0	0	0	70	3	65	2
	Paraguay	300	2	0	0	0	0	0	0	435	6	0	0
	Salta	0	0	0	0	0	0	0	0	200	2	0	0
	San Juan	0	0	0	0	0	0	0	0	162	3	73	1
	Santa Fe	0	0	0	0	0	0	0	0	400	1	0	0
	Santiago del Estero	0	0	0	0	0	0	0	0	16	1	0	0
	Tucumán	0	0	0	0	0	0	0	0	100	2	82	2
No Caja	Jujuy	100	2	0	0	0	0	0	0	0	0	25	1
	Misiones	0	0	0	0	0	0	0	0	130	3	0	0
Chile	Mendoza	0	0	0	0	0	0	0	0	25	1	10	1
	Total	800	6	572	4	0	0	268	3	1,679	36	330	15

Note: A = one-time contributions; B = annual contributions.

Table 5.7. Loans and patriotic loans, 1799–1801 (pesos)

	Buenos Aires		Charcas		La Paz		Paraguay	
	C	D	C	D	C	D	C	D
1797	0	0	0	0	0	0	0	0
1798	0	0	0	0	0	0	0	0
1799	6,098	NA[a]	0	0	3,400	NA[a]	14,594	0
1800	0	0	0	0	200	0	0	14,594
1801	0	0	80,900[b]	80,900	0	0	0	0
1802	0	0	0	0	0	0	0	0

Source: TePaske et al., The Royal Treasuries of the Spanish Empire in America.
Note: C = cargo; D = data.
a. These entries were not balanced out in the original source.
b. Of this amount, 66,400 pesos were interest-bearing loans (5 percent annually).
  The remaining 14,500 pesos were extended as patriotic loans (AGNA, IX, 8-7-12).

REDISTRIBUTION OF POWER AND INCOME AT THE MUNICIPAL LEVEL

During the British Invasions of the Rio de la Plata (1806–1807), the cabildo of Buenos Aires expanded its sources of revenue. The cabildo's extraordinary revenues included not only donativos but also loans and the enforcement of a new excise tax. The invasion of the viceregal city by the English troops additionally ignited an unprecedented political crisis. Viceroy Rafael de Sobremonte's (1804–1807) military failure during the first English Invasion resulted in his ousting. Under the constitutional principles established by Spanish pactismo, the cabildo of Buenos Aires became the legitimate authority. Changing political circumstances made the cabildo of Buenos Aires take on unprecedented financial, military, and political responsibilities. Not only did it prepare and finance the defense of the viceregal capital, but it also became a powerful player in viceregal politics. Thus, the politics of giving changed.

In this section, I will analyze the collection of donativos and loans at the municipal level from 1806 until the Napoleonic occupation of the Iberian Peninsula in 1808–1809. As in the past, donativos (and, after 1806, also loans and taxes) functioned as a mechanism for legitimately distributing power and income among different social groups. At the municipal level, however, the politics of giving was relatively inclusive, so instead of driving political and financial resources exclusively upward, it also benefitted the popular sectors that had been mobilized through the British Invasions of the Rio de la Plata.

"DOLLARS OF BUENOS AIRES"

T he first section of this chapter dis-
cusses the Atlantic and local circumstances that made possible the transformation of the cabildo of Buenos Aires into the legitimate political and
fiscal authority in the region. It is followed by an analysis and discussion
of the extraordinary revenues collected by the cabildo during the British
Invasions. Finally, this chapter compares the viceregal and municipal
politics of giving.

THE RIO DE LA PLATA IN 1806:
WAR AND FOREIGN INVASION

The cycle of warfare beginning in the early 1790s continued into the
nineteenth century. Although the Naval Wars against England ended
with the Peace of Amiens in 1802, two years later Spain was again at war
with Britain and facing even deeper financial disruptions. Diplomatically,
France's preeminence over Spain became increasingly clear. Napoleon,
consul of France since 1799, recognized Spanish Trinidad as a British
possession in 1802. When hostilities between France and Britain resumed,
Napoleon, seeking to raise funds, sold Louisiana to the United States,
disregarding previous agreements with Spain to never dispose of that
territory. Spain managed to maintain its neutrality (at least throughout
1803), though at a high price. Through a secret revision of the Treaty of San
Ildefonso, Napoleon demanded that the Spanish Crown provide an annual
subsidy of £3 million and allow French vessels to be resupplied at Spanish
seaports. Despite this support, England respected Spanish neutrality. But
in 1804, when Napoleon planned to invade Great Britain and counted on
Spanish military assistance, Great Britain declared war on Spain.[1]
The continuation of Atlantic warfare into the early nineteenth century created new challenges for the viceroys appointed to the Rio de la
Plata. Since the territorial defense and internal security of the area were
largely left in the hands of militias, at times of war local officials feared

a British invasion of the Rio de la Plata. From the mid-1780s onward, viceregal authorities reported their concerns to the Spanish court and repeatedly requested reinforcements, weapons, and military supplies. Local military leaders recognized that the number of professional troops and the available equipment were below the standards established by military regulations. For instance, in 1799 Rafael de Sobremonte, who by then served as subinspector general of regular troops and militias (*subinspector de armas*), unsuccessfully requested the posting of 1,059 additional men to complete the number of troops required in the area. In 1802 Sobremonte insisted on this matter, adding in his missives that men from this region were both uninterested in joining the military and reluctant to fulfill their militia service.[2] As demonstrated in the prior chapters, by the early 1800s the rewards and potential for advancement that had made careers in the military and militias attractive had become harder for creoles to obtain. This second exchange between Sobremonte and the minister of war additionally reveals that even under the threat of foreign invasion, the Spanish Crown was unwilling to finance long-term improvements to the existing defensive system in the Rio de la Plata. After all, the Spanish American subjects had successfully repelled the English attempts at seizing Cartagena (1741), Manila (1762–1764), and Havana (1761–1762) by relying on local financial and human resources.

Unlike creoles from the Rio de la Plata, Subinspector General Sobremonte was fully committed to advancing his military career by using all the means the Spanish imperial system offered to ambitious officers. In addition to his training and his professional assessment of the military situation in the area, which he systematically reported to the court, he contributed, voluntarily, 4 percent of his salary in donativos in 1799.[3] Still, in 1802 he had not yet been able to make it onto the list of military men who would advance to the rank of field marshal. Thus, after contributing donativos, he drafted a petition requesting his promotion. Two years later he was finally rewarded not only with the rank of field marshal but also with an appointment as viceroy of the Rio de la Plata, a position he held until 1807. While serving in the highest military and political office in the region, Sobremonte tried for a third time to obtain additional military reinforcements from Spain, arguing that in the event of an invasion, it would be dangerous to arm creoles and castas. Once again, the war ministry turned him down. However, Sobremonte's assessment of the invasion threat and the risks of heavily relying on plebeian militias proved accurate.

Upon hearing that Spain was at war with England, Viceroy Sobremonte decided to send the bulk of his meager number of troops to Montevideo, as it was there that he expected the British landing. He additionally sent patrols to inspect the coastline of the city of Buenos Aires and its hinterland. As a result of these orders, the viceregal capital was left practically defenseless. Late in May 1806, the viceroy received confirmation that an English expedition under the command of Sir Home Popham was sailing toward the Rio de la Plata from recently captured Cape Town. But there was little that he could do to resist the enemy.[4]

On 25 June 1806, British troops led by General Beresford landed in Quilmes, south of the city of Buenos Aires (instead of at Montevideo), and, after quickly defeating the meager local forces, began their march toward the capital. On 27 June, Buenos Aires capitulated and was occupied by the English. While they were subsequently expelled on 12 August, the first defeat did not dissuade the English, and they returned to the region in 1807. The second attempt to occupy the area combined forces from two expeditions, a contingent sent from Cape Town and another one from England, led by General Auchmuty. Both missions were sent to support Popham as the British government was still unaware of his failure. The troops from Cape Town arrived first and landed in Maldonado. After Auchmuty and his men joined them, they marched toward Montevideo, which was besieged and surrendered on 3 February 1807. A month later, a third mission under the leadership of General Whitelocke was dispatched to support Auchmuty, and still another expedition under General Craufurd, although intended for Chile, was rerouted in Cape Town toward the Rio de la Plata. From Montevideo General Whitelocke decided to attack Buenos Aires. On 28 June 1807, the English forces landed in Ensenada, south of the city of Buenos Aires, and advanced toward the capital from the west in three columns. Surprisingly, the city of Buenos Aires successfully resisted the attack. On 7 July 1807, the British capitulated and were forced to leave both shores of the Rio de la Plata.[5]

PACTISMO IN PRACTICE

Both British Invasions of the Rio de la Plata triggered a series of social, military, political, and financial transformations as the people of Buenos Aires mobilized manpower and financial resources first to resist and later to expel the enemy. In this and the following chapter, I will analyze the donativos collected during these years and examine the changes in political leadership and representation that occurred as a consequence of both Viceroy Sobremonte's actions and the rapid militarization of the area.

On 26 June 1806, upon receiving military briefs reporting the defeat of the Spanish army in their initial encounter with the English, Viceroy Sobremonte left the city of Buenos Aires and fled with his family to Córdoba. Accompanied by the cavalry, he took a large portion of his majesty's treasury with him, knowing that otherwise the British forces would seize it. After capturing the city, General Beresford negotiated the capitulation with those authorities he found at the fortress: the military commanders, the audiencia, and the bishop of Buenos Aires. The fourth article of the capitulation stated that the property and religion of the subjects would be respected. However, Beresford demanded that all privately owned vessels as well as the funds belonging to the Spanish king be surrendered.[6]

When General Beresford attempted to enforce this provision, he learned that a significant portion of the treasury had been shipped inland to be disposed of by the fleeing viceroy. He also realized that the authorities that remained in town were unable to order its return as this matter was beyond their jurisdiction. After a bitter meeting between Beresford and the cabildo to discuss this issue, the city councilmen agreed to send a missive to the viceroy requesting the return of the treasury. Otherwise, they feared, "the city would be exposed to even more insults and suffering," a euphemism employed to refer to confiscation of private property on the part of the invaders.[7] Early in July of 1806, the funds of the royal treasury were shipped back to Buenos Aires, and a week later most of it was sent on to England. According to the summary provided by Beresford in a letter sent to Lord Castlereagh, Sobremonte surrendered 1,291,323 pesos out of which 1,086,208 were dispatched to Britain, while 205,115 pesos remained in Buenos Aires to pay for the expedition's expenses. Ironically, the English seized in one blow more funds than the king of Spain regularly obtained out of his viceroyalty.

The shipment from and back to Buenos Aires of the treasury funds proves that authorities serving locally were able to legitimately make decisions regarding the king's moneys. The impressive sum surrendered by Sobremonte additionally demonstrates that the caja of Buenos Aires continued functioning as one of the major beneficiaries of the system of intertreasury transfers that financially held together the Spanish transatlantic monarchy. These facts did not conceal other important issues. Three weeks after the English occupied the viceregal capital, vecinos in

Buenos Aires became aware that they were members of a defeated, headless, and momentarily insolvent body politic. Across the Atlantic, the English celebrated in pamphlets and poetry the arrival of the "dollars of Buenos Aires."[8]

Whether shocked by the events or fearing retaliation, the *porteños* at first cooperated with the aggressor. But as soon as it became known that the English only had a small number of troops (1,641 men) to hold a city of 76,450 people, officials and vecinos began to draft various plans to expel them.[9] Viceroy Sobremonte was among those who planned to recapture the city. However, his previous actions had deprived him of much-needed popularity and political support. Pascual Ruiz Hiudobro, the governor of Montevideo, was also eager to drive out the English, as he was certain that they would take over his city as soon as Buenos Aires was secured. Porteño residents fashioned daring plots that included planting dynamite under the foundations of the fortress and blowing it up and kidnapping General Beresford during his regular horse rides across the city's hinterland. In the end, the plan that succeeded was that of Captain Santiago de Liniers, who, supported by Ruiz Hiudobro, gathered the professional troops remaining in the area and, with the help of volunteers recruited in Montevideo and in the suburbs of Buenos Aires, recovered the capital from the English on 12 August 1806.[10]

The following day, the people of Buenos Aires celebrated the return of the viceregal capital to the legitimate hands of the king of Spain. However, it was already known that fresh troops in support of Beresford were on their way to Buenos Aires. Thus, military and political authorities realized that they needed to mobilize resources and manpower to resist a second invasion. The task was immense and required a strong and committed leadership. Viceroy Sobremonte was unfit for the job as his actions (or rather inaction) during the first English occupation of Buenos Aires had made him extremely unpopular. In his absence, the cabildo of Buenos Aires took the political initiative and entrusted Santiago de Liniers, the military leader who had led the victory against the English, with the task of organizing the defense of the city. Jointly, the cabildo and Liniers began recruiting and training troops and raising the revenue needed to repel the imminent English invasion.

Drawing on the Spanish contractual political tradition, the city councilmen held their first meeting the day after the English were defeated and decided that "in the absence of the viceroy the Cabildo was authorized to call for a general congress of the judicial courts, ecclesiastical, military, and civil estates" for securing the recent victory. As already discussed in prior chapters, pactismo limited both the king's political authority and his subjects' obedience. Subjects could legitimately disobey and even revoke compacts binding them with authorities who violated the principles that sustained and fostered common good. The vecinos of Buenos Aires disapproved of Viceroy Sobremonte's fleeing at the verge of a foreign invasion and subsequently withdrew their obedience to him. The cabildo, which represented the city as an autonomous corporate body, emerged as the legitimate authority in the viceregal capital.[11]

The general congress convoked by the cabildo was held on 14 August 1806 in the city council meeting room. Major judicial, ecclesiastic, military, and administrative authorities as well as a large number of prominent vecinos were invited to participate in this meeting. The armed plebeian groups, who had found in the recent militarization not only a lifestyle but also a source of power, applied pressure by gathering outside the cabildo building. The congress discussed six points presented by the cabildo's notary, and although additional military and financial emergencies were on the agenda, the assembly left those matters in the hands of the Junta de Guerra.[12]

The cabildo, however, had made decisions about how to finance the resistance to an imminent second invasion before the meeting took place. Knowing that the bulk of the treasury had already been shipped to England, the city councilmen decided during the session held on 15 August that "in the lack of any other funds than those that may originate in the generosity of the vecinos, the Cabildo would cover with its own resources the expenses submitted to it."[13] From that day onward, the cabildo of Buenos Aires became the only institution capable of providing the financial resources to pay for the extraordinary expenses that the successful defense of the viceregal capital required. However, as the cabildo's regular revenues were insufficient, the city councilmen collected donativos, requested loans, and established a new excise. Thus, Atlantic warfare did not create the conditions for political and fiscal centralization but rather fragmented the viceroyalty both institutionally and fiscally.

Spanish American subjects generally resisted the imposition of new and uniform exactions as pactismo granted them the right to decide whether the king had a genuine need for imposing new taxes or increasing existing ones.[14] However, when new impositions were regarded as needed and enforced by legitimate authorities, subjects complied with them. In this case, the cabildo abierto, acting as the corporate representative of the community, successfully enforced the new excise, thereby creating a new and reliable source of revenue. In other words, the actions of the cabildo of Buenos Aires demonstrate that in spite of Bourbon centralization, Spanish American municipalities continued enjoying autonomous power to decide upon a variety of issues, including the removal of incompetent royal officers, the imposition of new taxes, and the budgeting for the military defense of the area. Similar to the North American assemblies, representative institutions in the Spanish Atlantic made use of their prerogatives, although they did so to sustain the authority of a monarch they regarded as legitimate.

DONATIVOS COLLECTED BY THE CABILDO: WHO AND HOW MUCH?

The new collection of donativos began on 27 August 1806. Asserting its political authority, the cabildo of Buenos Aires issued a *proclama* intended to mobilize the people's support. Although the first request was addressed only to the vecinos of Buenos Aires, on 26 January 1807 the city councilmen extended their request for funds to the other regions in the viceroyalty and even to the viceroy in Peru and the president in Chile. Soon afterward, subjects from the most distant areas sent funds and weapons to the cabildo of Buenos Aires. Their financial support boosted the finances of the municipality, which thereafter developed a financial system that transcended local boundaries. However, as the representative body of the local community the cabildo lacked the authority to tax beyond its jurisdiction. Nevertheless, by counting on the support, credit, and financial expertise of local merchant-bankers, it managed to transfer to Buenos Aires substantial funds from distant regions within and beyond the territorial confines of the Viceroyalty of Rio de la Plata.

Collections of donativos would continue until 1809. When it became known that Napoleon had occupied the peninsula and held the Spanish monarch captive, however, donativo funds were shipped to Spain to support the junta established in Seville. But most of the revenue collected locally and transferred from other regions to the cabildo of Buenos Aires in 1806, 1807, and 1808 remained in the viceregal capital and was utilized to pay for military expenses.[15] As in the past, an increase in revenue did not automatically imply the shipment of larger amounts of silver to Spain.

Donativos collected in the last years of the Spanish rule were different from the previous ones. Instead of being transferred to the local royal treasury, they were collected and dispensed by the cabildo of Buenos Aires. Additionally, the proclamas issued to excite the loyalty and generosity of the subjects and the lists of donors detailing the amounts of their contributions were published. Although the purpose of this publicity was to further stimulate the support of local and distant vecinos, it incidentally communicated to them that the royal coffers were empty, the capital city defenseless, and the viceregal authority in tatters.[16] Despite the odds, subjects from the Viceroyalty of Rio de la Plata continued supporting their monarch.

The cabildo's treasury records summarize the total funds collected in donativos from 1806 through 1809. The cabildo published a first list of donors and the amount of their contributions in December 1806. Unfortunately, the sources did not record either the transactions or the instruments employed to collect donativos in 1806. The ones collected in 1807 and 1808 were not published, nor were donors identified. However, the place of origin of the funds as well as the transactions employed to transfer them to Buenos Aires can be partially reconstructed from the information available in the briefs of the city council's meetings (*acuerdos del cabildo*).[17]

The figures in table 6.1 illustrate that between 1806 and 1807, when a second English invasion was feared, the cabildo collected the largest sums. Since the 1806 funds were exclusively collected within the boundaries of the city of Buenos Aires, they will be analyzed separately from the other ones, which additionally included contributions from other regions.

At first glance, what stands out about the 1806 donativo is the fact that one single city was able to collect 118,315 pesos in only four months (from late August to December). This extraordinary sum speaks of the legitimacy of the cause, the fear of a second invasion, and the prosperity enjoyed by a city that regularly received subsidies from other treasuries. It also indicates that a fiscal system that relied heavily on flexibility and improvisation was very effective at mobilizing the vecinos' financial support. In fact, per capita donativos increased significantly compared to earlier collections. At the viceregal level, donativos mobilized 0.52 pesos per capita in 1793–1795 and 0.71 pesos per capita in 1779–1801. In 1806, under the leadership of the cabildo but within the boundaries of the viceregal capital, per capita donativos increased to 1.54 pesos. That is, the 1806 donativos per capita doubled and tripled the yields of prior collections.

In 1806 all donativos were collected exclusively on a one-time basis. This practice shows that donativos at the municipal level represented for vecinos primarily a service to the common good rather than the starting point in a long-term process of individual and collective bargaining. Out of 438 contributions, only three relatively smaller ones originated in corporate groups (silversmiths, 112 pesos; the cathedral chapter, 291 pesos; and the Colegio de San Carlos, 100 pesos). The overwhelming number of individual donors additionally indicates that the cabildo was, at the municipal level, the exclusive corporate authority that represented the entire community of vecinos rather than particular interest groups. As in the past, a small number of wealthy donors mobilized remarkable funds, making apparent that unlike taxes, donativos were not uniformly enforced on the vecinos, not even when a foreign invasion was expected.

The surviving records are detailed enough to allow us to compare the size and number of the 1806 individual donativos with the 1793–1795 one-time contributions collected across the viceregal territory. As for the socioracial and occupational backgrounds of donors, the 1806 roster only identified city councilmen, ecclesiastics, and bureaucrats. Despite these shortcomings, I was able to identify the names of *comerciantes* (import and export merchants), *almaceneros* (wholesalers), and *tenderos* (retailers) by relying on different records.[18] Those donors whose occupation could not be identified (275 out of 535 individual donativos) were labeled as vecinos.

Records of donativo funds show that despite the disruptions caused by warfare, commerce was still the most important source of income in this port city as 90,164 pesos or 77 percent of the entire donativo came from men engaged in some sort of mercantile activity (table 6.2). The leading position of the porteño mercantile community confirms a trend already presented by previous donativo collections. However, in 1806 the funds provided by tradesmen followed a different pattern. Instead of investing their "idle" capital through the consulado, these donativos from the merchants of Buenos Aires were directly deposited into the cabildo's treasury. While in 1793 and 1799 a handful of prominent monopolists had contributed donativos of several thousand pesos, in 1806 eighty-four comerciantes, forty-four tenderos, and sixteen almaceneros contributed comparatively smaller amounts. Nine city councilmen serving in 1806 were also merchants. That is, 153 men contributed the bulk of this donativo (table 6.2).

The contributions of merchants ranged between 100 and 3,000 pesos, while 500 pesos was the most common amount they donated (twenty-five contributions). The almaceneros' donativos ranged between 10 and 1,000 pesos, and the most common contribution was 100 pesos (five contributions). The tenderos' donativos spanned between 10 and 1,500 pesos, but their most frequent contribution was 50 pesos (six contributions). These numbers indicate that despite warfare and changing commercial policies, the city of Buenos Aires still prospered from trade. Commerce attracted a variety of entrepreneurs of different means who, despite the volume and size of their businesses and their political differences, were willing to divert their savings to financially support the defense of the city and the preservation of Spanish rule. Their choices indicate that they believed their prosperity depended on the survival of the Spanish Atlantic monarchy.

In the past, a small group among the prominent monopolists found profitable investments in the donativos collected by the consulado. My analysis in previous chapters showed that these transactions functioned as interest-bearing loans backed by the avería. This type of secure investment was available not to just any investor, but only to a select group of merchants who supported monopolist policies. However, in 1806 all merchants, including those who profited from trade with neutral nations, were listed among the donors who financially supported the cabildo. For example, Tomás Antonio Romero, Antonio de Las Cagigas, and Manuel de Aguirre, who were slavers and outspoken supporters of trade with neutral nations, contributed 1,000 pesos each.

Instead of acting as an interest group represented by the consulado, comerciantes (monopolists or not), tenderos, and almaceneros were listed individually alongside other vecinos on the same donativo roster in 1806. Under swiftly changing political circumstances and under the leadership of the cabildo (a corporation they did not control), monopolists changed, at least temporarily, their attitude toward donativos by significantly reducing their pledges. For instance, Gaspar de Santa Coloma, who in 1793 invested 20,000 pesos through the consulado, contributed just 3,000 pesos in 1806. His was the largest single contribution provided by any individual donor. Nevertheless, it was still significantly smaller than his earlier donativo. In 1799 Anselmo Sáenz Valiente's donativo to the consulado's fund was 17,000 pesos, while the one he donated to the cabildo in 1806 was only 2,000 pesos. And Manuel de Arana, who also appeared among the strongest consulado investors in 1799 by pledging a 13,000-peso donativo, in 1806 reduced his contribution to 2,000 pesos. In past

CHAPTER 6

collections of donativos, the consulado offered the merchants corporate representation vis-à-vis the crown and the ability to bargain for financial and political benefits in exchange for their support. At the municipal level, however, that channel for political negotiation was not available. Thus, all merchants, including monopolists as well as supporters of neutral trade, contributed to the 1806 donativo not as investors represented by their mercantile corporation but as individual vecinos. In 1806 merchants did not conceal with their donativos an interest-bearing lending operation. Instead, they financially supported the defense of the region, a duty that vecinos ought to have fulfilled under the principles of Spanish pactismo.

As in the past, most individual contributions to the 1806 donativos (about 70 percent) were equal to or smaller than 100 pesos (table 6.3). However, the 1806 donativo also showed new trends. First, a few donors contributed amounts smaller than 1 peso. Second, while a large number of contributions fell below 100 pesos, the most common contribution among all donors was also 100 pesos (sixty-seven contributions). This figure, which is four times bigger than the most common contribution in 1793, reveals that commercial expansion supported by monopolists and trade with neutral nations, combined with the shipment of subsidies from other treasuries, brought to Buenos Aires a type of prosperity unknown in other regions of the viceroyalty. Finally, donativos equal to or larger than 200 pesos were more numerous in 1806 than in 1793, representing 30 and 15 percent of the total individual contributions, respectively.

It could be argued that affluence was the exclusive patrimony of the commercial classes. However, donativo funds provided by the vecinos of Buenos Aires who were not involved in trade show a similar trend (table 6.3). In 1806 contributions equal to or less than 100 pesos reached 86 percent of the total, a proportion similar to the one found among donors across the viceroyalty in 1793. However, the most frequent contribution was also 100 pesos (forty-one contributions), while individual donativos equal to or larger than 200 pesos represented 13 percent of the total. Whether engaged in trade or not, vecinos from Buenos Aires contributing to these donativos were wealthier than those who supported the crown across the viceroyalty during the previous wars, as they were capable of saving sums that exceeded the annual salaries paid to unskilled workers in the viceregal capital, which, according to recent estimates, ranged between 61 and 140 pesos.[19]

We arrive at a similar conclusion by analyzing the donativos provided by women. Although the number of their contributions was comparatively small (19 out of a total of 534), this was the first time that porteño women appeared listed as individual donors of small- and medium-sized contributions. Their donativos spread across a wide range (between 0.5 and 600 pesos). However, eight out of the total nineteen contributions were equal to or larger than 100 pesos, and the most frequent contribution was also 100 pesos (four contributions). Most of the large donativos came from the wives and widows of prominent merchants, including Josefa Lajarrota, who, following the lead of the comerciantes, opted in 1806 for a donativo of 600 pesos instead of investing, as she did in the past, a large sum through the consulado. The ecclesiastics, on the other hand, had already lost their interest in supporting the king financially after the implementation of the Consolidación decrees. The extension of these ordinances to the Spanish American possessions in 1804 further undercut their assistance. As a result, the 1806 donativos contributed by clergymen were small in size and number and almost insignificant compared to those from earlier collections of donativos.[20] As in 1799, they opted for distance (the lack of a gift) instead of engagement.

Compared to the 1793–1795 and the 1799–1801 donativos, contributions from bureaucrats in 1806 increased in number but not in size (table 6.4). They also followed the pattern set by the 1793 donativo; that is, most contributions originated in the revenue-collection agencies, which, as I have already discussed, were the branches where the largest profits were made. Compared to the donativos collected during the Naval Wars against England, officers serving in these agencies increased the number of their contributions. For instance, in 1806 all but one of the officers serving in customs contributed donativos, while in the treasury, two-thirds of the royal servants contributed as well. The numbers from the tobacco monopoly are deceiving as only two out the twenty-six donors were actually bureaucrats. The remaining donors were *estanqueros*, that is, the shopkeepers licensed to sell tobacco within the boundaries of the city of Buenos Aires.

The five leading officers serving in the customs department of Buenos Aires (the administrator, treasurer, two inspectors, and the overseer) pledged hefty donativos, ranging between 80 and 300 pesos, while the lower-ranking officers afforded smaller contributions (falling between 8 and 50 pesos). It is noteworthy that the leading customs officers received salaries of 2,000 to 3,000 pesos. Their donativos thus represented almost 10 percent of their annual income—a share that significantly surpassed the 4 percent discount to be enforced on bureaucratic salaries. Even the doorman from customs contributed a 1-peso donativo for financing the defense of the city against the English. The accountants from the royal exchequer and the court of audits also made substantial contributions to this donativo, ranging between 100 and 200 pesos.

As discussed in part 1, donativos collected at the viceregal level provided bureaucrats with the opportunity to advance their individual and corporate interests. These donativos additionally concealed the purchase of offices, which resulted in lengthy tenures. Counting among the beneficiaries of the politics of giving as managed at the viceregal or territorial level, royal officers were fully invested in financially supporting the continuation of Spanish rule. Nevertheless, the cabildo of Buenos Aires did not directly represent either their individual or their group interests but rather those of the local vecinos. Thus, the unstable political environment that followed the British Invasions explains the royal officers' interest in contributing donativos at the municipal level.

In 1806, during the brief English occupation of the viceregal capital, the cabildo of Buenos Aires was led by Francisco de Las Llagas Lecica. He was a criollo merchant and outspoken defender of trade with neutral nations. Simultaneously, his cousin Juan José Lecica held the office of prior at the consulado of Buenos Aires. During the English occupation of the viceregal capital, the Lecicas befriended General Beresford. Presumably, they knew that commercial vessels would follow the military expedition into the Rio de la Plata and were eager to take advantage of this unprecedented commercial opportunity. Upon Beresford's request, in fact, the Lecicas recommended men who would serve as customs officers under English rule. The list included the names of prominent slavers and supporters of neutral trade such as José Martínez de Hoz and Ventura Llorente Romero.[21] The Lecicas were willing to use municipal power to remove a branch of the royal administration in order to advance the commercial interests of the neutral-trade faction. The royal officers serving in revenue-collection agencies must have become aware of the Lecicas' intentions. After the English were expelled, the officers contributed numerous and large donativos, not only to court the members of the cabildo but also to fashion themselves as vecinos serving the common good. While they had no guarantee that their financial support would thwart the plans of the Lecicas and their faction, customs and treasury officers presumably thought it was worthwhile to express their allegiance by contributing donativos to the cabildo.

The rise of municipal power indicates that after 1806, it became crucial for interest groups to participate in cabildo politics. The English Invasion of Buenos Aires made apparent to the members of the monopolist faction led by Martín de Alzaga the risks involved in leaving the cabildo in the hands of the neutral-trade faction. Thereafter, the monopolist faction became interested in serving in the municipality. Merchants generally regarded holding municipal office as a burden rather than an honorable service to their local community. Indeed, Martín de Alzaga, who enjoyed one of the few grants that exempted vecinos from holding cabildo offices, would be elected as *alcalde de primer voto* in 1807.[22] His presence in the cabildo would boost the municipality's finances, and consequently, from 1807 onward, it would attract donativos not only from the Buenos Aires vecinos but also from the viceroyalty at large. Finally, the presence of Alzaga and other monopolists would also allow the cabildo to collect loans as well as a new excise.

DONATIVOS BEYOND THE CITY BOUNDARIES

As mentioned, the cabildo of Buenos Aires expanded the collection of donativos to the viceregal territory and, beginning in 1807, even beyond the viceregal boundaries in order to cover the extraordinary expenses incurred during the British Invasions. The cabildo treasury summaries indicate that donativos collected that year totaled 98,103 pesos. These records do not mention the place of origin of the funds or the transactions involved in transferring them to the viceregal capital. But based on the information recorded during the cabildo's meetings (*acuerdos*), I was able identify the origin and the transactions that made possible the collection of 83,265 out of the 98,103 pesos. The available information is displayed in table 6.5.

The cabildo of Buenos Aires became capable of expanding its fiscal capacity beyond the boundaries of the viceregal capital only when merchants who supported monopolist trade filled most of the municipality's seats. In 1807 the appointment of Martín de Alzaga to the office of alcalde de primer voto coincided with the election of Anselmo Sáenz Valiente and Esteban Villanueva as city councilmen.[23] Their presence in the municipal corporation generated confidence among those committed to supporting the Spanish monarch outside the city limits. Simultaneously, they inserted the cabildo into their far-reaching financial and commercial networks and boosted its solvency by collecting donativos and a new excise. Soon after they placed it within larger and more solvent financial networks, the monopolist merchants started to extend loans to the municipality.

As table 6.5 illustrates, the transfer of donativos from distant regions to Buenos Aires was carried out with the cooperation of prominent merchants from the viceregal capital. And, as in the past, they found in the transfer of donativo funds opportunities to capitalize and expand their businesses by simultaneously trading multiple financial obligations and by charging commissions for coin arbitrage. The information compiled in table 6.5 shows that large and small donativos collected outside the city were denominated in gold. As noted in the prior chapters, transfers in gold coins and gold disks generated commissions proportional to their karat. Additionally, donativos that came from the Alto Peruvian provinces and the Viceroyalty of Peru were first routed to other treasuries before they reached Buenos Aires, indicating that the bills of payment issued for the transfer of funds simultaneously pumped financial resources into the existing commercial routes. In many cases, donativos from one area encompassed the issuance of several bills. For instance, the 3,000-peso donativo from Cochabamba was transferred to Buenos Aires by the issue of two bills of payment, one against the merchant Sebastian de Torres and a second one against merchant and city councilman Martín de Alzaga. Continuing with established patterns of revenue collection and transfer, the postmaster general in 1807 also traded donativo bills from Arequipa in the Viceroyalty of Peru. Since his financial and trading networks overlapped with the relay system, the postmaster general was probably better positioned than average merchant-bankers to safely transfer funds that originated beyond the boundaries of the Viceroyalty of Rio de la Plata.

Anselmo Sáenz Valiente, another prominent merchant supporting the monopolist faction, developed the most extended financial web associated with the collection of donativos in 1807. Similar to the postmaster general's network, Sáenz Valiente's reached far into the Viceroyalty of Peru. He not only traded the majority of bills issued to collect the 1807 donativo but also engaged in transactions that required the coordination of several obligations at once. For instance, in March 1807 the cabildo of Buenos Aires had learned that the governor and cabildo of Potosí had collected donativos as well as received donativo transfers from other treasuries. These funds had been collected to support the war efforts against the English occupation of the viceregal capital. However, the governor and cabildo of Potosí were reluctant to transfer these funds to Buenos Aires unless they received the explicit approval of the viceroy. News about the institutional struggles taking place in Buenos Aires, especially the removal of Viceroy Sobremonte's military command, had reached Potosí, making the Potosino royal officers uncertain about the political intentions of the institutionally legitimate but politically independent cabildo of Buenos Aires. As such they continued to withhold the donativo funds. The viceroy of Peru adopted a similar position and communicated to the cabildo of Buenos Aires that donativos would only become available to the viceroy. The attitude of these royal officers reveals that viceregal patronage was essential not only to keep networks of loyalty in place, but also to enforce intertreasury transfers. Merchant Anselmo Sáenz Valiente engineered the financial solution to free up at least the donativo funds delayed at the Potosí treasury. He advanced 6,755 pesos to the cabildo of Buenos Aires, took a bill from it, endorsed it, and sent it to his business partner in Potosí, Juan de los Santos y Rubio. For this transaction, he charged the cabildo a 1.5 percent commission. That bill enabled Santos y Rubio to withdraw donativo funds from the Potosí treasury and simultaneously inject a financial instrument into Sáenz Valiente's trading network in the Alto Peru. Since a large share of the funds was denominated in gold, Sáenz Valiente additionally obtained commissions in coin arbitrage.[24]

In sum, these transactions reveal that men like Sáenz Valiente were aware that their prosperity and social existence were contingent on the continuation of Spanish rule over the Viceroyalty of Rio de la Plata. Merchant-bankers made their living and profited from the financing of a composite, decentralized, and transatlantic fiscal and commercial system. Finally, the ousting of the legitimate viceregal authorities must have made them aware that that it was crucial not only to capitalize but also serve in the cabildo of Buenos Aires, which after the British Invasions started to function as the de facto treasury for the viceroyalty.

TAXES AND LOANS

In its efforts to finance the imminent war with the English, the cabildo of Buenos Aires also established a new excise and solicited loans. Although borrowing and taxing counted among the legitimate prerogatives of the cabildo, during these years of political crisis the scale of its operations soared. On 30 September 1806, the cabildo started collecting a new excise on sugar, wine, and liquor, which generated additional revenue to be dispensed by the municipality. The tax schedule shows that this tax was designed to encourage the consumption of Spanish and domestically produced commodities, and it discriminated against those that reached the viceroyalty through trade with neutral nations. The new excise collected 2 reales per arroba on domestic and 6 reales per arroba on imported sugar. Domestic and Spanish liquor was taxed 12 reales per barrel, while liquor imported from non-Spanish territories was taxed 4 pesos per barrel. Domestic and Spanish wines were taxed at 6 reales per barrel and imported wines 2 pesos per barrel.[25]

The sources do not reveal any information about the bureaucratic structure deployed to efficiently collect this tax. Nevertheless, it yielded increasing revenues annually (table 6.6). Compared to the revenue generated in the viceroyalty, the excise performed very well. In the eighteenth century the Viceroyalty of Rio de la Plata generated 4.29 pesos per capita in revenue, while in 1808 the excise collected in the city of Buenos Aires generated 121,490 pesos, that is, a per capita revenue of 1.7 pesos.[26] The revenues produced by the excise tax demonstrate that the cabildo was capable of financing its debt by creating an exaction that affected consumption instead of property or income. Moreover, the income yielded by this tax, especially between 1807 and 1808, indicates that it was not resisted. While the imperial finances collapsed, the cabildo of Buenos Aires paradoxically strengthened its revenues, and, by relying on the income generated by the excise and donativos, it simultaneously developed an efficient system to finance the unprecedented military expenses.

Prior to 1806, municipal borrowing had never surpassed 20,000 pesos per year.[27] Additionally, most of the funds came from modest lenders who expected annual interest payments and/or the rapid repayment of their principals, typically in one or two years. After the first English Invasion, the size of the loans as well as the profile of the lenders changed. As the figures on table 6.7 show, in the course of three years, the cabildo collected from lenders 829,100 pesos. These were interest-free loans also known at the time as patriotic loans or *suplementos*, and the repayment of the principal was guaranteed by the Potosí situado. In other words, city councilmen paid for daily and extraordinary municipal expenses with the revenues generated by the cabildo (including donativos and the new excise), while simultaneously the Potosí situado paid loans back to lenders, the majority of whom were merchants of the monopolist faction. This policy was implemented after monopolist merchants started serving as city councilmen.

Table 6.7 also shows that the majority of cabildo lenders were prominent merchants who, during the British Invasions, opted for capitalizing the cabildo instead of searching for loan opportunities in the consulado. Additionally, corporate institutions such as the Real Compañía de Filipinas and even the consulado of Buenos Aires, loaned their entire treasury deposits to the cabildo. The financial decisions made by merchants during collections of donativos demonstrate that under the new political circumstances, they preferred to fund the municipality instead of the consulado.[28] For instance, Manuel de Arana, Esteban Villanueva, José Martínez de Hoz, and Anselmo Sáenz Valiente, who figured among the largest contributors to the 1793 and 1799 donativos brokered by the consulado, were listed in 1806–1808 among the most generous patriotic lenders. As discussed in chapter 2, donativos facilitated open-ended bargaining, while loans (mutuum) created stricter contractual obligations. Since the cabildo not only represented the merchants' interests but those of the entire community, the merchants preferred a "harder," legally binding type of arrangement to channel large funds into the municipality's coffers. They avoided canonical sanctions by extending to the municipality interest-free loans. Yet the capitalization of the cabildo was critical not only to pay for extraordinary military expenses but also to make possible the successful circulation of financial instruments issued to transfer donativo funds from distant regions to the viceregal capital. These instruments circulated through networks of trust, trade, and credit created and sustained by the merchants of Buenos Aires. In other words, trade, credit, and revenue collection continued to be intertwined, although in the early 1800s they converged in the cabildo of Buenos Aires instead of in the royal treasury or the consulado.

I was unable to find sources on interest-free loans other than their notation on the cabildo minutes. However, one transaction did receive more attention on the part of the city councilmen and, therefore, produced additional paperwork. This transaction further illuminates the policies enforced by the monopolist faction after they took control of the cabildo.[29] The 40,000 pesos the consulado of Buenos Aires loaned free of interest to the municipality originated in the confiscation of the cargo of a ship caught in contraband trade (table 6.7). The vessel was the frigate *Maria*, which belonged to Tomás Antonio Romero, and it had been captured by a corsair. The cabildo asked Anselmo Sáenz Valiente, who acted as proxy for the corsair's captain, to negotiate with Romero the transfer of those funds from the consulado to the cabildo's treasury.[30]

Other financial details of the transaction are unknown. However, it is clear that monopolists serving as city councilmen took various steps to capitalize the municipality, including transferring funds from other institutions such as the consulado. Moreover, the cabildo's capitalization caused financial loses to slavers like Romero—whose property had been confiscated—while simultaneously discriminating against merchants who traded with neutral nations by taxing their imports at a higher rate.

The cabildo of Buenos Aires additionally received funds loaned at a 5 percent annual interest rate. These sums were modest compared to those provided through patriotic loans (table 6.8). Most of these funds were from traditional cabildo lenders who expected the punctual payment of interest and repayment of their principal in three to four years. Many of these loans were advanced by the tutors of minors who invested capital inherited by their wards or by husbands seeking to increase the size of their wives' dowries.

In both cases, most of the loans managed by the cabildo were collected upon the request of the royal treasurers who, facing mounting bills and shrinking funds to disperse, turned to the municipality for help. Requests of funds from the royal administration reversed the trend of previous years when the cabildo relied on transfers from the royal treasury for financing its own projects.[31] Remarkably, discredited royal officers did not attempt to raise funds themselves but rather trusted the cabildo's recently acquired leadership and prestige to respond to their urgent financial needs. The cabildo's expanded fiscal capacity (manifested in the collection of loans, donativos, and the enforcement of the new excise) provided the municipality with the financial backing needed to secure the servicing and repaying of impressive loans. Thus, through these turbulent years the cabildo functioned as the main financial broker for the crown as it collected funds destined to pay not only for the expenses incurred by the city of Buenos Aires but also those of the viceregal administration. Moreover, no portion of these funds was shipped to Spain, and consequently they boosted the municipality's financial independence as well as local and regional trade and manufactures.

The cabildo's financial brokerage was sustainable due to the involvement of the merchants of Buenos Aires who, by means of their financial expertise and political experience, plugged municipal finances into the viceregal and transatlantic system of trade and revenue. While the excise and the 1806 donativos were collected locally, donativos that followed came from distant regions. Transferring these funds required trade in financial instruments endorsed by the merchants of Buenos Aires. After they boosted the municipality's finances, merchants began lending impressive funds to it. Yet the loans they advanced after 1806 were free of interest and backed by the Potosí situado, which continued to be transferred to the Buenos Aires treasury through the networks of trade and credit the merchants controlled and trusted. Thus, monopolist merchants deployed different strategies in lending to different corporate institutions. Unlike the consulado, the cabildo did not exclusively represent their corporate interests but those of the vecinos at large. Thus, they did not call this transaction a donativo, nor did they initiate negotiations vis-à-vis the cabildo. Instead, they boosted the cabildo's finances and participated in municipal politics in order to secure the continuation of the Spanish rule over the region and simultaneously enforce policies detrimental to merchants engaged in neutral trade. In the post–British Invasions political conjuncture, the cabildo instead of the consulado became the institution that best served the short-term interests of the merchants of Buenos Aires.

Although impressive, the financial resources managed by the cabildo were quickly depleted as they were destined to pay for a rapidly growing military budget. Yet prior to the wars of independence, men serving in the cabildo of Buenos Aires displayed honed political, administrative, and financial skills. The cabildo's annual income and expense summaries provide additional evidence for the city councilmen's financial competence (table 6.9). Although the cabildo's revenues grew steadily from the beginning of the nineteenth century, in the triennium of 1806–1808 its expenses swelled. However, the municipality managed to raise sufficient funds to pay for the extraordinary expenses caused by the British Invasions of Buenos Aires and even kept a positive balance through those difficult years and beyond.

Unfortunately, we have no records accurately itemizing the cabildo's expenses for 1806–1808. The cabildo's *propios y arbitrios* only provide yearly totals, and the acuerdos recorded the expenses the municipal officers agreed to pay for. For several items, the acuerdos do not reveal the amounts and dates of disbursements. However, the available information sufficiently documents the new role taken on by the cabildo. Immediately after the English were expelled, the municipality began paying for military salaries, uniforms, supplies, dowries for orphaned children, pensions for widows of soldiers who died defending the city, and medicine to care for the wounded (table 6.10).

Following the British Invasions of the Rio de la Plata, the cabildo of

Buenos Aires functioned not only as the de facto viceregal treasury but also as the institution that facilitated the transfer of income from consumers, donors, and taxpayers toward the recently created racially heterogeneous plebeian militias that received pensions, dowries, and salaries from the municipality. In other words, at the municipal level the politics of giving benefitted vecinos who served the common good, whether or not they were also donors.

CONCLUSION

During the British Invasions, the cabildo of Buenos Aires emerged as the only institution capable of meeting unprecedented military and financial challenges, as, in the absence of imperial authorities, it was the only institution capable of legitimately representing the local community. In order to finance warfare, the cabildo called for a congress to debate and agree on the policies to be implemented. The congress, or cabildo abierto, gathered representatives of the commercial elites, religious corporations, military leaders, and royal judicial authorities. The recently created plebeian militias followed this debate from outside the building, and according to several witnesses, they pressured the elites to depose Viceroy Sobremonte. As a second English Invasion was expected, the congress additionally made decisions on how to finance the defense of the city. By agreeing to collect donativos and loans, the congress continued with the customary practices regularly implemented by the Spanish Crown during times of financial distress. The outcome of the donativo was predictable: a small fraction of the population agreed to advance to the cabildo substantial funds. Unlike the prior collections of donativos, however, vecinos set aside their corporate identities, and the majority of them contributed as individual members of the community represented by the cabildo.

Also unlike prior collections of loans and donativos, petitions drafted by prominent corporate groups requesting royal favor did not follow the British Invasions of the Rio de la Plata. In fact, there was no room for this type of bargaining since the cabildo emerged as the leading institution throughout this process. Nevertheless, the cabildo represented a community that was unequal and hierarchical. It rewarded those vecinos who served the common good by paying for the provisioning, outfitting, and salaries of the standing militias and by giving away pensions and dowries to veterans, their widows, and orphans. As discussed in the following chapter, these resources were allocated following racial and social hierarchies.

The cabildo also innovated as it established an excise. The new excise was not resisted. On the contrary, it yielded significant funds that allowed the cabildo to strengthen its finances and simultaneously take sizeable loans. However, the cabildo was not completely financially independent as it backed its loans with future situados. Nevertheless, the cabildo emerged as major financial broker for the crown. It taxed, it collected donativos, it administered the situado, it took loans, and, last but not least, it took full responsibility for all the bills generated throughout the British Invasions.

The rise of the cabildo of Buenos Aires additionally strengthened the leadership of the viceregal capital over the viceregal territory. This trend began with the Bourbon reforms but accelerated with the imperial and revolutionary wars of the early nineteenth century. As we have seen, in 1807 the cabildo received substantial donativos from distant regions in the viceroyalty as well as from the Viceroyalty of Peru and the presidency of Chile. The strength displayed by the municipality in the early nineteenth century was the outcome of a process that began in the last decades of Spanish rule. While bureaucratic reforms aimed at tightening the grip on the imperial administration, local, corporate, and representative institutions were not wiped out but rather plugged into wider networks of power and revenue. The insertion of the cabildo of Buenos Aires into the viceregal financial system was made possible by the active participation of the monopolist merchants whose businesses held together a composite monarchy. As demonstrated in the previous chapters, the monarchy strengthened old and even created new corporations that were instrumental in achieving its political, economic, administrative, military, and fiscal aims. The cabildo was one more of those institutions. However, since it represented not just one group but all the vecinos, anyone with political ambitions had to secure the loyalty of its leaders.[32]

Cabildo politics was more complex than consulado politics as it represented the interests of the entire community of vecinos. Additionally, city councilmen served for only one year, and although they could be reappointed, their continuation in office was not guaranteed. The monopolist faction was well aware of that fact, and immediately after the English were repelled, they started to serve in the cabildo. In fact, the presence in the cabildo of prominent members of the mercantile community such as Martín de Alzaga, Anselmo Sáenz Valiente, and Esteban Villanueva turned the municipality into an efficient treasury. The financial capital, credit, and expertise commanded by these men made it possible for the cabildo to collect donativos beyond the city boundaries, enforce the new excise, and raise impressive loans. In sum, the king needed the partnership of his most wealthy subjects to survive politically and financially.

However, the members of the monopolist faction seized the cabildo not only to provide financial services for the crown but also to isolate and punish the faction supporting trade with neutral nations. From the municipality, and with the purpose of protecting and promoting communal well-being, they taxed commodities imported through neutral trade at a higher rate than those produced locally and imported from Spain. They additionally transferred to the cabildo treasury funds originating from the auction of confiscated goods brought into the region through trading practices they considered illegitimate.

Far from isolating Spanish American subjects and institutions, Atlantic warfare created many opportunities for partnership and profit. Groups and institutions whose interests became more tied to the financial support of the crown advocated strongly for the preservation of Spanish rule. Simultaneously, military service opened for plebeian groups new channels to serve the king and preserve his rule. Thus, warfare did not turn the Spanish monarchy into an oppressive or more absolutist system. Instead, warfare created new and expanded existing channels through which Spanish American subjects actively sustained a system that represented their interests. Once articulated through the cabildo, these channels widened to include the non-elites.

Table 6.1. Donativos collected by the cabildo of Buenos Aires, 1806–1807

	Totals from propios (pesos)[a]	Totals in pesos (donor or transaction known)
1806	113,957	118,315[b]
1807	98,103	83,265
1808	32,012	30,620[c]
1809	300	0
Total	244,372	332,200

a. *Cuenta general de cargo y data, 1806–1809*, in AGNA, IX, 19-9-5; IX, 19-10-1; and IX, 19-10-3.

b. Donativo collected in Buenos Aires in 1806 (*La reconquista y defensa de Buenos Aires*, 271–76).

c. *Acuerdos del extinguido cabildo*, series 4, vols. 2 and 3.

Table 6.2. Donativos by socio-occupational group in pesos and percentages, 1806

Socio-occupational categories	Pesos[a]	Percentage
Comerciantes	63,620.00	55
Vecinos	18,515.25	16
City councilmen (merchants)	13,300.00	11
Tenderos	10,553.00	9
Bureaucrats	3,954.00	3
Ecclesiastics	3,722.00	3
Almaceneros	2,691.00	2
Women	1,748.50	1
Silversmiths	112.00	< 1
Colegio de San Carlos	100.00	< 1
Total	118,315.75	100

a. Several pledges were smaller than 1 peso; thus, donations were not rounded up (4 reales made 0.5 pesos, and 2 reales made 0.25 pesos).

Table 6.3. One-time donativos by size, 1793–1795 and 1806

	1793 One-time		1806 All		1806 Vecinos			1793 One-time		1806 All		1806 Vecinos	
Range	n.	%	n.	%	n.	%	Range	n.	%	n.	%	n.	%
< 1	0	0	9	2	9	3	276–300	11	2	19	4	5	2
1–5	85	14.0	87	16	58	21	301–350	0	0	2	< 1	0	0
6–10	109	18.0	59	11	35	13	351–400	6	1	4	1	1	< 1
11–15	60	10.0	15	3	10	4	500	16	3	43	8	7	3
16–20	39	6.0	32	6	22	8	600	1	< 1	2	< 1	1	< 1
21–25	95	15.5	27	5	19	7	700	1	< 1	1	< 1	0	0
26–30	3	0	9	2	6	2	800	1	< 1	1	< 1	0	0
31–35	2	0	4	< 1	3	< 1	900	0	0	0	0	0	0
36–40	2	0	17	3	8	3	1,000	6	1	16	3	3	1
41–45	0	0	3	< 1	0	0	1,500	0	0	15	3	0	0
46–50	68	11.0	42	8	25	9	2,000	6	1	9	2	0	0
51–75	5	1.0	1	< 1	0	0	2,500	0	0	0	0	0	0
76–100	49	8.0	70	13	44	16	3,000	1	< 1	3	< 1	0	0
101–125	5	1.0	1	< 1	0	0	4,000	1	0	0	0	0	0
126–150	3	< 1.0	9	2	3	1	5,000	0	0	0	0	0	0
151–175	3	< 1.0	2	< 1	0	0	6,000	5	1	0	0	0	0
176–200	19	3.0	24	5	15	6	7,000	0	0	0	0	0	0
201–225	1	< 1.0	6	1	< 1	< 1	8,000	1	< 1	0	0	0	0
226–250	2	< 1.0	3	< 1	1	< 1	9,000	0	0	0	0	0	0
251–275	0	0	0	0	0	0	10,000	3	< 1	0	0	0	0
							15,000	1	< 1	0	0	0	0
Total	550	90	420	78	258	94		60	10	115	22	17	6

Table 6.4. Donativos from bureaucrats, 1793–1795, 1799–1801, and 1806

Buenos Aires	Political				Judicial				Customs			
	One-time		Annual		One-time		Annual		One-time		Annual	
	pesos	n.	pesos	n.	pesos	n.	pesos	n.	pesos	n.	pesos	n.
1793–1795	0	0	0	0	1,000	1	360	6	0	0	2,039	23
1799–1801	6,000	1	0	0	400	1	890	6	0	0	284	3
1806	0	0	0	0	582	2	0	0	1,258	27	0	0
Number of bureaucrats, 1803	15				19				28			

Buenos Aires	Treasury				Tobacco Monopoly				Postal Service			
	One-time		Annual		One-time		Annual		One-time		Annual	
	pesos	n.	pesos	n.	pesos	n.	pesos	n.	pesos	n.	pesos	n.
1793–1795	485	1	2,464	20	0	0	1,884	61	0	0	1,000	8
1799–1801	400	2	572	4	0	0	268	3	50	2	0	0
1806	1,970	43	0	0	144	0	0	0	0	0	0	0
Number of bureaucrats, 1803	64				26				9			

Table 6.5. Donativos collected by the cabildo of Buenos Aires, 1807

Region/Contributor	Pesos	Instrument, Merchant, Coin
Andahuaylas, vecinos	1,000	Routed to Potosí; bills and gold traded by Sáenz Valiente; bill against Jose Manuel Ocampo.
Arequipa, vecinos	7,095	Bill of 1,992 pesos against Juan Antonio de Lecica, another bill against Lucas Islas Valdes, the rest managed by the postmaster general.
Buenos Aires, vecinos		
Domingo Achaval	500	
Esteban Villanueva	2,500	
Gabriel Real de Azua	1,080	
Jose Antonio de Irigoien	200	
Jose Rubio	48	Traded in gold.
Juan de la Grava	500	
Juan Evangelista Terrada	400	
Manuel Alvarez	400	
Manuel Jose Ocampo	1,000	
Mariano Antesana	500	
Cabildo of Tarija	860	Bill against Martínez de Hoz.
Catamarca, vecinos	1,603	Several bills, merchants not named.
Charcas		
Marques Valle de Toxo	1,000	Bill against Sáenz Valiente.
Lawyer from La Plata	200	Bill against Sáenz Valiente.
Vecinos	4,031	Bill against Sáenz Valiente.
Chile		
Presidency of Chile	10,229	1,000-peso bill against Manuel Ortiz Basualdo.
Bishop of Chile	194	Unknown.
Chucuito, vecinos	1,458	Routed to Potosí, freed by Sáenz Valiente.
Cochabamba, vecinos	3,000	Bill issued against Sebastian de Torres.
	500	Another bill issued against Martín de Alzaga.
Córdoba, vecinos	4,378	Several bills against Buenos Aires merchants.
Corrientes, vecinos		
Isidoro Martinez	1,000	Bill against Matias Cires.
Governor of Arequipa	1,000	Routed to Puno.
Huamanga, vecinos	7,000	Routed to Cuzco.
Jujuy, vecinos	1,025	Bill against Dionisia Chaurri, widow of merchant Agustin Pinedo.
La Rioja		
Cabildo	100	Bill against Esteban Villanueva.
Vecinos	802	Unknown.
Mendoza		
Clergy	300	Bill against Pedro Garcia Díaz.
Vecino	120	Bill against Pedro Garcia Díaz.
Oruro, vecinos	2,028	Deposited by the postmaster general.
Paraguay		
Bishop of Paraguay	500	Bill against Juan Bautista de Otamendi.
Vecinos	6,839	Twelve bills against merchants from Buenos Aires.
Potosí, vecinos		
Jose Santos Rubios	194	Gold traded by Sáenz Valiente.
Luis de Orueta	500	Bill against Tomas de Balenzategui.
Tomas Mealla	100	Endorsed bill against Martínez de Hoz.
Manuel Rodo	100	Endorsed bill against Martínez de Hoz.
Baltasar Arce	50	Endorsed bill against Martínez de Hoz.
Mariano de Ibarguren	200	Gold traded by Ortiz Basualdo.
Juan de Ibieta	194	Gold traded by Vicente Echeverria.
Patricio Torrico	70	Unknown.

continued on page 192

Table 6.5 continued

Priest of Tapacari	150	50 pesos in gold and one bill for 100 pesos.
Regidor and Cabildo Pilasa y Paspaya	700	Bill against Sáenz Valiente.
Salta, vecinos	10,205	4,225-peso bill against Ignacio de Rezábal.
Santa Fe, vecinos		
Mariano Comas	100	Bill against Sáenz Valiente.
Francisco Antonio Candioti	1,000	Bill against Lecica.
Santiago del Estero, vecinos	1,849	Several bills, merchants not named.
Subdelegado Pacages	200	Gold traded by Damian de Castro.
Tucumán, vecinos	628	Bill against Manuel Posse.
Viceroyalty of Peru		
Archbishop of Lima	2,000	Deposited in local treasury at disposal of viceroy.
Ecclesiastical cabildo of Lima	2,000	Deposited in local treasury at disposal of viceroy.
Total	83,265	

Table 6.6. Revenue collected through the new excise tax, 1806–1809

Year	Pesos
1806 (three months)	4,413
1807	53,413
1808	121,490
Subtotal (1806–1808)	179,316
1809	91,006
Total	270,322

Source: Ensink, Propios y arbitrios del cabildo de Buenos Aires.

Table 6.7. Patriotic loans collected by the cabildo of Buenos Aires, 1806–1808

Date	1806	Pesos
5 September	Esteban Villanueva	20,000
30 October	Martín Gregorio Yániz, two loans	20,000
		40,000
	Subtotal 1806	80,000
	1807	
28 January	Consulado[a]	40,000
16 June	Joaquín de Arana	1,400
	José Xavier Amenábar	2,000
	Joaquín Pinto	3,000
	Juan Evangelista Terrada	3,000
	Diego Agüero	4,000
	Jaime Alsina	4,000
	Ramon Ximénez	4,000
	Francisco Tomás de Estrada	5,000
	José Ramón de Ugarteche	6,000
	Manuel de Aguirre	6,500
	Cabildo's own funds	8,000
	Francisco de Telleechea	8,000
	Juan José Lecica	8,000
	Tomas de Balenzategui	8,000
	Esteban Villanueva	10,000
	Pablo Villarino	12,000
	Ventura Marco del Pont	13,000
	Juan de Llano	13,200
	Anselmo Sáenz Valiente	18,000
	Manuel de Arana	20,000
	José Martínez de Hoz	32,000
12 August	Francisco Tomás de Estrada	5,000
	Subtotal 1807	229,100
	1808	
22 January	From the Real Compañía de Filipinas	200,000
	Manuel de Arana	20,000
26 March	Collected among vecinos[b]	200,000
12 May	Collected among vecinos[b]	100,000
	Subtotal 1808	520,000
	Total 1806–1808	829,100

Source: Archivo General de la Nación (Argentina), *Acuerdos del extinguido cabildo de Buenos Aires*, series 4, vols. 2 and 3.
a. Funds confiscated from a ship involved in contraband trade.
b. Names of and amounts provided by individual lenders unknown.

Table 6.8. Interest-bearing loans (at 5 percent annually) extended to the cabildo of Buenos Aires, 1807–1808

Date	1807	Pesos
3 June	Juan José Ignacio de Gardezábal's tutor, on his behalf	4,000
12 August	Francisco Tomás de Estrada, from his wife's dowry	5,000
	José Laguna, from his wife's dowry	11,000
2 September	Antonio Cordero, from his wife's dowry	1,000
	Dolores Segurola's tutor, on her behalf	8,000
	Subtotal 1807	29,000

	1808	
20 January	Esteban Romero	10,000
22 January	José Laguna	6,000
1 February	Fernando Domato's tutor, on his behalf	150
	Subtotal 1808	16,150
	Total 1807–1808	45,150

Source: Archivo General de la Nación (Argentina), *Acuerdos del extinguido cabildo de Buenos Aires*, series 4, vols. 2 and 3.

Table 6.9. The cabildo of Buenos Aires's income and expenses by year, 1800–1809 (pesos)

Year	Income	Expenses	Balance
1800	26,725	16,050	10,675
1801	26,532	19,389	7,143
1802	37,777	21,979	15,798
1803	44,514	42,026	2,488
1804	43,875	42,000	1,875
1805	157,894	134,468	23,426
1806	337,641	306,641	31,000
1807	353,128	279,983	73,145
1808	281,255	239,627	41,628
1809	226,551	213,955	12,596

Source: O. Ensink, *Propios y arbitrios del cabildo de Buenos Aires.*

Table 6.10. The cabildo of Buenos Aires's extraordinary expenses, 1806

Date	Expenses from August to December 1806	Pesos
15 August	Gave fifteen dowries of 1,000 pesos to orphaned daughters of military men.	15,000
16 August	Awarded sums of 25 pesos to soldiers, wounded soldiers, and widows.	
	Agreed to pay for supplies for the troops.	
	Agreed to pay for the uniforms of the Compañía de Miñones.	
	Agreed to pay for medicines used to take care of the wounded.	
17 August	Agreed to sponsor the battalion of Patriotas de la Unión and pay for all its expenses.	
26 August	Agreed to pay for the renovations needed to turn the fortress into a comfortable home for Santiago Liniers.	
1 September	Agreed to pay for all the supplies needed to take the British prisoners inland.	
2 September	Agreed to pay for the salaries of soldiers conducting British prisoners inland.	
5 September	Awarded Liniers with a uniform with golden buttons, a golden scepter, and a supplement of 4,000 pesos.	4,000
15 September	Agreed to pay for the expense of crafting medals to be distributed as awards among Pueyrredón's soldiers.	
	Agreed to buy horses for defending the city.	
	Agreed to give an extra payment of 4 pesos each to men volunteering to join the navy.	
25 September	Paid for saddles for the Cuerpo de Húsares.	8,100
4 October	Gave a 300-peso award to the captain of the Royal Artillery and a monthly supplement of 40 pesos.	300
	Agreed to repay all expenses incurred by vecinos during the first invasion.	
27 October	Agreed to pay for the uniforms of 300 Patricios.	
5 November	Paid Pueyrredón's expenses during first English Invasion.	9,213
12 November	Gave annual pensions to widows (viudedades): one of 500 pesos, one of 300 pesos, three of 100 pesos, and eleven of 72 pesos.	1,892
18 November	Paid for uniforms for the Cuerpo de Arribeños.	1,500
24 November	Paid for half of the saddles for the new Cuerpo de Húsares.	2,700
28 November	Paid for uniforms for the Cuerpo de Patriotas de la Unión.	8,000
	Paid for 400 quintales of bread made for feeding the troops.	3,200
2 December	Paid for uniforms for the Cuerpo de Arribeños.	5,000
18 December	Paid for uniforms for the Cuerpo de Indios y Negros.	1,000
	Paid for moving the family of the captain of the Royal Artillery to Buenos Aires.	700
23 December	Paid for uniforms for the Cuerpo de Cazadores.	1,000
29 December	Paid for crafting more medals to be given as awards.	
30 December	Paid to fix a home to be used as a barrack.	95
	Paid to cover various expenses from the time of the British occupation.	689
	Total expenses 1806	62,389

Source: Archivo General de la Nación (Argentina), Acuerdos del extinguido cabildo de Buenos Aires, series 4, vols. 2 and 3.

GIVING TO AND TAKING FROM THE CABILDO

The Politics of Giving after 1806

O n 5 January 1809, Interim Viceroy Santiago de Liniers urged the cabildo of Buenos Aires to come up with 100,000 pesos to pay the troops. This request hardly surprised the city councilmen, as they had been financing the viceroyalty's military expenses since 1806. However, there was something unusual about the viceroy's imperative request. Instead of offering the situado as collateral, which had already been pledged to back the cabildo loans, he proposed to exchange the funds he had requested for silver bars and nuggets deposited in the royal treasury. The city councilmen responded that they would do their best to collect 100,000 pesos among the vecinos, although they were certain that it would be almost impossible, as "specie had become extremely scarce in Buenos Aires due to the increased number in expenses and sacrifices made by the vecinos since the terrible year of 1806." In any event, the cabildo commissioned *regidor* and merchant Francisco de Telleechea to visit the royal coffers to estimate the value of the silver bars and nuggets. Later on that day, Francisco de Telleechea reported back that only about 54,000 pesos was in bars and nuggets with the remainder in "challises and other sacred ornaments previously belonging to the Jesuits."[1]

Viceroy Liniers's vital need of funds stemmed from the fact that a few days earlier, creole, black, and casta militias had been deployed to keep a conspiracy led by Martín de Alzaga from fully unfolding. Alzaga was a Spanish merchant and outspoken defender of the monopolist-trade faction. Counting on the support of other powerful men and the Spanish militias, he had planned the ousting of Liniers for 1 January 1809. Alzaga and his supporters distrusted Liniers not only because he was a Frenchman and advocate for neutral trade but also because he opposed demobilizing the popular militias deployed to expel the English.

Viceroy Liniers's exchange with the cabildo of Buenos Aires provides perhaps the best summary of the political and financial situation of Buenos Aires at the beginning of 1809. First, the militias created and deployed during the British Invasions had not been discharged. Instead, they had become powerful political players and a permanent burden on the city finances. Second, while Viceroy Liniers enjoyed the political and military support of the popular militias, he was financially dependent on the cabildo. Finally, monopolist merchants who clustered in the cabildo of Buenos Aires not only opposed Viceroy Liniers's popular politics and budgetary largesse but also his support for trade with neutral nations.

These and other circumstances impacted the collection of new donativos in 1808–1809 and 1810 and thereafter changed the politics of giving. As discussed in the previous chapter, the military expenses that followed the British Invasions were paid for by donativos, the new excise tax, and loans brokered by the cabildo of Buenos Aires. At the local level, the payment of these expenses facilitated the distribution of income from wealthier to poorer vecinos primarily in the form of pensions, salaries, and dowries. Similarly, the institutional changes that followed the invasions of Buenos Aires made it possible for the popular militias to engage in politics more frequently by utilizing channels not available to them in the past.[2] Between both British Invasions, popular militias had been deployed to decide the fate of Viceroy Sobremonte, and in 1809 they supported Viceroy Liniers against Alzaga and his faction. In other words, popular militias found in local politics a new role that transcended their military service.

On July 1809 Viceroy Baltasar Hidalgo de Cisneros arrived in Buenos Aires to replace Liniers. He held a permanent appointment and came directly from Madrid, the center of monarchical patronage. His authority was legitimate, and his presence should have resolved the leadership crisis that began with Sobremonte's ousting and the subsequent rise of Liniers. As illustrated by the cases of Governor Viedma and Viceroy Avilés (discussed in the previous chapters), collections of large donativos within the districts they served evidenced their capacity for leadership. The collection of new donativos provided Liniers and Cisneros with similar opportunities to gauge their leadership skills.

In this chapter, I argue that military service coupled with their role as beneficiaries of the politics of giving enfranchised the militias. Thereafter, popular militias not only enjoyed economic and political rights but also embraced their duty to support politically and financially the system that guaranteed those rights. In other words, popular militias became active vecinos, and from 1808 onward, they also became donors. Donors expressed their political preferences by contributing to donativos collected either by Liniers or Cisneros. That is, donors not only financially supported the system that best represented their interests but also the leader they regarded as the most suitable for representing, voicing, and preserving their rights.

Before analyzing the new changes in the politics of giving, I will summarize the social, political, military, and institutional changes that took place in Buenos Aires in the early 1800s.

THE COST OF POPULAR POLITICS
AND THE ELITES' REACTION TO IT

As discussed in chapter 6, the cabildo of Buenos Aires paid for the militias' uniforms, rations, and salaries. Additionally, in 1807 the cabildo started granting pensions to the widows of militiamen and wounded soldiers and dowries to their orphan daughters. In 1807 the cabildo assigned *viudedades* (pensions for widows, which occasionally included orphaned children) for a total of 7,756 pesos. The cost doubled the following year to 15,502 pesos, and in 1809 it increased again to 17,435 pesos. Pensions for the wounded started at 2,387 pesos in 1807, doubled in 1808 (5,382 pesos), and almost tripled in 1809 (6,617 pesos). Dowries absorbed 1,667 pesos in 1807, 1,120 pesos in 1808, and 2,706 pesos in 1809. Additionally, following the expulsion of the English, the city councilmen paid for grants of freedom to recognize the service of slaves who had participated in the British Invasions. However, they significantly reduced the number of grants afterward. In 1807 the cabildo spent 15,177 pesos on grants of freedom but spent only 2,477 and 984 pesos in 1808 and 1809, respectively.[3]

In previous years, the popular militias, in particular those staffed by blacks and castas, had tested their power and their ability to influence the decision-making process. Their influence was crucial first in forcing Viceroy Sobremonte to hand over his military command to Liniers and later in securing the complete ouster of the incompetent viceroy.[4] The black and casta militias had also neutralized Alzaga's plot aiming to overthrow Liniers. By 1809, Viceroy Liniers and the cabildo were aware of the importance of punctually paying the salaries of these highly politicized militias as they had been reminded by one of the commanders that most of the men serving in them were indigent, and if deprived of their salaries, they would likely return to criminal activities.[5]

Changes in urban labor organization taking place in the last quarter of the eighteenth century explain both the popular sectors' perceived propensity for criminal activity as well as their embrace of the militias. During those years, the importation of large numbers of African slaves into Buenos Aires coincided with the destruction of the guild system. These transformations not only exposed the urban popular sectors to a fragile and volatile labor market but also cut them loose from the institutions and practices that had facilitated their subordinate incorporation into the old regime. Workshops had provided Spanish and casta workers with control over labor recruitment, training, and production standards. Additionally, they had functioned as sources of mutual aid and corporate identity. Urban authorities even found in guilds effective mechanisms for controlling vagrancy, laziness, and crime. As the guilds crumbled, members of the elite and slave masters frequently complained about the "insolence" of slaves and plebs as well as their lack of respect for their superiors. The decline of the guilds coincided with the need to create popular militias and military units to repel the English. In this context, free black, casta, and creole artisans and laborers found in military mobilization social mobility, training regimes, group identities, income, and social benefits in the form of pensions and dowries. Black slaves even found a path to freedom by serving in the militias. Black, casta, and creole militias additionally created bonds of loyalty and patronage with military leaders like Santiago de Liniers and Cornelio Saavedraz, who had allowed in their units popular elections to select and promote officers.[6]

The fear and distrust of the popular sectors overlapped with a growing suspicion of the activity of foreigners. During the infamous "French Conspiracy" of 1795, which coincided with the radical stages of the French and Haitian revolutions, elites in Buenos Aires suspected the unfolding of a slave rebellion led by foreign, especially French, guild masters and merchants. Even Santiago de Liniers was suspected to be involved in this conspiracy, not as a marginal supporter, but as one of the ringleaders.[7] Ten years later, the rapidly changing political and military circumstances had permitted his rise to the highest ranks in the viceroyalty, making him, to the eyes of elite Spaniards, the living proof of the breakdown of the existing hierarchical social order.

Martín de Alzaga was among those who despised Liniers, his supporters, and his popular politics. Like many other prominent merchants in Buenos Aires, Alzaga had emigrated at young age from the Basque country to Buenos Aires to join the ranks of *mozos*—who helped already established Spanish merchants—hoping that one day he would become such a merchant. Alzaga's was a success story. Through thriftiness, hard work, the protection of Spanish monopolist trade, and the sponsorship of Gaspar de Santa Coloma (one of the most successful Spanish merchants in the city), Alzaga climbed the ranks in commerce and became one of the most powerful men in the consulado of Buenos Aires. Throughout the 1790s, Alzaga counted among the most outspoken opponents of trade with neutral nations. In 1799 he led the faction that resisted in the consulado the reopening of neutral trade, venting his anger against all who disagreed with him. At the time of the French Conspiracy, Alzaga served as alcalde de primer voto in the cabildo of Buenos Aires and conducted the most brutal investigation, which included the application of torture during the suspects' interrogation sessions. However, he fell short of incriminating Liniers, who, due to his social standing and the immunities granted to him by the military fuero, managed to keep Alzaga at bay.[8]

The British Invasions offered Alzaga the opportunity to display his military leadership skills, as he successfully commanded the Spanish militias that were instrumental to the expulsion of the enemy. However, in 1807 the rise of Liniers, his support for free-trade policies, and the increasing power of popular black and casta militias brought Alzaga back to local politics. That year, he was elected alcalde de primer voto even though he had enjoyed a royal grant that exempted him and other merchants from municipal service since 1797.[9] A series of bold political moves fashioned by Liniers infuriated Alzaga and the monopolist faction. After the English were expelled, Liniers authorized trade with foreigners by making shady deals with his followers. Additionally, he promoted and assigned leading military positions to men who had been arrested during the French Conspiracy. These circumstances, combined with the financial decline of the consulado, sparked Alzaga and his faction's interest in serving as city councilmen. While Liniers thrived on popular legitimacy, Alzaga and the monopolist merchants turned the cabildo into their new financial and political stronghold.[10] From this corporation, they continued dispensing financial services for the king.

The Napoleonic invasion of the Iberian Peninsula in 1808 provided good reasons to question Liniers's loyalties and encouraged Alzaga to plot his ouster. Had his plan been successful, Liniers would have been replaced by a junta similar to the ones already set up in Spain to rule on behalf of King Ferdinand VII. In fact, soon after it became known in the region that Napoleon had imprisoned the Spanish monarch, the governor of Montevideo had erected a junta not only to confirm the city's loyalty to the Spanish king but also to challenge Liniers's authority on the other side of the Rio de la Plata. Alzaga's rebellion was planned for 1 January 1809, the day the city councilmen delivered to the viceroy the list of newly elected municipal officers for his confirmation. Since Alzaga had been reelected to serve for a third time, the conspirators expected Liniers's rejection, and, counting on the support of the Spanish militias, they planned to turn Liniers's refusal into a legitimate excuse to force his ouster. However, informants had made Liniers aware of Alzaga's plot. On 1 January 1809, the deployment of black and casta militias kept the conspiracy from fully unfolding, and consequently Alzaga and his allies were arrested and exiled to Patagonia.[11]

Five days after the black and casta militias had been deployed to thwart Alzaga's coup, Viceroy Liniers requested from the cabildo the 100,000 pesos mentioned at the beginning of this chapter. However, the city councilmen did not rush to raise the requested funds to pay for the militias' salaries. Instead, they took the time to inspect the precious metals the viceroy had offered in exchange for coins and simultaneously reminded him that no more specie could be found in the city, even though in the aftermath of Alzaga's conspiracy the mobs that stormed and sacked the homes of his followers had found and seized impressive sums in cash.[12]

Liniers faced a number of political and fiscal choices in January 1809. There was no doubt that he counted on the unconditional support of the casta and black militias, the Buenos Aires popular classes, and the many members of the mercantile community who profited under his patronage. Yet even at the height of his popularity, he was still financially dependent on the cabildo, which, after the British Invasions, had been swiftly turned into the financial stronghold of the monopolist faction and the de facto treasury. The implementation of new taxes would have freed him of his financial constraints. The cabildo's successful enforcement of the new excise in 1807 could have served as a valid precedent. However, Liniers did not proceed to tax the Spanish subjects. Instead, he opted for collecting donativos, which, despite the city councilmen's claims about the scarcity of specie, yielded in the viceregal capital 121,281 pesos over the course of six months. A separate donativo collected by his successor, Viceroy Cisneros (1809–1810), raised another 62,685 pesos. Liniers's choice raises a fundamental question. Was there in the Spanish imperial system any institution other than the cabildo endowed with the legitimate authority to tax?

THE INSTITUTIONAL CHANGES AFTER 1806

The rise to preeminence of the cabildo of Buenos Aires coincided with the eclipse of the authority of the viceroy and the political and financial decline of the consulado. As previous chapters have demonstrated, through the 1790s the merchant guild had become an essential financial intermediary between the crown and its subjects. I mentioned that the consulado contributed a total of 200,000 pesos in wartime donativos during the War against the French Convention and the Naval Wars against England. However, during the British Invasions the consulado was only capable of contributing a 40,000-peso loan. Those funds came from the auctioning of the cargo of one of the vessels caught engaging in contraband trade, which belonged to Tomás Antonio Romero, a merchant who had expanded his operations by engaging in trade with neutral nations. The weakening of the consulado of Buenos Aires's financial role came as a consequence of both changes in trade policy and the continuous demands for financial support during this long period of international warfare. While in the early 1790s the merchant guild was capable of collecting sufficient revenues to pay interest on as well as to repay the principal of loans it had solicited on behalf of the crown, by 1799 the guild had difficulty managing its increased debt by exclusively relying on its ordinary resources. In the early nineteenth century, as a consequence of the hostilities against England, the crown demanded additional funds from the consulado. For example, in 1804 the king required that the merchant guild contribute 20,000 pesos to reopen trade with neutral nations and specifically requested that the merchants profiting from it provide the donativo. But as it was impossible for the politically split consulado to establish in advance which merchants would benefit from this measure, a loan from private parties was needed to pay the sum. On 14 July 1805, in addition to the avería, the consulado was ordered to collect another import and export duty of 1.5 percent on all merchandise traded in Buenos Aires and a tax of 0.5 percent on the silver exported through the Viceroyalty of Rio de la Plata. These sources of revenue were destined to boost the funds of the Caja de Consolidación recently established in Buenos Aires, and as such they had to be transferred from the consulado to the royal treasury every month. As a result of these policies, the consulado lost a portion of its own revenue, and, unsurprisingly, when the following year it was ordered to solicit a loan, hardly any investors were willing to contribute. Lenders were unwilling to advance their capital to an institution that was already financially crippled. In May of 1807, the consulado was unable to meet interest payments due on past loans. Finally, in August of 1808, when Viceroy Liniers solicited contributions for the new donativo, the merchant guild excused itself from pledging as otherwise it would have gone bankrupt.[13] Politically, the British Invasions brought more contention to an already divided consulado. While some merchants who profited under trade with neutral nations were willing to negotiate with the English, others, led by Manuel Belgrano, suggested that the corporation should immediately leave the city (carrying its files and royal seals) and settle in Córdoba, the provisional seat of the viceregal authority.[14]

The political leadership and patronage of the viceroys also deteriorated through these years. The political and military actions of Viceroy Sobremonte during the British Invasions of the Rio de la Plata generated distrust among subjects and eventually led to his removal from office and imprisonment. As British troops occupied Buenos Aires in June 1806, Viceroy Sobremonte left for Córdoba, carrying the royal treasury with him. Afterward, he attempted to justify his actions by stating that Córdoba was a reliable area in which to recruit an army to recapture Buenos Aires, and he claimed that it was in the king's interest to avoid his own capture and consequent capitulation to the enemy. However, Córdoba proved to be a poor choice as there were neither units of the regular army stationed in the area (only militia) nor sufficient resources for quickly financing Sobremonte's military campaign. Furthermore, when he surrendered the royal treasury to the British, Viceroy Sobremonte gave away the only funds at his disposal to pay an army. Consequently, he was forced to rely mainly on the cooperation and generosity of the vecinos of Córdoba.

From Córdoba, Viceroy Sobremonte issued mandates that added confusion to his already questionable actions. On 15 July 1806, he declared the city of Córdoba the provisional capital of the viceroyalty and invited the royal authorities in Buenos Aires to join him. The royal bureaucrats were perplexed by this order because if the viceroy actually intended to expel the invaders, the bureaucrats would be better off waiting for him in Buenos Aires. Both the audiencia and the consulado debated the viceroy's proposal but ultimately chose not to change their residence. Instead, they temporarily suspended their meetings.[15] In sum, Viceroy Sobremonte's exit from the viceregal capital left the audiencia and consulado with no other option but to temporarily shut down.

On 4 July 1806, Montevideo posed an open challenge to Viceroy Sobremonte's political and military authority. On that date, Governor Ruiz Huidobro called for an extraordinary meeting of the local cabildo to debate their course of action during this crisis. The governor and cabildo decided that they would organize a military expedition to recapture Buenos Aires, as they feared that the enemy would attempt to occupy the city after strengthening their position in the viceregal capital. In the course of that meeting, the cabildo of Montevideo opined that there was no legitimate authority representing the king of Spain in the Viceroyalty of Rio de la Plata because the viceroy was absent, the audiencia's sessions were suspended, and the cabildo of Buenos Aires had sworn allegiance to the British king. The critical situation demanded a strong command, and therefore, in the name of the king, the cabildo of Montevideo conferred upon Governor Ruiz Huidobro the rank of captain general (usually reserved only for viceroys) and the power and authority to defend the city. Invested with extraordinary powers, Governor Ruiz Huidobro began organizing military forces, collecting funds through donativos, and establishing contact with Captain Santiago de Liniers to plan the expulsion of the English.[16] Hence, the city of Montevideo, represented by its cabildo, emerged as an alternative power to that of Viceroy Sobremonte even before the cabildo and city of Buenos Aires asserted their independent political and financial authority. In sum, confusing signals sent by the viceroy weakened royal patronage, and thus, the institutions that represented the people before the king and sustained Spanish domination in the area emerged as legitimate representative and executive institutions.

While organizing his military campaign in Córdoba, Viceroy Sobremonte requested from Governor Ruiz Huidobro soldiers, weapons, and funds. The governor of Montevideo withheld his men and resources, arguing that he needed them to defend his city. Later, when the viceroy was informed of Liniers and Ruiz Huidobro's joint plan to expel the enemy, he ordered them to wait for him and his forces before entering Buenos Aires. Both Governor Ruiz Huidobro and Liniers disobeyed him and continued with their original plan. In August 1806, while the capital was being recovered, Viceroy Sobremonte and his troops reached Pontezuelas, on the outskirts of Buenos Aires. For a second time, Sobremonte had missed his chance to participate in victorious military operations while the local militias preserved the region under Spanish rule.[17]

Between the first and the second invasions, Viceroy Sobremonte's leadership did not improve but rather deteriorated even faster. As soon as the English capitulated, the audiencia resumed its sessions, although legally it had to wait for the viceroy to move his seat back to Buenos Aires (and reestablish the city as the viceregal capital). Additionally, in the absence of the viceroy the cabildo convoked the general congress of 14 August 1806, inviting judicial, ecclesiastical, and military authorities as well as prominent vecinos. In the course of that meeting, the recently created militias and the people of Buenos Aires stormed the cabildo building demanding that the congress confer the military command of the viceroyalty on Captain Liniers. In other words, they requested that the general congress strip Viceroy Sobremonte of his military authority. Under popular and military pressure, and under the leadership of city councilman Francisco de Las Llagas Lecica, who, as discussed in chapter 6, supported trade with neutral nations, the congress agreed to send a message to the viceroy suggesting that he should delegate the military command of the viceroyalty to Captain Liniers. Viceroy Sobremonte first rejected this proposal, not only because he regarded it as insulting, but also because he believed that no one but the king had the authority to divest him of his powers. But after exchanging missives with the audiencia, the bishop of Buenos Aires, and other vecinos, Viceroy Sobremonte became aware that not only his authority but also his life would be at risk if he returned to Buenos Aires. On 28 August 1806, he officially delegated his military command to Captain Liniers and simultaneously granted his political powers to the audiencia, which in turn named Regent Lucas Muñoz y Cubero as *superintendente de ejército y real hacienda* (superintendent of the army and royal finances).[18]

Although this decision saved Viceroy Sobremonte's life, it did not preserve his authority. In the following months, the cabildo of Buenos Aires (instead of the audiencia) made most of the executive and financial decisions concerning the defense of the viceregal capital, while Captain Liniers expanded his military leadership by creating popular militias. Additionally, the cabildo of Montevideo feuded with that of Buenos Aires over which one of the two should bear the title of *reconquistador*, which symbolized the leadership over a region that had been under the occupation of foreign troops.[19] Once deprived of its head, sovereignty fragmented into numerous pieces, each of which claimed the right to exercise de facto the different aspects of the king's authority.

After delegating his powers, Viceroy Sobremonte's political misfortunes continued. At the end of 1806, in his last attempt to recover (at least partially) his badly tarnished reputation, he decided to take his troops to the Banda Oriental, seeking both the support of the subjects on the other side of the Rio de la Plata as well as an opportunity to successfully repel the enemy in the event of a second invasion. Upon his arrival, he was rejected by the people of Montevideo and, as a consequence of his unpopularity, remained outside the city walls in charge of organizing the external defense of this bastion. Despite his efforts, however, Sobremonte and his meager troops were unable to stop the English, who, after dispersing them, besieged Montevideo and forced its surrender on 3 February 1807. For a second time, the defeated viceroy became a fugitive trying to avoid being captured by the enemy.[20]

On 6 February 1807, the cabildo of Buenos Aires met to discuss the situation in Montevideo. As had happened at the general congress of 14 August 1806, the people of Buenos Aires assailed the cabildo's meeting room and demanded the ouster of Viceroy Sobremonte. The cabildo consulted the audiencia on this matter, which first hesitated, pointing out the illegality of such a measure. However, on 10 February 1807 a general junta composed of the military commanders, the bishop, and the corporations (cabildo, consulado, and audiencia) decided to temporarily depose Viceroy Sobremonte, inform the king of their decision, and wait for his majesty's final verdict. The general junta dispatched a detachment to find and arrest Viceroy Sobremonte, who on 23 February 1807 was confined at a country house belonging to the Bethlemite order in the city of San Fernando, north of Buenos Aires.[21]

After Sobremonte was imprisoned, the audiencia became the political authority in the viceroyalty and confirmed Liniers's military powers. On June 1807 a royal decree arrived in Buenos Aires, ordering Viceroy Sobremonte's imprisonment and the appointment of Pascual Ruiz Huidobro, the highest-ranking military officer in the region, to the office of viceroy. The governor of Montevideo was unable to fill this appointment because he had been captured and sent to England during the second English Invasion. Another royal ordinance promoted Santiago de Liniers to the rank of brigadier in recognition of his performance during the first English Invasion of Buenos Aires. The audiencia appointed Santiago de Liniers as the interim viceroy, as, in the absence of Ruiz Huidobro, he held the highest military rank. Santiago de Liniers continued as interim viceroy until July of 1809, when Viceroy Baltasar Cisneros arrived in Buenos Aires to replace him.[22]

The rise of the cabildo of Buenos Aires from a marginal to a prominent financial position additionally endowed the municipality with an unprecedented share of political power. The cabildo of Buenos Aires made most of the executive decisions regarding the military defense of the region during both British Invasions and hosted the meetings that led to the stripping of the viceroy's political and military authority and his eventual removal from office. Thus, from this point onward anyone with political ambitions needed to have the support of (or even control over) the cabildo of Buenos Aires.

In fact, the porteño merchants had controlled the municipality by regularly holding municipal offices in the early 1770s. However, their attitude toward this institution was ambivalent. While the city was still small, the merchants were interested in becoming city councilmen, as the office conferred prestige without demanding much work. However, through the 1780s increases in urban population resulted in a complex city life. Municipal administration became a time-consuming burden, and consequently the wealthiest merchants began to avoid this form of public service by requesting royal exemptions. In 1794 the establishment of the consulado of Buenos Aires provided the merchants with a forum for channeling their corporate interests, and participation in the cabildo thereafter became even less attractive.[23]

Factional struggles within the consulado coupled with its financial decline shifted the attention of the merchants back to the cabildo. From the first years of the nineteenth century, prominent merchants including members of the Alzaga, Santa Coloma, Sáenz Valiente, and Villanueva clans began serving in the municipality.[24] The presence of such successful businessmen among the city councilmen undoubtedly boosted the municipality's credit, and consequently by 1806 the members of the merchant community did not hesitate to invest their substantial savings through this institution. The enormous funds managed by the cabildo in the early 1800s demanded not only good credit but also financial expertise. As the cabildo became the most important financial institution, porteño merchants (who were also lenders) began serving as city councilmen. For example, Esteban Villanueva, who during the British Invasions loaned 30,000 pesos to the cabildo, held the offices of alcalde de primer voto in 1807 and síndico in 1808. Likewise, Anselmo Sáenz Valiente, who had invested 18,000 pesos in loans advanced to the cabildo, served as alcalde de segundo voto in 1806, and Francisco de Telleechea, another merchant-lender, was elected alcalde de primer voto in 1805 and *primer regidor* in 1809.[25] As mentioned in the previous chapter, Sáenz Valiente's trustworthiness, trade credit, and financial expertise were instrumental in freeing up and transferring donativo funds collected in distant regions following the British Invasions. For Sáenz Valiente and Villanueva, investments of this size were hardly new, as they had loaned substantial funds to the crown through the donativos brokered by the consulado in 1793 and 1799. However, their presence and their money radically transformed the role of the municipality and the nature of municipal service. While in the last decades of the eighteenth century the cabildo was only expected to efficiently promote public works, hygiene, and civic festivities, in the early nineteenth century it became the political and financial stronghold of the porteño mercantile elite, the financial broker for the crown, as well as the viceroyalty's purse.

Politically, the role fashioned by the cabildo serves as another example of the local, regional, and Atlantic institutional coordination needed to preserve a composite monarchy. It additionally demonstrates that within the Spanish political system, the interests of the people were differently represented before the king. For example, when the municipality convoked the general congress of 14 August 1806, it claimed that the cabildo had the power to call that meeting because the "viceroy was absent and the Audiencia had not yet resumed its functions."[26] Because of the lack of legitimate royal authorities, the cabildo felt authorized to create a local representative body to lay out a political, military, and financial course of action. This strategy, far from being innovative, referred to the traditional role of cabildos as "representatives of the community" and defenders of the "common good," which under the Habsburg dynasty constituted one of the pillars of a flexible system sustained by the active participation of subjects.[27] However, the community represented by the cabildo of Buenos Aires and the congress was a forum not for challenging monarchical authority but for preserving it.[28] Even when the cabildo suggested that Viceroy Sobremonte should completely delegate his authority, it claimed that this decision "best served the king."[29] When the cabildo created a representative assembly that ruled while the viceroy was a fugitive and then ousted him due to his incompetence, it was simply upholding the traditional right of the local community to modify the compact that united it with the person of the king. While decided locally, the decisions made by the cabildo that represented the viceregal capital influenced politics at the territorial level as well. Although this practice prioritized popular constitutional values over monarchical prerogatives, it was legitimate under the principles of Spanish pactismo. Further evidence of the city councilmen's monarchical allegiance can be found in their incessant efforts to raise funds: first to keep the Viceroyalty of Rio de la Plata under Spanish rule and later to support the captive king in Spain. In 1809 the cabildo of Buenos Aires was nothing but a corporate institution of the old regime, sustaining the political and financial interests of the Spanish monarch.

THE POLITICS OF GIVING TRANSFORMED

While still upholding the authority of the Spanish monarch, the city of Buenos Aires nevertheless experienced profound transformations in the early 1800s. Scholars of the early independent period have pointed out that the military and social mobilizations experienced during the British Invasions forever changed colonial politics both in Buenos Aires and in the Viceroyalty of Rio de la Plata. The unprecedented militarization begun in 1806 not only increased the power and standing of the military and the militias but also provided opportunities for castas and creoles to access a prestigious occupation by pursuing a military career.[30] From then on, they voluntarily joined the militias and, through salaries, pensions, and other benefits, became beneficiaries of the politics of giving. Moreover, it was within the boundaries of the militias that alternative forms of representation and legitimacy emerged, as militias elected their officers by holding public assemblies. Furthermore, within the militia structure, professional promotions were dispensed on the basis of merit, individual talent, and skill, and thus the impact of inherited honors and services as well as that of patronage lessened.[31] In other words, the Spanish political culture had in place multiple and effective conduits not only for promoting the advancement of different social groups but also for representing their interests and channeling their political action.

Negotiations carried out in the fiscal sphere followed these rules as well. Many examples discussed in the previous chapters evidence that those subjects who provided financial services for the monarch obtained political, legal, and economic grants. At the viceregal or territorial level, the system was primarily opened to elites who successfully advanced their individual and corporate interests. Smaller imperial players occasionally entered this system, but competition made it increasingly costly for them to obtain any advantages in exchange for their financial support. However, groups that had been outcompeted in the past found in the institutional realignment that followed the British Invasions channels to voice their claims, advance their interests, and enjoy a share of the revenues distributed by the cabildo of Buenos Aires. Once included as beneficiaries of the municipal politics of giving, creoles and castas would come to sustain the system financially as well. In other words, a political voice transformed them into donors.

The collection of donativos after 1806 demonstrates that at the municipal level, negotiations became more inclusive as they drew into the politics of giving anyone capable of acting as a vecino. In Castile, the status of vecino was achieved not only through legal procedures but also by fulfilling basic requirements such as permanently residing in the area or performing essential community duties, including service in the militia and the payment of taxes. Active vecindad was, in theory, widely accessible. In practice, however, it created its own dynamic forms of exclusion. In the case of Buenos Aires in the sixteenth and seventeenth centuries, the city functioned primarily as a frontier settlement, antagonistic to neighboring Indians and Portuguese. Under those circumstances, vecindad was an exclusive right only shared by native-born Spaniards. During the union of the crowns of Portugal and Castile (1580–1640), these rules were temporarily overlooked, but they were reinstated afterward, and consequently foreign immigrants were again regarded with suspicion and their activities closely supervised. The French Conspiracy of 1795 serves as an extreme example of this type of change. Foreign and internal migrants who had been living and working in the city for decades became the targets of radically exclusionary perceptions by others. In the late eighteenth century, these developments also coincided with the empire-wide erection of ethnic and racial barriers among the diverse social groups that inhabited the imperial cities.[32] In Buenos Aires, changing forms of vecindad also coincided with a sharp increase in the importation of African slaves and the destruction of the guild system that had permitted the subordinate incorporation of economically disfranchised social groups into the urban community.[33] As a result, Indians, Africans, and castas who might have been considered potential vecinos (and, by extension, Spaniards) were regarded as permanently foreign to the community.

The British Invasions of Buenos Aires gave creole, casta, and black workers—that is, the groups recently excluded from achieving vecindad—

the opportunity to provide outstanding militia services for the local community and the king. Although they received for their services monetary compensations, social benefits, and, in some cases, even their freedom, they resisted being demobilized. Instead, they actively participated in the popular and factional politics that followed the 1806 crisis. Moreover, the analysis that follows demonstrates that they increased their stakes in the system by contributing donativos in 1809 and 1810. Their political imaginaires scripted their political involvement as they became aware that military service coupled with financial support in the form of donativos granted them access to Spanish-style channels to political voice and social advancement.

Unlike the donativo funds collected between both British Invasions, the funds collected in 1808 were not spent locally but shipped to Spain. Additionally, instead of being brokered by the cabildo of Buenos Aires, Viceroy Liniers and his replacement, Viceroy Cisneros, led the efforts at collecting donativos to support the war against Napoleon. Thus, the politics of giving demonstrates that the political participation of popular sectors not only widened existing channels of representation but also made possible, through the patronage of viceroys, the effective transfer of income from the popular sectors to the crown. In the process, however, the plebeian groups that provided these donativos gained the rights associated with vecindad.

Donativo funds collected by Liniers and Cisneros were gathered and kept in separate accounts and sent to Spain in separate shipments.[34] These viceroys were not simply following established administrative procedures. On the contrary, the separation of funds mirrored the political choices available to donors, who advanced their financial support for the captive king through the hands of the viceroy they perceived as the best broker for their interests. Moreover, their political and financial choices ultimately strengthened or weakened each one of these leaders' patronage and political outlook.

Upon learning that Bonaparte had captured King Ferdinand VII, Liniers started the collection of a new donativo, which between August 1808 and February 1809 yielded 170,334 pesos out of which 121,281 originated in Buenos Aires (table 7.1). Even though he had already collected the bulk of this donativo, on 5 January Liniers still requested funds from the cabildo to pay for the militias' salaries. In fact, he did not use donativo funds because they had been collected for the purpose of sending them to Spain. Later that year they were shipped to the metropolis on the frigate *Prueba*.[35] Although the raids that followed Alzaga's aborted conspiracy revealed that monopolist merchants who supported him had in their homes impressive funds, they did not want to surrender them to the cabildo for the payment of the popular militias. Liniers, on his part, opted to withhold the donativos as well. From his point of view, the cabildo was financially responsible for covering military expenses, and thus he urged the city councilmen to come up with the funds. By requesting that the municipal body pay for the militias, he acknowledged their newly acquired status as vecinos. Simultaneously, by shipping the donativo funds to Spain, he intended to demonstrate to authorities there that he was in fact a loyal Frenchman and that his popular politics supported the captive Spanish monarch.[36]

Table 7.1 shows that in accord with past trends, the bulk of the donativo collected in Buenos Aires came from a small number of well-off donors. In this case 512 individual contributions made up slightly more than half of the donativo (62,679 pesos), while the remaining half was contributed either by corporate groups or individual donors channeling their donations to a common fund. Contributions to this donativo ranged between 3 and 2,000 pesos, and the majority of them were equal to or smaller than 100 pesos (392 contributions). Donativos of 50 pesos were as frequently advanced as those of 100 pesos (sixty-eight contributions). It could be argued that donors quickly exhausted their savings after contributing to the 1806 donativo. However, in 1806 the majority of funds came from men engaged in commerce, while in 1808 only ten donors were either merchants, almaceneros, or tenderos. The occupation of the remaining donors cannot be identified. But judging by the smaller amounts of their contributions, they were likely to be from the middle rather than upper classes.

Bureaucrats, merchants, military men and militias, and ecclesiastics had traditionally been committed to contributing donativos. They had frequently employed these channels to communicate and bargain with the monarch for corporate benefits. As noted in the previous chapters, the politics of giving became more competitive, and consequently in the 1790s the creole militias almost did not obtain any benefits at all. In 1806 bureaucrats and ecclesiastics contributed smaller funds to the donativo collected by the cabildo, which, in both cases, represented only 3 percent of that total, while military and militiamen did not contribute in 1806 at all. Presumably, at the municipal level they regarded their military service as sufficient proof of their commitment to sustaining the monarch and the common good. Additionally, since the 1806 donativo was collected soon after the English were repelled, it was not yet clear if militiamen would continue to receive salaries and other benefits.

However, in 1808–1809 these groups significantly increased their donativos in order to support the captive king (table 7.2). Bureaucrats increased their pledges to represent 7 percent of the total, while the ecclesiastics lifted theirs to 6 percent.

Donativos from military and militiamen, however, reached an unprecedented 54 percent of the total. While commerce had always been the main source of profit and the preferred social and occupational identity among porteños, the recent military mobilization stimulated the pride of these vecinos who had recently become soldiers. Moreover, out of the 65,349 pesos contributed by men serving in the military and the militias, 21,698 pesos came from black, casta, and creole battalions.

As already noted, it had become impossible to demobilize militias as, under unstable labor market conditions, they found in the military service not only new sources of social standing and prestige but also regular employment, income, and benefits. At 12 pesos per month, military salaries were very competitive in a city where unskilled workers were generally paid between 61 and 140 pesos annually.[37] Pensions for widows and wounded soldiers were also attractive, and following the hierarchical color lines, they paid 144 pesos per year for Spanish widows and 8 to 12 pesos monthly for Spanish soldiers, while Indians, *morenos*, and pardos received half that pay.[38] It should not be surprising to find among donativo contributors "twenty-nine widows from the Reconquista" who, along with the soldiers, had become fully invested in supporting a system that rewarded their services and represented their interests (table 7.1).[39] Moreover, freed pardos and slaves also found it appropriate to advance their own savings for backing a king who, ironically, was in captivity while they were enjoying their recently acquired freedom. Lay and ecclesiastic slave masters, male and female alike, also felt compelled to contribute donativos on behalf of their *criados*, the umbrella term utilized to refer to domestic slaves and servants. Their attitude perhaps indicates that as heads of households confronting the social transformations brought to this slave-owning city by warfare, they were attempting to assert their control over their dependents by brokering their participation in the politics of giving.

While newcomers built up their political capital, many well-established imperial players also increased their donativos and their stakes in the politics of giving. As I have mentioned, bureaucrats increased their pledges relative to the 1806 donativo. However, we see no uniform trends across the different government branches. For instance, Viceroy Liniers contributed a donativo of 1,000 pesos. His was a generous donation although it fell short of the 6,000 pesos contributed by Viceroy Avilés in 1799. A larger number of audiencia judges contributed to this donativo. As in the past, however, most of them kept their pledges at 300 pesos, which represented about 10 percent of their reduced salaries. As for the revenue-collection agencies, all the customs officers contributed to this donativo, and even several unpaid employees from that office (*agregados* and *mozos de confianza*) made smaller donations. For the first time, officers who served at the *resguardo* (coast guard patrol), which functioned as a subdivision within customs, contributed donativos (table 7.3).

Fewer officers serving at the treasury contributed donativos to support the captive king, although those who did significantly increased the sizes of their contributions. Again, accountant Pedro José Ballesteros provides a good example of the choices available to bureaucrats under rapidly changing political circumstances. In 1793, while he held an interim position, he contributed a donativo of 166 pesos that came from annuities he collected in Spain. Since a detailed roster for the 1799 donativo did not survive, we do not know if he contributed to that donativo. However, in 1806 he had obtained a permanent junior position at the *tribunal de cuentas*, the court in charge of resolving accounts, and he donated 100 pesos to the donativo collected that year. While he was advancing through the bureaucratic ranks, his donativos were not impressive, though they were effective. However, by 1808 he had been promoted to a senior accounting position at a time when royal patronage had become more erratic. His larger stake in the preservation of Spanish rule increased his donativo to 500 pesos.

The available evidence shows that Ballesteros was not the only one who perceived that the rapidly changing political scenario demanded more assertive expressions of loyalty. All officers serving in the customs and coast guard patrol offices also made contributions to this donativo. Viceroy Sobremonte, who had been recently deposed due to his incompetence, was unemployed and unsalaried. However, he made a bold move and contributed a donativo of 1,728 pesos in coins and silver bars.[40]

Contributions to this donativo from the ecclesiastics were larger than the ones they advanced in 1799 and 1806. However, the 7,654 pesos they contributed in 1808 represented only a fraction of their 1793 donativo.

On this occasion, they opted for mild support instead of distance, their most common attitude since the enforcement of the Consolidación decrees. The nuns from the convent of Saint Catherine contributed their first donativo and even allowed their own criados to financially support this cause (table 7.1). While a captive king must have been a reason compelling enough to cause them to financially support the monarchy, the records reveal that ecclesiastics did not support the crown as strongly as they did during the War against the French Convention.

Finally, the number and sizes of contributions from women increased, and for the first time, they donated their jewelry and silver plate (table 7.1). Their stronger presence on the donativo roster coincided with the appearance of children as donors. In the past, politically ambitious fathers had contributed donativos on behalf of their children, indicating that they were seeking either the transfer of an office to the next generation or the purchase of future appointments. In 1808 two boys were listed as individual contributors instead of their wards making contributions on their behalf. For instance, the "boy" Roque Jose Fierro donated with the authorization of his father a small necklace with two topazes and a small diamond ring, and the son and daughter of Maria Isabel Gonzalez de Charri donated 2 pesos each. In the first case, it is notable that Roque's father allowed him to relinquish his property, while in the second case, we know of no male adult figure either supervising or authorizing the children's pledges. Additionally, one entry makes reference to children contributing together with an undisclosed number of "other individuals" a total of 64 pesos. Since neither the children's nor the adults' names are listed, this group of donors was probably made up of plebeians.[41] The rapid and radical politicization of the city of Buenos Aires reached deeper into the homes of the vecinos, thereby stimulating women and children to donate their coin, jewelry, and silver plate in support of the captive king. Their participation additionally evidences that Viceroy Liniers's power rested on a broad popular base that included not only the salaried militias but also other groups.

As for the transactions involved in meeting this donativo, the sources are not very revealing. The available sources did not record how the donativos collected in the different regions across the viceregal territory reached the treasury in Buenos Aires. However, a few references hint that as in the past, not all donativos were advanced in coin, nor were they exclusively managed locally. For instance, Pedro Sarrieta donated a *vale real* worth 150 pesos, which was held in Cádiz by Jose Fonseca. Fonseca must have been a merchant-banker underwriting vales reales because in order to make this donativo contribution, Sarrieta requested him to issue a bill of payment against the Suprema Junta sustaining the authority of Ferdinand VII. The merchant Juan Writh issued a 1,000-peso bill of payment against his partner in Cádiz "for covering [military] expenses in the metropolis."[42] It does not emerge from the sources whether Writh's partner endorsed the bill and deposited it in the Cádiz treasury or instead directly supplied the army. In sum, donativos collected in Buenos Aires continued to financially bind men and businesses not only throughout the Viceroyalty of Rio de la Plata but also across the Spanish Atlantic.

Once in power, Viceroy Cisneros collected separately 62,685 pesos in donativos between August 1809 and February 1810. However, the bulk of these funds came from the cabildo of Buenos Aires and two Spanish militias, the Batallón de Gallegos and the Batallón de Cantabros de la Amistad. The cabildo of Buenos Aires contributed a corporate donativo of 20,000 pesos as well as individual donativos originated with the city councilmen serving in 1809, which together totaled 4,975 pesos. That is, 40 percent of the financial support mobilized by Viceroy Cisneros came from the merchants of Buenos Aires who had recently moved their political and financial power to the cabildo in order to effectively oppose Liniers's commercial and popular politics. As for the Spanish militias, the Gallegos and Cantabros de la Amistad respectively contributed 12,138 and 10,853 pesos, or 19 and 17 percent of the total donativo collected by Cisneros. Undoubtedly, Cisneros became the financial and political broker for the Spanish faction, which had also developed a strong military identity during and after the British Invasions of the Rio de la Plata.

As for the sizes, contributions ranged between 1 and 2,000 pesos, and, mirroring the 1806 donativo, the donativo collected by Cisneros included several large donations provided by prominent merchants. The most generous individual donor was Tomas Balenzategui, who contributed 2,000 pesos. Luis de Gardezabal, Francisco de Telleechea, and José Martínez de Hoz contributed 1,000 pesos each. The latter also added to his donativo 218 pesos originating from the sale of one of his slaves. Three out of ten city councilmen as well as several merchants contributed 500 pesos each. The transactions involved in this donativo additionally signal the stronger presence of merchants. Two transactions were recorded in gold, and one of them even converted the donativo sum into pesos fuertes, utilizing as the exchange rate its current value in Cádiz. Another donativo was met by a bill of payment against a merchant from

Cádiz, while two other merchants contributed 1,000 and 500 hides each. Finally, Jose Garcia del Barrio donated 200 shoe soles, which unfortunately remained unsold due to their poor quality. [43] As in the past, different types of transactions cleared in the royal treasury when it came time to collect donativo contributions.

In summary, donativos mirrored in the fiscal sphere the institutional changes and political struggles that developed in the viceregal capital in the aftermath of the British Invasions. The process of their collection demonstrates that donativos were malleable and inclusive channels of negotiation and representation that, depending on the place, institution, and circumstances, expanded or contracted. As corporate identities declined, donors joined factions, followed their leaders, and supported with their contributions not only a wider imperial cause but also antagonistic local interests. Viceroy Liniers, who advocated for neutral trade and the inclusion of the popular militias into the politics of giving, mobilized the support of urban plebeian groups. Viceroy Cisneros became the political broker for the traditional beneficiaries of the politics of giving, and as such he received the support of the monopolist merchants and the Spanish militias. By channeling their financial support one way or the other, donors additionally boosted or diminished their leaders' capacity for brokerage and bound their interests to a leader's political success. At critical times, in other words, financial networks of loyalty and trust cut through and therefore held together territories, institutions, and loci of power that made up the composite Spanish monarchy.

CONCLUSION

Donativos collected following the British Invasions represented a transformative political experience for donors as their collection coincided with the vecinos' engagement in a more active type of vecindad. Historians have argued that this type of vecindad shared many characteristics with modern citizenship, for those who fulfilled the duties of vecinos acquired rights and improved their juridical statuses. As already mentioned, the prospect of social improvement stimulated political mobilization and participation in a community that, aiming at the preservation of the "common good," periodically demanded from its members the performance of services beyond those serving individual, family, and corporate interests. Thus, services promoting the well-being of the community facilitated the transformation of the traditional corporate and hierarchical body politic into a locally defined community made up of individuals entitled to similar rights. Moreover, actions taken to improve the communal circumstances of vecinos increased their autonomy vis-à-vis both outsiders and royal representatives and stimulated their identification with the interests of the patria. Thus, vecinos simultaneously became locally defined patricios or patriotas.[44]

As I have demonstrated in this chapter, the military and militia services provided during the British Invasions not only by Spaniards but also by creoles, blacks, and castas transformed them into active vecinos. This political mobilization constituted a new experience for the latter as they became entitled for the first time to be rewarded for their services. Through their contributions to the common good, creole and casta militias obtained both social compensations, in the form of an increase in their statuses, and material ones, represented by their appropriation of an increasing share of the cabildo revenues. Once included in the system, they began exercising their vecindad more actively, and consequently they financially supported and preserved the scheme that represented their interests by contributing donativos. For political novices, donativos provided exceptional opportunities for both expressing their support as well as exercising their newly acquired rights. Because they were not detrimental to a donor's status, donativos had traditionally been the contribution preferred by subjects entitled to full rights. Additionally, with each donativo donors increased their bargaining capital and their chances to obtain rewards in exchange for their financial support. Moreover, donativos created an unending chain of reciprocal obligation between donors and recipients, thereby strengthening the bonds uniting the people and the king.

However, the community of donors experienced the most profound transformations through the donativos collected at the municipal level as these diminished the influence of certain corporate bodies such as the consulado and the Catholic Church and promoted donors' participation primarily as individuals. Simultaneously, these donativos increased the bargaining power of creole and casta militias, which had traditionally used practices generally associated with modern forms of political association and representation. These practices included summoning periodical assemblies for debating their agendas, holding elections for selecting their commanders, and advancement through the ranks on the basis of merit. It is noteworthy that in Buenos Aires, artisans willing to develop a guild system systematically engaged in these practices as well. In other words, in Buenos Aires in the early 1800s donors who engaged in active vecindad militarily, politically, and financially also accumulated significant experience in both old-regime and modern forms of political representation at their workplaces and through their militia service. Thus, Spanish subjects conceptualized modern citizenship not in a vacuum but in reference to their experience as donors, vecinos, workers, patriotas, and soldiers.

As for the politics of giving, the new forms of political mobilization and representation that emerged after 1806 created new channels for the distribution of power and income. Donativos, loans, and the excises collected by the cabildo from the wealthiest vecinos of Buenos Aires funded the salaries, pensions, dowries, and grants of freedom enjoyed by the creole and casta militiamen and their families. Their inclusion into the community of vecinos also transformed their statuses. In 1808 they voluntarily contributed almost 20 percent of the funds collected in donativos by Viceroy Liniers. Viceroy Liniers's popular politics widened representation to include the political and financial support not only of the creole and casta militias but also of their wives, widows, and children. However, Liniers's politics was detrimental to the interests of the monopolist faction and the corporate groups who found channels of representation at the viceregal level. Under the municipal and popular politics of giving, the monopolist merchants lost their ability to obtain from the crown corporate financial and political grants in exchange for their financial support. Instead, they contributed individually donativos and interest-free loans that ultimately subsidized the well-being of politically emboldened and ever more socially insolent popular sectors. However, once they controlled the cabildo, the monopolists took measures that forced other vecinos to become financially responsible for the fiscal burden created by the military expenses incurred during the British Invasions. As I discussed in the prior chapter, the cabildo enforced an excise that affected not only all consumers but also discriminated against the merchants who profited from neutral trade.

Finally, the new politics of giving effectively transferred donativo funds to Spain. As we have seen, in the periods 1793–1795 and 1799–1801 only a portion of the wartime donativos were shipped to Spain. In the 1806–1807 period donativos, loans, and taxes collected by the cabildo of Buenos Aires exclusively paid for local expenses. From 1808 onward, however, all donativo funds collected by both Viceroy Liniers and Viceroy Cisneros were shipped to Spain. But while the popular militias obtained a share of the power and revenue generated by the politics of giving managed by the cabildo, merchants and bureaucrats momentarily lost both their capacity to communicate effectively with the king as well as their ability to channel donativo funds into their pockets. These changes ultimately demonstrated that, paradoxically, the Spanish monarch exercised his absolute fiscal authority over the Viceroyalty of Rio de la Plata more effectively while in captivity than when he was free to negotiate with his powerful financial brokers.

Table 7.1. Donativos collected by Viceroy Liniers in support of King Ferdinand VII, 1808–1809

From Buenos Aires	Pesos	Percentage
Bureaucrats	9,039	7.0
Ecclesiastics	7,654	6.0
Military and Militias	65,349	54.0
Vecinos	31,526	25.0
Women	4,689	4.0
Nuns from the convent of Saint Catherine	1,000	1.0
College of San Carlos	26	< 1.0
Marquis of Sobremonte	1,728	1.5
Twenty-nine widows from the reconquista	66	< 1.0
Criados from the convent of Saint Catherine	10	< 1.0
Individual criada from the convent of Saint Catherine	12	< 1.0
Gaspar de Santa Coloma on behalf of his twenty-five criados	50	< 1.0
Isabel Gil Campana on behalf of her criados	28	< 1.0
Children and other individuals	64	< 1.0
Free pardos and slaves	40	< 1.0
Subtotal	121,281	100.0
From Other Treasuries		
Cabildo and vecinos from Paraguay	16,590	33.0
Cabildo and vecinos from Mendoza	1,844	4.0
Cabildo and vecinos from Córdoba	10,050	20.0
Cabildo and vecinos from Salta	1,756	4.0
Vecinos from San Nicolas de Los Arroyos	216	< 1.0
Archbishop of Charcas	18,597	38.0
Subtotal	49,053	100.0
Total	170,334	

Source: AGI, Buenos Aires 96.

Table 7.2. Donativo collected among black, casta, and creole militias during the Napoleonic Wars, 1808–1809

Militias	Pesos
Cuerpo de Arribeños	4,992
Cuerpo de Artillería de Indios Pardos y Morenos	991
Cuerpo de Húsares	5,024
Cuerpo de Patricios	8,694
Batallón de Indios, Pardos y Morenos de Infantería	950
Escuadrón de Migueletes de Caballería	1,047
Total	21,698

Source: AGI, Buenos Aires 96.

Table 7.3. Donativos from bureaucrats, 1793–1795, 1799–1801, 1806, and 1808–1809

Buenos Aires	Political				Judicial				Customs			
	A (pesos)	n.	B (pesos)	n.	A (pesos)	n.	B (pesos)	n.	A (pesos)	n.	B (pesos)	n.
1793–1795	0	0	0	0	1,000	1	360	6	0	0	2,039	23
1799–1801	6,000	1	0	0	400	1	890	6	0	0	284	3
1806	0	0	0	0	582	2	0	0	1,258	27	0	0
1808–1809	1,100	2	0	0	2,400	9	0	0	1,524	30[a]	0	0
									240	?[b]	0	0
Number of bureaucrats, 1803	15				19				28			

Note: A = one-time contribution; B = annual contribution.
a. Includes three officers from the resguardo.
b. Lump sums from officers serving at the resguardo.

Buenos Aires	Treasury				Tobacco Monopoly				Postal Service			
	A (pesos)	n.	B (pesos)	n.	A (pesos)	n.	B (pesos)	n.	A (pesos)	n.	B (pesos)	n.
1793–1795	485	1	2,464	20	0	0	1,884	61	0	0	1,000	8
1799–1801	400	2	572	4	0	0	268	3	50	2	0	0
1806	1,970	43	0	0	144	26	0	0	0	0	0	0
1808–1809	3,475	29	0	0	0	0	0	0	300	3	0	0
Number of bureaucrats, 1803	64				26				9			

Note: A = one-time contribution; B = annual contribution.

222

EPILOGUE

On 21 June 1810, the first junta established in Buenos Aires began collecting a new donativo to finance military campaigns against the interior provinces. Since its establishment in the month of May, the authority of the Buenos Aires junta had been challenged by Spaniards residing in Montevideo and Córdoba unconvinced of the junta's professed loyalty to King Ferdinand VII. In the course of six months, this donativo yielded 16,542 pesos, a few ounces of gold, some cattle, and one slave.[1] These funds would not even cover a fraction of the salaries paid to the troops, which, according to the request Viceroy Liniers had sent to the cabildo in 1809, cost about 100,000 pesos annually.

After 1810 the collection of donativos no longer yielded sufficient funds. However, revolutionary authorities continued requesting them until 1816. Along the way, donativos lost their fiscal efficacy, although they preserved their capacity to mobilize political support. The revolutionaries systematically published donativo rosters in the *Gazeta de Buenos Aires*, the official newspaper. This publicity not only mobilized popular support but also set the boundaries between those who were true patriotas and those who were not. By adding political statements to the donativo rosters, the revolutionary leaders continued communicating with the people through these channels. Likewise, donors also utilized the published donativo rosters as a conduit to express their political preferences.

The donativo roster drafted in 1810 contains many of these features and reveals the social and ethnic backgrounds of revolutionary donors. Out of 427 donors, only 291 contributed donativos in coin. The remaining ones either promised to maintain one soldier without actually disclosing how or donated a few head of cattle or other military supplies such as *galletas*, the flatbread provisioned to soldiers. In the past, the fiscal success of donativos had never required the mobilization of large numbers of donors. However, the size of their contributions mattered. Throughout the revolutionary period, coin and supplies were advanced in small amounts and on an irregular basis, making more evident the new donativos' diminished fiscal efficacy.

Monetary contributions to the 1810 donativo ranged from 2 reales to

2,391 pesos; 86 percent of the individual contributions were smaller than 50 pesos, while the most frequent contributions were small, 4 or 8 pesos. These figures reveal a significant drop from the previous collections of donativos in which the mode was 25 pesos when collected in the Viceroyalty of Rio de la Plata and 100 pesos when collected within the boundaries of the prosperous city of Buenos Aires.

In 1810 donativos from the creole militias represented almost 30 percent of the total donativo. Their attitudes confirm a trend that had started in the aftermath of the British Invasions, which had turned militiamen into vecinos with full rights. Militias supported with their military service and monetary contributions a political system that represented their interests and provided for them a variety of benefits. Fourteen donors identified themselves simply as patriotas. This term had always referred to emotional expressions of allegiance to the community of birth and had been associated with a strong commitment to communal well-being. In the early revolutionary years, however, references to patria transcended the local community to include the common and, in this case, revolutionary cause sustained by the Americanos and to exclude those who opposed it, that is, the Spaniards.[2] Patriotas contributing donativos revealed their virtuous commitment to the junta and its cause. However, patriotas frequently donated funds on behalf of their children and other dependents, thereby revealing both their investment in the future generation of revolutionaries and their commitment to maintain a community led by hard-working, morally bound, and independent male heads of households.[3] Financially speaking, however, their contributions had a modest impact on the revolutionary finances.

The absence of the honorary titles "don" and "doña" as well as the occasional references to manual trades reveal that a large number of revolutionary donors were members of the urban working classes. Additionally, a few very young pardos and slaves were listed among the contributors, confirming that the revolutionaries drew their support from the younger members of the racially heterogeneous urban working classes. For example, Francisco Campana, a carpenter, contributed 8 pesos in donativos, while his wife donated half that sum. The slave Maria Eusebia Segovia contributed 1 peso, while the "ten- or twelve-year-old" pardo Santos Gonzalez and the "six- to seven-year-old" pardo Patricio Rodigral contributed donativos of 4 reales each. Another "five-year-old" pardo contributed 1 peso, while the parda Basilia Aguero, whose age was not noted, donated just 2 reales.[4] Their presence on the roster as well as that of other youngsters who, in the absence of any references to their ethnicity, were presumably white additionally indicates that politicization reached deep into the porteño homes. The references to their trades additionally reveal that through their services to the community both as virtuous workers and donors they intended to access a political voice and rights.

Other references confirm the lack of financial resources of the plebeian donors. Widows who had been traditionally the heads of poor urban households appeared among donors, usually contributing very small amounts. For instance, Juana Pavon, a forty-four-year-old widow, contributed 2 pesos. Her contribution was followed by the statement "That's what she has for clothing." Mariano Medrano, a priest from the district of La Piedad, also contributed 8 pesos "on behalf of the humblest members of his congregation." Three orphaned but legitimate daughters of Lieutenant Blas Zavala, ages eight, seven, and six, donated one ounce of gold. They had been among the beneficiaries of pensions and dowries distributed after the expulsion of the English. While their patriotism and economic survival bound them to the revolutionary authorities, their commitment to sustaining their cause presumably impoverished them even further.[5]

Except for the creole battalions and the cathedral chapter, corporate affiliations were completely missing from the donativo roster, indicating that the social transformations that had begun with the British Invasions had eroded the hierarchical corporate order that had characterized Spanish rule. Such transformations put an end to the old politics of giving as, at the local level, it was no longer possible for powerful corporate groups to exchange their financial support in exchange for grants.

In sum, the 1810 donativos revealed that revolutionary social changes promoted an egalitarian ethos that prioritized the interests of individual patriotas instead of those of powerful corporate subjects. However, the political beneficiaries of this new, more inclusive politics were not immediately transformed into homogeneous taxpayers. Evidence of this incomplete process can be found in the confiscating policies implemented by the revolutionary authorities. These measures facilitated the short-term financial survival of the revolutionary cause. However, they simultaneously alienated the support of wealthy entrepreneurial citizens and dislocated the commercial and financial networks that had integrated the city of Buenos Aires not only with the interior provinces but also with the Atlantic trade.

Throughout 1811, the junta demanded from Spanish merchants forced loans. The following year, the revolutionary authorities implemented a thorough survey of wealth, which forced merchants to draft legally endorsed declarations of property in the form of *declaraciones juradas*. Merchants were to include in their declarations all the capital in their hands as well as their obligations either contracted from or extended to residents in Spain, the Viceroyalty of Peru, or any of the regions that had fallen under the royalist forces commanded by General Goyeneche, the military commander sent from Spain to control the rebellious American territories. The drafting of these declarations was accompanied by periodic inspections of the merchants' accounting books and personal correspondence. Notaries were also ordered to surrender their books. Additionally, the revolutionary authorities encouraged whistle-blowers to denounce property owners who concealed their assets by giving out rewards. Merchants, like Martín de Alzaga, who resisted these measures were imprisoned. By October 1812, these confiscating measures yielded their first fiscal results and brought into the treasury more than 700,000 pesos.[6] Despite their fiscal success, these measures disrupted well-established mercantile and financial networks that had sustained the Spanish-sponsored prosperity for decades.

In 1813 the revolutionary government took further steps toward extracting fiscal contributions from those who had come to be referred to as "the exclusive owners of the wealth of the country." A second survey of wealth, this time entirely based on commercial assets owned and traded by the merchants of Buenos Aires, aimed at enforcing homogenous contributions from all property owners. The result of this measure is unknown as it was strongly resisted by the merchants, who put forward all sorts of excuses and legal claims to prevent the authorities from seizing their capital.[7] Resistance and evasion followed the excuses. For instance, a group of merchants hid their cash and underdeclared their assets. Others transferred their assets to proxies abroad (especially in Brazil and in Spain) or their Spanish American–born relatives and friends who, due to their support for the revolutionary cause, enjoyed exemptions from and reductions in these contributions. Many more sought the "cooperation" of low-ranking fiscal officers in order to file fraudulent declarations of wealth, which resulted in lower contributions. Indirect evidence suggests that capital flight was widespread. In 1819 the revolutionary authorities enforced regulations intended to retain 50 percent of the capital involved in the transfer of assets to foreign individuals and institutions by both inheritance and bequest.[8]

Revolutionary leaders like Juan Martín de Pueyrredón, who in 1812 served as a member of the First Triumvirate (the executive that replaced the junta) and four years later became *director supremo*, was also known for having brokered tax cuts for his Spanish friends and relatives. Corrupt officers were investigated for bragging about the shares they had obtained from fraudulent taxpayers or for showing consumption patterns that did not correspond to their income. The case of Juan Rebollo, a clerk (*escribiente*) at the tax assessment office, speaks of a certain degree of impunity among tax-collecting authorities as he was charged with corruption after he was heard bragging about the purchase of a black female slave valued at 260 pesos.[9]

Those merchants who actually met the payments for the new contributions took their capital away from other rolling obligations, thereby negatively affecting the local capital and credit markets. For example, in 1813 under the new tax schedule Flora Azcuenaga de Santa Coloma's contribution was set at 6,000 pesos. In order to pay for it, she took 5,000 pesos from one of the loans her husband had advanced to the cabildo, while the remaining 1,000 came from other private parties who had also borrowed from him.[10]

In order to finance warfare, revolutionary authorities who supported free trade and the preservation of private property ownership paradoxically implemented policies that not only violated property rights but also were detrimental to commercial growth and the development of entrepreneurship. Far from continuing with inherited Spanish policies, the revolutionary authorities took a divergent path and heavily relied on compulsory measures. After 1810 in the Rio de la Plata, Spanish-style partnership between the monarch and ambitious subjects was replaced by tax evasion, capital flight, favoritism, and the corruption of tax collectors.

As discussed in the first chapter of this book, France, England, and Spain implemented constitutionally legitimate fiscal measures in the eighteenth century. Parliamentary England successfully increased taxation, which made it possible for the crown to service its permanent debt at comparatively lower interest rates. Increases in taxation and expenditure as well as political and financial concessions were openly negotiated in parliament. Although the process was time consuming and corrupt, it was regarded as legitimate because members of parliament debated and consented to these policies. Transparency resulted in a more efficient allocation of economic rights, which fostered institutional stability and economic growth. Since England was a partially composite parliamentary state, the constitutional arrangements that guaranteed success in the metropolis failed across the British Atlantic. While loyal to their king, North Americans resisted increases in taxation consented to through a parliamentary process in which they did not have voice. In sum, English constitutional principles were effective at coordinating interests of subjects and king in the metropolis but incapable of accomplishing the same in the North American colonies.

In France, the absence of a national representative assembly made it very difficult for the French monarchs to enforce and expand taxation uniformly. Regional corporate bodies sharing sovereignty with the crown protected taxpayers against taxation. But while the French monarch's power to increase revenue was limited, his capacity to spend was unconstrained because France had no equivalent of the English parliament. Consequently, the French kings systematically created fiscal deficits that they generally balanced by breaching contracts and violating property rights. Under these circumstances, the French monarchs primarily secured very expensive loans that made long-term financing difficult. The French government redistributed privileges inefficiently and secretly. Instead of coordinating and mainstreaming competing private interests, the French distribution system promoted fiscal and institutional instability, which resulted in resistance to taxation and civil disobedience. Under such conditions, economic growth stalled.

My analysis of collections of loans and donativos demonstrates that in the 1793–1808 period, subjects successfully resisted and reversed attempts to enforce uniform taxation and fiscal equality. Instead, the monarch collected loans and donativos that opened for subjects conduits for voicing and debating their interests. In other words, Spanish kings partnered with their subjects and shared with them the spoils of empire. Without uniform taxation and parliamentary representation, the Spanish monarchs accomplished empire-wide what the English monarchs achieved only narrowly.

Partnerships took many forms. Sometimes, the monarch paid premium commission rates to the merchants who made possible the transfer of revenue across the viceregal treasuries. On other occasions, the king granted merchant-bankers the right to tax in order to guarantee the interest payment on the loans they advanced to the monarch. Most importantly, the participation of these financial partners made it possible for subjects to make contributions not only in coin but also through the renegotiation of a variety of credit instruments including bills of payment, ordinance bills, and bills of exchange. Merchants charged commissions for trading with commercial paper as well as for engaging in coin arbitrage. Simultaneously, they kept different areas in the Viceroyalty of Rio de la Plata commercially, fiscally, and financially integrated.

Unlike the French system, the Spanish state's redistributive role did not stifle competition, nor did it necessarily constrain economic growth. Loans and donativos demonstrate that bureaucrats across the ranks as well as bigger and smaller merchants competed for opportunities for social and professional advancement that were contingent on the preservation of Spanish rule in the Americas. As a result, the output of loans and donativo yields increased over time. However, the increase in revenues generated by loans and donativos did not automatically guarantee their transfer to the metropolitan treasuries. On the contrary, a large share of these funds remained in the viceregal territory and boosted the existing financial and commercial networks. In the case of Paraguay in the early 1800s, donativos and loans were even transferred within the same treasury from one ramo to another in order to be spent locally to better finance not only the administrative and military apparatus but also the commercial expansion that trade with neutral nations had brought to this area. Imperial partners exercised a significant degree of control over the revenue-collection system. Subjects positively engaged with it as this fiscal system was not detrimental to their status and was capable of distributing rewards. Indeed, donors and lenders of small, medium, and large sums took advantage of these opportunities. The Spanish way of bargaining was neither absolutely transparent nor equal as donors were not certain when and how they would be rewarded. But in any case, they trusted the system and they considered it legitimate and fair. The fiscal efficacy of the system supports this claim.

Thus, the competition for rewards resulted in an unequal but fair allocation of benefits. Individuals and groups capable of providing significant monetary contributions, essential financial or political services, or a combination of both were better positioned to obtain their share of the imperial wealth and power. In such a system, powerful Spanish bureaucrats who contributed and successfully collected large loans and donativos within their administrative districts bargained better than Spanish American–born administrators with strong professional qualifications. Occasionally, the system allowed creole administrators to bargain successfully. However, their success generally encompassed larger financial investments on the part of creole bidders. The examples of the creole militias and creole judges best illustrate these trends.

The opportunities for profit generated by the transfer of revenues across the treasuries served as stimuli for merchants to compete as well. Situadista factions vied for a share of this profitable system that, as demonstrated by collections of donativos, included not only large and small merchant-bankers who traded on a regional scale but also those who, like the post-master general, integrated regional and transatlantic businesses. Within the consulado of Buenos Aires, the monopolist faction competed against the merchants who supported trade with neutral nations. Their eagerness to profit from imperial trade also made it possible for the crown to collect its own share of the wealth generated by the empire. Unlike the French system, this type of competition made evident that merchants preferred to continue with their businesses instead of exclusively becoming rentiers. Additionally, trade with neutral nations opened new opportunities for businessmen willing to diversify their investments by relying on relatively smaller initial outlays of capital. Merchants who invested in the rope and cordage industries, the administrator of the Guarani missions in the late 1790s, as well as those who traded a variety of bills that made possible the collection and transfer of donativo funds within and out of Paraguay sustain this point. Overall, the Spanish redistributive system was success-ful not only because it engaged big businessmen and powerful adminis-trators, but also because it remained attractive to the middling groups. Their positive engagement with it ultimately made the upward transfer of power and wealth not only possible but also broadly accepted. Thus, the Spanish monarch was the ultimate and absolute arbiter of multiple and flexible bargains.

At the municipal level, the Spanish system enjoyed a broader base of support. Corporate identities faded vis-à-vis the cabildo. Unlike the Spanish imperial officers, but similar to the North American assemblies, cabildos at the local level had the power to tax uniformly and to inde-pendently decide on their expenses. Following the British Invasions of the Rio de la Plata, revenues collected by the cabildo were primarily spent lo-cally. However, the case of the cabildo of Buenos Aires after 1806 demon-strates that its success depended on the cooperation of merchant-bankers. In fact, it was only after the merchants of Buenos Aires transferred to this institution their financial expertise that it became possible for the cabildo not only to collect donativos but also to implement a new excise tax and borrow. The presence of the merchants in the cabildo of Buenos Aires made it possible for the municipality not only to function as the local treasury but also to establish trustworthy, legitimate, and profitable financial connections across and beyond the viceregal territory. The cabildo's integration into the existing commercial and trading networks made possible its capitalization. At the municipal level, however, principles sustaining the redistributive power of the cabildo included all who contributed to the common good, even those of lesser means. Consequently, the rewards legitimately distributed by the cabildo included salaries, pensions, and dowries paid to the creole and casta militias that had defended the city against the English invaders. The political crisis that followed the British Invasions also made apparent that merchants played a crucial role in the preservation of the empire. The inhabitants of Buenos Aires remained loyal to their king even after they decided to oust Viceroy Sobremonte. However, the other viceregal territories, especially the Alto Peruvian provinces, cast doubt on the cabildo's legitimacy and were reluctant to send their funds to finance the capital's military expenses. Only after the merchants of Buenos Aires began serving in the cabildo did distant provinces relinquish their donativo funds. In other words, their presence made possible the enforcement not only of financial but also political contracts beyond the local jurisdiction of the cabildo. Locally, however, the new system of redistribution gained a large number of supporters, and under the tenure of Interim Viceroy Liniers, popular sectors defended their right to appropriate a share of the power and wealth dispensed by the municipality.

In 1808 the king became a captive of Napoleon and subsequently lost his capacity to enforce imperial contracts. In the Viceroyalty of Rio de la Plata, the imprisonment of Ferdinand VII coincided with the arrival to Buenos Aires of the new, legitimately appointed viceroy Cisneros, who collected donativos to support the captive Spanish king. Donativos collected during the Napoleonic wars demonstrate that old and new systems for the distribution of power and wealth coexisted and competed. Those groups who had traditionally supported the monarch through the old system (which primarily included Spanish monopolist merchant-bankers and bureaucrats) channeled their financial support through the hands of Viceroy Cisneros. On the other hand, the new beneficiaries of the locally based politics of giving (which included merchants who supported trade with neutral nations as well as the popular and racially heterogeneous groups who had been recently incorporated into the system as full-right vecinos) financially supported the king by relying on the patronage of the popular Viceroy Liniers. In both cases, the funds collected in donativos were shipped to Spain. Ironically, when the Spanish king's capacity to arbitrate was compromised due to his captivity, all subjects did their best to finance the military efforts aimed at restoring his power. Presumably, they were aware that without the Spanish king's fair justice, his willingness to bargain, and the binding power of his authority, the different territories that made up his empire and the subjects who thrived under his rule would be split and impoverished.

APPENDIX

DONATIVOS IN KIND PLEDGED DURING THE
WAR AGAINST THE FRENCH CONVENTION

A.1. Wheat pledged during the War against the French Convention,
1793–1795

Wheat	Fanegas
Bishop of Buenos Aires	1,000
Cathedral chapter of Buenos Aires	1,000
Crisótobal de los Barrios, vecino from La Paz	50
Dominican convent of Buenos Aires	100
Total	2,150

A.2. Yerba maté pledged during the War against the French Convention, 1793–1795

Yerba Maté	Arrobas
Corregidor, cabildo, and caciques from Concepción (Misiones)	500
Indian community of San Luis (Misiones)	800
Total	1,300

A.3. Tobacco pledged during the War against the French Convention, 1793–1795

Tobacco	Arrobas
Narciso Martínez, Spaniard from Concepción (Misiones)	2.0
Juan Esteban de Arriola, Spaniard from Concepción (Misiones)	1.0
Ramon Galiano, Spaniard from Concepción (Misiones)	1.0
Pascual Galiano, Spaniard from Concepción (Misiones)	1.0
Tomás Abando, Spaniard from Concepción (Misiones)	1.0
Luis Galiano, Spaniard from Concepción (Misiones)	1.0
Josef Ignacio Obando, Spaniard from Concepción (Misiones)	1.0
Gerónimo Figueredo, Spaniard from Concepción (Misiones)	1.0
José González, Spaniard from Concepción (Misiones)	1.0
Lorenzo Arce, Spaniard from Concepción (Misiones)	1.0
Josef Venancio Oguendo, Spaniard from Concepción (Misiones)	1.0
Juan Bentura Benítez, Spaniard from Concepción (Misiones)	1.0
Juan Josef Maldonado, Spaniard from Concepción (Misiones)	0.5
Total	13.5

A.4. Cloth pledged during the War against the French Convention, 1793–1795

Cloth	Varas	
	One-time	Annual
José Antonio Barrios, Mercedarian friar from Santos Apóstoles	200	0
Francisco Xavier Palello, Indian from San Miguel (Misiones)	72	0
Sebastián Cabral, Spaniard from Concepción (Misiones)	25	0
Agustín Balbuena, Spaniard from Concepción (Misiones)	25	0
Tomás López de Villamayor, Spaniard from Concepción (Misiones)	25	0
Manuel Antonio Mascarena, Spaniard from Concepción (Misiones)	25	0
Francisco Mon Blas, schoolteacher from San José (Misiones)	12	0
Corregidor and cabildo from Santos Apóstoles (Misiones)	0	1,000
Miguel Ximénez, Spaniard from Concepción (Misiones)	0	50
Total	384	1,050

A.5. Animals pledged during the War against the French Convention, 1793–1795

Animals	Cows	Rams	Horses
Sebastián Ayala, Spaniard from San Carlos (Misiones)	10	0	0
Lorenzo Leyba, Spaniard from Concepción (Misiones)	1	0	0
Manuel Torales, administrator from San Carlos (Misiones)	0	0	2
Juan Esteban de Arriola, Spaniard from Concepción (Misiones)	0	0	2
Mateo Ruiz, Spaniard from Concepción (Misiones)	0	0	2
Juan Miguel Palomo, Spaniard from Concepción (Misiones)	0	0	2
Ramón Galiano, Spaniard from Concepción (Misiones)	0	0	1
Antonio Pacheco, Spaniard from Concepción (Misiones)	0	0	1
Francisco Vázquez, Spaniard from Concepción (Misiones)	0	0	1
José Antonio Castillo, Spaniard from Concepción (Misiones)	0	0	1
Silvestre Duarte, Spaniard from Concepción (Misiones)	0	0	1
Juan Josef Maldonado, Spaniard from Concepción (Misiones)	0	0	1
Romualdo Benítez, Spaniard from Concepción (Misiones)	0	0	1
Francisco Trinidad, Spaniard from Concepción (Misiones)	0	0	3
Juan Pereyra, Spaniard from Concepción (Misiones)	0	0	1
Luis Ayala, Spaniard from Concepción (Misiones)	0	0	1
Joseph Albarado, Spaniard from Concepción (Misiones)	0	0	2
Xavier Torales, Spaniard from Concepción (Misiones)	0	0	2
Manuel Sosa, Spaniard from Concepción (Misiones)	0	0	1
José Castillo, Spaniard from Concepción (Misiones)	0	0	4
Cristóbal de los Barrios, vecino from La Paz	0	200	0
Total	11	200	29

MILITARY STRENGTH IN THE VICEROYALTY OF RIO DE LA PLATA

A.6. Units of the Ejército de Dotación stationed in the Viceroyalty of Rio de la Plata, 1730–1800

Region	Unit
Banda Oriental frontier	Blandengues de la Frontera
Buenos Aires	Escuadrón de Dragones de Buenos Aires
Chaco frontier	Dotación de los Fuertes de la Frontera
Lujan frontier	Piquetes de la Frontera
Montevideo	Regimiento Fijo de Buenos Aires and artillery companies
Santa Fe frontier	Blandengues de la Frontera

Source: Marchena Fernández, Ejército y milicias en el mundo colonial americano.

A.7. Militias created in the Viceroyalty of Río de la Plata, 1760–1810

City	Militia	Type	Intendancy
Asunción	Regimiento de Caballería Provincial	cavalry	Paraguay
Asunción	Compañía de Artillería Provincial	artillery	Paraguay
Buenos Aires	Asamblea de Milicias	cavalry	Buenos Aires
Buenos Aires	Regimiento de Milicias	cavalry	Buenos Aires
Buenos Aires	Asamblea de Milicias	infantry	Buenos Aires
Buenos Aires	Compañías de Pardos Libres	infantry	Buenos Aires
Buenos Aires	Compañías de Morenos Libres	infantry	Buenos Aires
Buenos Aires	Regimiento de Milicias Provinciales Disciplinadas	infantry	Buenos Aires
Charcas	Compañías Provinciales de Infantería	infantry	Charcas
Cochabamba	Regimiento de Milicias Provincial de Caballería	cavalry	Cochabamba
Colonia	Regimiento Miliciano de Caballería Provincial	cavalry	Buenos Aires
Colonia	Compania de Artillería Miliciana Disciplinada	artillery	Buenos Aires
Corrientes	Regimiento Miliciano Provincial	cavalry	Buenos Aires
La Paz	Regimiento de Milicias Provincial de Infantería	infantry	La Paz
Lujan frontier	Compañía de Milicias Disciplinadas de Luján	infantry	Buenos Aires
Maldonado	Cuerpo de Milicias	infantry	Buenos Aires
Mendoza	Compañía de Artillería Provincial	artillery	Córdoba
Mendoza, San Juan, & San Luis	Cuerpo de Milicianos de Cuyo	cavalry	Córdoba
Montevideo	Compañías de Pardos Libres	infantry	Buenos Aires
Montevideo	Batallón de Milicias de Infantería	infantry	Buenos Aires
Montevideo	Regimiento de Milicias	cavalry	Buenos Aires
Montevideo	Compañías de Artillería Miliciana	artillery	Buenos Aires
Potosí	Compañías de Artillería Miliciana	artillery	Potosí
Potosí	Regimiento Provincial de Caballería	cavalry	Potosí
Salta, Tucumán, & Santiago	Cuerpo de Milicianos de Tucumán	cavalry	Salta
Santa Cruz	Batallón Provincial de Infantería de Santa Cruz	infantry	Cochabamba
Santa Fe	Regimiento Miliciano de Caballería de Santa Fe	cavalry	Buenos Aires
Tarija	Regimiento Miliciano de Caballería de Tarija	cavalry	Potosí

Source: Marchena Fernández, Ejército y milicias en el mundo colonial americano.

NOTES

INTRODUCTION

1. Archivo General de la Nación Argentina, Buenos Aires (AGNA), IX, 8-7-12.

2. Ibid. For the gracias al sacar, refer to Ann Twinan, *Public Lives, Private Secrets: Gender, Honor, Sexuality, and Illegitimacy in Colonial Spanish America* (Stanford, CA: Stanford University Press, 1999). *Adulterinos* refers to the children born out of adulterous relations.

3. Archivo General de Indias (AGI), Buenos Aires, legajo 37.

4. For both cases, refer to AGNA, IX, 8-7-12.

5. Ibid.

6. I am following Keith Michael Baker's view of political culture. He sees politics

> as the activity through which individuals and groups in any society articulate, negotiate, implement, and enforce the competing claims they make upon one another and upon the whole. Political culture is, in this sense, the set of discourses or symbolic practices by which these claims are made. It comprises the definitions of the relative subject-positions from which individuals and groups may (or may not) legitimately make claims one upon another, and therefore of the identity and boundaries to which they belong. It constitutes the meanings of the terms in which these claims are framed, the nature of the contexts to which they pertain, and the authority of the principles according to which they are made binding. It shapes the constitutions and powers of the agencies and procedures by which contestations are resolved, competing claims adjudicated and binding decisions enforced. (Baker, *Inventing the French Revolution: Essays on French Political Culture in the Eighteenth Century* [Cambridge: Cambridge University Press, 1990], 4–5)

7. Using postcolonial theory and the *cuadros de mestizaje*, Magali Carrera has analyzed the tensions and anxiety created by social mobility, hybridity, and ambiguity in New Spain. Refer to her *Imagining Identity in New Spain: Race, Lineage, and the Colonial Body in Portraiture and Casta Paintings* (Austin: University of Texas Press, 2003).

8. Giovanni Levi, "Reciprocidad mediterranea," *Hispania* 60, no. 204 (2000): 103–26.

9. In reference to France, James Van Horn Melton states that royalist theory is different from despotism because absolutism developed in a social order that limited royal authority in principle and in practice. The monarch ruled over a constitutional order that was prescribed by God and therefore immutable. As God's representative, the king had to preserve the social order by following the principles of justice and

religion, which guaranteed for every individual and corporate body that which was considered fitting and proper. The functions of kinship were juridical rather than administrative (Melton, *The Rise of the Public in Enlightenment Europe* [Cambridge: Cambridge University Press, 2001]).

10. In my doctoral dissertation, I questioned the use of the term *absolutism* in the Spanish world. Coined in the early nineteenth century, the term mainly referred to the political system of France under Louis XIV, which was, in the early 1800s, regarded as despotic (meaning that it encroached on individual and corporate rights), autocratic (as decision making was centralized, stifling dialogue with other powers), bureaucratic (working independently from society), and continental (that is, opposed to the English constitutional tradition). However, in early modern Europe politicians and ideologues did not use the term *absolutism* but rather discussed the "absolute power of the king." Absolute power did not allow monarchs to act arbitrarily or despotically; it simply meant that when exercising their powers, kings could not be limited by the people or the aristocracy. Absolute powers denied local representative assemblies and corporate bodies the right to resist the king's authority. See Viviana L. Grieco, "Politics and Public Credit: The Limits of Absolutism in Late Colonial Buenos Aires" (PhD diss., Emory University, 2005). Also refer to Nicholas Henshall, *The Myth of Absolutism: Change and Continuity in Early Modern European Monarchy* (London: Longman, 1992); Andrew Lossky, "The Absolutism of Louis XIV: Reality or Myth?" *Canadian Journal of History* 19, no. 1 (1984): 1–15; James B. Collins, *The State in Early Modern France* (Cambridge: Cambridge University Press, 1995); and William Beik, *Louis XIV and Absolutism: A Brief Study with Documents* (Boston: Beford/St. Martin's, 2000), introduction. Most recently, Regina Grafe has thoroughly questioned the application of the absolute paradigm to early modern Spain (see Grafe, *Distant Tyranny: Markets, Power and Backwardness in Spain, 1650–1800* [Princeton, NJ: Princeton University Press, 2012]).

11. Cynthia E. Milton regards poverty as a site of negotiation and contestation within which different colonial actors defined their rights and obligations. By studying poverty, she additionally shows how the rights and expectations of subjects and king changed over time (Milton, *The Many Meanings of Poverty: Colonialism, Social Compacts, and Assistance in Eighteenth-Century Ecuador* [Stanford, CA: Stanford University Press, 2007]).

12. The Spanish definition of *pueblo* included not only the commercial, political, and intellectual elites but also the plebeian groups, which appeared on the sources as "la gente menuda, menesterales y labradores" (Monica Quijada, "El pueblo como actor histórico: Algunas reflexiones sobre municipalismo y soberanía en los procesos políticos hispánicos," in *El lenguaje de los ismos: Algunos conceptos de la moderninad en América Latina*, ed. Marta Casaús Arzú [Guatemala: F & G Editores, 2010]).

13. In Grafe's own words: "What is missing from the theories so far is a more appropriate concept of governance that goes beyond the simplistic notions of predation and constitutional regimes. It has to be able to capture a variety of organizational and institutional solutions to the problems of rule, representation and commitment to public and private property rights within the context of the premodern European state,

which was not a linear trajectory to more state autonomy everywhere, as it turned out" (*Distant Tyranny*, 25).

14. For collections of donativos in Spanish America previous to the 1780s, refer to Ronald D. Hussey, "Analysis of a Document Concerning a 'Voluntary Donation' in Guatemala in 1644," *Hispanic American Historical Review* 24, no. 4 (1944): 699–708; Robert S. Smith, "A Peruvian Donativo Gracioso in 1717," *Hispanic American Historical Review* 27, no. 3 (1947): 496–500; and John L. Phelan, *The Kingdom of Quito in the Seventeenth Century: Bureaucratic Politics in the Spanish Empire* (Madison: University of Wisconsin Press, 1967), 109–11.

15. Refer primarily to the works of Carlos Marichal, including "Beneficios y costes fiscales del colonialismo: Las remesas americanas a España, 1760–1814," *Revista de Historia Económica* 15, no. 3 (1997): 475–505; "Las guerras imperiales y los prestamos novohispanos, 1781–1804," *Historia Mexicana* 39, no. 4 (1990): 881–907; and *La bancarrota del virreinato: Nueva España y las fiananzas del imperio Español, 1780–1810* (Mexico City: El Colegio de México, Fideicomiso Historia de las Américas, Fondo de Cultura Económica, 1999).

16. For a reevaluation of intertreasury transfers, refer to Maria Alejandra Irigoin and Regina Grafe, "The Spanish Empire and Its Legacy: Fiscal Redistribution and Political Conflict in Colonial and Post-colonial Latin America," *Journal of Global History* 1, no. 2 (2006): 241–67.

17. For a discussion of entrepreneurial middle classes, refer to Jay Kinsbruner, *The Colonial Spanish-American City: Urban Life in the Age of Atlantic Capitalism* (Austin: University of Texas Press, 2005).

18. I do not believe that corruption was nonexistent in Spanish America. Unlike the practices associated with corruption, however, donativos were performed neither informally nor illegally. The literature contending with corruption is extensive. My arguments are primarily based on the following works: Hilton L. Root, *The Fountain of Privilege: Political Foundations of Markets in Old Regime France and England* (Berkeley: University of California Press, 1994); Zacarías Moutoukias, *Contrabando y control colonial en el siglo XVII: Buenos Aires, el Atlántico y el espacio peruano* (Buenos Aires: Centro Editor de América Latina, 1988); Horst Pietschmann, "Burocracia y corrupción en Hispanoamérica colonial: Una aproximación tentativa," *Nova Americana* 5 (1982): 11–37; Tamar Herzog, *Upholding Justice: Corruption, State and the Penal System in Quito (1650–1750)* (Ann Arbor: University of Michigan Press, 2004); Anthony McFarlane, "Political Corruption and Reform in Bourbon Spanish America," in *Political Corruption in Europe and Latin America*, ed. Walter Litle and Eduardo Posada Carbó (New York: Palgrave Mcmillan, 1996); Kenneth Andrien, "Corruption, Self-Interest and the Political Culture of Eighteenth Century Quito," in *Virtue, Corruption and Self-Interest: Political Values in the Eighteenth Century*, ed. Richard K. Matthews (Bethlehem, PA: Lehigh University Press, 1994); and Horst Pietschmann, "Corrupción en las Indias españolas: Revisión de un debate sobre la historiografía en la Hispanoamerica colonial," in *Instituciones y corrupción en la historia*, ed. Manuel González Jiménez, Horst Pietschmann, Francisco Comín, and Joseph Pérez (Valladolid: Instituto de Historia Simancas, 1998).

19. Marta Irurozqui, "De como el vecino hizo al ciudadano en Charcas y de como el ciudadano conservó al vecino en Bolivia, 1809–1830," in *Revolución, independencia y las nuevas naciones de América*, ed. Jaime Rodriguez O. (Madrid: Fundación Mapfre Tavera, 2005); Tamar Herzog, "Early Modern Spanish Citizenship: Inclusion and Exclusion in the Old and New World," in *New World Orders: Violence, Sanction and Authority in the Colonial Americas*, ed. John Semolensky and Thomas J. Humphrey (Philadelphia: University of Pennsylvania Press, 2005).

20. François-Xavier Guerra, *Modernidad e independencias: Ensayos sobre las revoluciones hispánicas* (Madrid: Editorial MAPFRE, 1992); François-Xavier Guerra, "'Voces del pueblo': Redes de comunicación y orígenes de la opinión en el mundo hispánico, 1808–1814," *Revista de Indias* 62, no. 225 (2002): 357–83; François-Xavier Guerra, "El apogeo de los liberalismos hispánicos: Orígenes, lógicas y límites," *Bicentenario* 3, no. 2 (2004): 7–40; François-Xavier Guerra, "La ruptura de la monarquía hispánica: Vivencias y discursos americanos," *Jahrbuch für Geschichte Lateinamerikas* 37 (2000): 73–99; François-Xavier Guerra, "The Spanish-American Tradition of Representation and Its European Roots," *Journal of Latin American Studies* 26, no. 1 (1994): 1–35; François-Xavier Guerra, Annick Lempérière, et al., *Los espacios públicos en Iberoamérica: Ambigüedades y problemas, siglos XVIII–XIX* (Mexico City: Centro Francés de Estudios Mexicanos y Centroamericanos, Fondo de Cultura Económica, 1998); Jaime Rodriguez O., *The Independence of Spanish America* (Cambridge: Cambridge University Press, 1998).

CHAPTER 1

1. As the costs of fighting exceeded the monarchs' own income, they were obliged to strike deals with their subjects in return for increased revenues. Depending on the severity of the fiscal crisis and the political forces at play, monarchs strengthened their prerogatives or shared their political power. Therefore, fiscal crises were always turning points in economic and political developments. For a further discussion of this issue, refer to Philip Hoffman and Kathryn Norberg, eds., *Fiscal Crises, Liberty, and Representative Government* (Stanford, CA: Stanford University Press, 1994). I am using Hoffman and Norberg's definition of fiscal crisis: "a jump in expenses beyond both revenues and the ability to borrow" (*Fiscal Crises*, 2). Although the practice of paying taxes became more acceptable by the eighteenth century, in the early modern times new levies were generally regarded as "robbery." The prevailing viewpoint was that taxes were an episodic matter, requested in response to a specific need. Once the need had been met, it was believed that it no longer made sense for rulers to continue asking for contributions regularly (Juan Gelabert, "The Fiscal Burden," in *Economic Systems and State Finance*, ed. Richard Bonney [Oxford: Oxford University Press, 1995], 539–76).

2. The transformation of domain states into fiscal states has been discussed by many scholars. I am following primarily the works of John Brewer, Richard Bonney, and W. M. Ormrod. For England, see John Brewer, *The Sinews of Power: War, Money and the English State* (London: Unwin Hyman, 1989), and the discussion that followed his work in Lawrence Stone, ed., *An Imperial State at War* (London: Routledge, 1994).

For the European outlook and comparative perspective, refer to Richard Bonney, ed., *Economic Systems and State Finance* (Oxford: Oxford University Press, 1995); and Richard Bonney, ed., *The Rise of the Fiscal State in Europe, c.1200–1815* (Oxford: Oxford University Press, 1999).

3. The Bank of England was created in 1695. It was the first genuine bank integrating public credit with public currency banking. Before the creation of national banks, loans were managed through two instruments: repayable loans and annuities. Through repayable loans (also called purchases of money), the lender purchased the right to an annual payment stipulated in the contract until the capital was fully repaid. Annuities, on the other hand, did not repay the principal. Instead, the lender periodically received a payment (once a year or every four to six months) representing 7 to 10 percent of the capital invested. The right to the payment died with the lender. Annuities became the first forms of consolidated debt. When the state was unable to repay its loans, it could transform them into annuities. In the seventeenth century, interest rates dropped in republics and constitutional monarchies. The United Provinces paid between 3 and 4 percent, the Swiss Confederation about 5 percent, and England 6 percent. Spain and France still had to pay premium for their money (Martin Korner, "Public Credit," in *Economic Systems and State Finance*, ed. Richard Bonney [Oxford: Oxford University Press, 1995], 507–38). Interest rates in Spain and France will be discussed subsequently.

4. Douglas C. North, William Summerhill, and Barry Waingast, "Order, Disorder and Economic Change: Latin America versus North America," in *Governing for Prosperity*, ed. Bruce Bueno de Mesquita and Hilton L. Root (New Haven, CT: Yale University Press, 2000).

5. The quote is from Brewer, *The Sinews of Power*, 210. The author also argues that the aristocracy and gentry primarily opposed the fiscal state during the early stages of its development (between 1688 and the 1720s). As the state grew in size, the landed classes also found bureaucratic and military opportunities in addition to the strictly financial ones. The increase in the number of offices in the army, navy, and civil administrations provided a comfortable and prosperous way of living for the landowners that staffed them, and in many cases, their salaries compensated for the higher taxes (Brewer, *The Sinews of Power*, chap. 7).

6. English parliamentary-approved legislation facilitated its economic transformation. Parliament sanctioned the expansion of large landed estates resulting from enclosure, the manipulation of grain prices, the decline of guilds and urban trade monopolies, the creation of an efficient bureaucracy to collect excise taxes, and capital-intensive manufacturing in the countryside. Thus, parliament functioned as a market for rights to control the economy (Root, *The Fountain of Privilege*).

7. The Albany Congress was a meeting of representatives from seven of the thirteen British North American colonies (Connecticut, Maryland, Massachusetts, New Hampshire, New York, Pennsylvania, and Rhode Island) to discuss improving their relations with the Indian tribes as well as common defensive measures against the French. Delegates discussed Benjamin Franklin's Albany's Plan of Union, which would have created a unified colonial entity. The plan was rejected by both the colonies and the British Colonial Office.

8. John Elliott, *Empires of the Atlantic World* (New Haven, CT: Yale University Press, 2006).

9. Kings taxed the wealth available, and in France it was the land. At the end of the old regime 69 percent of the twenty-seven million Frenchmen worked in agriculture. In the 1700s, 55 percent of the English and only 40 percent of the Dutch farmed. Before Colbert's fiscal reforms, trade provided less than 26 percent of revenues. Additionally, urban tax exemptions made trade difficult to tax in France, and the dispersion and diversity of the French commerce made excises and tariffs costly to levy (Philip Hoffman, "Early Modern France," in *Fiscal Crises, Liberty, and Representative Government*, ed. Philip Hoffman and Kathryn Norberg [Stanford, CA: Stanford University Press, 1994], 226–52).

10. Richard Bonney, "France, 1494–1815," in *The Rise of the Fiscal State in Europe, c.1200–1815*, ed. Richard Bonney (Oxford: Oxford University Press, 1999), 122–76.

11. The bibliography concerning tax privileges and immunities is immense. For a synthesis, refer to Kathryn Norberg, "The French Fiscal Crisis of 1788 and the Financial Origins of the Revolution of 1789," in *Fiscal Crises, Liberty, and Representative Government*, ed. Philip Hoffman and Kathryn Norberg (Stanford, CA: Stanford University Press, 1994), 253–98.

12. See Michael Kwass, *Privilege and the Politics of Taxation in Eighteenth-Century France* (Cambridge: Cambridge University Press, 2000). The taille was the main direct tax collected in France from the fourteenth century onward. Nobles owning "commoner" land paid the taille réelle. The dixième (tenth) was an income tax introduced during the War of Spanish Succession. It was abolished when peace resumed. In the 1750s, it was replaced by the vingtième, which became a permanent tax. The crown took a more aggressive stance in surveying the patrimony of its subjects when it introduced the vingtième. In many regions, this tax was enforced after land surveys were conducted (Collins, *The State in Early Modern France*).

13. In the sixteenth century, the crown borrowed through a system that could have originated public credit. In 1522 the king gained access to long-term credit by having the city government of Paris issue perpetual annuities backed by royal tax revenues that the crown placed under the city's control (*rentes sur l'Hôtel de Ville*). The investors trusted the reputation of the Parlement of Paris to protect their interests. The city served as a financial intermediary for another issue of annuities in 1536, and the system was also extended to other cities. However, the king defaulted on his loans, and in Lyon he seized tax revenues pledged to lenders and employed military force to extract new loans from city councilors. In Paris, the *rentes* also degenerated into forced loans. By the end of the sixteenth century, public credit had virtually disappeared, and the king's councilors and venal officeholders had to borrow in their own names on behalf of the king. Rentes perpetuelles provided investors an annual income terminated by repayment of the capital or interest on a loan, while rentes viagères yielded an annual income terminated by the death of one or more persons named in the contract. In the second case, investors abandoned their capital and therefore received higher interest rates. Tontines were instruments created by Lorenzo Tonti, a Neapolitan banker who advised the French king. Tontines were allocated

to a group of investors who subscribed to a royal loan and abandoned their capital in return for an annual payment. As the individuals in the group died, their payments were distributed among the survivors, usually with a percent deducted for the king. The king established "classes" of individuals according to age so that the youngest received the lowest payment and the oldest the highest. Higher life expectancy made all life annuities expensive to service. For instance, a woman who died at the age of ninety-six in the last year of her life received 73,500 livres for an original investment of 300. And they were open to speculation as well. Genevan bankers found a way to make huge profits by purchasing a host of annuities and settling them on the heads of healthy Swiss maidens. Then they pooled the annuities and sold shares in Paris and Amsterdam at high profits (Hoffman, "Early Modern France"; and Norberg, "The French Fiscal Crisis"). For a discussion of different financial instruments available to early modern states, also refer to Korner, "Public Credit."

14. Venality of office was a very complex system that attracted bidders until the end of the eighteenth century. Although new sales and taxes imposed on officeholders generated income, the permanently alienated offices drained the treasury of revenues through the payment of salaries or gages (annual interest paid for the money advanced in the purchase of the office). Venality of office became a fiscal burden that resembled consolidated debt and required servicing through the setting aside of a large share of the regular revenues. When the king was desperate for funds, he could create new offices or refinance old ones. If he created new ones, the value of existing offices diminished. Officeholders generally purchased the newly created offices in order to secure their positions and obtained a higher annual payment. If the king defaulted on his payments, they could extract from him privileges such as the right to bequeath their offices to their heirs in return for an annual fee (*paulette*; see Collins, *The State in Early Modern France*). Regarding interest rates, the clergy and provincial estates provided loans with an interest set at 4 to 5 percent annually. Similar gains were expected from the refinancing of venal offices and rentes perpetuelles. Other sources of credit were very expensive. In the eighteenth century, tontines paid around 9 percent, life annuities paid on average 10 percent, and the lottery paid 10 to 11 percent. On average, the crown paid for its loans 7.5 percent annually, while the private interest rate was set around 2.5 percent. The British crown paid on average 3.8 percent annual interest for its loans, and when similar instruments are compared, one can see that the French monarchy paid usually 2 percent more. Additionally, while the Dutch and British monarchs moved toward consolidating their public debt through perpetual loans, the French king continued offering life annuities and tontines (see Norberg, "The French Fiscal Crisis").

15. Scholars who study state finances agree in that the early modern state "bankruptcies" were not actually such, as monarchs did not entirely lose their credit or any of their assets. Unilateral cessations of payments were followed by the consolidation and rescheduling of the floating debt at lower interest rates. The kings of Spain and France in the seventeenth and early eighteenth centuries took recourse to these mechanisms to secure new understandings with their debtors. By means of the visa in France and the *medio general* in Spain, the government called in outstanding obligations

and reduced both capital and interest. In return for past financial services investors received newly issued bonds at a discounted price. Losses and defaults sent many lenders into bankruptcy and, in the long run, pushed interest rates higher. Republics and constitutional monarchies, on the other hand, respected property rights, generated public confidence, and secured lower interest rates. Additionally, parliamentary consensus over taxation made revenues more predictable and borrowing less risky. States benefiting from lower interest rates exported capital, and consequently London, Amsterdam, and Geneva emerged as the financial centers dominating government loans (Korner, "Public Credit").

16. Warfare had an ambiguous impact on royal finances. It put tremendous stress on revenues, while at the same time creating opportunities for expanding existing taxes and creating new ones. From the mid-eighteenth century onward, it became harder for the French kings to balance their budgets through extraordinary means (dixième, new excise taxes, and borrowing). When Louis XIV died, debt surpassed ordinary considerations. However, the tough polices of the Duke of Orleans (discussed subsequently) saved the monarchy. In 1734, due to the War of the Polish Succession (1733–1738), military and naval expenses rose significantly again. Between 1733 and 1736, the king sold life annuities, extracted greater subsidies from the clergy and the pays d'état, borrowed money, and imposed the dixième. By 1740, most traces of war had been erased, and service on the national debt had been reduced. The following year, however, expenses exceeded income again due to the War of the Austrian Succession (1740–1748). Once again, the king financed this war by extraordinary means. By 1751, the percentage of the budget used to service debt looked as if it might decline. However, after 1755 the situation worsened. The Seven Years' War (1756–1763) cost about 1 billion livres, and the crown had to borrow at a high interest rate (10 percent). Servicing the national debt absorbed more than half of the annual budget. Soon thereafter, the French entered the U.S. War of Independence (1775–1783), and the crown was forced to take more loans and issue more life annuities. After the 1750s, however, the crown had more difficulty relying on tax increases to balance the budget (Richard Bonney, "The Eighteenth Century II: The Struggle for Great Power and Status and the End of the Old Fiscal Regime," in *Economic Systems and State Finance*, ed. Richard Bonney [Oxford: Oxford University Press, 1995], 315–90).

17. Norberg studied and compared three major financial crises that occurred in eighteenth-century France in 1720, 1763, and 1788. She found that these crises were severe and caused political resistance. However, only the last one sparked a revolution. In 1720 the regent did not hesitate to apply despotic measures (visa and chambre de justice), but the Parlement of Paris declined to register the king's edicts. But their language of resistance was not radical at all. Consequently, despite the crisis, the monarch's regalian rights emerged intact. In 1760 the king's ministers, in their efforts to strengthen public confidence, avoided the visa but applied other drastic measures including moratoria and partial write-downs. These measures, Norberg argues, created not confidence but confusion among investors and failed to restore fiscal health. Additionally, the king increased old and created new taxes: the vingtième was extended for ten more years, exemptions from the taille enjoyed by venal

officeholders were suspended, postal fees and custom duties were increased, and new excise taxes were established. The parlements opposed these policies aggressively by calling themselves the defenders of the "ancient constitution" (Merovingian) of France against despotism. The struggle between the king and courts brought the question of the royal finances into the public domain, sparking a public controversy. However, the courts were neither strong nor independent enough to overturn the king. Finally, in 1788 the magistrates opposed fiscal policies using a new language. Appeals to reason and nature replaced their conservative constitutionalism, and their resistance was more damaging than in the past as they exposed the king's bad credit and made levying new taxes virtually impossible. Taxpayers also contributed to the crisis as they massively avoided paying their taxes. Political thinkers not only demanded consent over taxation but also considered taxes as mechanisms that precluded the extreme accumulation of wealth and social inequality. In sum, the fiscal exigencies of 1788 coupled with political and ideological resistance necessitated the creation of a sovereign representative body able to consent to taxation in the name of the nation (Norberg, "The French Fiscal Crisis"). It is noteworthy that from the 1750s onward, elite groups, in particular the judges of the parlements, criticized absolutism more frequently by using constitutional rhetoric (such as during the Jansenist controversy). When the same language was used to oppose taxation, however, it became more radical as it concerned the interests of all Frenchmen (Kwass, *Privilege and the Politics of Taxation*).

18. Root notes that *cronyism* and *corruption* are not interchangeable terms. Corruption is an informal, illegal method of redistribution. Cronyism, on the other hand, is legal, formal, institutionalized, and socially sanctioned. The distribution of privileges was a practice associated with cronyism but was not necessarily corrupt, as it did not imply engaging in illegal deal making. Corrupt practices included the bribing of officials in charge of enforcing certain laws or taxes as well as the ability of political actors to influence the outcome of elections by buying votes. These methods were more prevalent in England than in France. Corruption and cronyism cause market imperfection. However, corruption is open to market forces and allows a relatively more efficient allocation of resources. Its main inefficiency lies in its transaction costs (the price of making deals). Cronyism, on the other hand, excludes many potential bidders. Additionally, it is inherently unstable because individual and private relations become critical in maintaining confidence in contracts; that is, contracts secured by cronyism depend on the continuation of secret interactions between cronies and power brokers (Root, *The Fountain of Privilege*, chap. 3).

19. For example, Marichal estimates that from the 1750s to the 1780s, New Spain sent on average 1 million pesos annually to the metropolitan treasury (*La bancarrota del virreinato*).

20. The Marquis of Ensenada proposed these reforms to Ferdinand VI. The catastro and the única contribución were first launched in the province of Guadalajara. This experiment showed that the single-tax scheme would be not only profitable but also less cumbersome than the existing tax system. In 1749 the king ordered the introduction of the catastro throughout Spain, and by 1756 the task was complete. The following year the king obtained authorization from the pope to collect the tax from the clergy.

However, the clergy and nobility objected to these measures, and the project was eventually abandoned. In the 1760s the crown tried again to move away from indirect taxes, and the idea of a single-tax scheme was therefore revived. Opponents insisted on revising the catastro, and thus, the tax was never implemented due to constant disagreements and delays. The 1770s saw one more attempt to enforce a single contribution, and again it failed. For a further discussion of this issue refer to Juan Gelabert, "Castille, 1504–1808," in *The Rise of the Fiscal State in Europe, c.1200–1815*, ed. Richard Bonney (Oxford: Oxford University Press, 1999), 201–41. In the eighteenth century, land surveys and registers of land leases became popular throughout Europe. Although they were expensive to administer, cadastral reforms found supporters because taxes on the rent of land (which rise and fall with the improvement or neglect of cultivation) were considered fair (Richard Bonney, "Revenues," in *Economic Systems and State Finance*, ed. Richard Bonney [Oxford: Oxford University Press, 1995], 422–505).

21. The wealth of Castile was mainly agrarian. However, the land and the products of the land were not taxed directly except for the two-ninths of the tithe paid to the crown as *tercios reales*. Consequently, a large part of Castile's wealth remained outside the reach of the state. Thus, the crown's revenues were extracted mainly from the market sector of the economy and, within that sector, from noncereal foodstuffs and manufactured goods. Revenues were divided into ordinary and extraordinary. Ordinary rents were mainly taxes collected as regalian rights. They included the alcabala (excise tax), custom duties, and monopolies. Extraordinary rents were divided into regalian rights and concessionary grants. The former included rights created or appropriated ad hoc by the monarch (such as the royal prerogative to sell offices and the royal fifth charge on the silver output from the American mines). Concessionary grants required the consent of the papacy (Cruzada bulls, *maestrazgos*) or the Cortes (*servicios ordinarios, extraordinarios*, and *millones*). *Servicios* fell on the *pechero* (tax-paying commoner), while the nobility and clergy were exempted from direct personal levies. The servicios were fixed grants made voluntarily by the *reino* in response to specific royal needs and on specific terms granted by the Cortes. The distinction between ordinary and extraordinary revenues was important for contemporary accounting. It separated the sources that could be applied to known permanent expenses from those uncertain revenues that could be used only to pay the current account. The "ordinary rents" were the essential foundation for the consolidation of debt, and their yield determined the size of public debt (I. A. A. Thompson, "Castile: Polity, Fiscality and Fiscal Crisis," in *Fiscal Crises, Liberty, and Representative Government*, ed. Philip Hoffman and Kathryn Norberg [Stanford, CA: Stanford University Press, 1994], 140–80).

22. The *contribución de frutos civiles* was meant to transfer the burden of taxation from peasants to landowners by fiscal and administrative mechanisms intended to prevent the latter from recouping the tax via the rent on land. The bibliography regarding the Spanish financial crisis in the late eighteenth century is extensive. The classics include Jacques Barbier, "Peninsular Finance and Colonial Trade: The Dilemma of Charles IV's Spain," *Journal of Latin American Studies* 12 (1980): 21–37; Miguel Artola, *La hacienda del antiguo régimen* (Madrid: Alianza, 1982), chaps. 4 and 5; Pedro Tedde

de Lorca, "Las crisis bancarias en España: Una perspectiva histórica," in *El sistema financiero de la economía española: Once estudios,* ed. José Luis García Delgado, Andrés Pedreño Muñoz, Juan Velarde Fuertes (Madrid: Colegio de Economistas de Madrid, 1989); and Marichal, *La bancarrota del virreinato.*

23. For a good synthesis of the creation of the Banco de San Carlos, refer to Gisela von Wobeser, *Dominación colonial: La consolidación de vales reales en Nueva España, 1804–1812* (Mexico City: Universidad Nacional Autónoma de México, Instituto de Investigaciones Históricas, 2003). For a detailed account, see Pedro Tedde de Lorca, *El Banco de San Carlos, 1782–1829* (Madrid: Alianza, 1988).

24. By 1788 the debt amounted to almost the entire income of one year (Von Wobeser, *Dominación colonial,* 21).

25. The idea of seizing "idle" (*manos muertas*) property belonging to the Catholic Church or lay corporations was supported by several Spanish enlightened thinkers. Campomanes, Jovellanos, and Olavide wrote extensively about the social advantages of these measures aimed at increasing the overall agricultural productivity of the nation by dividing large estates into smaller plots. When the Consolidación was implemented, however, it lacked those social and economic overtones, as its main purpose was to provide the crown with fresh funds destined to back the vales reales. The Consolidación affected not only real estate property but also the liquid capital either possessed by or invested through the institutions included in the decree (ibid., chap. 1).

26. The monetary shipments from the Spanish American colonies represented about 15 percent of the crown's ordinary revenues between 1763 and 1783. Through the 1790s they increased to 25 percent. Between 1802 and 1804 they rose again, reaching 40 percent, and in 1810–1811 the colonies provided 50 percent of the ordinary revenues. From the 1780s onward, 75 percent of the funds shipped from the Americas came from the Viceroyalty of New Spain. Figures are from Marichal, "Beneficios y costes ciscales del colonialismo." The rebellions will be discussed subsequently.

27. The bibliography concerning the Bourbon fiscal reforms is quite impressive. The classics include Richard Garner and Spiro E. Stefanou, *Economic Growth and Change in Bourbon Mexico* (Gainesville: University Press of Florida, 1993); John TePaske et al., *The Royal Treasuries of the Spanish Empire in America* (Durham, NC: Duke University Press, 1982); Jacques Barbier and Herbert Klein, "Las prioridades de un rey ilustrado: El gasto público bajo el reinado de Carlos III," *Revista de Historia Económica* 3, no. 3 (1986): 473–96; Jacques Barbier and Herbert Klein, "Revolutionary Wars and Public Finance: The Madrid Treasury, 1784–1807," *Journal of Latin American Studies* 41, no. 2 (1981): 315–39; Jacques Barbier and Herbert Klein, "Recent Trends in the Study of Spanish American Colonial Public Finance," *Latin American Research Review* 23, no. 1 (1988): 35–62; and Barbier, "Peninsular Finance and Colonial Trade." For the Viceroyalty of Buenos Aires, see Tulio Halperin Donghi, *Guerra y finanzas en los orígenes del estado argentino (1791–1850)* (Buenos Aires: Editorial de Belgrano, 1982); Herbert Klein, "Structure and Profitability of Royal Finance in the Viceroyalty of Rio de la Plata," *Hispanic American Historical Review* 53, no. 3 (1973): 440–69; and Samuel Amaral, "Public Expenditure Financing in the Colonial Treasury: An Analysis of the Real Caja de Buenos Aires Accounts, 1798–91," *Hispanic American Historical Review* 64, no. 2 (1984): 287–95.

28. From the 1750s to 1780, New Spain sent on average 1 million pesos annually to the metropolitan treasury, while in the same period, it sent about 3 million annually to the military situados in the Caribbean. During the War with England (1779–1780), the average shipment to the Caribbean possessions rose to 8.5 million pesos per annum, while that sent to the metropolis doubled. By the 1790s, both the metropolitan treasury and the Caribbean situados received from New Spain on average 5 million pesos annually. In order to provide those funds, the viceroy frequently requested loans and donativos (especially from the 1790s onward), as the ordinary revenues did not yield enough funds for sustaining both the demands of the metropolis and the possessions in the Caribbean (Marichal, "Las guerras imperiales y los prestamos novohispanos"). Marichal's most important contributions to this topic are compiled in his latest book, *La bancarrota del virreinato*.

29. Between 1780 and 1810, the Viceroyalty of New Spain sent to the metropolis about 30 million pesos in loans and 5 million pesos through donativos (Marichal, *La bancarrota del virreinato*, 284).

30. Toward the end of the eighteenth century, the Mexican subjects of the Spanish king paid on average 4 pesos per capita in taxes annually, while in Spain the average was 2.9 pesos. French subjects paid on average 3.2 pesos, while the British paid 9.2 pesos annually. Taxation in England represented 24 percent of per capita income, in France 12 percent, and in Mexico 20 percent (ibid., chap. 2).

31. Elliott, *Empires of the Atlantic World*; North, Summerhill, and Weingast, "Order, Disorder and Economic Change."

32. For the early modern meaning of the term *absolutism*, refer to note 10 of the introduction.

33. Ruth MacKay, *The Limits of Royal Authority: Resistance and Obedience in Seventeenth-Century Castile* (Cambridge: Cambridge University Press, 1999), 10.

34. Ibid, 4.

35. The share of royal revenue subject to grants by the Cortes increased from 25 percent in the 1560s to 70 percent in the mid-seventeenth century. Simultaneously, the estates in Navarre and the Basque provinces increased their power. In 1665 the crown stopped summoning the Cortes out of weakness rather than strength (Grafe, *Distant Tyranny*).

36. Following Drelichman and Worth, Grafe states that interest rates increased from 7.6 to 9.5 percent. (In the eighteenth century, the crown additionally improved the market of annuities, which paid close to face value [ibid.].)

37. Spanish historic territories borrowed at lower interest rates than the crown, 2–4 percent, which were lower than what the Dutch provinces paid in the seventeenth and eighteenth centuries (ibid., chap. 1).

38. Irigoin and Grafe, "The Spanish Empire and Its Legacy," 247: "The system was obviously less conditioned by historical exemptions than its European counterparts, but that did not create a more modern fiscal system in the sense of one that was more rationally bureaucratic, centralized, and based upon clear universal rules as to who had to pay what, where and when. In practice, the imperial fiscal system differed from that in Spain (or Castile) primarily because the labor and silver 'discovered' in America

meant that the fiscal base expanded instead of contracted." See Maria Alejandra Irigoin and Regina Grafe, "Bargaining for Absolutism: A Spanish Path to Nation-State and Empire Building," *Hispanic American Historical Review* 88, no. 2 (2007): 173–209.

39. Maria Alejandra Irigoin and Regina Grafe, "A Stakeholder Empire: The Political Economy of Spanish Imperial Rule in America," *Economic History Review* 65, no. 2 (2012): 609–51. I would like to thank the authors for sharing this article with me prior to its publication.

40. In the sixteenth century and due to the trade and mining booms, the Americas contributed on average 18 percent of the revenue collected by the Spanish central treasury. Yearly contributions fluctuated significantly. In the seventeenth century that average dropped to 10 percent, and for most of the eighteenth century it decreased to 5 percent, though it was 12 percent in the late 1700s. These numbers speak of overall significant transfers, but they are far from reflecting the extractive capacity imagined by Spain's foes (Grafe, *Distant Tyranny*).

41. Irigoin and Grafe, "Bargaining for Absolutism," 201.

42. On August 17, 1780, Charles III ordered the collection of a donativo in the American possessions, stipulating that Indians and castas should contribute 1 peso per family (hearth), while nobles and Spaniards should pay 2 pesos. Out of a total of 843,474 pesos, 75 percent came from the contributions of Indians and castas. For a summary of the royal ordinances contending with loans and donativos collected in New Spain, refer to Marichal, *La bancarrota del virreinato*, app. 3. Nobles and castas were expected to contribute the same amounts in New Granada in 1781 when the decree concerning the donativo was published (John L. Phelan, *The People and the King: The Comunero Revolution in Colombia, 1781* [Madison: University of Wisconsin Press, 1978], 29).

43. Natalia Silva Prada, "Contribución de la población indígena novohispana al erario real: El donativo gracioso y voluntario o 'rigorosa pension' de 1781 y su impacto en recaudaciones posteriores," *Signos Históricos* 1 (1999): 28–58.

CHAPTER 2

1. José Canga Argüelles, *Diccionario de hacienda para el uso de los encargados de la suprema dirección de ella*, vol. 2, *Donativo* (London: Imprenta Española de M. Calero, 1826).

2. Ibid. Canga Argüelles lists among the voluntary donativos those approved by the Cortes in 1653, the one provided by the merchants of Andalusia in 1684, the one offered by the archbishops and bishops of Spain in 1784, the one that came from all the "classes of the nation" during the War against the French Convention (1793–1795), and the one promoted by Francisco de Saavedra in 1798.

3. Ibid.

4. Ibid., vol. 4, *Préstamos*.

5. In 1798 he served as *procurador general* and *síndico* in Gijón; in 1799 he began serving at the Caja de Amortización de Vales Reales; in 1803 he became *secretario de estado*; and in 1810 he was appointed as secretario de hacienda.

6. Robert I. Burns, SJ, ed., *Las Siete Partidas*, vol. 4, *Family, Commerce and the Sea* (Philadelphia: University of Pennsylvania Press, 2001), 1008.

7. Ibid., 4:1022.

8. Ibid.

9. If fools, madmen, or spendthrifts made donations, they would be invalid. In the case of heretics and criminals, the donation would be valid if it took place before they had perpetuated their crimes.

10. Manuel Josef de Ayala, *Diccionario de gobierno y legislación de Indias* (Madrid: Ediciones de Cultura Hispanica, 1989); and Fabian de Fonseca and D. Carlos de Urrutia, *Historia general de la real hacienda* (Mexico City: Imprenta de Vicente Garcia Torres, 1850).

11. Fonseca and Urrutia, *Historia general*, 4:429–50.

12. For gifts in archaic societies refer to the classic works of Maurice Godelier, *The Enigma of the Gift* (Chicago: University of Chicago Press, 1999); and Marcel Mauss, *The Gift: Forms and Functions of Exchange in Archaic Societies* (London: Cohen and West, 1954).

13. Valentin Groebner, *Liquid Assets, Dangerous Gifts: Presents and Politics at the End of the Middle Ages* (Philadelphia: University of Pennsylvania Press, 2002), 1.

14. Ibid., 5.

15. Natalie Zemon Davis, *The Gift in Sixteenth-Century France* (Madison: University of Wisconsin Press, 2000). According to Davis, the "gift mode" drew upon Christian charity, noble liberality, favors of friendship, and neighborly generosity. In all four traditions, donors acted voluntarily, and recipients were expected to express their gratitude and bound to reciprocate. The Christian charitable tradition included gift exchanges among rich and poor, laity and clergy, and living and dead. However, noble liberality was reserved for wealthy households. Favors of friendship referred to exchanges based on love and sympathy instead of utility. And neighborly generosity represented the solidarity that bound peasants and artisans.

16. Lords additionally gifted in kind and hospitality. They occasionally gave away small amounts of money. Peasants presented their lords with gifts "suitable to their stations," including fish, fruits, capons, and goslings. These gifts were not the equivalent of rents in kind as they were infrequent and respectful actions taken when one needed a favor (ibid., 68).

17. Gesture and language distinguished the "gift mode" from the sale and contract modes. Plates illustrating sales and contracts featured the parties leveled and standing, while in the case of gifts, either donor or recipient appeared at a lower plane, bowing, or kneeling, indicating either the superior social status of the donor and/or the gratitude and obligation to reciprocate on the part of the beneficiary (ibid., chap. 4).

18. Courtesy manuals recommended reciprocating neither too soon (out of pride) nor too late (which would humiliate the donor) (ibid., 108).

19. Jacques Le Goff, *Your Money or Your Life: Economy and Religion in the Middle Ages* (New York: Zone Books, 1988). Le Goff and other scholars have pointed out that the association between usury and the Jews promoted anti-Semitism.

20. Gerardo Landrove Diaz, *La regulación de la usura en el ordenamiento jurídico español* (Santiago de Compostela: Imprenta Paredes, 1967–1968).

21. Bernard W. Dempsey, *Interest and Usury* (Washington, D.C.: American Council on Public Affairs, 1943). The author emphasizes the works of Lessius (1554–1623), Luis de Molina (1536–1600), and Juan de Lugo (1593–1660). For the changes in monetary theory emerging from Salamanca, refer to Marjorie Grice-Hutchinson, *The School of Salamanca: Readings in Spanish Monetary Theory, 1544–1605* (Oxford: Clarendon Press, 1952).

22. Amalia Kessler, "Enforcing Virtue: Social Norms and Self-Interest in an Eighteenth-Century Merchant Court," *Law and History Review* 22, no. 1 (2004): 71–118.

23. The Cinco Gremios Mayores of Madrid associated the five most important merchant guilds, namely silk, canvas, jewelry, broadcloth, and spices. In Spain, they managed public debt and tax farming and became the largest military contractors. As bankers, they additionally took loans from private parties, paid interest to lenders from their own profits, and rewarded different types of investors with different interest rates. See Rafael Torres Sanchez, "Military Provisioning as the Driving Force behind the Growth of Spain's First Multinational: The Cinco Gremios Mayores during the Eighteenth Century" (paper presented at the European Network in Universal and Global History, Third European Congress, London School of Economics & Political Science, 14–17 April 2011); Jesus Cruz, *Gentlemen, Bourgeois and Revolutionaries: Political Change and Cultural Persistence among the Spanish Dominant Groups* (Cambridge: Cambridge University Press, 1996); and Jorge Pinto Rodriguez, "Los Cinco Gremios Mayores y el comercio colonial en el siglo XVIII," *Revista de Indias* 51, no. 192 (1991): 293–326.

24. José de Barrenechea, *Moral y economía en el siglo XVIII: Antología de textos sobre la usura; Zubiaur, Calatayud, los Cinco Gremios Mayores y Uría Nafarrondo* (Vitoria-Gasteiz: Gobierno Vasco, Departamento de Justicia, Economia, Trabajo y Seguridad Social, 1995).

25. In the sixteenth and seventeenth centuries the kings of Spain occasionally collected donativos. They were usually enforced along with other measures such as voluntary and occasionally forced loans. Philip IV and Charles II frequently used these mechanisms, and therefore, they became regular features of the Castilian treasury. When donativos were aimed at particular groups, they generally targeted officeholders, merchants of the consulados, the Catholic Church (*subsidio ecclesiástico*), and cabildos. There were at least four collections of donativos in the 1650s, three in the 1660s, and four in the 1670s. For a discussion of these issues, refer to Antonio Dominguez Ortiz, "La desigualdad contributiva en Castilla durante el siglo XVII," *Anuario de Historia del Derecho Español* (1951–1952): 1222–72. See also Manuel Garzón Pareja, *La hacienda de Carlos II* (Madrid: Instituto de Estudios Fiscales, Ministerio de Hacienda, 1980), 331–93; and José Canga Argüelles, *Diccionario de hacienda*, 2 vols. (Madrid: Pirámide, 1984). For collections of donativos in Spanish America prior to the 1780s, refer to Hussey, "Analysis of a Document Concerning a 'Voluntary Donation' in Guatemala in 1644"; Smith, "A Peruvian Donativo Gracioso in 1717"; and Phelan, *The Kingdom of Quito in the Seventeenth Century*, 109–11.

26. The Spanish Crown traditionally relied on German, Dutch, Genoese, and Portuguese bankers for managing its debt. In the 1640s, the crown lost access to important international lines of credit due to the Dutch revolt, the separation of the Portuguese territories, and the persecution of Portuguese Jewish bankers by the Inquisition. Consequently, credit became more national and decentralized. Donativos and advanced payments from Castilian tax farmers and municipal institutions (cabildos) shifted credit to Castilian private and corporate hands. Thus, funds from private savings, increasing numbers of taxes, and municipal rents were channeled toward servicing public debt (Thompson, "Castile: Polity, Fiscality and Fiscal Crisis"). For the role of municipalities as sources of public credit, stressing both the political and financial aspects, see Felipe Ruiz Martin, "Procedimientos crediticios para la recaudación de los tributos fiscales en las ciudades castellanas en los siglos XVI y XVII: El caso de Valladolid," in *Dinero y crédito (siglos XVI al XIX): Actas del Coloquio Internacional de Historia Económica*, ed. Alfonso Otazu (Madrid: Editorial Moneda y Crédito, 1978), 37–47; and José I. Martinez Ruiz, "Donativos y emprestitos sevillanos a la hacienda real (siglos XVI y XVII)," *Revista de Historia Económica* 2, no. 3 (1984): 233–44.

27. Economic expansion generally caused the growth of regalian rents (alcabalas, custom duties, and monopolies), while economic stagnation required shifting toward concessionary revenues. Servicios, in addition to being constitutionally limiting, were fixed in quantity and resented because they usually fell on an impoverished population. Fiscal crises in Castile were constitutionally limiting. When regalian rents stagnated or decreased, the crown needed the consent of the Cortes to establish new or increase existing servicios. Additionally, as public debt reached different sectors of society (and affected the interests of many groups) the Cortes became more involved in the financial and fiscal arrangements concerning it. In sum, in Castile fiscal stress weakened the king's absolute prerogative to tax and his freedom to deal with creditors unsupervised. It is noteworthy that the influence of the Cortes on government was limited by their lack of legislative powers. However, they were financially influential. The Nueva Recopilación declared that "no impositions, contributions or other taxes are to be imposed on the whole kingdom without the Cortes being summoned and without their consent being granted by the *procuradores*" (Thompson, "Castile: Polity, Fiscality and Fiscal Crisis," 146). For a discussion of the relationship between fiscal strategies and politics in Castile in the sixteenth and seventeenth centuries, refer to Thompson, "Castile: Polity, Fiscality and Fiscal Crisis"; and I. A. A. Thompson, "Castile: Absolutism, Constitutionalism and Liberty," in *Fiscal Crises, Liberty, and Representative Government*, ed. Philip Hoffman and Kathryn Norberg (Stanford, CA: Stanford University Press, 1994), 181–225.

28. For alternative forms of representation, see Hanna P. Pitkin, *The Concept of Representation* (Berkeley: University of California Press, 1972).

29. Dominguez Ortiz discussed these aspects of donativos in "La desigualdad contributiva en Castilla." During the 1640s crisis, subjects defaulted on their taxes, and the fiscal system virtually collapsed. "Barter fiscality" (a reversion to nonmonetary demands for men, hay, transport, and foodstuffs for the troops) and donativos

replaced regular taxation. Localized and unequal taxation was at odds with the ideal of a national fiscal system based on uniform, permanent, and socially equitable taxes (Thompson, "Castile: Polity, Fiscality and Fiscal Crises").

30. Dominguez Ortiz, "La desigualdad contributiva en Castilla."

31. Examples can be found in Dominguez Ortiz, "La desigualdad contributiva en Castilla"; Garzón Pareja, *La hacienda de Carlos II*; and Thompson, "Castile: Polity, Fiscality and Fiscal Crisis." In 1629 the encomenderos from Quito obtained from the king the right to inherit their encomiendas from to two to three successive generations in exchange for a substantial donativo (Phelan, *The Kingdom of Quito*, 109).

32. John Coatsworth quantified the incidence of rural rebellions in Mesoamerica and the Andes from 1700 to 1899. He found that the number of village uprisings increased in both regions throughout the eighteenth century. Rebellions in Peru reached an early peak in the 1730s but then declined in the 1750s. In both areas, the number of rebellions increased again in the 1760s, but, unlike any other area, uprisings in Peru rose again in the 1770s, leading to the Túpac Amaru movement in the 1780s. Until the Hidalgo rebellion of 1810, there was no generalized upheaval in Mexico, while in the Andes, the number of village uprisings dropped sharply after the Túpac Amaru rebellion. From the 1840s through the 1870s, Mexico experienced an upsurge in village revolts and large-scale caste wars (John Coatsworth, "Patterns of Rural Rebellion in Latin America: Mexico in Comparative Perspective," in *Riot, Rebellion and Revolution: Rural Social Conflict in Mexico*, ed. Frederick Katz [Princeton, NJ: Princeton University Press, 1988], 21–62). For New Granada and Peru, refer to John R. Fisher, Allan J. Keuthe, and Anthony McFarlane, eds., *Reform and Insurrection in Bourbon New Granada and Peru* (Baton Rouge: Louisiana State University Press, 1990).

33. William B. Taylor, *Drinking, Homicide, and Rebellion in Colonial Mexican Villages* (Stanford, CA: Stanford University Press, 1979).

34. In Mexico, most of the revolts studied by Taylor arose from purely local grievances. The imposition of new taxes or abuses by tax collectors were less important in sparking rebellions than any changes in the lifestyle and autonomy of the village, such as the redrawing of community boundaries, prohibitions on fiestas, or the threat of external authorities (lay or ecclesiastic). Peasant villages appear to have been in a state of continuous latent conflict over scarce resources with competing groups. Normally, the potential conflict was repressed through accommodations among the groups, and rebellion was most likely to occur when customary agreements broke down (Taylor, *Drinking, Homicide, and Rebellion*). In eighteenth-century Peru, income came from three sources: taxes on mining, taxes on commerce, and Indian tributes. The Indian *tributo*, although a head tax, was paid by the community as a whole. In order to raise the cash needed to meet the tributo obligations, caciques hired Indians from their communities for the local haciendas and *obrajes* or employed them as pack drivers. Additionally, they devoted part of the communal land to cash crops. Thus, the mita system and the tributo were the only mechanisms available to tap Indian labor for the colonial centers of production. In the second half of the eighteenth century, the *reparto de mercancías* was legalized and became another system for extraction of payments in coin, labor, and kind from the Indians. Fiscal issues constantly lay

at the root of colonial social unrest as they not only affected different social sectors but also created tension between the different arms of the colonial government. For example, Indians who were more willing to pay tribute than meet their obligations owed to the church caused competition between corregidors and parish priests. In the 1770s, taxes on production and trade increased, creating a greater burden on the entire population of Peru. The alcabala was raised twice and expanded over traditionally exempted products. Customhouses were opened on the main commercial routes, and a project to extend the tributo to mestizos and mulattoes was approved. These measures caused a significant increase in revenues. However, they also sparked the wave of insurrection that swept across the viceroyalty, culminating in the Great Rebellion of 1780–1781 (Scarlett O'Phelan Godoy, *Rebellions and Revolts in Eighteenth-Century Peru and Upper Peru* [Cologne: Böhlau, 1985], chaps. 1 and 2). For the fiscal origins of the Comunero Revolt, refer to Phelan, *The People and the King*, chap. 2. A full discussion of the Quito insurrection is available in Anthony McFarlane, "The 'Rebellion of the Barrios': Urban Insurrection in Bourbon Quito," *Hispanic American Historical Review* 69, no. 2 (1989): 283–330. For an analysis of the long-term economic causes of the rebellion, see Kenneth Andrien, "Economic Crisis, Taxes and the Quito Insurrection of 1765," *Past and Present* 129 (1990): 104–31. For the role of illegitimate curacas, refer to Sergio Serulnikov, *Subverting Colonial Authority: Challenges to Spanish Rule in Eighteenth-Century Southern Andes* (Durham, NC: Duke University Press, 2003).

35. Anthony McFarlane, "Rebellions in Late Colonial Spanish America: A Comparative Perspective," *Bulletin of Latin American Research* 14, no. 3 (1995): 313–38; and Anthony McFarlane, "Civil Disorders and Popular Protests in Late Colonial New Granada," *Hispanic American Historical Review* 64, no. 1 (1984): 17–54.

36. Colin MacLachlan's work skillfully connects political ideas with institutional and social change. The author points out that the Bourbons faced many difficulties in ruling their empire as they attempted to replace a system of authority that was spiritual, flexible, and based on respect, loyalty, and fidelity with a material one based on prosperity and obedience (MacLachlan, *Spain's Empire in the New World: The Role of Ideas in Institutional and Social Change* [Berkeley: University of California Press, 2003]).

37. McFarlane, "Rebellions in Late Colonial Spanish America," 323. According to MacLachlan, the enlightened belief that a rational organization of the state and society would eliminate both economic backwardness and politics (perceived as the source of all evils by Bourbon reformers) supported the change from Habsburg to Bourbon political principles. However, when confronted with the reality of the New World, the reformers immediately found out that the elimination of politics was not an easy task (MacLachlan, *Spain's Empire in the New World*).

38. Phelan, *The People and the King*, 163.

39. Visitador Areche's decree of 16 November 1779 aimed at extending tribute liability to mestizos, cholos, and zambiagos. For a thorough discussion of the new fiscal impositions in Bourbon Peru, refer to O'Phelan Godoy, *Rebellions and Revolts in Eighteenth-Century Peru*; and D. Cahill, "Taxonomy of a Colonial Riot: The Arequipa Disturbances of 1780," in *Reform and Insurrection in Bourbon New Granada and Peru*,

ed. John R. Fisher, Allan J. Keuthe, and Anthony McFarlane (Baton Rouge: Louisiana State University Press, 1990), 255–91.

40. For Katari's rebellion, see Sergio Serulnikov, "Disputed Images of Colonialism: Spanish Rule and Indian Subversion in Northern Potosi, 1777–1780," *Hispanic American Historical Review* 76, no. 2 (1996): 189–226.

41. Phelan, *The People and the King*, 110. In the Spanish world, tributes were associated with dishonor and servitude. Nobles were exempt from direct taxation, while commoners (*pecheros*) were not. The association between nobility and tax exemption was so strong that in dubious cases, the tax rolls were used to prove noble birth (Dominguez Ortiz, "La desigualdad contributiva en Castilla"). In Spanish America, all Spaniards were exempt from direct taxation while Indians, some blacks, and free mulattoes paid tributes. As the fiscal needs of the state increased, it became necessary for the crown to find ways of raising revenues without affecting the social ranks. For a discussion on the importance of honor in Spanish America, see Lyman Johnson and Sonya Lipsett-Rivera, eds., *The Faces of Honor: Sex, Shame, and Violence in Colonial Latin America* (Albuquerque: University of New Mexico Press, 1998).

42. For the sources of Spanish *pactismo*, refer to the preliminary essay by Luciano Pereña in Francisco Suárez, ed., *De iuramento fidelitatis* (Madrid: Consejo Superior de Investigaciones Científicas, Escuela Española de La Paz, 1979). Also see Guerra, *Modernidad e independencias*; Monica Quijada, "*Potestas Populi* in Hispanic Political Thought," *Mexican Studies/EstudiosMexicanos* 24, no. 2 (2008): 185–219; and MacLachlan, *Spain's Empire in the New World*.

43. Levi, "Reciprocidad mediterranea."

44. On the common good, refer to the preliminary essay by Pereña in Suárez, *De iuramento fidelitatis*; and MacLachlan, *Spain's Empire in the New World*.

45. Quijada argues that while Francisco de Vitoria insisted that leadership ought to be delegated by the community, he additionally argued that the king's power comes from God, marking a difference between power (received from God) and authority (granted by the community). Francisco Suárez, on the other hand, argued that the only sources of legitimate power were man's natural liberty and the consent of the community. Once the community transferred its sovereignty, however, it was irrecoverable except when the existence of the community was at stake. This clause preserved order and hierarchy within the community. Other thinkers such as Domingo de Soto, Fernando Vázquez de Menchaca, and Juan de Mariana defended the principle that power exclusively resided in the community and was transferred to the prince by consent (Quijada, "*Potestas Populi* in Hispanic Political Thought").

46. Ibid., 215. For imaginaire as a concept, refer to page 191.

47. Refer to the scholarship of François-Xavier Guerra cited in the introduction, note 20. Also Antonio Annino, ed., *Historia de las elecciones en Iberoamérica, siglo XIX* (Buenos Aires: Fondo de Cultura Economica, 1995).

48. Federica Morelli, "Entre el antiguo y el nuevo régimen: El triunfo de los cuerpos intermedios; El caso de la Audiencia de Quito, 1765–1830," *Historia y Política* 10 (2003): 163–90; and Federica Morelli, "Origenes y valores del municipalismo iberoamericano," *Araucaria: Revista Iberoamericana de Filosofía, Política y Humanidades* 18 (2007): 116–29.

49. During the Napoleonic crisis, sovereignty reverted to the people. In Spanish America, the abstract concept of the people materialized in tangible institutions: the cities, the juntas, and the cabildos. In addition to representing the people, in the eighteenth century cabildos strengthened their fiscal capacities, their jurisdictional power over neighboring rural areas, and their ability to administer local justice (Federica Morelli, "El espacio municipal: Cambios en la jurisdicción territorial del cabildo de Quito, 1765–1830," in *Dinámicas de antiguo régimen y orden constitucional: Representación, justicia y administración, siglos XVIII y XIX*, ed. Marco Bellingeri [Torino: Otto Editore, 2003]).

50. Jaime Rodriguez O., *La independencia de la América española* (Mexico City: Fondo de Cultura Económica, 1996).

51. Bartolomé Clavero, *Tantas personas como estados: Por una antropología política de la historia europea* (Madrid: Tecnos, 1986).

52. It is noteworthy that by 1806, bureaucratic circumstances and fate had already weakened viceregal authority. As demonstrated by Susan Socolow, the sudden death in office of two viceroys coupled with the inability of the crown to secure permanent appointments reduced their time in office from five to two years, and consequently five viceroys commanded the region between 1795 and 1804 (Socolow, *The Bureaucrats of Buenos Aires, 1769–1810: Amor al real servicio* [Durham, NC: Duke University Press, 1987]).

53. I discuss the constitutional meaning of these events in my doctoral dissertation (Grieco, "Politics and Public Credit," chaps. 7 and 8).

54. Before expelling the judges of the audiencia, the junta circumscribed its political and ceremonial authority and limited its judicial capacity. The loyal judges were less influential than the royal oidores. The inherited distribution of power (*cuatro causas* as opposed to division of powers), coupled with the lack of constitutional innovation, allowed the cabildo of Buenos Aires to preserve and expand its authority and simultaneously legitimate the transition from the colonial to the revolutionary regime. Cabildos in Buenos Aires were abolished in 1821 (Marcela Ternavasio, *Gobernar la revolución: Poderes en disputa en el Rio de la Plata, 1810–1816* [Buenos Aires: Siglo XXI Editores, 2007]).

55. Bonney, ed., *The Rise of the Fiscal State in Europe*.

56. In Castile citizenship was a natural right. Vecindad conferred the right to royal protection, access to land, local justice and local officeholding, selective forms of punishment, tax exemptions, and market privileges. Vecinos' duties included residence in the community, service in the local militia, payment of taxes, and financing public expenses. By the early modern period, one was additionally required to be a Christian, reside in the community, and establish ties with other residents in order to achieve the status of vecino (Herzog, *Defining Nations: Immigrants and Citizens in Early Modern Spain and Spanish America* [New Haven, CT: Yale University Press, 2003]).

57. Herzog states that unlike in Castile, formal procedures for achieving citizenship disappeared from the Spanish American municipal record. Consequently, vecindad was discontinued as a natural right and became a fully social construction.

58. Popular mobilization has been most recently discussed by Gabriel Di Meglio, *¡Viva el bajo pueblo! La plebe urbana de Buenos Aires y la política entre la Revolución de Mayo y el rosismo* (Buenos Aires: Prometeo Libros, 2006).

59. For the impact of slavery in the city of Buenos Aires, refer to Lyman L. Johnson, *Workshop of Revolution: Plebeian Buenos Aires and the Atlantic World, 1776–1810* (Durham, NC: Duke University Press, 2011).

60. Mark D. Szuchman, *Order, Family, and Community in Buenos Aires, 1810–1860* (Stanford, CA: Stanford University Press, 1988); and Bianca Premo, *Children of the Father King: Youth, Authority, and Legal Minority in Colonial Lima* (Chapel Hill: University of North Carolina Press, 2005).

61. Johnson, *Workshop of Revolution*, 275.

62. Viviana L. Grieco, "Family and Political Authority in Early Nineteenth-Century Buenos Aires: Rituals, Practices, and Texts, 1806–1816," *Colonial Latin American Historical Review* 17, no. 1 (2008): 63–96.

63. For the militarization of Buenos Aires as a source of revolutionary legitimacy refer to Tulio Halperin Donghi, "Militarización revolucionaria en Buenos Aires, 1806–1815," in *El ocaso del orden colonial en Hispanoamérica*, ed. Tulio Halperin Donghi and Herbert Klein (Buenos Aires: Editorial Sudamericana, 1978), 123–58. Also refer to Pilar González Bernaldo's works, including "Producción de una nueva legitimidad: Ejército y sociedades patrióticas en Buenos Aires entre 1810 y 1813," *Cuadernos Americanos* 17 (1989): 134–56; "La Revolución Francesa y la emergencia de nuevas prácticas de la política: La irrupción de la sociabilidad política en Rio de la Plata revolucionario, 1810–1815," *Boletín del Instituto de Historia Argentina y Americana "Dr. E. Ravignani,"* 3rd ser., 3 (1991): 7–28; "Las pulperías de Buenos Aires: Historia de una expresión de sociabilidad popular," *Siglo XIX* 7, no. 13 (1993): 27–54; "La 'identidad nacional' en el Rio de la Plata post-colonial: Continuidades y rupturas con el antiguo régimen," *Anuario IHES* 12 (1997): 109–22; and *Civilidad y política en los orígenes de la nación Argentina: Las sociabilidades en Buenos Aires, 1829–1862* (Buenos Aires: Fondo de Cultura Económica, 2001).

64. Irurozqui, "De como el vecino hizo al ciudadano en Charcas."

65. Ibid.

66. Hilda Sabato, "On Political Citizenship in Nineteenth Century Latin America," *American Historical Review* 106 (2001): 1296. The literature on elections and the emergence of modern citizenship is broad. For a general overview, refer to Sabato, "On Political Citizenship in Nineteenth Century Latin America." Note that Johnson sees elections as widespread practices among the artisans.

67. Gabriel Di Meglio, "Patria," in *Lenguaje y revolución: Conceptos políticos clave en el Rio de la Plata, 1780–1850*, ed. Noemí Goldman (Buenos Aires: Prometeo Libros, 2008).

PART TWO

1. For a discussion of Spain's diplomacy in the 1790s, refer to Gonzalo Anes, *El siglo de las luces* (Madrid: Alianza, 1994), chaps. 6 and 8.

2. For the crown's financial strategy during the 1790s, see chapter 1.

3. Primary sources for this database include AGNA, Sala IX, Tomas de Razón, Libro 60 (AGNA, IX, 8-7-12). In this bound volume of four hundred pages, royal officers recorded most of the donativos collected from 1793 through 1801. Additionally, I have found the following rosters at the AGI in the volumes of viceregal correspondence: Buenos Aires 85, Duplicado 154; Buenos Aires 88, Duplicado 235; Buenos Aires 90, Duplicado 55; Buenos Aires 93, Duplicado s/n; Buenos Aires 94, Duplicados 1 and 2; Buenos Aires 96, Duplicado s/n and 45; Buenos Aires 97, Duplicados 49, 50, 54, 78, and 80; Buenos Aires 109, Duplicado 8. Fortunately, the libro manual recording donativos collected between 1793 and 1796 survived. The information available in this volume reveals the multiple mechanisms at play in the transfer of funds to the treasury in Buenos Aires (AGNA, XIII, 42-1-2). For the early nineteenth century, sources are scattered. Donativos for the British Invasions of Buenos Aires were mainly collected through the cabildo. Most of the information for this database comes from the Archivo General del Nación Argentina, *Acuerdos del extinguido cabildo de Buenos Aires, serie IV, tomo II, 1805–1807* (Buenos Aires: Archivo General del Nación Argentina, 1926). Records of donativos are very rich sources as they registered not only the sums donated but also the name, sex, social status, and occupation of donors as well as the type of payment they were willing to make.

4. Regarding currency, those amounts that were not listed in *pesos de ocho reales* were converted following the guidelines provided by Humberto Burzio, *Diccionario de la moneda hispanoamericana*, 2 vols. (Buenos Aires: Fondo Histórico y Bibliográfico José Toribio Medina, 1952). As for the amounts in pesos, those that included reales were rounded off to the next peso if the number of reales was four or more. For example, a donativo of 16 pesos 3 reales was computed as 16 pesos, while one of 16 pesos 5 reales was computed as 17 pesos.

5. The *libro de tomas de razón* recorded the different type of services subjects provided to the crown. In addition to donativos, these books complied the service records for bureaucrats and military men (*fojas de servicios*). Libros de tomas de razón recorded temporal as well as spiritual donations. The libro manual was the accounting book the royal treasurers utilized to record the financial instruments and transactions transferring donativos across the different cajas. For donativos in kind, see the appendix.

CHAPTER 3

1. After the Jesuits were expelled in 1767, the territory of the Guarani missions was divided into two separate governorships. Reunified in 1770, the mission towns were divided again in 1784. Seventeen of them fell under the jurisdiction of the intendancy of Buenos Aires, and the remaining thirteen were incorporated into Paraguay. In 1803 the Governorship of Misiones was erected as an independent jurisdiction, but in 1805 it was again reincorporated into Paraguay.

2. As noted in the introduction to part 2, the earliest entry in the libro manual appears on 26 June 1793, while annual contributions continued until the peace was made known in Buenos Aires on 4 September 1795 (twenty-six months). In the libros

de tomas de razón, donativos stopped in December 1794, the closing date for accepting offers (eighteen months).

3. Irigoin and Grafe, "The Spanish Empire and Its Legacy."

4. John Lynch documents the impressive growth in revenue collected by customs after the enforcement of free trade in 1778, which more than doubled from the previous year (increasing from 20,000 pesos to 53,974 pesos in 1778) and reached an average of 400,000 pesos between 1791 and 1794 (Lynch, *Spanish Colonial Administration, 1782–1810: The Intendant System in the Viceroyalty of Rio de la Plata* [London: Atlone Press, 1958], 121–22 and 146–47). According to Marichal, the Viceroyalty of New Spain collected 1,559,000 pesos in donativos during the War against the French Convention. Population estimates for the late eighteenth century are 5.9 million for New Spain and 500,000 for the Viceroyalty of Rio de la Plata (Rodriguez O., *The Independence of Spanish America*, 8). For revenue per capita refer to Irigoin and Grafe, "A Stakeholder Empire."

5. All salary discounts recorded in the libro manual were prorated until the end of the war.

6. The yearly subtotals in the cartas cuentas in pesos were the following: 1793: 39,664; 1794: 153,738; 1795: 57,020. Refer to Te Paske et al., *The Royal Treasuries of the Spanish Empire in America*, vol. 3. These figures are also available online at https://home.comcast.net/~richardgarnero5/cajafiles.html.

7. For situados across the Spanish empire, refer to Irigoin and Grafe, "The Spanish Empire and Its Legacy." For the Viceroyalty of Rio de la Plata in the seventeenth century, see Zacarías Moutoukias, "Corruption and Commerce in Seventeenth-Century Buenos Aires," *Hispanic American Historical Review* 67, no. 4 (1988): 771–801; also, Moutoukias, *Contrabando y control colonial en el siglo XVII*. For the eighteenth century, see Jorge Gelman, *De mercachifle a gran comerciante* (La Rábida: Universidad Internacional de Andalucía, Sede Iberoamericana de la Rábida, 1996); and Eduardo Saguier, *Genealogía de la tragedia argentina*, 2:2:chap. 19. Internet resource, http://www.er-saguier.org.

8. For factional struggles over the appointment of situadistas, refer to German Tjarks, *El consulado de Buenos Aires* (Buenos Aires: Universidad de Buenos Aires, Facultad de Filosofía y Letras, 1962), 2:chap. 16.

9. AGNA, XIII, 42-1-2.

10. States were co-opted by elites in a patrimonial fashion when, out of fiscal need, the monarch created privileges and monopolies. In doing so, the monarch lost political and economic initiative. Absolute and parliamentary rule were generally regarded as state technologies capable of taming elites as monarchs found in these systems mechanisms for suppressing aristocratic power. However, this model fails to explain early modern European historical processes since scholars have found that administrative centralization did not necessarily imply the marginalization of powerful interest groups. On the contrary, early modern European monarchs co-opted elites with or without representative institutions when, by expanding their spheres of influence, they simultaneously created opportunities for nobles and aristocrats to become entrepreneurial

through military service and victualing, office holding, lending, and tax farming. In William Beik's words, elites "basked in the sun" under Louis XIV (Beik, *Absolutism and Society in Seventeenth-Century France: State Power and Provincial Aristocracy in Languedoc* [Cambridge: Cambridge University Press, 1985]).

11. Tjarks, *El consulado de Buenos Aires*, 2:chap. 16.

12. The libro manual did not record bonuses for the fifty-seven transfers from regional cajas to Buenos Aires, although, in many cases, the percentage paid in bonuses and commissions was openly stated. Transfers totaled 133,846 pesos, that is, about 50 percent of the entire donativo. The situadistas did not have a monopoly over the Potosí–Buenos Aires route as several merchants who transferred only middle-ranged sums also operated within it (AGNA, XIII, 42-1-2).

13. AGNA, XIII, 42-1-2. In a letter sent to the viceroy, the governor of Salta stated that he would wait until the situado came by to ship the donativos down to Buenos Aires (AGNA, IX, 8-7-12).

14. The largest donativo transfers from the Alto Peruvian provinces to Buenos Aires included the following: one from Charcas of 15,000 pesos deposited in Buenos Aires on 6 February 1794; two from La Paz, one of 22,155 pesos deposited on 20 December 1793 and the other one of 12,238 pesos deposited on 27 June 1794; three transfers from Potosí, one of 19,476 pesos, another one of 12,166 pesos, and a third one of 11,120 pesos, deposited in Buenos Aires on 27 June 1794, 12 August 1794, and 11 December 1795, respectively. Most of the smaller transactions (thirty-nine in total) associated with donativos collected in the Rio de la Plata provinces cleared in Buenos Aires between June and October of 1793 (AGNA, XIII, 42-1-2).

15. Post offices opened in Catamarca, Córdoba, Corrientes, Jujuy, Mendoza, Parana, La Rioja, Salta, San Juan, San Luis, Santa Fe, Santiago del Estero, and Tucumán. The *carrera* (route) to Potosí started in Buenos Aires and traveled through Córdoba, Santiago del Estero, Tucumán, Salta, Jujuy, Chichas, and Porco. The route to Chile connected Buenos Aires with Córdoba, Mendoza, and Uspallata. Tucumán, Mendoza, Catamarca, La Rioja, and San Juan were integrated through their own route (*carrera de la travesía*), and Buenos Aires connected with Paraguay through Santa Fe, Corrientes, and Misiones.

16. The Basavilbasos were married to other prominent merchant families from Buenos Aires (Santa Coloma and Azcuenaga) and ranked among the most successful merchant families in the region (Susan Socolow, *The Merchants of Buenos Aires, 1778–1810: Family and Commerce* [Cambridge: Cambridge University Press, 1978]).

17. Raquel Bisio de Orlando, "La renta de correos de Buenos Aires hasta 1810," in *Memoria del X Congreso del Instituto Nacional de Historia del Derecho Indiano*, ed. Instituto de Investigaciones Jurídicas de la UNAM (Mexico: Instituto de Investigaciones Jurídicas, 1995), 169–85.

18. Socolow, *The Bureaucrats of Buenos Aires*.

19. For instance, the postmaster of Sicasica as well as the one in Oruro utilized the postal revenue to finance regional trade and silver mining.

20. Similar cases support my decision to prorate annual donativos through the end of the war.

21. Socolow, *The Merchants of Buenos Aires*, 59.

22. AGNA, XIII, 42-1-2.

23. AGNA, XIII, 42-1-2.

24. Julia Sarrail, "Globalization and the Guarani: From Missions to Modernization in the Eighteenth Century" (PhD diss., Harvard University, 2010). After 1784, the thirteen Paraguayan mission towns fell under the jurisdiction of the intendancy of Paraguay, and thus, the administrator lost a share of the regional trade that was thereafter managed through Asunción.

25. AGNA, XIII, 42-1-2. Similar financial instruments were also utilized to transfer donativo funds from the Banda Oriental to the Buenos Aires treasury. An undisclosed number of troops from the Cuerpo de Blandengues of the Banda Oriental contributed 213 pesos in donativos by issuing a bill exchange against their supplier (*habilitador*) in Buenos Aires. As already discussed, these mechanisms resembled those employed since the seventeenth century by military leaders in partnership with merchants who financed their own mercantile operations by drawing on the funds that were supposed to pay for the salaries of the rank and file under their command.

26. Carlos Sempat Assadourian, *El sistema de la economía colonial: El mercado interior, regiones y espacio económico* (Mexico: Editorial Nueva Imagen, 1983).

27. AGNA, IX, 8-7-12.

28. AGI, Buenos Aires 120, Duplicado 353, Arredondo to Gardoqui, 18 September 1794, Buenos Aires; AGI, Buenos Aires 122, Duplicado 120, Melo de Portugal to Gardoqui, 10 March 1796, Buenos Aires.

29. Irigoin and Grafe, "A Stakeholder Empire."

30. Kendall W. Brown, "Price Movement in Eighteenth Century Peru: Arequipa," in *Essays on the Price History of Eighteenth-Century Latin America*, ed. Lyman L. Johnson and Enrique Tandeter (Albuquerque: University of New Mexico Press, 1990), 173–200; Johnson, *Workshop of Revolution*, chap. 7.

31. In Buenos Aires, grocery stores capitalized at under 500 pesos, and many of them did so below 200 pesos. Sellers of small retail stores made the terms of sale attractive by selling the stores in installments. Entrepreneurs of very limited means accessed the lower echelons of the commercial economy by heavily relying on credit. As in the case of smaller, independent merchants, competition and risk ruined many fortunes (Kinsbruner, *The Colonial Spanish-American City*, chap. 6).

CHAPTER 4

1. For a discussion of the fortunes made by the merchants of Buenos Aires as well as their politics through this and other wars, refer to Socolow, *The Merchants of Buenos Aires*.

2. The letters exchanged between the merchants of Buenos Aires and Diego Paniagua (the deputy in Madrid) show that negotiations concerning the erection of a consulado in Buenos Aries accelerated from June 1793 onward. On 11 December 1793, Paniagua reported that his negotiations were successful. The decree dated 6 February 1794 finally established the merchant guild in Buenos Aires, and on 13 February 1794,

Viceroy Arredondo notified the king of the merchants' contribution of 100,000 pesos (AGI, Buenos Aires 120, Duplicado 282). For the correspondence between the porteño merchants and their deputy, refer to Archivo General de la Nación (Argentina), *Consulado de Buenos Aires: Antecedentes, actas, documentos; Años 1785–1795*, vol. 1 (Buenos Aires: Kraft Ltda., 1936). For a discussion of the earlier negotiations, see Socolow, *The Merchants of Buenos Aires*, chap. 6; and German Tjarks, *El Consulado de Buenos Aires*.

   3.   AGI, Buenos Aires 120, Duplicado 282.

   4.   These financial operations and the political opportunities associated with them have been studied primarily for the consulado of Mexico City. Refer to Guillermina del Valle Pavón, "El apoyo financiero del consulado a las guerras españolas del siglo XVIII," in *El crédito en Nueva España*, ed. Maria del Pilar Martinez López Cano and Guillermina del Valle Pavón (Mexico City: Instituto Mora, El Colegio de Michoacán, El Colegio de México, Instituto de Investigaciones Históricas–UNAM, 1998). Tjarks, who has extensively studied the consulado of Buenos Aires, argues that revenue as well as loans and donativos channeled through this institution constituted a burden because instead of being invested locally, they were shipped to Spain. Additionally, Tjarks states that this policy was at odds with the consulado's charter as it diverted its revenues from public works and charity. He does not seem to fully grasp the financial and political significance of these transactions (Tjarks, *El Consulado de Buenos Aires*, 1:chaps. 2, 6.

   5.   The receipts detailing the annual payment of interest can be found in AGNA, IX, 31-s/a-5.

   6.   For information on Gaspar de Santa Coloma and other porteño merchants, refer to Socolow, *The Merchants of Buenos Aires*. Maria Josefa Engracia de la Jarrota y de la Quintana was born in 1747 and died in 1822. She was the daughter of Maria Josefa de la Quintana y Riglos and Domingo Alonso Ortiz de Rosas, both members of prominent merchant clans. In 1777 she married Agustin Casimiro de Aguirre, who, in addition to being the nephew of Viceroy Juan José de Vértiz, was the representative for a very prominent Spanish mercantile firm in Buenos Aires. His business included partnerships with merchants in Potosí, Cádiz, and Lima. Aguirre died in 1790, and Maria Josefa managed his estate thereafter. Maria Catalina de la Quintana was the daughter of Jose Ignacio de la Quintana y Riglos (brother of Josefa Lajarrota's mother) and Petrona Nicolasa de Aoiz. She was probably born in 1766, but she died unmarried before 1797; in that year, when the consulado paid her loan and interest back, her investment was handed over to his father because she had already passed away. The donativo therefore provided investment opportunities for single women and widows. Genealogical data about these women was collected from different sources including Enrique Udaondo, *Diccionario biográfico colonial argentino* (Buenos Aires: Editorial Huarpes, 1945); Carlos Jáureguy Rueda, *Matrimonios de la catedral de Buenos Aires, 1747–1823* (Buenos Aires: Fuentes Históricas y Genealógicas Argentinas, 1989); Vicente O. Cutolo, *Nuevo diccionario biográfico argentino, 1750–1930* (Buenos Aires: Elche, 1968–1985); Universidad Nacional de Buenos Aires, *Documentos para la historia argentina, Vol. 10: Territorio y población; Padrones de la ciudad y campaña de Buenos Aires (1726–1810)* (Buenos Aires: Instituto

de Investigaciones Históricas, 1955); "Genealogía hombres de mayo," in *Revista del Instituto Argentino de Ciencias Genealógicas* (Buenos Aires: Instituto Argentino de Ciencias Genealógicas, 1961); Roberto Vazquez Mansilla, *Matrimonios de la Iglesia de Nuestra Señora de la Concepción de Buenos Aires, 1737–1865* (Buenos Aires: Fuentes Históricas y Genealógicas Argentinas, 1988).

7. For a discussion of the coordination of the interests of lenders, borrowers, and monarchs, refer to Stephan R. Epstein, *Freedom and Growth: The Rise of States and Markets in Europe, 1300–1750* (London: Routledge, 2000), chap. 2. The quote is on page 26.

8. Although Gabriel Paquette does not discuss the financial brokerage of Spanish American consulados, his analysis sheds light into the complex negotiations and compromises between the crown and corporate institutions seeking licensed privilege. See Gabriel Paquette, "State-Civil Society Cooperation and Conflict in the Spanish Empire: The Intellectual and Political Activities of the Ultramarine Consulados and Economic Societies, c. 1780–1810," *Journal of Latin American Studies* 39 (2007): 263–98.

9. For supralocal forms of representation promoted by the Bourbons, refer to Annick Lempériére, "La representación política en el imperio español a finales del antiguo régimen," in *Dinámicas de antiguo régimen y orden constitucional: Representación, justicia y administración en Iberoamérica, siglos XVIII–XIX*, ed. Marco Bellingeri (Torino: Otto editore, 2000). The charter of the Banco de San Carlos established that individual and corporate bondholders in possession of at least twenty-five bonds had the right to send their deputies to the bank's general assembly; however, this "imperial" type of representative assembly never came together (Pedro Tedde, *El Banco de San Carlos* [Madrid: Alianza Editorial, 1988]).

10. For the role of diputaciones, see AGNA, XIII, 47-6-23.

11. For the risk involved in eighteenth-century Spanish American commerce, refer to Jeremy Baskes, "Risky Ventures: Reconsidering Mexico's Colonial Trade System," *Colonial Latin American Review* 14, no. 1 (2005): 27–54.

12. AGI, Buenos Aires 120, Duplicado 282.

13. In chapter 2, I pointed out that eighteenth-century merchants adopted a virtuous attitude toward their businesses for both social and commercial reasons. See also Kessler, "Enforcing Virtue."

14. Francisco Tomás y Valiente, *Gobierno e instituciones en la España del antiguo régimen*, 165–66; and Sharon Kettering, *Patrons, Brokers and Clients in Seventeenth-Century France* (Oxford: Oxford University Press, 1986).

15. Tomás y Valiente, *Gobierno e instituciones*. The sales of offices included provisions allowing purchasers to resell or bequeath appointments as they became the holder's private property. Generally, three transfers (or *renuncias*) were allowed, each one of them less profitable for the crown because each time it collected a smaller percentage in fees. The sale of appointments lasted only for one lifetime (Socolow, *The Bureaucrats of Buenos Aires*, chap. 4; and Mark A. Burkholder and Dewitt S. Chandler, *From Impotence to Authority: The Spanish Crown and the American Audiencias, 1687–1808* [Columbia: University of Missouri Press, 1977]).

16. For example, refer to Linda Arnold's works on Mexico and those by Jacques Barbier on Chile. Also see Burkholder and Chandler, *From Impotence to Authority*.

17. Alberto Gallo, "La venalidad de oficios públicos en Brasil en el siglo XVIII," in *Dinámicas de antiguo régimen y orden constitucional: Representación, justicia y administración en Iberoamérica, siglos XVIII–XIX*, ed. Marco Bellingeri (Torino: Otto editore, 2000).

18. Brewer, *The Sinews of Power*.

19. Socolow, *The Bureaucrats of Buenos Aires*.

20. Several incumbents who had purchased or inherited their offices refused to give them up. Also, petitions for bureaucratic appointment based on the service provided by the petitioners' ancestors continued (Socolow, *The Bureaucrats of Buenos Aires*).

21. While the total number of bureaucratic positions for all regions and branches in the Viceroyalty of Rio de la Plata is unknown, partial estimates are available. After the Bourbon Reforms, high-end political appointments across the viceregal territory (excluding corregidors, *subdelegados de Indios*, and the administradores of mission towns) increased to thirty-one offices. In Buenos Aires, the number of appointments across all government branches grew from 14 in 1767 to 136 in 1790 and 142 in 1810. For political appointments, refer to Ernesto J. A. Mader, *Nómina de gobernadores civiles y eclesiásticos de la Argentina durante la época española (1500–1810)* (Corrientes: Universidad Nacional del Nordeste, Instituto de Historia, Facultad de Humanidades). For Buenos Aires, see Socolow, *The Bureaucrats of Buenos Aires*.

22. AGNA, IX, 8-7-12, p. 126.

23. Depending on the area, intendants remained in office for longer or shorter periods of time: Buenos Aires, 5.3 years; Paraguay, 6.5 years; Córdoba, 6.3 years; Salta, 4.2 years; La Plata, 5.2 years; Cochabamba, 5.6 years; La Paz, 3.4 years; Puno, 3.0 years. Only two intendants (Jose del Pino Manrique and Francisco de Paula Sánz) were appointed to Potosí, and they served for six and twenty-one years, respectively. Their tenure was taken into consideration when estimating the average. The average tenure for each intendancy was estimated utilizing the information provided by Lynch, *Spanish Colonial Administration*, app. 1.

24. The intendants of Potosí received 10,000 pesos annually as they bore additional responsibilities at the mining center (Lynch, *Spanish Colonial Administration*).

25. Lynch documents the reduction of salaries although he does not explain the reasons behind this policy that contradicted Bourbon bureaucratic professionalization strategies.

26. AGI, Buenos Aires 90, Del Pino to Caballero, 25 May 1803, Buenos Aires.

27. For biographical information on this and other audiencia ministers, refer to Mark A. Burkholder and D. S. Chandler, *Biographical Dictionary of Audiencia Ministers in the Americas, 1687–1821* (Westport, CT: Greenwood Press, 1982). For salaries of audiencia judges, refer to Socolow, *The Bureaucrats of Buenos Aires*, chap. 6.

28. AGNA, XIII, 42-1-2.

29. The general administrator, Manuel de Basavilvaso, contributed 435 pesos; the renta's accountant, 150 pesos; and the first official, 100 pesos. The remaining funds came from five lower-ranked officers whose individual contributions were prorated according to their ranks.

30. Treasurers from the Royal Mint in Potosí made all the contributions in this

branch. As for Buenos Aires, the senior accountants from the Tesorería General de Ejército y Real Hacienda contributed 500 pesos each annually, while the eleven *subalternos* (subordinates) in this office jointly donated another 500 pesos. For Medrano and Pinedo, see Socolow, *The Bureaucrats of Buenos Aires*.

31. AGNA, IX, 8-7-12.

32. Melchor Mesa, a vecino from Potosí, donated 1,000 pesos for himself and another 1,000 for his son. Ventura Carpio, a vecino from La Paz, donated 305 pesos exclusively for his son. Since he was not an officeholder, he was probably trying to engineer for his son upward social mobility. For these and several other cases, refer to AGI, Buenos Aires 120, Duplicado 288; and AGNA, XIII, 42-1-2.

33. AGI, Buenos Aires 90, Duplicado 55, Joaquín del Pino to Antonio Caballero, 25 May 1803, Buenos Aires. Even though the count donated 1,000 pesos in 1793, he mentioned 2,000 pesos in contributions, indicating that he donated funds also in 1799. Francisco Ortega y Barrón also requested this position, and his case will be discussed in the following chapter.

34. AGNA, IX, 8-7-12.

35. AGI, Buenos Aires 120, Duplicado 288. Ballesteros received a salary of 1,000 pesos, half of what was paid to the accountants holding permanent positions. For Ballesteros's bureaucratic career, see Socolow, *The Bureaucrats of Buenos Aires*.

36. As stated previously, the bulk of the donativo was collected between 1 July and 31 December 1793. The royal decree establishing the mandatory discount of 4 percent of all salaries was issued in San Idelfonso on 17 August 1794. In the Viceroyalty of Río de la Plata, such measures should have been put into practice from 1 February 1795 onward. The letter in which Viceroy Melo de Portugal discussed this issue was dated on 5 September 1795 (AGI, Buenos Aires 122, Duplicado 50).

37. Irigoin and Grafe, "A Stakeholder Empire."

38. For inspections and corruption investigations, refer to Socolow, *The Bureaucrats of Buenos Aires*, chap. 8.

39. AGNA, IX, 8-7-12, p. 36.

40. AGNA, XIII, 42-1-2.

41. For a thorough discussion of this point, refer to chapter 2.

42. As the figures provided by Juan Marchena Fernández show, from the 1750s onward middle-ranking officialdom was taken over by American-born men, although the highest ranks remained in the hands of Spaniards (Juan Marchena Fernández, *Oficiales y soldados en el ejército de América* [Seville: Escuela de Estudios Hispano-Americanos, C.S.I.C., 1983], chap. 3).

43. Many of these officers stayed in the Indies and became members of the Ejército de Dotación because in the Americas they found better opportunities for career advancement in addition to superior salaries. On many occasions, due to the lack of men in arms, both soldiers and officers of the Ejército de Refuerzo were forced to stay in the Americas (Marchena Fernández, *Oficiales y soldados*, chaps. 3 and 9). For the figures regarding the Ejército de Refuerzo, see Juan Marchena Fernández, *Ejército y milicias en el mundo colonial americano* (Madrid: Editorial MAPFRE, 1992), chap. 4.

44. In most cases, militias existed only on paper, as they were rarely mobilized.

Recruitment was generally left in the hands of an officer from the regular army who toured around the city and countryside looking for those qualified to join the service. Wealthy members of the local elites, generally merchants and landowners, were offered the ranks of colonels, captains, and lieutenants. As for the troops, they were organized following ethnic categories and received some basic training on Sunday mornings (Marchena Fernández, *Ejército y milicias*).

45. Jose Alfredo Rangel Silva, "Milicias en el Oriente de San Luis Potosí," in *Las armas de la nación*, ed. Manuel Chust and Juan Marchena (Madrid: Iberoamericana, 2007).

46. For a discussion of the transformation of the army in the Americas, see the work of Juan Marchena Fernández. Summaries of his research can be found in his *Oficiales y soldados en el ejército de América* and *Ejército y milicias en el mundo colonial americano*. Spanish-born officers frequently married local elite women. Young members of the local elite found in a military career, in addition to a regular salary and retirement benefits, opportunities for social advancement not available to them in the royal bureaucracy. Admission to the military also denoted "purity of blood" (*pureza de sangre*), thereby conferring additional social standing on the officers. The judicial immunities and privileges provided by the fuero militar gave men an extra incentive to join the army. For a discussion of the extent of military privileges in civil and criminal cases, refer to Lyle N. McAlister, *The "Fuero Militar" in New Spain* (Gainesville: University of Florida Press, 1957). For the regional cases, refer to Manuel Chus and Juan Marchena, eds., *Las armas de la nación: Independencia y ciudadanía en Hispanoamérica (1750–1850)* (Madrid: Iberoamericana, 2007). For colored militias, refer to Ben Vinson III, *Bearing the Arms for His Majesty: The Free-Colored Militia in Colonial Mexico* (Stanford, CA: Stanford University Press, 2003).

47. Juan Beverina, *El Virreinato del Rio de la Plata: Su organización militar* (Buenos Aires: Círculo Militar, 1992); and Marchena Fernández, *Oficiales y soldados*. Also, see the tables in the appendix.

48. For instance, the 456 pesos contributed in annual donativos by the regular army in Potosí came from the 8th Company of the 3rd Battalion of the Ejército de Buenos Aires temporarily posted in the area. And, the 3rd and 4th Corps of Surveyors (Partidas de Demarcación), who were drawing the boundaries between the Spanish and Portuguese territories, sent their donativos through the Paraguay treasury.

49. For abuses of power on the part of Spanish military men, refer to Sergio Serulnikov, "Patricians and Plebeians in Late Colonial Charcas: Identity, Representation and Colonialism," in *Imperial Subjects: Race and Identity in Colonial Latin America*, ed. Andrew B. Fisher and Matthew D. O'Hara (Durham, NC: Duke University Press, 2009).

50. For instance, in Potosí militia soldiers each contributed on average 25 pesos in donativos. As already discussed, this amount represented a significant share of the annual salaries paid for skilled and unskilled laborers in the late eighteenth century. For *pardo* militias, refer to Vinson, *Bearing the Arms for His Majesty*; and José Luis Belmonte Postigo, "El color de los fusiles: Las milicias de pardos en Santiago de Cuba en los albores de la Revolución Haitiana," in *Las armas de la Nación: Independencia*

y ciudadanía en Hispanoamérica, ed. Manuel Chust and Juan Marchena (Madrid: Iberoamericana, 2007), 37–51.

51. For salaries, refer to chapter 3.

52. For a discussion of changing creole identities in the eighteenth century, refer to Serulnikov, "Patricians and Plebeians in Late Colonial Charcas."

53. Roberto Marfany, "El Cuerpo de Blandengues de la frontera de Buenos Aires: 1752–1810," *Humanidades* 23 (1933): 313–74.

54. The first commander of the Cuerpo de Blandengues donated 115 pesos, followed by the second commander, who pledged 80 pesos. Six captains made contributions of 50 pesos each, while the same number of lieutenants contributed 32 pesos. Second lieutenants (*alferezes*) made individual donativos of 25 pesos, whereas all cadets contributed only 10 pesos apiece. Finally, each military chaplain contributed 20 pesos. Each one of the six companies that made up this force donated between 500 and 550 pesos. These sums were collected by the captains among sergeants, drummers, corporals, scouts, and soldiers. Although the donativo roster only recorded lump sums, it is possible to estimate how much each soldier individually contributed as a few Blandengues soldiers, who were posted in Montevideo, sent their donativos later on. These soldiers contributed 5 pesos each. That sum was presumably the standard amount donated by the rank and file (AGI, Buenos Aires 120, Duplicado 288; AGNA, IX, 8-7-12, Tomas de Razón, Libro 60).

55. In theory, juro holders could redeem juros at any time by requesting the royal treasury to repay the principal of the original loan. Throughout the seventeenth century, the crown had trouble redeeming annuities, especially at their face value. In the eighteenth century, however, the crown lowered the interest paid on juros and retired a large portion of them through redemptions (Grafe, *Distant Tyranny*).

56. Kenneth Andrien, "The Sale of Juros and the Politics of Reform in the Viceroyalty of Peru, 1608–1695," *Journal of Latin American Studies* 13, no. 1 (1981): 1–19.

57. Ann Twinam has studied in detail the process of obtaining *cédulas de gracias al sacar* and the social implications of granting such privileges. She has also pointed out that recipients of legitimations were more socially accepted and successful at the local than at the imperial level. Doña Francisca del Risco's case shows such limits: after obtaining her cédula de gracias al sacar, she applied for a title of nobility but was rejected as she did not meet the criteria for selection (service to the monarchy and sufficient wealth to maintain their noble position) (Twinan, *Public Lives, Private Secrets*). For personal information about Vicente Tardio de Guzmán, refer to Edberto O. Acevedo, *Las intendencias altoperuanas del Virreinato del Río de la Plata* (Buenos Aires: Academia Nacional de la Historia, 1992).

58. For the marquises of Toxo, see Josep M. Barnadas et al., *Diccionario histórico de Bolivia, 2 vols.* (Sucre: Grupo de Estudios Históricos, 2002).

59. Andrien, "The Sale of Juros and the Politics of Reform."

60. Between 1720 and 1790, the native Andean peoples of Peru and Bolivia repeatedly rebelled against colonial authorities. On two occasions, these movements, led by popular *kurakas*, became well organized and mobilized people outside their original regional boundaries. The first one started in 1742, and its leader was Juan

Santos Atahualpa. His movement controlled the jungle zone bordering Peru's central highland, and his guerrilla armies resisted the Spanish military incursions over a period of ten years. The second period of widespread revolt took place from 1780 to 1782 and spread through the highlands of southern Peru and Bolivia. The leaders of these movements were Jose Gabriel Condorcanqui, who took the name of Túpac Amaru II, Tomas Katari, and Julian Apasa, also known as Túpac Katari. In this case, the Spanish military quickly defeated the insurrection, though at a high cost in human lives. In 1781 violence reached the highest point as the rebels, led by Túpac Katari, surrounded and pillaged the city of La Paz on two occasions. Many factors have to be considered in order to explain the "age of Andean insurrection" (1742–1782). The economic exactions endured by the Indian communities in the form of tributes, labor drafts (mita), and forced commercialization of the peasant economies through *repartos de mercancías*, although very important, do not fully explain the Indian rebellions. Additionally, insurrections were not strictly Indian as castas and Spaniards also participated in them, though to a lesser extent. Recent historiography has pointed toward the program of political rationalization enforced by the Bourbon kings as a major aspect of peasant forms of contention because it imposed a stricter surveillance on the Indian economic activities, political arrangements, and religious practices. Indians made use of a variety of strategies to pursue their aims (i.e., legal appeals to royal courts, rioting, murder of certain unpopular officials or anyone considered Spaniard, and widespread rebellion) and elaborated different programs including Inca political restoration, the subordination of non-Indians to Indian rule, and the anticolonial cry for self-rule. None of the revolts followed a unique religious program either. Many of them simply rejected Catholicism, while others sought to fix abuses on the part of the parish priests. A summary of the major historiographical trends around the issue up to the 1980s can be found in Steve Stern, ed., *Resistance, Rebellion and Consciousness in the Andean Peasant World, 18th to 19th Centuries* (Madison: University of Wisconsin Press, 1987). Works by Sergio Serulnikov and Sinclair Thompson have explored deeply the political agendas of peasants in the eighteenth century: Serulnikov, "Disputed Images of Colonialism"; Sergio Serulnikov, "Customs and Rules: Bourbon Rationalizing Projects and Social Conflicts in Northern Potosi during the 1770s," *Colonial Latin American Review* 8, no. 2 (1999): 245–74; Sinclair Thompson, "'We Alone Will Rule . . .': Recovering the Range of Anticolonial Projects among Andean Peasants (La Paz, 1740 to 1781)," *Colonial Latin American Review* 8, no. 2 (1999): 275–99.

61. AGNA, IX, 8-7-12.

62. According to Thompson, anticolonial programs used at different times a variety of strategies, including the repudiation or displacement of the Spanish king, rejection of Indian political subordination, and assertion of Indian autonomy. Tactics included peasant radicalism, racial antagonism, violence, and communal power. Even when Indians sought to eliminate or dominate Spanish colonists or achieve legal equality with the Spaniards, they did not necessary reject the authority of the king. The restoration of Inca rule as opposed to that of the Spaniards was one of the possible political aims available to the Aymara- and Quechua-speaking Indians (Thompson, "'We Alone Will Rule'").

63. The cartas cuentas from Charcas did list the ramo of censos de Indios. However, indigenous communities from Charcas did not contribute donativos (TePaske et al., *The Royal Treasuries of the Spanish Empire in America*).

64. Larson describes the structural antagonisms occurring between small- and large-scale producers of the Cochabamba Valley. Landlords, especially those who collected and speculated with the tithe, made the largest profits in times of crisis. In seasons of abundance, however, they had to settle for narrow gains due to both a stagnant agriculture and the competition from the peasants of the region. Rapid demographic growth coupled with a more efficient collection of tribute put additional financial pressure on the indigenous communities of Cochabamba (Brooke Larson, "Rural Rhythms of Class Conflict in Eighteenth-Century Cochabamba," in *Essays on the Price History of Eighteenth-Century Latin America*, ed. Lyman L. Johnson and Enrique Tandeter [Albuquerque: University of New Mexico Press, 1990]). Indians from the *subdelegación* of Tapacari contributed 230 pesos, while those from Hayopaya donated 218 pesos. Each community contributed as follows: Tapacari, 73 pesos; Calliri, 45 pesos; Sipesipe, 37 pesos; Tinquipaya and Collcapirgua, 75 pesos; Palca, 80 pesos; Machacamarca, 39 pesos; Charapaya, 57 pesos; Marochata, 12 pesos; Yani, 30 pesos.

65. The missions prioritized economic activities that were less labor intensive, such as hunting wild cattle and exporting lower quality yerba maté instead of the *caaminí* kind (Sarrail, *Globalization and the Guarani*).

66. Other mission towns contributed the following donativos: Santo Angel, 561 pesos; San Lorenzo, 300 pesos; Santo Tomé and Yapeyú, 338 pesos; San Nicolas, 500 pesos; San Cosme, 141 pesos; Santiago, 194 pesos; San Ignacio Guazú, Santa Maria de la Fe, and Santa Rosa, 97 pesos each.

67. For the income of cabildos, refer to Kinsbruner, *The Colonial Spanish-American City*, chap. 4. The cabildos' financial operations will be discussed in chapters 6 and 7.

68. For the financial role of the Catholic Church, see Arnold J. Bauer, "The Church in the Economy of Spanish America: *Censos* and *Depositos* in the Eighteenth and Nineteenth Centuries," *Hispanic American Historical Review* 63, no. 4 (1983): 707–33; and Asuncion Lavrin, "The Role of Nunneries in the Economy of New Spain in the Eighteenth Century," *Hispanic American Historical Review* 46, no. 4 (1966): 371–93.

69. Religious institutions favored corporate one-time donativos, while a few ecclesiastics contributed individual donations.

70. Smaller orders, such as that of the Predicadores, could only afford a one-time donation of 200 pesos divided into four equal shares among the monasteries located in the cities of Córdoba, La Rioja, Santiago del Estero, and Tucumán. Except for the sisters of the convent of Saint Claire in Cochabamba, no monetary gifts were made by nuns.

71. AGI, Buenos Aires 120, Duplicado 288.

72. The Carmelite nuns of Cochabamba chose a different path. They decided to admit into their cloister free of charge "a noble girl called Luisa de San Carlos to serve in perpetuity as a chaplain for the Spanish Kings" (AGI, Buenos Aires 120, Duplicado 288; also see AGNA, IX, Tomas de Razón, Libro 60, p. 245).

73. The fear experienced in Buenos Aires during the French Revolution, especially

when the French Convention was established, is very well depicted by Johnson's study of the so-called Conspiración de los Franceses of 1795 (Lyman Johnson, "Juan Barbarin: The 1795 Conspiracy in Buenos Aires," in *The Human Tradition in Colonial Latin America*, ed. Kenneth Andrien [Wilmington, DE: Scholarly Resources, 2002], 259–77).

74. On 2 July 1793, Viceroy Arredondo communicated to the crown that he had received the royal order announcing the War against the French Convention and requiring these prayers (AGI, Buenos Aires 80, Duplicado 39). For a discussion of the English press as supporters of public debt, refer to Brewer, *The Sinews of Power*.

75. For a full description of these procedures, see chapter 2.

76. The quote is from AGNA, IX, 8-7-12. Davis describes peasants' gifts to their lords as "suitable to their stations." These gifts in kind were different from annual rents delivered in kind as they were infrequent, respectful actions taken to cement personal bonds (Davis, *The Gift in Sixteenth-Century France*).

77. The interruption of the Atlantic trade due to warfare resulted in a sharp decline in the price of exports (especially hides) and an increase in the price of imports, thereby making regional manufactures such as textiles and wine more competitive. Additionally, Atlantic warfare momentarily interrupted the export of silver, which instead circulated within the viceregal economic space. Under these circumstances, merchants from Buenos Aires expanded both their trade in local and regional commodities as well as their involvement in lending and trade credit. Gelman estimates that trade in yerba maté resulted in gains of 32 percent annually in Buenos Aires, while in Potosí, that margin even doubled. Domingo Belgrano Peri, Gaspar de Santa Coloma, as well as other merchants from Buenos Aires increased their trade in local commodities and sought financial investments during Atlantic warfare in the 1780s and 1790s (Gelman, *De mercachifle a gran comerciante*; and Socolow, *The Merchants of Buenos Aires*).

78. AGNA, IX, Tomas de Razón, Libro 60.

79. Hat makers, weavers, and builders were listed as small donors. For their contributions and this quote, refer to AGNA, IX, 8-7-12.

CHAPTER 5

1. AGI, Buenos Aires 125, Duplicado 190, Viceroy Olaguer Feliú to Francisco de Saavedra, 24 December 1798.

2. The royal ordinance issued on 20 June 1798 and the royal decree of 27 May 1799 were quoted by Viceroy Avilés in a letter sent to Minister Soler on 5 June 1799 (AGI, Buenos Aires 126, Duplicado 13).

3. AGI, Buenos Aires 126, Duplicado 13.

4. Lynch, *Spanish Colonial Administration*, 143.

5. Jerry Cooney, "Oceanic Commerce and Platine Merchants, 1796–1806: The Challenge of War," *Americas* 45, no. 4 (1989): 509–24.

6. Barbier, "Peninsular Finance and Colonial Trade."

7. Jerry Cooney, "A Colonial Naval Industry: The 'Fábrica de Cables' of

Paraguay," *Revista Historia de América* 87 (1917): 105–26; and Jerry Cooney, "Forest Industries and Trade in Late Colonial Paraguay," *Journal of Forest History* 23, no. 4 (1979): 186–97.

8. Indian towns that fell under the jurisdiction of the intendancy of Paraguay but had not belonged to the Jesuit missions owed labor services (encomiendas) instead of tributes. Each Indian provided in labor the equivalent of 36 reales annually. Out of that sum, encomenderos gave to the crown 15 reales plus the costs of shipping them to Spain. Another 6 reales per Indian went to pay for the salaries of the priests serving at those parishes, while encomenderos kept the rest. The Indians had to work for approximately two months per year to cover such demands. Paraguayan encomiendas, like many other ones granted in marginal areas, remained in the hands of private parties until the eighteenth century. For a discussion of this issue, refer to Edberto O. Acevedo, *La intendencia del Paraguay en el Virreynato del Rio de la Plata* (Buenos Aires: Ediciones Ciudad Argentina, 1996); and J. E. Saeger, "Survival and Abolition: The Eighteenth-Century Paraguayan Encomienda," *Americas* 38, no. 1 (1981): 59–85. The total population of the Paraguayan Pueblos de Indios increased from 7,727 in 1782 to 13,678 in 1799, while those from the ex–mission towns declined from 45,159 in 1767 to 15,917 in 1808 (Ernesto J. A. Maeder, "La poblacion del Paraguay en 1799: El censo del Gobernador Lazaro de Rivera," *Estudios Paraguayos* 3, no. 1 [1975]: 63–86).

9. Jerry Cooney, "Neutral Vessels and Platine Slavers: Building a Vicergal Merchant Marine," *Journal of Latin American Studies* 18, no. 1 (1986): 25–39. For Tomás Antonio Romero, see Hugo Galmarini, "Comercio y burocracia colonial: A propósito de Tomás Antonio Romero," *Investigaciones y Ensayos* 28/29 (1980): 407–39/387–424.

10. Juan Carlos Garavaglia and Diane Meléndez, "Economic Growth and Regional Differentiations: The River Plate Region at the End of the Eighteenth Century," *Hispanic American Historical Review* 65, no. 1 (1985): 51–89.

11. For a discussion of trade disruptions during the 1790s, refer to John Fisher, "The Imperial Response to 'Free Trade': Spanish Imports from Spanish America, 1778–1796," *Journal of Latin American Studies* 17, no. 1 (1985): 35–78; and John Fisher, "Commerce and Imperial Decline: Spanish Trade with Spanish America, 1797–1820," *Journal of Latin American Studies* 30, no. 3 (1998): 459–79. Also see Socolow, *The Merchants of Buenos Aires*, chaps. 6 and 7, and the postscript published in the Spanish translation of this book. The consumer price index elaborated by Lyman Johnson indicates that in the city of Buenos Aires from 1776 to 1811 the cost of living changed as follows (1776 = 100): The creation of the viceroyalty started a period of price inflation that reached its highest point in 1781 with an index number of 171. Afterward the index fell, returning in 1787 to the level of 1776 and then falling below that level in the following years. In 1794 Johnson recorded the lowest price index of 85.2. However, in the remaining years of the colonial period prices increased steadily, especially at the turn of the century when the severe drought ruined the harvest throughout the pampas. As opposed to the low price indexes present during the collection of the 1793 donativo, the ones that coincided with the second collection were dramatically higher: 114.4 in 1798, 112.0 in 1799, 129.4 in 1800, and 153.8 in 1801 (Lyman Johnson, "The Price History of Buenos

Aires during the Viceregal Period," in *Essays on the Price History of Eighteenth-Century Latin America*, ed. Lyman L. Johnson and Enrique Tandeter [Albuquerque: University of New Mexico Press, 1990]).

12. According to the treasury summaries compiled by TePaske and colleagues, between 1799 and 1801 the Buenos Aires caja received 367,838 pesos in donativos (TePaske et al., *The Royal Treasuries of the Spanish Empire in America*).

13. Francisco Esteban Garcia, the proxy for Tomas Villota, who was the situadista designated for the Alto Peruvian treasuries, deposited in Potosí a large share of donativos from La Paz, Charcas, and Cochabamba as well as the loans collected at the first two cajas. Merchants Tomas Carrasco and Manuel de Antesana managed smaller shares of those funds (AGNA, IX, 7-8-12).

14. Ibid.

15. Ibid.

16. Socolow, *The Merchants of Buenos Aires*.

17. AGNA, IX, 7-8-12. For Francisco Tadeo Diez de Medina, see Burkholder and Chandler, *Biographical Dictionary of Audiencia Ministers in the Americas*.

18. I have discussed this point in chapter 4.

19. AGNA, Intendencia del Paraguay, 1798–1800; AGNA, IX, 5-4-6.

20. After the expulsion of the Jesuits in 1767, the territory of their missions was divided into two separate governorships, reunified in 1770, and divided again in 1784. Seventeen pueblos fell under the jurisdiction of the intendancy of Buenos Aires, and the remaining thirteen were incorporated into Paraguay. In 1803 the governorship of Misiones was erected as an independent jurisdiction, but in 1805 it was again reincorporated into Paraguay.

21. For arribadas in the Rio de la Plata, refer to Moutoukias, *Contrabando y control colonial en el siglo XVII*.

22. For Pacheco and other Portuguese merchants in the Rio de la Plata, refer to Marcela Viviana Tejerina, "Los Portugueses al servicio de España y sus vinculos comerciales con el Brasil," in *Navegación y comercio Rioplatense*, ed. Hernan Arsdubal Silva (Bahía Blanca: Universidad Nacional del Sur, 1998), 2:135–79.

23. AGNA, IX, 7-8-12.

24. Lynch argues that Rivera was trying to block Avilés's attempts to abolish encomiendas. His thesis has been revised by the works of James Schofield Saeger. Refer to Lynch, *Spanish Colonial Administration*, 110–15; and Saeger, "Survival and Abolition."

25. AGNA, IX, 5-4-6, letter from Avilés to Rivera, 19 July 1799.

26. The original donativo subscriptions were also filed along with the receipts. All of them were signed by the corregidor, the members of the indigenous cabildo, the caciques, the resident priest, and the local administrador. In some cases, the caciques signed on behalf of the illiterate members of the cabildo. For examples, see AGNA, Intendencia del Paraguay, 1798–1800, IX, 5-4-6.

27. AGNA, Intendencia del Paraguay, 1798–1800, IX, 5-4-6.

28. Ibid.

29. The correspondence exchanged between Rivera and Avilés indicates that

funds generated by donativos and loans were moved to the otras tesorerías branch (ibid.).

30. Saeger, "Survival and Abolition."

31. According to Stern, Andean kurakas offered Philip II a "dazzling bribe" of 100,000 ducats to end the encomienda system. I wonder if that "bribe" was actually a donativo. See Steve J. Stern, *Peru's Indian Peoples and the Challenge of the Spanish Conquest* (Madison: University of Wisconsin Press, 1982), 45.

32. Cooney, "A Colonial Naval Industry"; and Cooney, "Forest Industries and Trade in Late Colonial Paraguay."

33. Johnson, *Workshop of Revolution*.

34. The same document established that the consulado would back the loans taken at an interest rate of 5 percent with its own revenues (Archivo General de la Nación [Argentina], *Consulado de Buenos Aires*, 4:63).

35. For the politics of the merchants in Cádiz and the drafts issued against American treasuries, see Fisher, "The Imperial Response to 'Free Trade.'" In 1799 merchants supporting trade with neutral nations were led by Antonio de Las Cagigas, who held the office of síndico at the consulado, while Martín de Alzaga was the head of the monopolist group as well as the director of the merchant corporation. In 1802 the monopolists were still collecting signatures to put an end to individual grants that continued neutral trade. For a detailed account of the struggles dividing the merchant community, refer to Socolow, *The Merchants of Buenos Aires*, chap. 6. The royal ordinance abolishing neutral trade was issued on 20 April 1799.

36. As discussed in the prior chapter, the avería was earmarked to pay interest on the loans advanced by consulado investors. The receipts issued by the consulado indicate that investors punctually receive their dividends (AGNA, IX, 31-s/a-5).

37. Bernarda Lezica belonged to the Lezica clan, one of the most powerful and successful merchant families of colonial Buenos Aires. Most of the Lezica women married prominent merchants. For instance, six out of seven surviving daughters of Bernarda Lezica and Francisco de Segurola married merchants. The seventh one became a nun. Segurola was among the wealthiest men in Buenos Aires. At the time of his death in 1790, the net value of his estate was 395,077 pesos. For more information about the Lezica clan and Francisco de Segurola's businesses, refer to Socolow, *The Merchants of Buenos Aires*.

38. The term *comerciante* referred to those engaged in the import and export of goods. Almaceneros were the wholesalers, and tenderos were retailers. The categories were not mutually exclusive as some merchants expanded their business into the wholesale and retail trades. Additionally, each category included businesses of wide-ranging sizes.

39. Cooney, "Forest Industries and Trade in Late Colonial Paraguay."

40. Cooney, "A Colonial Naval Industry."

41. Futuras were appointments unavailable at the time the sale was performed but expected to be held in the future by purchasers.

42. For the powerful families of Jujuy, refer to Gustavo L. Paz, "'El orden y el desorden': Guerra y mobilización campesina en la campana de Jujuy, 1815–1821," in

*Desafíos al orden: Política y sociedades rurales en la revolución de independ*encia, ed. Raul Fradkin and Jorge Gelman (Rosario: Prehistoria, 2008), 83–121.

43. Both examples and quotes are from AGNA, Intendencia del Paraguay, 1798–1800, IX, 5-4-6.

44. Like many other noble families from Valencia, the marquises of San Joaquin y Pastor diversified their sources of income to include loans in the form of censos they frequently extended to private parties as well as to municipal authorities in Spain. For a discussion of the financial strategies of the noble houses from Valencia, see Jorge Antonio Catala Sanz, *Rentas y patrimonios de la nobleza valenciana en el siglo XVIII* (Madrid: Siglo XXI Editores, 1995).

45. The sums of 4 percent salary discounts that entered the ramo were minimal. In the case of La Paz, the *data* (expenditures) column lists 10,396 pesos, but it is not clear whether that sum came from this or another ramo as the *cargo* (income) does not show an equivalent amount (TePaske et al., *The Royal Treasuries of the Spanish Empire in America*).

46. In the previous chapter, I discussed Joaquin de Alós's donativo and his subsequent promotion from the intendancy of Paraguay to the governorship of Valparaiso in 1796. He served in Valparaiso until the end of the Spanish domination in 1811.

47. Gullermo Furlong, "Lazaro de Rivera y su breve cartilla real," *Humanidades* 34 (1954): 15–69.

48. "D. Lázaro de Rivera reclama al Duque de Alcudia el pago de unos atrasos (S. Ildefonso, 23 August 1794)," in *Paraguay siglos XVII y XVIII: Selección de textos, transcripción y revisión,* ed. Antonio M. García Español (Tarragona: Universidad Rovira i Virgili), AGI, Estado 81, num. 2; see also http://www.docstoc.com/docs/44598847/ PARAGUAY-SIGLOS-XVII-XVIII.

49. For the length of the average tenure, see Lynch, *Spanish Colonial Administration*, app. 1.

50. For a discussion of Cañete's conflicts, refer to Lynch, *Spanish Colonial Administration*, 256–57.

51. AGI, Buenos Aires 90, Duplicado 61, Del Pino to Caballero, 27 August 1803, Buenos Aires.

52. Burkholder and Chandler, *From Impotence to Authority.*

53. As part of an empire-wide plan to reduce audiencia expenses, the salary of the regent of Buenos Aires was reduced from 6,000 to 5,250 pesos, while all other judges found their 4,000- to 5,000-peso salaries fixed at 3,500 pesos (Socolow, *The Bureaucrats of Buenos Aires*, 162).

54. Ibid., chaps. 7 and 8.

55. Judge Campuzano, who disregarded the established regulations and married into a powerful local family, was transferred to the audiencia in Guatemala, and in 1812 he became the regent of the audiencia of Cuba, where he served until his death in 1818 (Burkholder and Chandler, *Biographical Dictionary of Audiencia Ministers in the Americas*).

56. AGNA, IX, 8-7-12.

57. The media annata was a tax charged on the wages paid to officeholders. It was

the equivalent of half of an officer's annual income. Its continued enforcement since the creation of the Viceroyalty of Rio de la Plata in 1776 demonstrates that despite the Bourbons' emphasis on the professional qualifications of the royal officers, the crown expected them to profit from their positions. Montepíos created pension funds for widows, children, and widowed mothers of those who had served the crown well. Officers contributed substantial funds to the montepío. Upon joining the montepíos in Buenos Aires, for instance, all members were to pay one and one-half months' salary as their initial contribution. Additionally, whenever a bureaucrat received a salary increase he was charged with another payment to the montepío to cover the difference between his old and new salary (Socolow, *The Bureaucrats of Buenos Aires*).

58. For slow bureaucratic advancement in Buenos Aires, see Socolow, *The Bureaucrats of Buenos Aires*, chap. 5.

59. At the time of its establishment in 1778, only six officers staffed this agency, but by the turn of the century, that number increased to twenty-eight. Simultaneously, it became harder for these officers to advance (Socolow, *The Bureaucrats of Buenos Aires*).

60. Written statements of consent for contributing donativos were filed in the officers' *fojas de servicio* (service records) along with other paperwork that certified their service. For these statements, refer to AGNA, IX, 8-7-12.

61. For slow advancement in the aduana of Buenos Aires, refer to Socolow, *The Bureaucrats of Buenos Aires*, chap. 5.

62. AGNA, IX, 8-7-12.

63. For Vilanova's bureaucratic network, refer to Socolow, *The Bureaucrats of Buenos Aires*. Other members of powerful bureaucratic networks included Antonio Pinedo and his brother-in-law, Felix Pedro de Casamayor, both treasurers simultaneously serving in revenue-collection agencies in Buenos Aires. Pinedo gave two donativos of 500 pesos each during both wars. Casamayor contributed 500 pesos during the War against the French Convention (AGNA, IX, 8-7-12).

64. As already mentioned in chapter 2, Viedma contributed in one-time and annual donativos 1,400 and 3,000 pesos, respectively, while the Count of San Miguel de Carma contributed 1,000 pesos.

65. For the Royal Tobacco Monopoly, see Socolow, *The Bureaucrats of Buenos Aires*, app. D. The privileges associated with office holding in the tobacco monopoly included judicial immunities (*fuero de hacienda*), the right to carry weapons, tax exemptions (they did not pay municipal taxes or tolls when transporting tobacco), and exemptions from military service and housing and maintaining troops in wartime (Rafael Escobedo Romero, "Los empleados de la renta del tabaco durante los siglos XVII y XVIII: El imán del privilegio," *Hispania: Revista Española de Historia* 67, no. 227 [2007]: 1025–40).

66. The contador entre las partes was the accountant in charge of settling differences among litigants over common accounts. Occasionally, the same officer held also the position of *tasador de costas* or appraiser of legal fees.

67. AGI, Buenos Aires 37, Derechos Reclamados for Francisco Ortega y Barrón, 1795.

68. AGI, Buenos Aires 90, Del Pino to Caballero, 25 May 1803, Buenos Aires.

69. AGI, Buenos Aires 127, Duplicado 247, Avilés to Soler, 20 May 1801, Buenos Aires.

70. The excellent work of Roberto Di Stefano thoroughly describes the multiple strategies employed by the members of the religious establishment to consolidate and perpetuate their economic power and political leadership. Refer to Roberto Di Stefano and *Historia de la iglesia argentina: Desde la conquista hasta fines del siglo XX* (Buenos Aires: Grijalbo-Mondadori, 2000); and Roberto Di Stefano, *El púlpito y la plaza: Clero, sociedad y política de la monarquía católica a la república rosista* (Buenos Aires: Siglo XXI, 2004).

71. For these statements, refer to AGNA, IX, 7-8-12. Archdeacon Josef Roman y Cabezales donated thirty *doblones de a diez y seis*. These gold coins represented 240 silver pesos. The paperwork recording his donativo did not reveal any special interests or concerns, although we may wonder if he obtained any monetary compensation by depositing gold coins into the royal treasury. As discussed in chapter 3, coin arbitrage provided merchants transferring donativo funds across different treasuries with extra income. Perhaps this benefit was also extended to religious men willing to relinquish gold coins by means of donativos.

72. AGNA, IX, 8-7-12.

73. For a discussion of interest rates paid by trade in commercial paper, see Socolow, *The Merchants of Buenos Aires*; and Tjarks, *El Consulado de Buenos Aires*.

74. Irigoin and Grafe demonstrate that earlier in the century (1729–1733), shipments of silver to Spain represented 11 percent of the revenue collected in the Viceroyalty of Rio de la Plata. Toward the end of the century (1796–1800), however, they dropped to 5.2 percent.

CHAPTER 6

1. For a summary of the diplomatic alliances and treaties signed by European powers, refer to Peter J. Bakewell, *A History of Latin America: Empires and Sequels, 1450–1930* (Oxford: Oxford University Press, 1997); also, Artola, *La hacienda del antiguo régimen*; and Carlos E. Roberts, *Las Invasiones Inglesas* (Buenos Aires: Talleres gráficos, 1938).

2. Sobremonte stated that only 876 men were enlisted in the infantry, whereas the military regulations established that there should be 2,065 (Roberts, *Las Invasiones Inglesas*, 100–101). For a summary of regular troops and militias available at the beginning of 1806, refer to J. L. R. Fortin, *Las Invasiones Inglesas* (Buenos Aires: Editora Cía. Lamsa, 1967), chap. 1. From the mid-eighteenth century onward, British policy toward the Spanish possessions in the Americas did not follow a single trajectory but rather combined a vast array of strategies. In times of warfare, the Caribbean was the most active front, as the British navy captured Spanish vessels and occupied many of the islands. When peace resumed, so did piracy and contraband trade. After the U.S. War of Independence, the British ministry, the admiralty, the foreign office, and many members of parliament discussed projects that included fostering the independence of the Spanish possessions and even the

military occupation of certain areas. In these discussions, the opinions of a variety of nonpolitical figures were considered, such as those of the disaffected Jesuits living in Rome, some British explorers, and colonial officers. Men like Francisco de Miranda, who combined the skills and ambitions of a politician, a propagandist, and an adventurer, were heard and supported in London as well. However, due to the factional nature of parliamentary politics it is hard to assess which one of these projects was truly at the core of the official strategy of the foreign office. In any case, it seems that a cautious approach to the matter dominated the discussions, and when considered, it was always subordinated to the more crucial issues of the empire such as the preservation of India and the competition from the continental powers, in particular France. For a discussion of the changing attitudes of the British government toward South America in general and the Rio de la Plata in particular, see Klaus Gallo, *Great Britain and Argentina: From Invasion to Recognition, 1806–1826* (New York: Palgrave, 2001), chaps. 2 and 3. Sobremonte's donativo was listed on the 1799 roster (AGNA, IX, 7-8-12). His petition for a promotion was sent to Spain along with the viceregal correspondence (AGI, Buenos Aires 90, Duplicado 320, Del Pino to Caballero, 25 May 1803, Buenos Aires).

3.   AGNA, IX, 7-8-12.

4.   A thorough discussion of the measures taken by Viceroy Sobremonte in June 1806 can be found in Juan Beverina, *Las Invasiones Inglesas al Rio de la Plata (1806–1807)* (Buenos Aires: Taller gráfico de L. Bernard, 1939), 1:chaps. 8 and 9.

5.   Detailed accounts of the military operations can be found in Roberts, *Las Invasiones Inglesas* and Beverina, *Las Invasiones Inglesas al Rio de la Plata.*

6.   Viceroy Sobremonte had given the orders to take the treasury away from the capital city in the event of an invasion. Refer to Sobremonte's orders given to Joaquin Mosquera on 4 April 1805 and reproduced in Beverina, *Las Invasiones Inglesas al Rio de la Plata,* 1:app. 6. Viceroy Sobremonte's orders and actions followed the defense plan elaborated in 1797 by Viceroy Olaguer Feliú and the governor of Montevideo. Among other provisions, the 1797 plan established that the military efforts should concentrate on the Banda Oriental, and in case of an invasion, the treasury should be shipped inland. However, the plan did not mention that the viceroy should abandon the city as well. For this plan, refer to Roberts, *Las Invasiones Inglesas,* 97–102. The text of the capitulation is reproduced in Instituto de Estudios Históricos sobre la Reconquista y Defensa de Buenos Aires, *La reconquista y defensa de Buenos Aires, 1806–1807* (Buenos Aires: Editores Peuser, 1947), 194–95.

7.   Beresford met with the cabildo on 28 June 1806. The documents regarding this meeting as well as the letters exchanged by the city councilmen and the viceroy regarding the return of the treasury are reproduced in Beverina, *Las Invasiones Inglesas al Rio de la Plata,* app. 12–13. The Compañía de Filipinas, although enjoying the protection of the Spanish king, was a privately owned company. The English considered these funds to be public.

8.   On 17 July 1806, Beresford dispatched a British vessel carrying the treasury that was captured in Buenos Aires. The letter reproducing a summary of the funds as well as a reproduction of the pamphlet "Dollars from Buenos Aires" can be found

in Roberts, *Las Invasiones Inglesas*, 155; and Instituto de Estudios Históricos sobre la Reconquista y Defensa de Buenos Aires, *La reconquista y defensa de Buenos Aires*, 211.

9. I am using Johnson's latest population estimates for 1810, based on crude birth rates (Johnson, *Workshop of Revolution*, 30).

10. Viceroy Sobremonte's actions, as well as those of Liniers, will be discussed subsequently. Montevideo was more likely to be the target of an invasion due to the deeper waters surrounding its shores. After Buenos Aires surrendered, additional English forces as well as supplies were expected to land in Montevideo. Aware of this matter, Governor Ruiz Huidobro promptly prepared a campaign to recover Buenos Aires (Beverina, *Las Invasiones Inglesas al Rio de la Plata*, chap. 12).

11. Archivo General de la Nación (Argentina), *Acuerdos del extinguido cabildo de Buenos Aires*, series 4 (Buenos Aires: Archivo General de la Nación, 1926), 2:264–69.

12. The congress discussed and agreed on the following issues: (1) the celebration of a Te Deum to thank God for his intervention during the past military actions; (2) the provision of twelve dowries for the daughters of those killed in combat who were willing to enter convents; (3) the informing of king and viceroy that the city was recovered; (4) the distribution of pension funds (viudedades) to the widows of military men; (5) the organization of troops to resist the forthcoming English expedition; and (6) an inventory of the weapons and military supplies available (ibid.).

13. Ibid.

14. Refer to chapter 2.

15. Refer to the acuerdos held on 26 August 1806 and 26 January 1807 (Archivo General de la Nacion [Argentina], *Acuerdos del extinguido cabildo de Buenos Aires*, series 4, vol. 2.

16. The donativos and proclamas were published by the Imprenta de los Niños Expósitos. For a thorough discussion of the militarization of the city of Buenos Aires, see the classic works of Halperín Donghi, *Revolución y guerra: Formación de una elite dirigente en la Argentina criolla* (Buenos Aires: Siglo Veintiuno Editores, 1972), pt. 2, chaps. 1 and 2; and also Halperín Donghi, *Guerra y finanzas en los origenes del estado argentino (1791–1850)* (Buenos Aires: Editorial de Belgrano, 1982), introduction and chap. 2. For the militarization of Buenos Aires as a source of revolutionary legitimacy, refer to Pilar González Bernaldo's works, including "Producción de una nueva legitimidad"; "La Revolución Francesa y la emergencia de nuevas prácticas de la política"; "Las pulperías de Buenos Aires"; and "La 'identidad nacional' en el Rio de la Plata post-colonial."

17. The donativo collected in Buenos Aires in 1806 was published in different volumes. See Instituto de Estudios Históricos sobre la Reconquista y Defensa de Buenos Aires, *La reconquista y defensa de Buenos Aires*, 271–76; and Enrique Williams Alzaga, *Documentos relativos a la actuación de Martin de Alzaga en la reconquista y defensa de Buenos Aires (1806–1807)* (Buenos Aires: F.A. Colombo, 1948), 73–80. For the regional origin of the donations collected in 1807 and 1808, see Archivo General de la Nación (Argentina), *Acuerdos del extinguido cabildo de Buenos Aires*, series 4, vols. 2 and 3.

18. I relied on the following sources: *Expediente sobre exceptuar del servicio de milicias al comercio (1798)*, available in AGNA, IX, 4-7-5, and the almanac, published

in Madrid from 1801 through 1808, *Almanak mercantil o guía de comerciantes* (Madrid: Imprenta de Vega y Compañía, 1801–1808). Socolow also made available to me her own file consisting of the names of all the merchants she identified in Buenos Aires for her research on this group. The term *comerciante* referred to those engaged in the import and export of goods. Almaceneros were the wholesalers, and tenderos were retailers. The categories were not mutually exclusive as some merchants expanded their business into the wholesale and retail trades. Additionally, each category included businesses of wide-ranging sizes.

19. Scholars generally encounter many difficulties in estimating salaries in premodern societies. In addition to their payments, workers often received rations and housing. Depending on the trades, the days at work throughout the year also varied. Despite these obstacles, Johnson concludes, based on extensive research, that in Buenos Aires unskilled workers received 123 pesos a year if they worked for 245 days at 4 reales per day. At 2 reales per day, their annual pay was set at 61 pesos. Unskilled workers working 280 days at 4 reales per day received salaries of 140 pesos annually, while those who received 2 reales daily made 70 pesos annually (Johnson, *Workshop of Revolution*, 240).

20. There was only one outstanding individual contribution of 3,000 pesos made by the bishop of Buenos Aires, followed by that of the cathedral chapter, which donated 291 pesos as a group. Six other pledges that fell below 200 pesos each made the total 3,722 pesos, a modest sum for a wealthy corporation (Williams Alzaga, *Documentos relativos a la actuación de Martin de Alzaga*).

21. Jose Maria Sáenz Valiente, "Los alcaldes de Buenos Aires en 1806," *Boletín del Instituto de Investigaciones Históricas* 17, nos. 58–60 (1943): 99–140; and Julio Cesar Gonzalez, "El real consulado de Buenos Aires durante las Invasiones Inglesas (1806–1807)," *Anuario de Historia Argentina* 2 (1940): 223–75.

22. Exemptions from cabildo service are discussed by Sáenz Valiente, "Los alcaldes de Buenos Aires en 1806."

23. Archivo General de la Nación (Argentina), *Acuerdos del extinguido cabildo de Buenos Aires*, series 4, vols. 2 and 3.

24. Acuerdo del Cabildo, 23 June 1807 in Archivo General de la Nación (Argentina), *Acuerdos del extinguido cabildo de Buenos Aires*, series 4, vol. 2.

25. Ibid.

26. Irigoin and Grafe, "A Stakeholder Empire," table 1.

27. Oscar Ensink, *Proprios y arbitrios del cabildo de Buenos Aires, 1580–1821* (Madrid: Instituto de Estudios Fiscales, 1990).

28. The decline of the consulado will be discussed in the following chapter.

29. As already mentioned, merchants who had been exempted from serving in the cabildo after 1806 started to be elected for municipal offices. In addition to Martín de Alzaga and Anselmo Sáenz Valiente, members of the Santa Coloma, Elorriaga, Cires, and Belaustegui clans took municipal appointments after 1807. For the names of the cabildo members, refer to Archivo General de la Nación (Argentina), *Acuerdos del extinguido cabildo de Buenos Aires*, series 4, vol. 2.

30. The Archivo General de la Nación (Argentina), *Acuerdos del extinguido cabildo*

de Buenos Aires recorded the available details for this transaction. For Tomás Antonio Romero, see Hugo Galmarini, "Comercio y burocracia colonial."

31. After the first English Invasion, the cabildo's minutes recorded frequent requests for funds coming from royal treasurers. When Viceroy Sobremonte delegated his military and political authority to Santiago Liniers and the audiencia, both of them relied on the cabildo's funds to pay for their increased expenses.

32. Lynch discusses the dynamism of cabildos at the end of the eighteenth century. He states that cabildos cooperated with rather than confronted the intendants and developed more efficient collection of taxes, which allowed them to expand their involvement in municipal public works. Refer to John Lynch, "Intendants and Cabildos in the Viceroyalty of Rio de la Plata, 1782–1810," *Hispanic American Historical Review* 35, no. 3 (1955): 337–62. Halperín Donghi has discussed the leadership of the city of Buenos Aires and its long-term consequences for the region; refer to *Guerra y finanzas en los origenes del estado argentino*, introduction and chap. 2.

CHAPTER 7

1. Archivo General de la Nación (Argentina), *Acuerdos del extinguido cabildo de Buenos Aires*, series 4, 3:410–12.

2. For popular politics in Buenos Aires, refer to Gabriel Di Meglio, *¡Viva el bajo pueblo!*

3. Pensions and dowries were items also listed among the cabildo's military expenses. Despite a decline of such expenses in the 1807–1809 triennium, pensions and dowries absorbed a larger share of the cabildo's military budget. In 1807 dowries represented less than 1 percent of the military expenses, but they increased to 3 percent in 1809. Viudedades increased from 4 percent in 1807 to 13 percent in 1808 and reached 20 percent in 1809. Pensions for the maimed and wounded started just above 1.0 percent in 1807 but absorbed 4.5 percent of the military expenses in 1808 and 7.0 percent in 1809 (Grieco, "Family and Political Authority in Early Nineteenth-Century Buenos Aires"). For the funds the cabildo disbursed in pensions, dowries, and grants of freedom, refer to *Estado general que de orden del excmo. cabildo de esta capital forma en su contaduria, para demostrar los caudales que por lo correspondiente al nuevo impuesto de ciudad y al donativo con que le ha auxiliado su generoso y fiel vecindario, y demas provincias del virreynato, han entrado en la tesoreria de proprios y arbitrios desde el 12 de agosto de 1806 . . .* , Buenos Aires, 10 de febrero de 1810, reproduced in D. Miguel Lobo, *Historia general de las antiguas colonias hispano-americanas desde su descubrimiento hasta el año de 1808* (Madrid: Imprenta y Librería de Miguel Guijarro, 1875), vol. 3.

4. The general congress held on 14 August 1806 demanded the relinquishing of military command by Viceroy Sobremonte to Liniers, and the general junta of 10 February 1807 finally ousted him (see following discussion). For military mobilization of the urban plebs in Buenos Aires, refer to Gabriel Di Meglio, *¡Viva el bajo pueblo!*; and Johnson, *Workshop of Revolution*.

5. Authorities in Buenos Aires regarded popular mobilization as well as the creation

of militias with increased fear and suspicion. For an example of their viewpoint, see the report written by the audiencia's judges on the independence movement: "La revolución de mayo juzgada por los oidores de la real audiencia de Buenos Aires" (document from the AGI), *Revista de Derecho, Historia y Letras* (Buenos Aires) 43 (1912): 325–47. The comment about the precarious existence of the men serving in the militias came from Idelfonso Pasos, who led the Arribenos unit (quoted in Johnson, *Workshop of Revolution*, 263).

6. For the rise of Liniers and the popular militias, refer to Halperín Donghi, "Militarización revolucionaria en Buenos Aires," in *El ocaso del orden colonial en Hispanoamérica*, ed. Tulio Halperin Donghi and Herbert S. Klein (Buenos Aires: Sudamericana, 1978), 121–57; and González Bernaldo, "Ejército y sociedades patrióticas en Buenos Aires entre 1810 y 1813," in *Imagen y recepción de la Revolución Francesa en la Argentina, 1789–1989*, ed. Comité Argentino para el Bicentenario de la Revolución Francesa (Buenos Aires: Grupo Editor Latinoamericano, 1990), 27–51.

7. Johnson, *Workshop of Revolution*, chap. 5.

8. Socolow, *The Merchants of Buenos Aires*; Johnson, *Workshop of Revolution*.

9. Sáenz Valiente, "Los alcaldes de Buenos Aires en 1806."

10. I discussed this process in chapter 6.

11. Spaniards from Montevideo rescued Alzaga and his followers from Patagonia. Once relocated to Montevideo, Alzaga continued challenging the Buenos Aires regime.

12. In one case, the mobs found 300,000 pesos.

13. For a discussion of these measures, refer to Tjarks, *El consulado de Buenos Aires*, chap. 6.

14. For a discussion of the political divisions within the consulado during this period, see González, *El real consulado de Buenos Aires durante las Invasiones Inglesas*.

15. For the letters exchanged between the viceroy and the consulado and the viceroy and the audiencia, refer to González, *El real consulado de Buenos Aires durante las Invasiones Inglesas*; and Beverina, *Las Invasiones Inglesas al Rio de la Plata*, 1:chap. 12.

16. The text of the cabildo of Montevidedo's meeting is reproduced in Beverina, *Las Invasiones Inglesas al Rio de la Plata*, 1:337; also see Roberts, *Las Invasiones Inglesas*, 178.

17. For the letters exchanged by Sobremonte and Ruiz Huidobro, see Beverina, *Las Invasiones Inglesas al Rio de la Plata*, 1:366–77.

18. For the general congress of 15 August 1806, see Archivo General de la Nación (Argentina), *Acuerdos del extinguido cabildo de Buenos Aires*, series 4, 2:264–69. The Laws of the Indies established that in the absence of the viceroy, the political authority must be exercised by the audiencia until the current viceroy returned or a new one was appointed. In 1788 the Superintendencia de Ejército y Real Hacienda was dissolved and the office of *superintendente* was from then on held by the viceroy. For the letters exchanged by Viceroy Sobremonte with the cabildo, audiencia, bishop of Buenos Aires, and vecinos, refer to Beverina, *Las Invasiones Inglesas al Rio de la Plata*, 2:chap. 1.

19. The cabildo of Montevideo additionally requested that Buenos Aires give it the captured English military flags and banners. For the disputes between the cabildos of

Montevideo and Buenos Aires, refer to Archivo General de la Nación (Argentina), *Acuerdos del extinguido cabildo de Buenos Aires*, series 4, 2:283–86; also see Beverina, *Las Invasiones Inglesas al Rio de la Plata*, 2:chap. 1.

20. Viceroy Sobremonte was able to recruit about three thousand men in Córdoba, nine hundred of whom were dispatched to escort the English prisoners inland. Later, seven hundred of his men were sent to Buenos Aires to support Liniers's troops, and four hundred more deserted upon leaving for Montevideo. By the time he confronted the British troops he had about one thousand men (Beverina, *Las Invasiones Inglesas al Rio de la Plata*, 2:chap. 3). Meanwhile, on 1 January 1807, the cabildo of Buenos Aires elected its new members and submitted the results to Viceroy Sobremonte for his approval. The viceroy disapproved the new election, arguing that the critical situation demanded the continuation in office of the 1806 city councilmen. The cabildo rejected the viceroy's position and pushed for the approval of the election. However, as it had not received a response from the viceroy (who was fleeing the English) by 26 February, the newly elected city councilmen began their terms in office after receiving the endorsement of the audiencia (Archivo General de la Nación [Argentina], *Acuerdos del extinguido cabildo de Buenos Aires*, series 4, 2:389, 396, 402, 407).

21. Archivo General de la Nación (Argentina), *Acuerdos del extinguido cabildo de Buenos Aires*, series 4, 2:462–71.

22. The royal ordinance of 23 October 1806 established that in the absence of the viceroy, the officer holding the highest military rank automatically became the interim viceroy. The royal ordinance of 3 March 1807 conferred the rank of brigadier on Captain Liniers. This ordinance arrived in Buenos Aires in June of 1807.

23. For a discussion of the porteño merchants' attitude toward the cabildo, refer to Socolow, *The Merchants of Buenos Aires*, chap. 6.

24. For example, Martín de Alzaga held the office of alcalde de primer voto in 1807 and 1808, Juan Antonio de Santa Coloma served as primer regidor in 1804 and 1808, and Francisco de Las Llagas Lecica became alcalde de primer voto in 1806 (Archivo General de la Nación [Argentina], *Acuerdos del extinguido cabildo de Buenos Aires*, series 4, vol. 2).

25. Martin Gregorio Yániz loaned 20,000 pesos while he served as *sexto regidor* in 1806, and Juan the Llano, who was *quinto regidor* in 1805, invested 13,200 pesos the following year. For a list of lenders who advanced funds to the cabildo in 1806–1808, refer to table 6.7.

26. Archivo General de la Nación (Argentina), *Acuerdos del extinguido cabildo de Buenos Aires*, series 4, 2:264–65.

27. The community was made up of the corporations and prominent individuals of the old regime, which were those that the cabildo invited to participate, including the bishop and cathedral chapter, audiencia, royal treasurers, members of the regular clergy, military commanders, and prominent vecinos. The general congress of 16 August 1806 was a variation of the cabildo abierto, which was a city council meeting open to the other prominent members of the community and therefore representative of the community as a whole. These meetings always claimed to better represent the priorities

of the community, and therefore they appeared as the "defenders of the common good." For a discussion of cabildos abiertos, refer to Phelan, *The People and the King*; and MacLachlan, *Spain's Empire in the New World*. For the political role of municipal government in Spanish America see also Federica Morelli, "Orígenes y valores del municipalismo iberoamericano," *Araucaria: Revista Iberoamericana de Filosofía, Política y Humanidades* 9, no. 18 (2007): 116–29; Gabriella Chiaramonti, "De marchas y contramarchas: Apuntes sobre la institución municipal en el Peru (1812–1861)," *Araucaria: Revista Iberoamericana de Filosofía, Política y Humanidades* 9, no. 18 (2007): 150–79; and Geneviève Verdo, "La ciudad com actor. Prácticas políticas y estrategias de pertenencia: El caso del Rio de la Plata (1810–1820)," *Araucaria: Revista Iberoamericana de Filosofía, Política y Humanidades* 9, no. 18 (2007): 189–95.

28. Unlike the cases of the Quito Rebellion of 1765 and the Comunero Rebellion of 1781, which opposed the king's orders by convoking cabildos abiertos, the congress held in Buenos Aires upheld the monarch's authority. For a discussion of these rebellions, refer to McFarlane, "Rebellions in Late Colonial Spanish America."

29. Archivo General de la Nación (Argentina), *Acuerdos del extinguido cabildo de Buenos Aires*, series 4, 2:438.

30. Before 1806 the mercantile and the bureaucratic careers were regarded as the most prestigious in Buenos Aires. The military elite, although respected, never enjoyed the highest esteem. Military families therefore engaged in endogamy, which contributed to their relative isolation from the rest of the society (Halperín Donghi, "Militarización revolucionaria en Buenos Aires"). Additionally, as Socolow notes, the merchants of Buenos Aires repeatedly tried (although unsuccessfully) to be relieved of serving in the militias (Socolow, *The Merchants of Buenos Aires*, chap. 6).

31. For the rise of republican legitimacy within the militias, refer to Halperín Donghi, "Militarización revolucionaria en Buenos Aires"; and González Bernaldo, "Ejército y sociedades patrióticas." However, both authors emphasize that as the revolutionary military and militias became more professional, they lost the popular and republican features of the earlier times.

32. The changes in vecindad in Buenos Aires have been studied by Herzog, *Defining Nations*. For a discussion of the erection of racial and ethnic barriers in the eighteenth century, refer to Twinan, *Public Lives, Private Secrets*; also refer to Carrera, *Imagining Identity in New Spain*.

33. For the increase in the importation of African slaves, refer to William Accre and Alex Borucki, *Francisco Ventura de Molina y los caminos de la escritura negra en el Rio de la Plata* (Montevideo: Ediciones Trilce, 2007). The destruction of the guild system has been thoroughly discussed by Johnson, *Workshop of Revolution*.

34. Copies of the donativo rosters can be found in AGI, Buenos Aires 96 and Buenos Aires 97.

35. AGI, Buenos Aires 96.

36. For a discussion of the collective strategies of Indians and slaves in New Granada during the Napoleonic occupation of Spain, see Marcela Echeverri, "Popular Royalists: Empire and Politics in Southwestern New Granada, 1809–1919," *Hispanic American Historical Review* 91, no. 2 (2011): 237–69.

37. Johnson, *Workshop of Revolution*.

38. Grieco, "Family and Political Authority in Early Nineteenth-Century Buenos Aires."

39. AGI, Buenos Aires 96.

40. Ibid.

41. Ibid.

42. Ibid.

43. AGI, Buenos Aires 97.

44. Irurozqui, "De como el vecino hizo al ciudadano en Charcas."

EPILOGUE

1. *Gazeta de Buenos Aires*, facsimile ed., vol. 1, no. 1 (Buenos Aires: Editorial Docencia, 2006).

2. Di Meglio, "Patria."

3. Chambers argues that in the transition from Spanish domination to republicanism, the more egalitarian concept of virtue replaced the status-based ideal of honor. The author also points to the limits of a system based on virtue (Sarah Chambers, *From Subjects to Citizens: Honor, Gender and Politics in Arequipa, 1780–1854* [University Park: Pennsylvania State University Press, 1999]).

4. *Gazeta de Buenos Aires*, vol. 1, no.1.

5. Ibid. For pensions and dowries distributed in the early revolutionary years, refer to Grieco, "Family and Political Authority."

6. Enrique Williams Alzaga, *Vida de Martín de Alzaga: 1755–1812* (Buenos Aires: Emecé, 1984).

7. José Martínez de Hoz and the widow of Alzaga claimed that they had no cash, as they had employed it to finance their trading operations in Lima. Martin Gregorio Yañez argued that the interruption of the trade with Spain left him unemployed, as he was simply an agent for the merchants of Cádiz. Others blamed the military occupation of Chile for the reduction of their businesses and filed for bankruptcy (Hugo Raul Galmarini, "La situación de los comerciantes españoles en Buenos Aires despues de 1810," *Revista de Indias* 44, no. 173 [1984]: 273–90).

8. Congressional resolution passed on 9 August 1819 (*Registro oficial, 1819*).

9. Hugo Raul Galmarini, "Los Españoles de Buenos Aires después de la revolución," *Revista de Indias* 46, no. 178 (1986): 561–92.

10. Galmarini, "La situacion de los comericantes españoles."

INDEX

Page numbers in italic text indicate tables.